A. Mahadema Sastri

The Vedanta-Sutras With Srikantha Bhashya

A. Mahadema Sastri

The Vedanta-Sutras With Srikantha Bhashya

ISBN/EAN: 9783337413699

Printed in Europe, USA, Canada, Australia, Japan

Cover: Foto ©Lupo / pixelio.de

More available books at **www.hansebooks.com**

THE VEDANTA-SUTRAS WITH SRIKANTHA BHASHYA.

Translation by

A. MAHADEVA SASTRI, B.A.

As appeared in

"THE LIGHT OF TRUTH"

OR

SIDDHANTA DEEPIKA AND AGAMIC REVIEW

Volumes 1 to 7

June 1897 – March 1907

The Vedanta-Sutras with Srikantha Bhashya

Contents

	Pages
First Adhyaya	
First Pada	3 - 48
Second Pada	48 - 70
Third Pada	70 - 94
Fourth Pada	94 - 110
Second Adhyaya	
First Pada	110 - 126
Second Pada	127 - 140
Third Pada	141 - 158
Fourth Pada	158 - 166
Third Adhyaya	
First Pada	166 - 175
Second Pada	176 - 196
Third Pada	196 - 233
Fourth Pada	234 - 252
Fourth Adhyaya	
First Pada	252 - 265
Second Pada	265 - 274
Third Pada	274 - 280
Fourth Pada	281 – 298

FIRST ADHYAYA – FIRST PADA.

BHASHYAKARA'S INTRODUCTION.

1. Bow! To Siva, the Paramatman (Supreme Spirit) who is Sat (Existence, Chit (Intelligence) and Ananda (Bliss) in essence denoted by the word *aham* (I, ego); the cause of the manifestation of the worlds.

2. Supreme Siva, that Great Atman (spirit the entire essence of all agamas scriptures), by whom the whole panorama of all the worlds has been painted on the wall of His Sakti (energy).

3. May He secure perfection (siddhi) to you, - He, the Paramatman (Supreme Spirit), endued with all excellences, to whom all this Universe of Chit and Achit (spirit and matter) is subservient.

4. Bow! to the Teacher (acharya), Sveta by name, the author of many an agama (scripture); bow! to the excellent Master (Guru), the generous giver of liberation (kaivalya).

5. Resplendent is Srikantha's work on the blessed Sutras of Vyasa, - his great commentary (Bhashya), a sweet composition, mighty in meaning (but) not too extensive.

6. This Sutra of Vyasa, the eye for the wise to see the Brahman with, made turbid by the former teachers, will be made clear by Srikantha.

7. This commentary (Bhashya) is a great treasure for those Aryas who are devoted to Siva, and who take a delight in tasting the sweet essence of the whole Vedanta.

Here begins an enquiry into the Upanishad Now: (1) For what end of man (*purushartha*) is this enquiry intended? The end of man consists verily in the attainment of happiness which is the object of unqualified love, or in the complete cessation of pain which is the subject of unqualified hatred. (2) Who is here the *adhikarin*, *i.e.*, who is the person qualified for the enquiry? The adhikarin is the person who is endued with such attributes as a thirst for the subject. (3) What is its *subject*? That forms the subject of an enquiry which, though known, is yet not quite so well-known, and which, therefore, hangs on the swing of doubt. (4) *After* what does this enquiry arise? What is it which, as necessary leading to the enquiry should precede that enquiry? It is with a view to eradicate these sharp bristles of doubts from the minds of enquirers that the following Sutra is introduced by Lord Vyasa, the crest-jewel of the Omniscient.

The Vedanta-Sutras with Srikantha Bhashya

SUTRA 1.

Now, then, arises a desire to know Brahman.

This Sutra forms one section (*adhikarana*). By an *adhikarana* or section is meant here a topic which is made up of the following members: (1) *Vishaya* or the subject, (2) *Samsaya* or the doubt, (3) *Purvapaksha* or the prima facie view or argument, (4) *Siddhanta nirnaya* or the demonstrated conclusion, and (5) *Sangati* or the connection.

Here the word "now" (*atha*) denotes *anantarya* or immediate succession, not *adhikara* or commencement as in "*atha Yoganusasanam*," "Now (let us begin) to treat of Yoga." We cannot, indeed, speak of commencing a desire to know Brahman as though it were something that can be done as a duty. In fact, desire can arise from a mere sense of loveliness in the object.

Neither can we interpret the word 'now' (*atha*) as meaning *mangala* or auspiciousness as said in the Smriti.

> The syllable 'Om' and the word 'Atha,' these two emerged at first from Brahman, breaking forth from his throat; whence both are auspicious:

For, auspiciousness can have no logical connection with "desire to know." As to the necessity of performing, in pursuance of the example of the wise, an auspicious act when commencing a science, that necessity can be met by the mere utterance of the syllables.

Nor does the word "now" (*atha*) indicate that now follows another side (of an argument); for there is no occasion to speak of another side, as no one side (of any subject) has been treated off before.

The use of "now" (atha) can have no reference to an antecedent circumstance such as, like the act of eating or of going, is merely accidental; for, here it is intended to speak of something which forms a necessary equipment; that is here held to be the antecedent condition which, when secured, forms a special qualification of the student and constitutes a necessary equipment for an enquiry into Brahman.

Now one may say: it is but right that the necessary antecedent (here implied) of Brahma-vichara is the Vedadhyayana or the learning of the Vedas, which, preceded by the sacramental rite of Upanayana performed in the case of Brahmanas and other castes at the age of eight and so on, consists in the getting up of the texts coming from the mouth of the teacher duly approached, and which leads (ultimately) to a knowledge of its contents, - this learning of the Vedas being obligatory in as much as it is enjoined in the special injunction "Veda should be learned;" for, Brahman, like Dharma, being known only through the Vedas, an enquiry into Brahman is not possible for him who has not learnt the Vedas. An enquiry into Brahman should therefore come immediately after the learning of the Vedas.

(We say): granted that such a study is necessary; but immediately after that study should come the Dharma-vichara or enquiry into Dharma, since such an enquiry is not possible without that study. It has accordingly been expounded by the Acharya (Teacher) – in the words "Now, then, (arises) a desire to know Dharma,"* - that after learning the Vedas from the Upadhyaya (Teacher) is the time for an enquiry into Dharma. [*Mimamsa-Sutra, I.1.1.] We do not hold that the Sastras treating respectively of Dharma and Brahman are quite distinct. On the other hand we hold that they form one (Sastra). From the Sutra, "Now then arises a desire to know Dharma," to the Sutra, "No return, because of the text," † it is but one Sastra, treating of Dharma and Brahman, of worship and the object of worship: the Sutra "Now then arises a desire to know Brahman," marks only the beginning of a section which forms an integral part of that one Sastra, like the Sutra "Now then as to the definition of *sesha* or the subsidiary." ‡ [† Vedanta-Sutras IV, iv, 22. ‡ Mimamsa-Sutra, III, I, 1.]

Or, because Dharma is a means to the knowledge of Brahman, and that such topics as *sruti* (direct statement), and *linga* (indication), and the exposition of the authorities such as *Veda-chodana* (scriptural injunction), *arthavada* (explanatory passage), *Smriti* (mediate revelation), - which are treated of in the science of Dharma – are also useful in the science of Brahman, it is right that the science of Brahman should come after the science of Dharma; for, the end cannot be achieved without the means. The authority as to Dharma being the means to the knowledge of Brahman is the divine sruti itself.

"This by Vedic study do the Brahmanas seek to know, by Yajna (sacrificial rite)* by Dana (gift), by tapas (austerity), by fast." [* Brihadaranyaka-Upanishad IV, iv, 22.]

It cannot be urged that, if Karma be the means to the knowledge of Brahman, Dharma alone should be investigated and practiced, and that the enquiry into the import of the Vedantic passages serves no purpose. For, when devoid of a longing for the fruits, Karma forms a means to the knowledge of Brahman by bringing about purity of mind, by way of removing sins. Accordingly the Smriti of the learned, beginning with the words "He who undergoes the forty samskaras (sacramental rites)" and ending with the words "He attains unity with the Brahman and goes to His loka," † declares that all Karmas beginning with the Garbhadhana (the ceremony connected with impregnation) constitute a means of (spiritual) regeneration by way of removing the dirt of sin. [† Gautama Dharmasutra, viii, 24, 25.]

(*Objection*): If all Karma should thus form but a complement (of something else), like the sprinkling of water upon the grains (in a sacrificial rite), then it would detract from the independence of the (several) Asramas or religious orders as to their fruits, - that independence which is declared by the Sruti in the words "all these attain to the heavenly regions." ‡ [‡ Chandogya Upanishad, ii, 23, 2.]

(*Answer*): Not so. Though those Karmas are independent which are done with a longing for such fruits as heavenly regions, still it holds good that those which are performed by the man who is free from such a longing constitute mere complementary factors by way of conducing to the purity of mind. In the case of such a man the fruit of Jnana (knowledge) is itself the fruit of Karma. Just as the sprinkling of water upon the grains helps to secure *Svarga*, as forming a factor in generating the *apurva* (unseen effect) of the sacrifices of

Dars'a Purnamasa, so Karmas help to secure moksha, through the attainment of Jnana; and therefore as forming *guna-karmas* (secondary factors) they are mere *angas* (subsidiaries).

(*Objection*): Since the Jyotishtoma and other sacrificial rites which are enjoyed by independent injunctions as obligatory cannot constitute the mere *itikartavyata* or the manner of bringing about another main act; it cannot be that they are complementary factors.

(*Answer*): This objection is untenable; for just as the Sautramani, the Brihaspatisava and the like which are enjoined as primary means by independent injunctions form also secondary constituents of the Agnichayana and the like, so also an act may be of the two-fold nature in virtue of a two-fold injunction.* Wherefore until knowledge springs up karma should be performed. [* One injunction enjoining it as a primary means and a second injunction enjoining it as a secondary factor.]

(*Objection*): Because of the text "(by yajna etc.) they seek to know," † karma should be performed till the dawn of a desire for knowledge. [† Bri. Up. IV, iv, 9.]

(*Answer*): There is no force in the objection; for, mere desire cannot constitute an object of human pursuit.

Wherefore it is but right that the science treating of Brahman should follow the enquiry into karmas which are the means by which to attain the knowledge of Brahman.

(*Objection*): How can the order of sequence, here defined, as to the sciences of Karma and Brahman be explained? If it be so because the agent is the same in both, then it may be that the agent is the same in both either because the one is complementary to the other, as the *aghara* (an oblation) is complementary to the (main sacrifice of) *Darsa* and *Purnamasa*; or because, they both form, like the five *prayajas* (certain oblations), two secondary factors of a third which is primary; or because, as in the case of *godohana*‡ and the life, the one is enjoined under a special circumstance as a substitute for the other; or because like the six constituent parts§ (of the Darsa-Purnamasa) they conjointly produce one single effect. We find no sruti or any other authority showing that the sciences bear such a relation to each other. Wherefore this definite order of sequence as to the sciences of Karma and Brahman is unjustifiable.

[‡ Referring to the injunction, "the priest should consecrate water in the vessel called chamasa, and in the case of one who desires to attain plenty of cattle, he should consecrate it in the vessel called *godohana* instead of *chamasa*."

§ These six parts are made up of the three main sacrifices in the Purnamasa known as the *agneya*, the *agnishomiya*, and the *upams uyaga*; and of the three main sacrifices in the Darsa known as the *agneya*, the *aindram-dadhi*, and the *aindram-payas*.]

(*Answer*): Indeed it may be so, if there were no authority, sruti and the like. We do find passages like the following in sruti, declaring a conjunction of Karma and Jnana:

"He who knows together both Vidya and Avidya"*

"On he goes, whoever knows Brahman and who has done good." †

"By truth verily this Atman can ever be attained, by tapas (austerity), by right knowledge, by Brahmacharya (devotion to Brahman)." ‡

[* Isopanishad 11; † Bri. Up. IV, iv, 9. ‡ Mundakopanishad III, 5, 5.]

Thus Karma and Jnana conjointly producing one effect, namely Moksha, it is but right that the two sciences should come in a definite order of sequence.

Though indeed the injunction as to the learning of the Vedas inculcates the mere getting up of the text, still there does arise an occasion for the two enquiries. By the learning of the Veda together with the Angas or auxiliary sciences, § one comes to know the literal meaning of the passages in the sruti. [§ These are: siksha (phonetics), grammar, metrics, nirukta (etymology), astronomy, and kalpa (liturgy).] Then finding apparent mutual contradictions in the passages, which treat of the Jyotishtoma and other rites constituting the Sthula-Upasana or coarser forms of worship, as well as in those passages which treat of Dahara-Vidya (contemplation of the Divine Being in the heart) and the like constituting the Sukshma-Upasana or finer form of worship the student aspiring towards higher aims of life engages of himself in an investigation of the subject. Hence no absence of an occasion for the enquiry.

(*Objection*):   In the passage, "the Atman should be learnt the Vedantic enquiry is directly enjoined.

(*Answer*):   No, because of the absence of conditions which go to make it an injunction. To explain Vedantic enquiry cannot be the subject of an *apurvavidhi*, an injunction which enjoins an act not known of before from any other source, for, the Vedantic enquiry is otherwise known as necessary. It is known as necessary by arguing thus: Vedantic enquiry, like the enquiry into the science of medicine, is a means to the understanding of the thing the Vedanta treats of, since the former is a scientific enquiry like the latter. Neither does it from the subject of a *niguna-vidhi*, - an injunction intended to restrict the act to only one of the several alternative ways of doing it, - like the threshing of rice (in a sacrifice); for, no other means (except the Vedantic enquiry) has been known in our experience to produce the same result. Nor does it form the subject of a *parisankhya-vidhi*, - an injunction which is intended to exclude all other alternatives, - for then it would be tantamount to this, that the Vedanta should be only enquired into and not learned by rote. In that case since the enquiry into the Vedanta is not possible for those who have not thus learnt Vedantic texts they can never attain the (Supreme) end of man. If, on the other hand, Vedantic enquiry should form the subject of a *parisankhya-vidhi* as excluding an enquiry into the karma-kanda or the ritualistic portion of the Vedas, then, too, in the absence of this latter enquiry, performance of Karma is not possible. As, without performing Karma, mental purity cannot be attained, there can be no dawn of knowledge. Wherefore the aforesaid proposition holds good.

Thus the Sastra known as the Upanishad which treats of the Para-Brahman-Who is unrivalled in His glory, as endued with the Supreme Sakti manifesting itself in the form of the Universe composed of *Chit* and *Achit*, - spirit and matter, the conscious and the inert;

The Vedanta-Sutras with Srikantha Bhashya

Who is the storehouse of all secrets contained in all the great scriptures; Whose supreme grandeur is declared by such choice synonymous designations applied to Him a Bhava, Siva, Sarva, Pasupati, Paramesvara, Mahadeva, Rudra, Sambhu and the like; by Whose grace, extended to all sentient beings subservient to Him according to the manner in which they approach and worship Him, all human aspirations are fulfilled, - should be enquired into after completing the enquiry into the blessed Dharma, which is taught in the form of Vedic injunctions constituting Divine commands; which comprises, in one whole, various forms of Divine worship; whose excellence is made known in many a laudatory passage; which is embellished with the several subsidiary parts furnished by the sruti etc; which is treated of even at a greater length in the Smriti, Itihasa, Purana and the wise sayings of the adepts, all these being in perfect accord with the original authority; which is composed of *vidhi* and *nishedha* (injunctions and prohibitions), *vikalpa* and *samuchchaya* (alternatives and conjunctions, *utsarya* and *apavada* (general and special rules), *badha* and *abhyuchchaya* (weakening exceptions and strengthening illustrations); which is the repository of all human ends and the means of attaining the supreme knowledge. Thus has been determined the meaning of the word "now".

The word 'then' (*atah*) indicates that what has preceded from the reason of what follows: because Dharma has been investigated by the student after having learnt the Vedas, therefore, having attained to the purity of mind by the observance of Dharma, and being endued with supreme Bhakti (devotion) quickened by true discrimination and such other attributes which then unfold themselves, he should also investigate Brahman leading to the highest good.

In the compound "Brahma-jijnasa", Brahman should be construed as the object of the verb "*Jna*" to know.

The *subject* (of discussion in this section) is the following passage:

"Having surveyed the worlds that deeds (done for reward) build up, He (the Brahmana) who loves God unto renunciation should betake himself. The un-create is not by the create (to be obtained). To find out That, he verily should to a teacher go – versed in the law, who takes his final stand on God, - *fuel samit* in hand."* [* Mundaka-Upanishad. I, ii, 12.]

The *doubt* arises in the following form: Is Brahman fit for enquiry or not?

And the *prima facie* view may be stated as follows: Brahman is not a subject fit for enquiry, there being no room for doubt concerning it. – How can there be no doubt? – Thus: the Sruti "This Atman is Brahman" † [† Mandukya-Upanishad, 2.] teaches that the very Atman that is immediately perceived as "I" is Brahman. How, then, can there be an occasion for slightest doubt? Furthermore, the aim of an enquiry is verily a knowledge of the subject of that enquiry. And to know is to define the object of knowledge. Now, does the knowledge, arising from Vedantic enquiry, define Brahman or not? If it could define Brahman, then it would militate against the notion that Brahman transcends all definition. If it could not define Brahman, then He is not known in His true light. A jar or any other object is said to be known when it is defined "such is the jar". Wherefore knowledge, too, concerning Brahman is not possible. And, moreover, we see no good (resulting from the enquiry). Liberation (Mukti) is not the end, in as much as the beginning less samsara is hard to set aside.

Such *prima facie* view presenting itself, we agree as follows: From all points of view the enquiry should be undertaken, because Brahman, being within the realm of doubt, forms the subject of enquiry; and further because a determinate knowledge of the subject conduces to a great end. There does arise a doubt for the very reason that such passages of Sruti as "This Atman is Brahman" speak of this very samsarin, bound by egotism (Shankara), as Brahman. It is indeed the possession in a great measure of the unsurpassed potencies of knowledge and bliss and the like, free from all taint of evil, that constitutes the nature of Brahman; and it is the being subject to the necessity of entering into and getting out of various bodies suited to the reaping of the fruits of actions ripening under the influence of the traces of beginning less ajnana (nescience) and thus becoming subject to boundless pain, that constitutes the nature of Jiva. How can the srutis speak of a unity of two such quite distinct entities? – How can a doubt not arise in this way? A doubt, moreover, can also arise on the following ground. Food is Brahman;" "Manas is Brahman; Vijnana is Brahman'* "The sun is Brahman;" † Narayana is the supreme Brahman;" - ‡ these and other passages speak of widely different things as Brahman. Which of these is Brahman? [* Chandogya-Upanishad VII, ix, iii. vii, & c. † Ibid III, xix, 1. ‡ Mahanarayana-Upanishad xi.5.]

Being thus in many ways subject to doubt, Brahman is a subject fit for enquiry. And then by the Great Grace of Siva, the Para-Brahman, the Great Teacher, highly merciful and all-benign, Who, ascertained by studying the Sruti and reflecting thereupon, is won over by proper Devotion and Knowledge (Bhakti and Jnana), – there accrues to the aspirant the great Good, the wealth of Liberation (Kaivalya-Lakshmi), all bonds (Pasa) being destroyed, his own nature as made up of unsurpassed intelligence and bliss directly perceived, while he is endued in his essence with the qualities similar to those of the Para-Brahman. Thus the Vedantic enquiry has a subject to treat of and a purpose to serve.

As to the objection that, because knowledge consists in defining the object of that knowledge, no knowledge concerning the indefinable Brahman can arise, - it is only due to a want of proper investigation; for, though no positive definition of Brahman – "He is so and so" – can be given, still it is possible to define Him indirectly by means of implication, by distinguishing Him from all others. Indeed, everywhere, to know a thing by definition is to know it as distinguished from all others. When Brahman is enunciated, defined and investigated by means of Vedantic texts, He is known to be that thing which is distinguished form all others of the same class or from other classes not possessing the given characteristics of Brahman. Wherefore it is right to enter upon this enquiry into Brahman.

What is not subject to doubt or is not productive of any good cannot indeed form, for the wise men, a subject of enquiry. So, (the two points) that Brahman, Who forms a subject of doubt owing to the so-called authoritative texts and arguments on the subject, is the subject of this enquiry of Vedantic-Sastra, and further that by worshipping Him the aspirant attains his end, the Mukti, which consists in the breaking of the bond (Pasa), as taught in the following passages: -

"The knower of Brahman reaches the Supreme;" * [* Taittiriaya-Upanishad, II, ii, 1.]

"Knowing Siva, he passes into peace for ever;" † [† S'vet.Up. 4-11.]

"Knowing that Isa they become immortal;" ‡ [‡ Ibid. 3-7.]

"A man, who has left all grief behind, sees the majesty, the Lord, the passionless, by the grace of the creator;" ‡ [‡ Ibid. 20.]

"Making Atman the arani, and pranava the upper arani, only by the churning of dhyana, the wise man burns up the bond (pasa); § [§ Kaivalya-Upanishad. 11.]

"Knowing God, he is released from all bonds"; || [|| S'vet. Up. 1-8.]

These two points have been propounded here in the first section.

Adhikarana. 2.

Now that the question arises as to what that distinguishing mark is which determines the nature of Brahman here enunciated, the blessed Sutrakara introduces the sutra which forms the second adhikarana or section and states the definition of that (Brahman):

Whence the birth etc. of this (I. i. 2.)

When the thing to be defined is known, definition serves no purpose; when the thing is not known, there is no seeking for its definition. So, what occasion is there for giving a definition of Brahman here? – No objection such as this need to be raised; for there does arise an occasion for a definition of Brahman, of whom a vague idea is formed by the study of Vedic texts.

The literal meaning of the Sutra is: Brahman is He from whom proceeds the evolution – *i.e.*, birth (*janma*), existence (*sthiti*), dissolution (*laya*), disappearance (*tirobhava*), and grace (*anugraha*)* - of this manifested universe made up of *chetana* and *achetana*, of spirit and matter, held together in indissoluble union.

[* Appaya-dikshita in his Sivarkamanidipika, a commentary on Srikantha-Bhashya, explains *Sthiti*, as the state of continuance of the universe between its emanation and dissolution; *tirobhava* as bandha or bondage, the root of the whole evil of *Samsara*, the inherent powers of *Jnana* and *Kriya* (knowledge and action) being veiled or hidden; and *anugraha* as deliverance from bondage. He cites also, with a view to refute; two other explanations of *tirobhava*: (1) the ceaseless continuance of worldly enjoyment as suited to each sentient being, (2) the return, at the time of pralaya, of chetana and achetana existence to their subtlest forms. This last explanation of the word seems to agree with the teachings of Saiva Agamas so far as Brahman's five-fold act (Pancha Kritya) is concerned.

In his Saundaryalahari, verse 24, Sri Sankaracharya, following the teaching of the agamas, describes this (*tirobhava*) stage of the universe as Isana's act of concealing (by way of merging) it as well as His own form in Sadasiva, and he describes *anugraha* as Sadasiva's act of projecting into manifestation Brahma the Creator, Hari the Preserver, Rudra the Destroyer, and Isana the Concealer, from out of Himself in whom they lay concealed after pralaya, and who once more emanates the souls into being with their respective pasas (or karma-bandha) with a view to further on the evolutionary progress of such souls as lag behind in their march towards moksa. Appayadiskshita's interpretation of *tirobhava* and *anugraha* emphasizes only one aspect of the evolution, that which refers to Jivas individuality, not to the universe as a whole.]

The texts which here form the subject of discussion are such as the following:

"From which indeed these creatures have their birth; by what, when born, they live; to what they do depart, they pass away; that strive to know." *

"The master of nature and of man; the lord of qualities; the cause of the bondage, existence and liberation of the world." †

"Truth, wisdom, and endless is Brahman." ‡

"Hail to the reality, the truth, the Supreme Brahman, dark and yellowish in person, having the semen above, diverse-eyed, hail to the Omnipresent." §

Now the doubt arises as to whether or not the birth etc., of the universe forms the definition or characteristic marks of Brahman.

[* Taittiriya-Upanishad.iii. 1. † Svet. Up. vi. 16. ‡ Tait-Up. ii. 1. § Mahanarayana-Upanishad. 23.]

(Purvapaksha): - They cannot constitute (the characteristic marks of Brahman), in as much as they do not inhere in Him. Moreover, in the passage "He saw that Bliss was Brahman" ‖ it is evident that the birth etc. of the universe are the characteristic marks of the Bliss. [‖ Tait. Upanishad. iii.6] Elsewhere, in the passage "Existent (*sat*) alone, my dear, this at first was" ¶ the *sat* or the existent is taught as the cause of the universe. [¶ Chandogya-Upanishad. vi. 2.] In one place – in the passage "Truth, wisdom, and endless is Brahman" – it is taught that the infinite Jnana or wisdom is itself Brahman, the cause of the universe; and in another place, in the passage,

"When the light of knowledge has risen, there is no day, no night, neither existence nor non-existence, Siva alone is there," ** [** Svet. Up. iv. 18.]

we are given to understand that the Being denoted by the word 'Siva' is the cause and therefore, Brahman, existing before all.

Now, it may be asked: in case of the Bliss etc. are Brahman, do they constitute Brahman each by itself, or all of them conjoined together? In the former case, we ignore what is directly revealed and commit other similar fallacies; and then, too, Brahman will be of an undefined nature. If it be held that each of them is the mark of a Brahman of a distinct kind, then a plurality of Brahman has to be admitted. If it be supposed that they conjointly constitute Brahman, even then, since they are mere attributes, they cannot constitute Brahman who possesses attributes, such as a knowledge as to the means of building the whole universe. Furthermore, the Sruti "One should know Maya to be the cause"* declares that the unintelligent Maya is the cause of the universe; and it does so rightly; for, if Brahman who is made of intelligence (Jnana) be the cause of the universe, He would be subject to vikara or change, - which runs counter to the teaching of the Sruti declaring that Brahman is "partless, actionless, tranquil"† and so on. Wherefore in no way is it possible to define Brahman, - to define Him as the cause of the universe and so on. [* Svet. Up. iv. 10. † Ibid. vi. 19.]

As against the forgoing prima facie view, we hold as follows:

Admitted that birth etc., as attributes inhering in the universe, do not pertain to Brahman; still, they rightly constitute the defining marks of Brahman as one closely connected with the universe. The Entity called Siva, possessed of the attribute of omniscience and so on and denoted by the eight appellations,‡ is said to be Brahman, the cause of the universe; and to that Entity alone Bliss and all other like attributes point. The attributes referred to are Omniscience (*Sarvajnata*), Ever-contentedness (*nityatriptata*), Begninningless Wisdom (*Anadibodhata*), Independence (*Svatantrata*), Never-failing Potency (*Nityaluptasaktita*), and Infinite Potency (*Anatasaktita*).

Omniscience (*Sarvajnata*) consists in all things becoming objects of direct perception – of stainless intuitive experience – independent of all external organs of sensation. It is known to inhere in Brahman, from such passages as: "Who perceives all and who knows all, whose penance consists of knowledge." § [§ Mundaka-Upanishad. 1.1.4] Thus the cause (of the universe) is Brahman who knows the appropriate ways and means of building up the several bodies suited to all sentient beings for the reaping of the fruits of their multifarious acts.

Ever-contentedness (nityatriptata) consist in being replete with unsurpassed Bliss, wherein there is not the slightest trace of distress. Hence the revelation "Bliss is Brahman." ‖ [‖ Tai. Up. iii. 6.] That Bliss (Ananda) which – introduced in the words "There is yet another Atman who is composed of Bliss,"* and carried to the culminating point of unsurpassed Bliss by repeated multiplication in the passages beginning with "Here follows the measuring of Bliss" and ending with "that is the unit of Brahman's Bliss"† - is the attribute of Para-Brahman is figuratively spoken of as Brahman Himself in the passage "Bliss is Brahman," because of the abundance of Bliss in Him. Brahman who delights in enjoying such a Bliss is said to be ever-contented. The enjoyment of this mighty Bliss on the part of Brahman is effected through *manas* only, not through external organs of sensation. Hence the passage,

"There is Brahman who is *akasararira* (whose body is light), *satyatman* (Himself the existent), *pranarama* (whose joy is life), *manaananda* (delighted in the mind), *santi-samriddha* (perfect in peace), and *amrita* (immortal)." ‡

[* Tait. Up. ii. 5. † Tait. Up. ii. 8. ‡ Tait. Up. i. 6.]

Here by akasa – literally, that which shines all round, the Light – is meant the *chid-ambara*, the ether of spirit, the spirit-light, but not the material akasa or ether, because the latter can mark no distinction (*i.e.*, the latter cannot serve to distinguish Brahman from other things in nature). The *chid-ambara* here referred to is that Supreme Power (Parama-Sakti), that highest cause, that ocean, as it were, from which spring up all the hosts of bubbles, the mundane eggs of all groups. Brahman, whose form is that supreme light, is spoken of in the sruti as "*akasa-sarira.*" That chid-akasa is the highest cause is known from such passages as the following:

"All these beings take their rise from Akasa and return into Akasa." §

"He who is called Akasa is the revealer of all forms and names" ||

[§ Chha. Up. III. ix. 1. || Chha. Up. VIII. xiv. 1.]

Satyatman: He who is the Satta or existence. *Pranarama*: He who delights in Prana, the *chid-ambara-sakti*, the Power of Spiritual light, the Basis of all, constituting Brahman's own essential nature. *Manaananda*: He whose joy is in Manas (mind), not in the external organs of sensation. Here, too, "Ananda" refers to the spirit-light the *chid-ambara*, the Prakriti or cause. Accordingly the Sruti says:

"Who could breathe if that Bliss, that Light, existed not."*

[* Tait. Up. III. vii. 1.]

Santi-samriddha: He who has attained to Sivata, to Siva's condition. *Amrita*: He who has been free from time without beginning.

Thus, it is seen that Brahman who is essentially Existence, Intelligence and Bliss, and whose essential nature is the Supreme Light, enjoys the Bliss of His essential nature by mind alone, independent of external organs of sensation, as implied by the epithet "Manaananda." This epithet also implies that the emancipated souls who have attained to the state of Brahman are possessed of the *antah-karana* or mind, the organ which acts independently of external organs, and by which they experience the unsurpassed bliss of their essential nature. Wherefore, *nityatripta* or ever-contented is Brahman, enjoying the infinite Bliss of His essential nature by manas which is pure *bodha-sakti* itself, the faculty of knowledge which can act independently of external organs. That is to say, for Him there is no necessity for the slightest joy of the world (samsara) external to Himself.

The possession of unsurpassed knowledge – which is *svatas-siddha*, self-existing or inherent, - constitutes what is called *anadibodhatva* or beginningless wisdom. Indeed, the *antah-karana*, jnana or knowledge, which is the organ whereby He enjoys the Bliss of His own essential nature, exists through eternity, without beginning. Wherefore, Brahman is one of beginningless wisdom, in as much as knowledge which repels samsara exists through eternity; He is ever free from the evil of samsara and is spoken of in the Sruti as "perfect in peace and immortal."

Independence (Svatantrata) consists in freedom from servitude to others and from other marks of inferiority, and in all things other than Himself being brought under his own control. Independence of Brahman as the impelling agent of the universe of matter and spirit is taught in such passages as the following:

"There are two, one knowing (Isvara), the other not knowing, both unborn, one strong, the other weak." †

"By knowing the enjoyer, the enjoyed, and the ruler & c." ‡

"But he, who controls both knowledge and ignorance, is another." §

The Vedanta-Sutras with Srikantha Bhashya

[† Sveta. Up. i, 9. ‡ Sveta. Up. i, 12. § Sveta. Up. v, 1.]

It is evident that because of His independence in all matters, Brahman is the author of all.

The never-failing-potency (*Nityaluptasaktitva*) consists in all potencies being inherent in His own nature. Accordingly, the Sruti says "His Higher Power (Para-sakti) is revealed as manifold, as inherent, acting as force and knowledge. * From this it follows that the potencies of the universe of spirit and matter are inherent in Brahman and that He is never without these specific attributes. [* Svet. Up. vi. 8.]

The possession of unlimited potentialities is what is called Endless Potency (*anantasaktita*). It is in virtue of these endless potencies that Brahman is the producer and the ruler of the world. Accordingly it is revealed to us that

"There is one Rudra only, - they do not allow a second – who rules all the worlds by His powers"; † [† Atharvasiras Upanishad.]

"Who rules all these worlds by His supreme powers of ruling and producing." ‡ [‡ Atharvasiras Upanishad.]

As possessed of endless potencies, Brahman can be the material cause of the infinite universe.

As to Brahman being the subject of eightfold appellation: The Supreme Brahman is the Being denoted by the eight appellations of *Bhava, Sarva, Isana, Pasupati, Rudra, Ugra, Bhima* and *Mahadeva*. Though He is denoted by all worlds, He is designated specially by Bhava and other like words, indicative as they are of His Highest being; it does not follow that He is not designated by other words than these eight.

Brahman is called Bhava because He exists everywhere at all times, the root – "bhu" meaning satta or existence. We are taught that Brahman is the Existent, running through all things. Accordingly, the Sruti says:

"Existent alone, my dear, this at first was, one only without a second." § [§ Chha. Up. vi. ii.]

"Truth (Existence), Wisdom, Endless is Brahman." ‖ [‖ Tait. Up. ii. 1.]

"He who is existent, who delights in Prana, whose joy is in manas." ¶ [¶ Tait. Up. i. 6.]

"The ineffable glory" ** [** Mahanarayana. Up. 24.]

and so on. As running through all things – as for instance "jar existing" cloth existing – it is evident that Brahman, the existent, constitutes the upadana or material cause of all. The jar, for instance, always associated as it is with clay, is said to be made out of clay, *i.e.*, has clay for its upadana. Thus Brahman, the existent, is designated by the word *Bhava*.

Brahman, the all-destroyer, is designated by the word *Sarva*, derived from the root "Sri" to destroy. Brahman is spoken of as the destroyer in the following passages:

"(Hail! Hail! Therefore, to the Destroyer, to the Great Devourer" * [* Atharva-Siras. Up.]

"To whom the Brahmanas and Kshatriyas (are as it were) but food" † [† Katha. Up. ii. 25.]

Brahman is denoted by the word "*Isana*," the Ruler, as endued with the unconditioned supreme sovereignty, as revealed in the passage, "Who rules these worlds with His powers of ruling." ‡ [‡ Atharva-Siras. Up.]

As the Isvara or Ruler must have some beings to rule over, Brahman is denoted by the word Pasupati, Master of Pasas or subject beings (souls). Thus, the Sruti says:

"Whom – the four-footed as well as two-footed souls (pasus) – Pasupati, the Lord of souls, rules." § [§ Taittiriya-Samhita. III.i.4,]

As Pasus (souls) are so-called because of pasa (bond), Pasu stands for both Pasu and Pasa. By this epithet, Brahman is shown to be the Ruler of *chit* and *Achit*, of matter and spirit.

Brahman is called Rudra as expelling the malady o samsara, as we are told in the passage:

"The knower of Atman crosses beyond grief" ‖ [‖ Chha. Up. VIII. 1.]

Brahman is called Ugru or Fierce, because He cannot be overpowered by other luminaries, as taught in the passage:

"Not there the sun shines, nor the moon and stars." ¶ [Sveta Up.]

As the regulator and the source of fear to all sentient begins, Brahman is known by the name of Bhima or Terrible, The Sruti says:

The Sruti says:

"By fear of Him does the wind blow." * * [Steva. Up. Tait-Up.]

As Great and Luminous, Siva is called *Mahadeva.* So the Atharva-Siras says:

"For what then, is He called Mahadeva? As having abandoned all things, He is adored for His Atma0Jnana or spiritual wisdom and for His yogic glory; wherefore He is called Mahadeva." †

That being called Siva known as free from all taunt of Samsara and as the repository of all that is good is, because He is of such a nature, the cause of the birth &c. of the whole world. Since a Being of such a greatness can be the twofold cause of the world. That (Being called Siva), endued as He also been proved to be the seat of Bliss and such other attributes; wherefore it is vain to raise the question whether Bliss etc., each constitute Brahman each by itself. From the passage "one should know Maya as Prakriti" it may be seen that Maya is the

Prakriti or cause, that says being Isvara essentially, as taught in the concluding part of the sentence"

"And know "Isvara as the possessor or the seat of the Maya." * [*Sveta UP. i. 10.]

Brahman, associated with the sukshma or subtle chit and Achit is the cause; and Brahman associated with the sthula, or gross chit and Achit is the effect. Wherefore the Siddhanta or demonstrated conclusion is that birth etc. of the universe form the distinguishing marks of Brahman.

Adhikarana 3(A).

Knowledge of a thing is obtained by means of its definition and the organ of perception. Now what is the pramana or organ of perception in the case of Brahman, the cause of the world? In answer to this question the Sutrakara says:

Because Sastra is the source (of our knowledge of Brahman) (I. i. 3.)

Because Sastra is the source, the *pramana*, the authority, or the organ of perception, therefore, there is Brahman who has been defined by (i.e., as the cause of) the birth etc. of the universe.

Now, the doubt arises as to whether Brahman, the cause of the universe, can be reached through Sastra alone or through other pramanas.

The prima facie view may be stated as follows: This world which is made up of parts is an effect, and that effect, involving variety, should have an appropriate agent. Thus may be inferred some agent endued with omniscience. Thus, not being reachable by Sastra alone, Sastra's aim is not Brahman: Sastra treats of things not revealed by other pramanas.

The demonstrated conclusion may be stated as follows: - Brahman, the cause of the universe, can be reached through Vedanta-Sastra alone; for such passages as

"None, who knows not the Vedas, can think of That, the Great." * [* Taittiriya-Brahmana III. xiii. 9.]

- teach the impossibility of (attaining to) a knowledge of Brahman except through Vedanta-Sastra.

As to the contention that the universe is an effect because it is made up of parts, and that it may therefore be inferred that the universe must have an appropriate agent, it is unreasonable to say so; for it is found that steeples and palaces and the like, which exhibit a complicated design, have more than one agent. Thus, it cannot be established that the universe has only one agent. By force of induction, we are further led to the conclusion that such an agent is subject to Karma, *i.e.* has to reap the fruits of his act.

Even if it could be established by *anumana* or *inference* – in virtue of the world being an effect – that the author of the world is one alone and distinct from itself, it cannot be proved that that one agent is endued with the potency of becoming both the efficient and the material cause of the universe. Thus it is proved that Brahman is reached by Vedanta-Sastra alone, and is founded on that (Vedanta-Sastra) alone as the authority.

Adhikarana 3(B).

Some hold that by this Sutra we are further taught that the attribute of omniscience which is so essential in the case of the world, propounded in the previous section (2nd adhikarana), can be predicated of Brahman as He is the source of all Sastras or Vedas. Such a double signification is no more a fault in a sutra whose aim is merely to indicate, than in a poem conveying (by slesha or pun) a double signification. Hence the introduction of a fresh adhikarana or section here.

Because He is the source of Sastra (I. I. 3.)

In this case the texts which form the subject of discussion are the following:

"What is (known as) Rig-Veda, Yajur-Veda, Sama Veda etc., is the breath of this Great Being" † [† Bri. Up. II. iv. 10.]

The *doubt* arises as to whether or not it is right to hold that Brahman is the author of the Vedas.

The Purvapaksha or the *primafacie* view may be stated as follows: It is not right to hold that Brahman is the author of the Vedas; because it contradicts the sruti which declares the eternality of the Vach in the passage.

"O Agni that assumes diverse forms, do thou impel (the sacrifice) to adore Indra by eternal word." * [* Taitt-Samhita II. vi. 11] If they were the creation of Brahman, the Vedas would have a personal author and, as such, would form no authority. Wherefore, how can Brahman be the author of the Vedas?

As against the foregoing, we hold as follows: - It is but right that Brahman is the author of the Vedas; for, from the Sruti,

"What is (known as) Rig-Veda, Yajur-Veda, Sama-Veda etc., is the breath of this Great Being,"

we understand that the mass of the Vedas has emerged as the breath from Brahman without any effort; and further we are taught that Paramesvara is the author of all Vidyas, in the following verse:

"Of these eighteen sciences of different paths, the original author was, as the sruti says, the wise Sulapani Himself."

Of the Vedas dissolved in Himself before creation, the Omniscient Paramesvara again becomes the author by composing them in the same order of syllables as before. Wherefore it is that the Vedas have no personal author and are at the same time the work of Isvara. The statements of persons who have likes and dislikes and so on may prove untrue. But ever true are the statements of Brahman, of Siva, who is free from all taint of evil tendencies, by whose unobstructed and unsurpassed knowledge is directly perceived whatever may happen to things in all the three periods of time, who is an authority in Himself (Svatah-pramana), who is the Supreme Lord and the Supreme Truth-speaker, who has attained all desires. For, in the passages "the Ruler of all Vidyas" † and "May that Divine Being endow us with the blessed wisdom (Subhi Smriti)" ‡ it is taught that Paramesvara is the founder of all sciences and is the cause of the blessed wisdom (Subhi Smriti). Wherefore, Paramesvara being the author of the Vedas which illumine all things, His omniscience is proved, in as much as it is impossible to reveal what is unknown. [† Mahanarayana-Upanishad, 21. ‡ Mahana-Upanishad, 12.]

Though in the case of the omnipresent Paramesvara, His omniscience has to be admitted in virtue of His contact with all things, still His being the author of the Vedas which illumine all things points to a peculiar feature: a lamp, for instance, illumines form alone, but not taste and so on, though these latter as well as form come in contact with its light; but not so does the Supreme Lord: He illumines all that is energized by His Sakti.

(*Objection*): Paramesvara's omniscience consists in His being aware of all things taught in the Vedas. Then we have to admit that even the Maharishis or the Great Sages who know the teaching of Vedas are omniscient. Then where is the distinction?

(*Answer*): Not so; Isvara their author, has more knowledge. In fact we see that authors of works such as Vyakarana are persons like Panini who know more than what is contained in their works. And the Veda, though illumining all things, does not point to all as the main object of its teaching: it teaches certain things indirectly, certain other things in a general way and some only in their special character, whereas Paramesvara, the witness of all, perceives all directly. This, we hold, is the difference between the Veda and the Isvara.

(*Objection*): It is not necessary that Paramesvara alone is the author of the Veda, as the passages of the Sruti like

"Having become Shat-hotri, Prajapati created all this, the Rik, Yajus and Sama," *

[* Taitt-Brahmana II.iii.2.]

give us to understand that Hiranyagarbha and the like are also its authors.

(*Answer*): No, because of the existence of the Vedas even before the birth of Hiranyagarbha. The Sruti says,

"He who first creates Brahman (Hiranyagarbha) and delivers the Vedas to him." †

[† Sveta. Up. vi. 18.]

He who is the author even of Hiranyagarbha and teaches Him all the Vedas, He alone is above all, the author of Vedas, the Supreme Teacher. Accordingly the Sruti clearly teaches,

"Rudra who is above all, the great Seer, who first glanced at Hiranyagarbha, the foremost-born among the Devas, may He endow us with blessed wisdom." * [* Mahanarayana-Upanishad. 12.]

This passage has to be explained thus: That Maharishi, the Great Sage, the author of the Vedas, who, in virtue of His omniscience, is superior to the whole universe of *chit* and *Achit*; that Rudra, that Para-Brahman, who at the time of creation cast upon Hiranyagarbha – the first among Gods including Indra, and just then emerging from Atman who is His Prakriti or cause, by the force of Divine will – His gracious glance by way of teaching the whole Veda which is the source of all knowledge; may that Great Teacher endow us also with the Smriti, with that ray of wisdom (bodha-kala) concerning Himself which brings about the cessation of the great evil, of the whole bondage of samsara; which leads to the attainment of Supreme Bliss and conduces to the highest wealth of immortality; and which, therefore, is the supreme good, resulting from the harmonious essential teaching of the Vedanta. Thus it has been demonstrated that Isvara is the author of all Vedas.

The teaching of the Sruti as to the eternality of the word (Vach) is not contradicted, in as much as the Vedas are said to have been composed by Isvara just as they had been before; and thus Isvara's authorship, too, of the Vedas is uncontradicted.

Adhikarana 4

For a knowledge of Siva, the Para-Brahman, expounded in the first adhikarana as the subject of enquiry, a definition of Brahman was needed; and a definition thereof was stated in the second adhikarana as That whence proceeds the emanation etc. of the universe. Then the question arising as to what was the authority for such a definition, it has been propounded in the third adhikarana that the Vedanta Sastra is the source of our knowledge of the subject, and that Brahman is the source of the Vedanta-Sastra. That indeed is the pramana or source of our knowledge of a thing, by which that thing is invariably known. Now, a question arises as to how the Vedantic texts can teach Brahman; and in answer thereto the fourth adhikarana is now introduced:

Him, verily, (the Vedanta teaches) with one accord (I. i. 4).

'Him' refers to Brahman, the subject of enquiry. The word 'verily' shows that all Vedantic texts taken collectively are here referred to. The word "*Samanvaya* (one accord)" shows that Brahman is the drift or the main subject of their teaching. The Sutra means: The Vedantic texts treat of Brahman in the main, as shown by the several *lingas* or tests of their ultimate import.

All the Vedantic texts form the *subject* of discussion in this adhikarana.

The *doubt* arises as to whether or not it is right to hold that the Vedantic texts teach Brahman (*a*).

(*a*) To understand in its full bearing the discussion that follows in this adhikarana it is necessary to bear in mind that the first issue which the mimamsakas or Indian theologians have taken up to settle in connection with the problem as to what is the maid drift of all the vedic teaching is the metaphysico-philogical question, what does a word denote? A solution of this latter problem has been attempted by an investigation of the various sources from which a child, - or, for that matter, anyone who does not know the meaning of a particular word – first learns the meaning of the word. The means of knowing what a word denotes are enumerated as follows:

(1) *Vriddha-vyavahara* or the behavior of one adult as induced by the speech of another; (2) *Vyakhyana* or explanation; (3) *Vakyasesha* (the remaining portion of the passage where the word occurs); (4) connection with another word of known meaning referring to the same thing; (5) grammar; (6) lexicon; (7) instruction by a trustworthy person.

An investigation of one or another of these processes led some to the conclusion that all speech primarily points to acts; while others hold that it refers to things as they are in themselves as well as to acts.

The next question whose solution hinges on the settlement of the foregoing question is, what is the drift of all vedic teaching? On this question the Indian philosophers may be classed in two groups:

I. Those who, like the karma-mimamsakas, hold that the whole Veda inculcates action only. – By an investigation of the first process of *vriddha-vyavahara* – in which the child, observing how one engages in an act when a word of command is uttered by another, is supposed to conclude that, from the words of the speaker, the hearer first understands that he has to do an act (in general), and then acts about doing the particular act commanded, - the mimamsakas concluded that all speech, and therefore the whole Veda, inculcates action primarily; that all else taught therein is subservient to action; that the Vedas describe Brahman or other things in their already existing state, only so far as these subserve an act enjoined; and that such descriptions of Brahman and other things connected with acts may or may not always correspond to truth.

II. Those who, like the Vedantins, - seeing that other processes, mentioned above, of acquiring the first knowledge of the relation of a word to the thing denoted by it show that a word may denote a thing in itself unrelated to any act, and that even, in vriddha-vyavahara, a knowledge of things as they are is imparted by the sentence uttered, - hold that the Vedas teach Brahman as He is in Himself, as well as karma or action. With reference to this question, the Vedantins may be subdivided into two groups: -

(1) The older or pre-Sankaric school of Vedantins, who hold that the Veda teaches Brahman as He is in Himself, but only as a complement of an injunction of an act *i.e.*, by way of supplying the object of the act of knowing primarily enjoined in the form "Brahman should be known."

(2) The modern Vedantins who, like Srikanthacharya, hold that, primarily, the Vedas both teach Brahman as He is in Himself and enjoin action. Most of these maintain that all acts of ritualistic and meditative worship of Brahman, are subservient to, as a preparation for, the Sakshatkara, a direct and intuitive perception of Brahman.

A full presentation of the course of reasoning, by which the several schools have established their respective conclusions, does not fall within the limited scope of this note. There exists a vast literature on the subject in Sanskrit.

Purvapaksha: (A) Everywhere the power which a word has to denote a thing depends upon the knowledge of their mutual relation. Without a knowledge of the special relation between a word and the thing denoted by it, no man can have an idea of the thing denoted by the word. And the knowledge of their relation is derived from *vriddha-vyavahara*, *i.e.*, from an observation of the speech and the behavior of the elders. This *vriddha-vyavahara* invariably points to something to be done as the ultimate import of words. To explain fully: seeing that immediately after hearing the words "bring the cow" "tie the cow" uttered by one elderly person, the other elderly person to whom the order is addressed engages in the act, the by-stander who seeks to ascertain the meaning of words concludes within himself thus: by all means, the person has engaged in the act on knowing that he has something to do, and the knowledge that he has to do something is derived from the words just uttered; otherwise, how to account for his activity following immediately after hearing the word of command? Then, on seeing the cow brought and tied, the by-stander understands what is the special act meant. Thus the ultimate import of words pointing to *Karya* or something to be done, the authority of *Sabda* or Revelation does not apply to Brahman who is *Siddha*, *i.e.*, who already exists.

(B) Moreover, it being possible to know by inference that this world which is an effect of a particular kind must have its appropriate agent such as Brahman, how can the authority of the Vedantic texts which should treat of things not knowable by any other means apply to Brahman?

(C) Or thus: the Vedantic texts all point to *Vidhis* or injunctions of acts, not to Brahman, as the main subject of their teaching if they should treat of both, then they would be teaching a double proposition. Wherefore it is not right to hold that Vedantic texts teach Brahman.

The *Siddhanta* maintains that it is right to hold that the Vedantic texts teach Brahman, in as much as by a proper collation of the several *tatparya-lingas*, or test-passages as to what the special aim of their teaching is, it is found that the Vedantic texts yield us a knowledge of Brahman.

(A) Now, as to the contention that, because the ultimate meaning of a word always refers to something that *has to be done*, Sabda or revelation does not point to Brahman, - *i.e.*, to what already exists, - we hold it is wrong to say so; for it is found that, even from the sentences (*b*), such as "a son is born to you", which denote things as they are in themselves, a knowledge of the relation between words and their meanings is obtained. Even in *vriddha-vyavahara – i.e.*, in cases where the import of words is learnt by watching the utterance of a word of command by one elderly person followed by action on the part of another, - the person who seeks to know the import of words concludes that the words of the speaker produces, in the mind of the person spoken to, a knowledge of the things themselves, in as much as the idea of something to be done which led to his own activity is found to have been preceded by a knowledge of the things themselves. Therefore, it may be concluded, that Sabda or revelation can signify things that are, as they already exists.

(*b*) This change of illustrations is intended to show that in vyavahara the first knowledge of *vyutpatti* or the relation of a word to the thing denoted by it may be obtained even from a sentence which does not include within it any word or particle indicative of command.

Or, why should we confine ourselves to *vriddha-vyavahara* alone? A knowledge of what a word means may be brought about in other ways. Children, for instance, often taught by their mothers etc., pointing out with their fingers or the like such objects as the moon and the cow, and using appropriate designations with reference to those several objects, come to know what objects the words severally designate (c). Persons, again, who are not conversant with poems and dramas, approach one who is well versed in them, and by an analysis of words they understand the signification of all words, in their respective bearings. Wherefore, since words can signify things already existing, Sabda or revelation constitutes an authority concerning them. Hence the authority of Vedantic-passages concerning Brahman.

(c) In *vriddha-vyavahara* the object of the speaker is not to instruct the child as to the meaning of words, the knowledge acquired by the child being merely accidental and not necessarily following from it and therefore liable to error; whereas the main object of the process described here is the instruction of the child. When the child thus learns the meanings of words, the things severally denoted by words in a sentence become known in their special relations to one another in virtue of *akanksha* or the contiguity of words arranged in a particular order. The special relation in which things spoken of in a sentence stand to one another is knowable solely from the mere contiguity of words. In studying the meaning of a verse composed of unfamiliar words, the student who is taught only the meaning of words in it separately can, in virtue of their contiguity, understand the meaning of the whole verse without being specially taught the mutual relations of things spoken of in the verse. There is thus no use whatever of the general notion that all things spoken of in a sentence are mutually related to one another; - a notion – which alone can, if at all, be said to be obtained from the *vriddha-vyavahara*.

(B) As to the contention that since the universe is an effect, it's appropriate agent, namely Brahman, can be arrived at by anumana or inference, - we say it has no foundation to rest upon; for, it being found that cars, steeples, palaces and the like which exhibit complicated designs have each a plurality of agents, it is not possible to establish by inference that the universe has only one agent. And it has been already shown that, by force of induction, the conclusion becomes inevitable that the agent is subject to karma and so on. Wherefore Brahman cannot be reached by anumana. And, moreover, it may also be conceded that even anumana or inference is an authority concerning Brahman when it is accordant with the Sruti.

(C) Indeed, (*d*) whatever the words point to by tatparya as the special aim of their teaching, to that alone their authority extends, but not to all things, unlike the case of *pratyaksha* or sensuous perception. If it be asked, what are the lingas or marks which determine that Brahman is the drift of the teaching of Vedantic texts, - we say in reply that such marks comprise *upakrama* (enunciation) and *upasamhara* (conclusion), *abhyasa* (repetition), *apurvata* (novelty), *phala* (the result), *arthavada* (persuasion) and *upapatti* (the rationale). Accordingly, here, that Brahman is the drift of the Vedantic teaching is established by such lingas or marks as upakrama. The determining, Vedantic teaching forms what is called the *sravana*, or "the process of hearing," of the Vedantic texts. Accordingly they say:

"Born of ignorance is pain, and knowledge is the remover thereof: the Sravana of all the Vedantic texts brings about that knowledge. Sravana consists in determining, by upakrama and other marks, that Siva, the Higher than the high, is the drift of the teaching of Vedic texts."

(*d*) In this paragraph, the Bhashyakara proceeds to show that Vedantic texts point to both Brahman and to an injunction of His worship s the main drift of their teaching, so that he may refute, in order, the views held respectively on the subject by other schools.

Upakrama (Enunciation) and *Upasamhara* (conclusion) together constitute one linga or mark in determining that Brahman is the drift of the Vedantic-texts. To say that Brahman is the drift of their teaching is to say that they treat of His essential nature and of His upasana.

The following passages constitute the *upakrama* and *upasamhara*, the enunciation and conclusion, in their respective contexts:

(a) [1] *Upakrama*: - "Existent alone, my dear, this at first was."

Upasamhara: - "That thou art."

(b) [2] *Upakrama*: - "By the grace of the creator, he sees the Majesty, the Lord."

Upasamhara: - "He who is Supreme, He is the Great Lord."

[[1] Chh. Up. 6, 2-8. [2] Mahanarayana Up. 12.]

The upakrama and upasamhara ay similarly be discovered in other instances (*e*).

[(*e*) In the passages quoted in the sixth and the subsequent adhikaranas.]

Abhyasa (repetition) may be seen in the following passages (*f*): -

"That thou art."

"All verily is Rudra."[3]

"To the spouse of Ambika, to the spouse of Uma." (3)

"He who verily is Rudra and who is, Brahman also, He is the Lord." [4]

[(*f*) These passages respectively emphasize by repetition the following points in connection with Brahman:
1. that Brahman is intelligent;
2. that He is the All;
3. that He is associated with chit-sakti.
4. that He is endued with all good qualities.
[3] Mahanarayana Up. 22-24. [4] Atharvasiras-Upanishad.]

Apurvata (novelty) consists in Brahman being not known from any other pramana or authority than the Veda (g). Brahma-Jnana (h) or knowledge of Brahman constitutes the phala or result. Arthavada (persuasion) consists in the description of the creation of the universe, its continuance, dissolution etc. Upapatti (the rationale) may be said to consist in proving that the Vedantic theory does not contradict any authority, or in supplying such arguments as are derived from the Brahman's possession of omniscience and the like attributes.

[(*g*) We may add the Smritis, the puranas etc. which are based upon the Vedas.

(*h*) Brahma-Jnana is the Sakshatkara of Brahman, who is unsurpassed Bliss in essence.]

The Vedantas do not point to Brahman alone as the special aim of their teaching, but it is understood that they point that they point also to a *vidhi* (*i*) or an injunction as to knowing Him, as witness such passages as,

"Atman verily, my Dear, should be perceived" [1]

[¹ Bri. Upanishad 4-5.

(*i*) Otherwise, owing to non-observance of upasana, the result thereof, namely, the attainment of Brahman, is not possible.]

As to the contention that, if the Vedantas aim at both, then we would be led to the conclusion that the Vedantas teach a double proposition, - we (*j*) say that the contention is groundless; for, just as by means of the eye which enables us to perceive rupa (form or color), the underlying substance (dravya) also is perceived, so Brahman also is taught by the Vedantas, though they aim at the injunction referred to and thus there is no self-contradiction involved in the Vedantas aiming at both.

[(*j*) The objection is answered from the stand point of the school holding that Brahman is taught in the Vedanta as a mere subsidiary factor concerned in the act of knowing, which is the main drift of the Vedantic teaching.]

(*Objection*): The Brahmajnana which is to be produced by the Sabda or revelation is obtained from the texts which treat of Brahman. Then, what is the use of an injunction concerning it.

(*Answer*): There is no inconsistency (*k*) in enjoining Brahmajnana or the act of knowing Brahman, not withstanding that we are led to the act otherwise. Take for example the case of *mantras* etc: although a knowledge as to the substances and Devatas concerned in a ritual has been obtained from a study of the mantras themselves treating of those substances and Devatas, still, the *prayoga-vidhi*-the tersely formulated statement of an injunction in all its details, - that those substances and Devatas should be thought of at the time of observance by means of mantras, impels us to a fresh act of knowledge. So also here. And this cannot be objected to on the ground that no such prayoga-vidhi is possible here, in the absence of Utpatti-vidhi (*l*), *viniyoga-vidhi*, and *adhikara-vidhi*. For, *utpatti-vidhi* being understood through implication by force of context, there naturally comes the Viniyoga-vidhi-prescribing the *modus operandi* in the form of sama or self-control etc – in connection with the injunction "Let him see the Atman." And then, on the principle of *Ratri-satra* (*m*) we may even supply the *adhikarin*, - the person, for whom the Brahmajnana is intended, - namely the seeker of moksha, as may be learnt from the arthavada-passages- passages explaining things that are subservient to an injunction – such as the following: "Knowing God, one is released from all pasas or bonds." Accordingly we come to the *prayoga-vidhi* in the following form: He who seeks moksha should equip himself with sama (tranquillity) and other attributes and acquire Brahmajnana.

[(*k*) The jnana derived by a study of the passages themselves which treat of Brahman is alleged to be quite different from that which is induced by injunction. Wherefore the injunction, they say, is not useless.

(*l*) *Utpatti-vidhi* is that in which the main sacrificial act as well as the substance by means of which the act can be effected is enjoined. *Adhikara-vidhi* is that which teaches the fruit attainable by means of the act. *Viniyoga-vidhi* is that which enjoins a minor or subsidiary act which subserves the major act of the sacrifice. *Prayoga-vidhi* is the formula of an injunction with all its subsidiary parts. The Utpatti-vidhi implied here in Vedanta is, "by means of Vedanta Brahmajnana should be acquired."

(*m*) In the passage in which the sacrifice called *Ratri-Satra* is enjoined it is not mentioned for what result it is intended. Elsewhere, however, it is said in an arthavada passage that he who performs *Ratri-Satra* can secure *pratishtha*, glory or renown. Thus, Ratri-Satra-nyaya consists in deriving the adhikara-vidhi from a section different from that in which utpatti-vidhi is found.

(*Objection*): - Brahmajnana cannot be a subject of an injunction. In the passage such as "Atman verily my dear, should be seen", it is not indeed right to construe Atman, i.e., Brahman who is eternal, immutable and quite pure – as karma-karaka, *i.e.*, as the direct object (of the act of seeing), - a construction which would be necessary if the passage should be interpreted as an injunction (of Brahmajnana): for, such a Brahman cannot undergo birth; He cannot be an object of *prapti* or attainment, nor can He be subjected to *vikara* (change), or *Samskara* (purification) (*n*). Neither is it possible on the principle of "*Saktu-nyaya*" (*o*) to resort to an injunction in the form "He should see by Atman," thus construing Atman as the instrument of action instead of as the direct object of the action. For, the two cases are different. To explain at length: a fresh change of state, by way of being reduced to ashes, being possible in the case of the flour in virtue of the act of throwing into fire, "flour" can be construed as an instrumental case in form, while in sense the flour continues as an object of the act. This does not apply in the case of Atman. Wherefore the Vedanta cannot be interpreted to enjoin Brahma-jnana.

(*Answer*): - No; for though birth etc, which should necessarily pertain to the object of an action are absent in Atman, an injunction is possible with a view to the result in the form of moksha accruing to the agent.

(*Objection*): - How is an injunction possible in the case of an act in which we will engage even without such an injunction?

(*Answer*): - The act to which we may thus be led even without such an injunction, is either intermittent or constant. In either case there is room for a *niyama-vidhi* and so on (*p*).

(*n*) Brahman being eternal, He cannot be newly brought into existence; being Brahman, - *literally*, vast or omnipresent, - He cannot be attained to as one removed by space before; as immutable, He is not subject to change of form or attribute; as ever quite pure. He cannot be subject to purification, become purer.

(*o*) *Sakta-nyaya*: In the injunction "let him offer flour," 'flour' in the accusative case in converted into an instrumental case so as to render the injunction one of a main sacrificial act (artha-karma). If 'flour' be taken in the accusative case as it is, then the injunction is reduced to one of a subsidiary act (guna-karma); and it cannot be a mere subsidiary act here, in as much as the flour once reduced to ashes cannot be used again for any other purpose, nor is there another act mentioned to which it may be considered as subsidiary. In this case, though the 'flour' be thus taken logically as an instrument, it can continue be the grammatical object of the verb.

(*p*) The Vedantic study is either intermittent and occasional as following from one's own choice; or obligatory and constant, as due to the injunction that one should never leave Vedic study. In the first case there is room for the *niyama-vidhi* enjoining that Vedantic study should always be pursued. In the latter it is a *parisankhya-vidhi* intended to exclude altogether the study of things alien to the Atman.

TABLE OF TATWAS AND THRIPADARTHA.

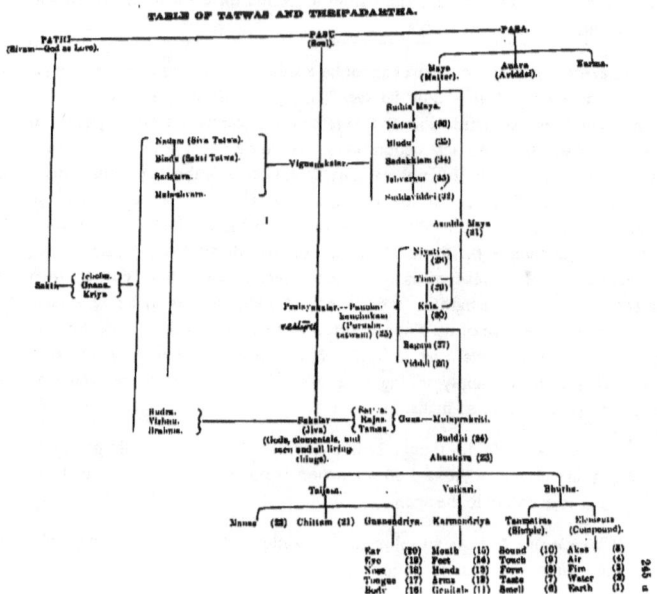

(*Objection*) (*q*): - In that case the drift of the Vedantic teaching being an injunction, it cannot be held that Vedantas teach Brahman. It has, however, been contended that just as by means of the eye, by which we perceive *rupa* or color, the underlying substance (*drayva*) is perceived, so also Brahman may be taught by Vedantic which point to an injunction as their special aim. But this contention is untenable; for the eye is a pramana or as organ of perception as regards everything that comes in contact with it. Not so is the Sabda or revelation. This latter becomes a pramana or authority only as regards that which constitutes the *drift* of all its teaching. Wherefore it is not possible for Vedanta both to teach who Brahman is and to enjoin the act of knowing Brahman.

(*q*) The Bhashayakara has thus far expounded the view of the so called Vedantins. He now proceeds by means of objections and refutations thereof such points as he does not approve of in the view just described and to establish in his own way the proposition that Vedanta both teaches Brahman and enjoins His Upasana. The first objection has been raised and answered with a view to show that the illustration of the eye is inappropriate owing to a difference between Veda and sensuous perception as to their authority concerning their respective revelations and that the same Proposition can only be established by an appeal to other instances in the Veda itself in which two different propositions are inculcated in the same sentence.

(*Answer*): - No; because we find that passage like "he should offer *samits* or fuel" * have a double aim, namely, to enjoin the five prayajas themselves and to enjoin also the order of their observance, therefore it is but right that the Vedantic texts also should both inform us as to what the nature of Brahman is and enjoin the act of knowing Brahman as leading to moksha. [* Taittiriya Samhita I. vi. 1.]

(*Objection*): - (*r*) Brahman being known from the text itself, an injunction of Brahmajnana is of no use, in as much as the aim of the injunction can be achieved without such an injunction , by the knowledge already obtained otherwise, (*i.e.* by an independent study of the texts themselves).

(*r*) Now the Bhashayakara opposes the doctrine of the injunction that Brahman should be known by means of Vedanta with a view to establish his own doctrine that the aspirant should meditate upon Brahman after acquiring a knowledge of Him by means of the Vedanta.

(*Answer*): - Not so; for, though Brahman is known indirectly (parokshatvena) from the texts, it is right that there should be an injunction of the act of jnana with a view to the sakshit-kara or an intuitive realization of Brahman. It may be asked, what is the difference? We answer: the knowledge produced by the texts (sabda) cannot cause sakshit-kara on the other hand; it is jnana, of the form of Upasana or continuous meditation, which alone can produce sakshat-kara. Accordingly the Sruti says:

> "By meditating, the Muni goes to the source of all beings, the witness of all" beyond all darkness." *

> "By churning with Jnana alone does the wise man burn up the bond (pasa)." *

> "Knowing the Deva, the Shining one, he is released from all bonds (pasas)." †

> "Knowing Him, the Lord, they become immortal." ‡

[* Kaivalya Upanishad. † Svet. Upanishad 1-8. ‡ Svet. Upanishad 3-7.]

Accordingly in the passage,

> "Brahman should be learnt from the passages of Sruti, reflected upon by reasoning, then after reflection meditated upon: these are the means to darsana or intuitive perception,"

the smriti shows that it is *nididhyasana* or intense meditation inseparably associated with the knowledge produced by *Sravana* and *Manana*, (*s*) – by the processes of learning and reflecting, - which produces sakshatkara or direct perception of Brahman. Wherefore Jnana, of the form of Upasana, calculated to produce the result of moksha, is enjoined in the following passages: -

> "In the self (*t*) should he see the Atman." §

"Sambhu should be contemplated in the middle of akasa." ||

"Seeing that all this (Universe) has its birth, its dissolution, and its being, in Him, every one, tranquil-minded, should worship Him." ¶

"Do thou worship, O prachina-yogya." *

[(s) Jnana is first produced by Sravana or hearing, and then strengthened by Manana or reflection and reasoning. The Jnana being the cause of nididhyasana or intense meditation of Brahman the latter is said to be inseparable from it.

(t) In the self; In the body, in the middle of the akasa of the heart.

§ Bri. Upanishad 4-5-23. || Atharvasikha-Upanishad. ¶ Chh. Upanishad 3-14. * Taitti. Upanishad 1-6.]

Similarly in such passages as "the knower of Brahman attains to the Supreme" the nature of Brahman His Upasana and the effect thereof are taught. Otherwise (u) how can either the attainment 'of all desires' as the result 'equally with Brahman' (v) who is described as the True, or the sikshat-kara of such a Brahman, be achieved? Such passages as

"Truth, wisdom, and endless is Brahman" †

"Bliss is Brahman" ‡

"Brahman is He whose body is akasa, who is the existent, who delights in Prana, whose joy is manas" §

"Hail to the Reality, the Truth, the Supreme Brahman, dark and yellowish in person, having semen above, diverse eyed," ||

[(u) *Otherwise*: It is but reasonable that the Vedanta should enjoin the Upasana of Brahman. Without the Upasana no sakshat-kara is possible, and the whole exposition of Brahman would be useless if no means of reaching Him be taught, if therefore, the scriptures which expound Brahman should serve any human end, it can be only by enjoining the means of reaching him. This reasonableness is one of the lingas showing that Vedanta enjoins Upasana.

(v) *All desires*: Equal to the aggregate of pleasures accessible to all beings from man up to Hiranyagarbha: Equally with Brahman: *i.e.*, the liberated soul enjoys all the bliss that Brahman enjoys.

† Taitti. Upanishad 2-1. ‡ Bri. Upanishad 3-9-28. § Taitti. Upanishad 1-6. || Mahanarayana 12.]

Propound – as shown by upakrama and other tatparya-lingas or marks showing what the special aim of Vedantic teaching is – Brahman as one who is by nature Truth, Wisdom and Bliss, who delights in Himself, in whom all taint of pain is absent, who is all good itself who is dark and yellowish because associated with the inseparable Parama-Sakti or Supreme-Energy, who is diverse-eyed as possessed of three eyes. Such passages as:

"He who knows (Brahman) seated in the cave, etc." ¶ [¶ Taitt. Upanishad 2-1]

"Thus do thou worship, O Prachina-yogya" ** [** Taitt. Upanishad 1-6]

Enjoin His Upasana which is inseparable from Jnana And Passages like, "he attains all desires" tell us of the attainment of all desires by the worshippers (Upasakas- Wherefore it is but just that there should be an injunction of Upasana inseparably associated with Jnana, in the following form: - A mumukshu or seeker of moksha, performing his own duties disinterestedly, eschewing all prohibited and interested acts, endued with the purity of mind resulting from the observance of acts enjoined in the Sruti and Smriti, saturated with Bhakti for Parama-Siva which is rendered possible by the subjugation of the body and the senses, - thus prepared, a mumukshu should know of Para-Brahman called Siva from the essential portion of the Sruti and meditate upon Him. The use of the epithet *Siva* here (in the Bhashya) is intended to show that the diverse-eyed Brahman is the repository of supreme purity and good and is therefore, for mumukshus, the sole object of Upasana. Accordingly in a passage in the Atharvasikha: –

"Siva alone, the source of good, should be meditated upon, abandoning all else." –

It is taught that the Being denoted by the word *Siva* should alone be meditated upon. Otherwise, how can the cessation of Samsara be brought about" Siva is the seat of the unsurpassed good when is free from all taint of evil, and a knowledge of Him leads to moksha as its result, as said in the passage:

"When men should roll up the ether like a hide, then only, without first knowing God, there could be an end of pain." * [* Svetasvatara-Upanishad 6-20.]

The passage:

"Siva alone, the source of all good, should be meditated upon, abandoning all else,"

Excludes all brings other than Siva as not worthy the aspirant's while to know or meditate upon. Wherefore those who are desirous of moksha has to know and meditate upon Siva alone, the Para-Brahman.

There can, therefore, be no opposition to the view that a harmonious concatenation of all tests which go to show what the drift of the Vedantic teaching is, prove that the Vedantas point both to Brahman and to an injunction of His worship.

Adhikarana – 5

With a view to prevent a possible objection that the aforesaid definition of Brahman is too wide as applying to Pradhana as well, the Sutrakara says:

Because of thinking, (Sat is) not the unrevealed (I. i. 5.)

The subject of discussion in this section is the following passage of the Chhandogya Upanishad:

"Sat (existent) alone, my dear, this at first was one only, without a second and It thought may I may be many." * [* Chh. 6-2.]

Here the *doubt* arises as to whether the Being spoken of as Sat, the Existence and said to have existed in the beginning and to be the cause of the whole of this universe, is Brahman or Pradhana.

(*Purvapaksha*): - It is but right that Pradhana is the cause of the world as described elsewhere in the Sruti:

"Unborn, one red, white and black, giving birth to manifold progeny similarly formed ...." † [† Mahanarayana Upanishad 12.] Here it is taught that the Sankhya's Prakriti, composed of *rajas*, *sattva* and *tamas* – as indicated by the red and other colors – is the producer of manifold progeny. In accordance with this passage we should understand that it is Pradhana which is the cause of the world, spoken of here (in the Chhandogya Upanishad) as the *Sat*. we may even explain that the Pradhana possesses, in virtue of *rajas* and *sattva* contained in it the powers of intelligence and action (Jnana-Sakti and Kriya Sakti) which are indispensable in the cause of the world. It stands to reason that the unintelligent Pradhana should become transformed (parinama) into the world, not the Supreme Lord, the Immutable Intelligence; - parinama (transformation) being only a vikara or modified form of the cause. Thus both reason and revelation lead us to the conclusion that it is the Pradhana which is spoken of as Sat and is the cause of the world.

As against the foregoing view, we hold as follows: the *unrevealed* i.e., the Pradhana established by pure *anumana* or inference, is not the thing spoken of as the *Sat* and described as the cause of the universe; but it is the intelligent Brahman (that is spoken of as Sat); for 'thought' is predicated of the Sat in the words "It thought, may I become many." ‡ [‡ Chh. Upanishad 6-2.] In the unintelligent Pradhana, indeed, there cannot exist thought which is the property of a conscious entity.

It is not right to contend that, because of the passage "Giving birth to manifold progeny similarly formed," it is the Prakriti of the Sankhya that is here spoken of as the cause of the universe. For, in Sutra I. iv. 8 we shall show that it is only that Prakriti which has the Supreme Lord for its impelling cause that can produce manifold progeny. Neither as it possible to maintain that, as made up of *rajas* and *sattva*, Pradhana is endued with the potencies of action and intelligence; for, the Prakriti which is made up of the three gunas cannot possess *sattva* and *rajas* quite exclusive of *tamas*. It being admitted that Prakriti is the *sattva*, *rajas* and *tamas* in a state of equilibrium; it is idle to say that when *tamas* becomes quiescent and *rajas* and *sattva* not excited, Pradhana becomes endued with intelligence and activity. The objection that the transformation of the Supreme *immutable* Lord would subject Him to vikara or change is a mere play of ignorance: there is no fear of our being led to such a conclusion, in as much as we hold that the Supreme Lord is the cause when invested with the potencies of subtle *chit* and *achit* in their undifferentiated state as to name and form and He is the effect when invested with the potencies of grosser *chit* and *achit* which are differentiated in name and form.

(*Objection*): - From the determinate exclusion implied in such passages as the "existent *alone*, my dear, this at first was, one alone, without a second" we learn that the thing spoken of as Sat, "the Existent" has no specific attributes. How can It be spoken of as the cause containing within it the universe in its subtle form?

(*Answer*): - The determination conveyed by "Existent alone" is not meant to exclude specific attributes; but it is meant to remove the idea that the cause is not the non-existent; there being persons who by ignorance cherish that idea, as set forth in the Sruti:

"Non-existent verily this at first was; thence, indeed, the existent sprang up." * [* Tait. Upanishad 2-7.]

Moreover, how can Brahman – as described in the passage:

"The existent alone, my dear, this at first was, one alone, without a second," –

be without specific attributes? In this passage the word 'was' shows a specific act, and the words "at first" show a specific time. The determination implied in "one alone" is indented to exclude an external ruler, and the words without a second" indicate that it is the *Upadana* or material cause of the universe. Hence also the specific attributes of Omniscience and infinite power; for how, without the specific attributes of Omniscience and all-powerfulness, can Brahman constitute the two fold cause of the universe? Or, (the same thing may be established in another way): it cannot be rightly held that the word 'Sat' which is made up of a *base* and *termination* refers to only one thing; the word 'Sat' being intended to denote two things by means of its base and termination. Accordingly, the learned have declared as follows:

"Sakti and Siva are denoted by the base and the termination of the word 'Sat'. These two constitute Brahman, as together forming, by their harmonious union, the essence of the whole universe."

The conclusion, therefore, is that the Supreme Lord Himself invested with the potencies (Sakti) of the Universe – *chit* and *achit* in their gross and subtle forms, - and thus forming the cause and the effect, is the thing denoted by the word 'Sat'

Again an objection is raised and answered:

If (you regard it) figurative, (we say) no, because of the word 'Atman.' (I. i. 6.)

(*Objection*): - It has been stated that, because no act of thinking is possible in Pradhana which is insentient, it is the sentient Supreme Brahman that is the cause, spoken of as the '*Sat*' or Existent. Now, this view is quite inconsistent. For, just as in the statements "that *light* thought" and "those *waters* thought," thought is figuratively predicated of insentient objects, so also it may be held that thought is figuratively predicated of Pradhana.

(*Answer*): - No, because of the word 'Atman' denoting a sentient being. The Sruti starts with the words "the existent, my dear, this at first was," and concludes thus, "He is the

Atman; That thou art." Even as to the light etc., the predicate of thought is not figurative, since the sentient Supreme Lord runs through them as their Atman or essential Soul.

(*Objection*): - It has been shown that, even admitting that the predicate of thought the insentient is figurative, it is not possible to maintain that the insentient Pradhana is the existent and is the cause of the Universe, because of the word "Atman" implying that the cause is a sentient being. Granted that the word 'Atman' cannot denote the insentient Pradhana; but the sentient Jiva or individual soul can be denoted primarily by the word 'Atman.' Wherefore, it is the sentient Jiva that is spoken of as the existent and the cause of the universe.

(*Answer*): -   In reply the Sutrakara says: -

(The Sat is not Jiva.) It being taught that the devotee thereof attains Moksha (I. i. 7.)

The passage,

"For him there is only delay so long he is not delivered (from the body)" * [* Chh. Upanishad. 6-2-...14.]

teaches that he who is devoted to the Being spoken of as the 'Sat' attains to Moksha. Wherefore neither Pradhana nor Jiva is referred to by the word 'Sat.' Not even they who hold Pradhana to be the cause can admit that the devotee of Pradhana attains to moksha holding as they do that Pradhana is a thing to be avoided. Neither can a devotee of Jiva attain Moksha, Jiva being excluded from the passage,

"Siva alone, the source of all good, should be contemplated, abandoning all else." † [† Atharvasikha.]

Again, the Sutrakara states quite clearly the reason for discarding Pradhana:

And (Sat is not Pradhana), there being no declaration that (the Sat) is to be abandoned. (I. i. 8.)

If the Pradhana were intended to be taught here, then it (Sat) would have been spoken of as a thing to be avoided. Whereas in the sentence "That thou art" the 'Sat' is spoken of as an object of contemplation leading to Moksha. Wherefore it stands to reason that Pradhana is not (the thing spoken of as 'Sat').

Moreover, in the case of Pradhana there is some inconsistency, as the Sutrakara says:-

Essence of inconsistency with the proposition. – (I. i. 9.)

There is another reason why Pradhana cannot be the thing denoted by the word 'Sat'; the reason being that it would involve a contradiction of the original proposition asserting that, the One being known, all is known. The passage "whereby the unheard of becomes heard"‡ asserts that the knowledge of the thing denoted by the word 'Sat' leads to a knowledge of all things, sentient and insentient, these latter being the effect of that one thing. This would be impossible if Pradhana were the cause, in as much as Pradhana cannot be the cause of the sentient existence. [‡ Chh. Upanishad 6-1.]

(*Objection*): - The cause, Pradhana being known, all this – the effect thereof – which is insentient and subject to change becomes known. When the clay, for instance, is known, its effect, the pot etc., is known.

What inconsistency, then, is found here? In reply the Sutrakara says: -

Essence of dissolution. – (I. i. 10.)

For the following reason, too, Pradhana is not the thing denoted by the word 'Sat'; for the passage

"Learn from me the true nature of sleep (svapna). When a man sleeps here, then, my dear son, he becomes united with the Sat, he is gone to his own (self). Therefore they say '*svapiti*,' he sleeps." * [* Chh. Upanishad, 6-8]

speaks of the dissolution of the sentient Jiva when he becomes one with the Sat. Dissolution means absorption. The sentient cannot attain dissolution in the insentient Pradhana. Wherefore 'Sat' does not refer to Pradhana.

It is the Supreme Lord that is referred to by the word 'Sat,' not Pradhana. So the Sutrakara says: -

The usage being the same. – (I. i. 11.)

Just as in this Upanishad the word 'Sat' is taken to mean the Supreme Lord, so in other Upanishads, too 'Sat' refers to the same thing (i.e., the Supreme Lord), as for example in the passages like.

"Purusha verily is Rudra, the *sat*, the adorable. Hail! Hail!!" † [† Mahana. Up.]

Wherefore it is verily the Supreme Lord who is denoted by the word 'Sat.'

In this (*i.e.*, the Chhandogya) Upanishad it is plainly said that everything takes its birth from the Atman referred to by the word 'Sat'. So the Sutrakara says: -

And it being also revealed. – (I. 1. 12.)

Here, too, the Sruti beginning with the words "From Atman is Prana, from Atman is akasa" concludes with the words "from Atman alone is all this." ‡ [‡ Chh. Upanishad. 7-25.]

Therefore Brahman Himself is spoken of as the cause of the universe and is referred to by the word 'Sat' not Pradhana.

Adhikarana. – 6

Here (in the adhikarana just closed) it has been objected that the definition of Brahman as the cause of the universe which can be learned from scriptures alone, is too wide as applying to the Tantric Pradhana as well; and arguments based on the sentiency of the cause of the Universe have been adduced with a view to show that the definition is not too wide as applying to Pradhana. The next adhikarana proceeds to show that as in the case of insentient Pradhana so also the definition is not too wide as applying to sentient Jiva either:

Anandamaya (is Paramesvara) because of repetition – (I. i. 13.)

In Ananda-valli, in the passage beginning with "From this Atman, verily akasa was born" and ending with "Beyond that Atman made up of intellect, there is another inner Atman which is blissful," * a certain Atman, blissful and hidden within *annamaya* (physical) and other sheaths, is spoken of as the cause of the whole creation including akasa.

Then *doubt* arises as to whether the 'blissful atman' is Jiva or Paramesvara.

The *prima facie* view is that it is Jiva, because the attributes of Jiva are found described here. For example, in the passage beginning with "From earth plants, from plants food, from food the person," † we find described the body made up of five members, and so on. Here *annamaya* refers to the physical body, *pranamaya* to prana within the physical body, *manomaya* to manas within prana, *vijnanamaya* to buddhi within manas; and *anandamaya* is the Jiva himself, the basis of all these, - of *annamaya etc*. The representation of annamaya and other Atmans as made up of head and so on is intended for meditation. Abundance of food etc., is described as the fruit of the meditation of *annamaya* etc., as Brahman. It may be asked how can Jiva, immersed in pain – in the ocean of samsara - be spoken of as *anandamaya*? But there is no room for any such objection. The word 'ananda' denotes Supreme Brahman, as said by the Sruti – "ananda is Brahman." ‡ [‡ Tait. Upanishad 2-4.] As the suffix maya implies modification (vikara), *anandamaya* refers to Jiva, who is the *karya*, - the effect or emanation – of Brahman. If *anandamaya* were to refer to Brahman who is ever endued with goodness, the prayer for purity offered in the words "may my annamaya, pranamaya, manomaya vijnanamaya, and anandamaya become pure" § would be useless. Wherefore this anandamaya Atman is Jiva, not Paramesvara. [§ Mahana. Upanishad. 57.]

As against this view, we hold that the Anandamaya Atman is the Paramesvara, because this Ananda or bliss is repeatedly spoken of as unsurpassed. Beginning with 'there arises this enquiry as to Ananda,' * the sruti speaks of several grades of bliss, ranging from human bliss to that of Prajapati, each higher grade being a hundred times superior to the one below it, and then concludes with "that is the unit of Brahman's bliss," thus declaring by repetition that Brahman's bliss stands unsurpassed at the head. The samsarin cannot be spoken of as such a repository of unsurpassed bliss. [* Tait. Upanishad 2-8.]

As to the question how, if Anandamaya be the Isvara, to account for His prayer for purity, - the answer is follows: Just as the highly lustrous moon attains clearness only on the disappearance of clouds which hide her, so, too, in the case of Him who is ever pure, purification consists in merely removing the *tirodhana-mala*, the dirt which acts as the veil concealing Him from our view. Wherefore Anandamaya is none other than Paramesvara.

(*Objection*): - Ananda itself is declared to be Brahman; and Anandamaya must be an effect or emanation thereon, since the suffix 'maya' implies vikara (change). If Anandamaya were Isvara, it would follow that Isvara is different from Brahman. If, thus, Isvara were a mere vikara or effect, He would also be non-eternal.

The Sutrakara states and answers the foregoing objection as follows:

If (you hold it is) not so because of the word implying vikara, (we hold you) not (right), because (it implies) abundance. – (I. i. 14).

(*Objection*): - Just as *Annamaya* and others are the vikaras or modified forms *anna* or food, etc., so also *Anandamaya* is a vikara or modified form of ananda. For instance, a jar or the lake which is formed of clay is only a modified form of clay. Accordingly since Paramesvara cannot be: vikara, Anandamaya is none other than Jiva.

(*Answer*): - No, because here the suffix 'maya' implies abundance. Only in the words 'annamaya,' 'pranayama' and 'manomaya,' '*maya*' means vikara or modified form. Vijnanamaya is the Jiva in whom Vijnana or intellection is in abundance; Anandamaya is Paramesvara in whom Ananda or bliss abounds.

(*Objection*): - As occurring in a section dealing with vikaras or modified forms, it is altogether but proper that the suffix 'maya' should be taken to mean viakarr.

In answer, the Sutrakara says:

Also because of the mention of a reason therefore (I. i. 15.)

The passage "He alone verily causes bliss" * declares Anandamaya as the cause of bliss with reference to Jivas. He alone who himself abounds in bliss can impart bliss to others. Wherefore Anandamaya is none other than Paramesvara. [* Tait. Upanishad 2-7.]

(*Objection*): - Though it has been said that Anandamaya is the Paramesvara in whom bliss is abundant, still, it will be found that He is quite distinct from Brahman; for, the words "Brahman is the tail, the basis" † show that He has Brahman for His basis. If it be admitted that Brahman, is distinct from the Paramesvara, the former becomes a dependent being and cannot, therefore, be the cause of the universe, and so on. Wherefore it is better to hold that Jiva is meant here. [† Tait. Upanishad 2-5.]

In reply the Sutrakara says:

And the very subject of the hymn is sung here. – (I. i. 16.)

The very Brahman spoken in the words of the Mantra, "Truth, Wisdom, and Endless – is Brahman" ‡ is described as Anandamaya in the passage "Another inner atman is Anandamaya, § as abounding in bliss. In the passage Brahman is the tail, the basis, the word

"Brahman" designates Pranava, which as the designation of Paramesvara, forms His basis. [‡ Tait. Upanishad. 2-1. § Tait. Upanishad. 2-5.]

On this subject some hold as follows: -

It is the *Paramakasa* or Supreme Light, the *Prakriti Atman*, that is spoken of in the Sruti as Anandamaya; but not the Para-Brahman, that Cause which is beyond the Universe and described, as "Truth, Wisdom, and Endless is Brahman." Anandamaya is the *Paramakasa* described as the Prakriti or the material cause of the universe including akasa or ether, as stated in the passage "From this Atman, verily, was akasa produced." * That the Atman here spoken of is of the form of Paramakasa is seen from the passage "If this akasa, the Ananda, did not exist &c." † And the passage "Brahman is the tail, the basis"‡ shows that Brahman is the basis of Ananda-akasa. Accordingly in the passage "That is the unit of Brahman's bliss" we find that the Ananda rests in Brahman. This very Ananda is again described as the Prakriti of all beings in passages like

"He knew that Ananda is Brahman, it is from Ananda verily are all these beings born." § [* Tait. Upanishad 2-1. † Tait. Upanishad 2-7. Tait. Upanishad 2-5. ‡ §Tait. Upanishad 3-6.]

And Ananda is here spoken of as Brahman in the words "Ananda is Brahman," because as an attribute of Brahman is not quite distinct from Brahman. The passage "This wisdom of Bhrigu and Varuna is based on the Paramakasa declares that Varuna's wisdom concludes with Paramakasa, which is an attribute of Brahman, and which is of the nature of Supreme Bliss, the Prakriti or material cause of the universe, otherwise known as the Supreme energy, the self-conscious Atman. Wherefore it is the Supreme energy (Paramasakti) – which is an attribute of Brahman, the Atman which is the Prakriti or the material cause the Supreme Light (Paramakasa), that is spoken of as Anandamaya. As the substance possessing Anandamaya as an attribute, the Supreme Brahman is spoken of as its basis. And Vijnanamaya is the Jiva, the worshipper thereof. The Sutrakara has introduced the Sutra 13, thinking that the Anandamaya-Atman is one with Brahman, because the former, the Anandamaya, which is of the nature of an attribute (dharma) and energy (Sakti) cannot be thought of as distinct from the latter, the Para-Brahman, the basic substance wherein it inheres as an attribute and energy.

Others, again, hold as follows: these five Atman, spoken of as *annamaya* and so on, are no doubt the five sentient Purushas or spiritual entities on the causal plane of being, designated as Brahma, Vishnu, Rudra, Isvara and Sadasiva and who are the impelling controllers of the five bhutas or cosmic elements hinted at by *anna* (food) etc., in as much as in such passages as "from this world departing, he becomes united with the physical (*annamaya*) Atman", the 'annamaya' and others occur in connection with Atman which denotes a sentient being, and are described as reachable one after another by the liberated soul departing from this world of samsara. The Brahman who is known as Paramasiva and who is the cause even of Sadasiva, *i.e.*, of the *Anandamaya* who is the basis of the Annamaya and other Atmans, - is spoken of as His (Sadasiva's) basis. The Anandamaya is not regarded as distinct from Brahman and is therefore spoken of as Brahman. Thus, all things considered, it may be concluded that Anandamaya is Paramesvara.

Adhikarana. – 7.

It has been established that the definition – arrived at by an accordant construction of the scriptural texts – of Brahman, the Supreme Siva, as the cause of the Universe, is not so too wide as applying to Pradhana and Jiva as well. Next the Sutrakara proceeds to discuss the passages which seem to declare that Hiranyagarbha, who is made up of the totality of Jivas is the cause of the Universe.

Not the other, becomes of incongruity. (I. i. 17.)

The following passage of the Mahopanishad forms the subject of discussion here:

"Whence proceeded the birth of the Universe, That Being by water sent forth the (bodies of) souls on earth, and (it was that Being) which by plants, entered into men and beasts, into all beings moving and unmoving." † [† Mahana. Up. 1.]

The doubt arises as to whether the Purusha spoken of as the cause of the birth etc. of the whole Universe is the Paramesvara or someone else.

Purvapaksha: - It is the Hiranyagarbha, because of His characteristic marks described here.

From the puranic passage:

"The three lokas having become one ocean, the Brahman in the form of Narayana reclines on the serpent-bed, expanded by the devouring of the three worlds."

we learn that Brahma lies in the ocean. This characteristic mark of His is found described in the passage:

"Whom within the ocean the sages weave." ‡ [‡ *i.e.* whom the sages see forming himself the whole universe as threads form themselves a cloth.]

In the opening passage of the whole section, "Prajapati moves in the womb within" * He is described as having entered into all beings, and in the conclusion the passage "the creator made the sun and the moon as before, also heaven and the earth" † declares that He is the cause. Wherefore it is but right that to the Hiranyagarbha who is thus referred to in the opening and concluding passages apply all the attributes described in the intervening passages. Moreover, reference has been made to the following passages which treat of Hiranyagarbha: [* Mahana. Up. 12. † Tait. Aranyaka. 3-13.]

"He was born of waters & c." "Hiranyagarbha at first was & c."

In the section first referred to here, it is certainly Prajapati that is treated of; for, we find it said that "Prajapati moves in the womb within; the unborn is born in many a form." In the section next referred to, it is said that "Prajapati is verily the Hiranyagarbha." Therefore it is verily the Hiranyagarbha who is described here as the cause of the birth of the world and so on.

As against the foregoing view we hold as follows: It is not the Hiranyagarbha as distinct from the Paramesvara, that is treated of here; for, the attributes of Paramesvara – such as being the cause of the origin of the Universe – cannot apply to the Hiranyagarbha. The Being spoken of at the beginning as the cause of the Universe, as the being "whence proceeded the birth of the Universe" is described to be higher than all and far transcending the darkness or the region of Prakriti, in the verses beginning with the following: -

> "There is verily none else higher and subtle than This which is higher than the high and greater than the greater which is one, unmanifest, of endless forms, the whole universe, the ancient, beyond the darkness." ‡ [‡ Mahana. Up. 18.]

This cannot apply to the Hiranyagarbha who is within the Mundane Egg. Moreover, moksha or immortality is said to result from a knowledge of Him, in the work.

> "They who knows Him become immortal."§ [§ Mahanarayana Up. 1.]

This, too, cannot refer to Hiranyagarbha, for, as a special distinguishing mark of Paramesvara, it is declared that He is the source of immortality in the following passage.

> "When like leather men can fold ether, men alone without, knowing Siva there can be an end of pain." * [* Svetasvatara Up. 6-2. *i.e.* There can be no end of pain without a knowledge of Siva.]

It is of no use to say that He (the Hiranyagarbha) is referred to in the opening and concluding passages. As inapplicable to Hiranyagarbha, the words "Prajapati" and "Dhata," denote the Paramesvara who is literally the Lord of creatures and the supporter of the Universe. In both the sections referred to – Taittiriya Aranyaka 3-13 and Taittiriya Samhita 4-1-8 – it is the Paramesvara Himself that is spoken of, because of His characteristic attributes – that He is the Lord of the Universe and far beyond it – described thus.

> "Who rules this, the two-footed and the four-footed"† "The sun-colored, beyond the darkness." ‡ [† Tait. Sam. 4-1-8. ‡ Tait. Aranyaka. 3-13.]

Wherefore He who is spoken of as Prajapati and the cause of the world is the Paramesvara, not the Hiranyagarbha.

As against the view that the Hiranyagarbha is the cause of the Universe since there is not distinction between Him and Paramesvara, the Sutrakara says:

And because of the mention of a distinction. (I. i. 13.)

A distinction between Paramesvara and Hiranyagarbha as cause and effect, is made in this Mahopanishad in the following passage: -

"The Rudra, the Great Sage (Maharshi) transcending the Universe, first saw the Hiranyagarbha, the first of the Devas then being born." § [§ Mahanarayana. Up. 12.]

Wherefore it may be concluded that the Isvara is the cause of the whole Universe including Hiranyagarbha.

The Sutrakara refutes another possible objection thus:

And in spite of his desire, no ground for inference. (I. i. 19.)

Everywhere in the Sruti Hiranyagarbha's desire concerning the creation of the Universe is spoken of in the words "Prajapati desired, may I produce the creatures," still there is no ground for the inference that he is the cause of the universe, for his desire concerns itself with the minor creation. Even this minor creation pertains to the Paramesvara Himself who takes the form of Hiranyagarbha's as the Sutrakara will say in the Sutra II. iv. 20.

The Sutrakara now proceeds to consider the view that the identity of Paramesvara and Hiranyagarbha should be admitted in as much as it is declared in the passage.

"Entering in the form of this Jiva, the Atman, the name and form will I differentiate," * that Paramesvara who has entered into the universe as its soul in the form of Hiranyagarbha is the creator of names and forms. [* Chhandogya Upanishad. 6-3.]

And herein (it) declares his relation to Him (I. i. 20.)

Herein, in the science of this very Upanishad, the mantric texts declare the Hiranyagarbha's subordinate relation to Paramesvara, in the words "Brahman is the Lord, the Lord of Brahma" † [† Mahana. Up. 21.] Wherefore, it follows that none but Paramesvara is the cause of the universe and that the Hiranyagarbha is subordinate to Him.

Adhikarana – 8.

By means of arguments adduced in the foregoing adhikaranas it has been established that Para-Brahman is the Being called Siva who is distinct from *chit* and *achit*, spirit and matter; who is omniscient, ever-contented, of beginningless wisdom, independent of never tailing power of infinite potentialities, the two-fold cause of the whole universe; who can be revealed only by the one accordant interpretation of the whole science of the Upanishad; who, by nature is without a second, self-luminous, and conjoined with the whole Universe; who is the existence, Intelligence and Bliss in essence; who constitutes the means by which it cut asunder the bond of samsara. The next adhikarana proceeds to point out that form of His on which to concentrate the mind and which constitutes for the aspirant an antidote for samsara.

The Vedanta-Sutras with Srikantha Bhashya

(He who is) within is Paramesvara because of the declaration of His attributes. (I. i. 21.)

The following passage in the Chhandogya forms the subject of discussion here:

"Now that Golden Person, who is seen within the sun, with golden beard and golden hair, golden altogether to the very tips of his nails, whose two eyes are like white lotus." ‡ [‡ Chh. Upanishad. 1-6.]

The doubt arises as to whether this golden person within the sun is Paramesvara or any particular Devata.

Now, Paramesvara who is the basis of all and who is everywhere, cannot be the person who is within the sun and of golden form. If it be held to be the form assumed by Him of His own accord, it must necessarily be the form containing three eyes. Such a form is not found here; we find described here only two eyes which are like blue lotuses.

Or, even if it were the body assumed of his own accord, it would certainly produce pain even in the case of Paramesvara as much as in the case of samsarins. Even in the case of a voluntary contact, it is in the very nature of fire to burn the thing in contact. Thus it is not proper to suppose that Paramesvara becomes united to a body. Wherefore the person (spoken of in the passage under discussion) is some Devata, not the Paramesvara. This is the argument that may be adduced on behalf of the *Purvapaksha*.

The *Siddhanta* maintains that it is the Paramesvara Himself – Why so? – Because of the mention of his attributes. In the passages "He is the master of all worlds and of all desires" and "His name is the 'Above', He has arisen above all sins"* it is the attributes of Paramesvara, the attributes of sinlessness and of mastery over all worlds and desires, are spoken of; for, it is revealed that [* Chh. Upanishad 1-6.]

"One indeed is Rudra, - they are never for a second, - who rules these worlds by His ruling energies. † [† Sveta. Upanishad 3-2.]

"The One who to many ordains the objects of desire." ‡ and so on. [‡ Svet. Upanishad 6-13.]

As to the contention that He who is the basis of all and who pervades all cannot be a dweller within the sun, we reply that the Paramesvara who is the basis of all and who pervades all things assumes some golden form in consideration of the devotees and dwells in the solar orb. Unlike us, by such a connection with the body the Isvara does not become subject to the evil of samsara. The blessed sruti itself declares both his connection with the body and his freedom from all sin. In fact, dependent as we are on the authority of sruti, we do not hold analogical reasoning very high. Even fire cannot burn those things in contact which are too powerful. The mention of two eyes of the three-eyed Paramesvara is meant merely to show its resemblance to white lotus; it does not mean the absence of a third eye. When we say, for instance, of a man having three sons, that two of his sons are like fire, the mention of the number 'two' does not imply the absence of the third; but it is meant to show the resemblance of the two sons to fire. So also here. Two of Paramesvara's eyes shine like the white lotus which has been blossomed by the sun, whereas the third eye, which is naturally closed, does not resemble the fully-blossomed lotus; it is like a closed lotus.

(*Objection*): - In the following passage,

"This Being who moves, the Dark-necked (Nilagirva) and Red, whom the cowherds and the water-carrying women have seen, and whom all beings see, He, when seen, makes us happy." * [* Tait. Samhita 4-5-1.]

We are given to understand that the dark-necked Paramesvara's visible to all beings. And from another passage "The three-eyed sun who by his splendor has pervaded the orb on all sides" we learn that he possesses three eyes. Therefore Aditya Himself is the Paramesvara visible to all and residing in the middle of the shining orb. Otherwise, how can the Sruti speak of the sun as dark-necked and three-eyed or designate Him a Brahman in the words "This sun is Brahman"† Wherefore it is the very Sun-god residing in the orb, spoken of as he "who is within the sun," that is referred to as the golden Purusha or spirit. [† Tait. Aranyaka 2-2.]

Against this view the Sutrakara says: -

And because of the mention of a distinction, He is another. (I. i. 22.)

The Paramesvara of golden form is quite distinct from the sentient Aditya, the personal soul of the solar orb, because of the distinction made in the sruti.

Who dwelling in the sun, inner than the sun, whom the sun knows not, whose body the sun is, who within controls the sun, - he is thy Atman, the inner Regulator (Antaryamin), the Immortal." ‡ [‡ Br. Upanishad 6-7.]

Here the word "immortal" denotes Siva, because it is said in the Jabala Upanishad in praise of Satarudriya that "these verily are the designations of the Immortal." § [§ Jabala. Up. 3.] From the attribute – described of Paramesvara – that He is unknown to the sun, we should understand that the Paramesvara is distinct from the Jiva. Wherefore it is the Paramesvara dwelling within the sun, the golden Isvara, - it is the Paramesvara as distinguished from the sentient sun that is spoken of here as "dark-necked, blood-red." * As the indwelling soul of the sun, he is spoken of by the sun. [* Tait. Samhita 4-5-1.]

(*Objection*): - The "dark-necked" dwelling within the sun is not the Paramesvara; on the other hand He is Narayana. Accordingly the lay poets, everywhere, declare: -

"To be always meditated upon is He, Narayana, who, dwelling within the sun's orb, is seated on the lotus-seat."

He alone can properly be said to have two eyes like the white lotus, because He is well-known as "the Pundarakaksha or the lotus-eyed." Why all the trouble of explaining it otherwise?

(*Answer*): - No; because the special characteristic marks of the Paramesvara which are found described in connection with the Golden Spirit (Hiranmaya Purusha), cannot be explained when applied to Narayana. Now it is proper to determine the drift of this passage of doubtful signification, - referred to in the Sutra, - by collating it with other passages which admit of no doubt.

In the Mahopanishad there is the following passage: -

"It is verily the sun (Aditya) that burns this orb, etc." † [† Tait. Samhita 4-5-1.]

Here the sun, the personal soul dwelling in the orb, is spoken of in the words "the person who is in this shining orb"; then the Golden Spirit, the Regulator within the sun, is referred to in the words "This Golden spirit who is within the sun."*; then again His vibhuti (glory) as the sun is spoken of in the words "The sun is the vigor, energy, strength and fame."*; then he is referred to as the Lord of all beings in the words "He is the Spirit, the Lord of all Beings."* then again in answer as it were to the question who He is, He is again described in the section which begins with "All is Rudra..."* and concludes thus: "to Him who is Golden-armed the Golden-Lord, the Lord of Ambika (the mother), the Lord of Uma."† As the mention of 'arm' in this description stands for other features as well, we should understand that it means the golden-colored. Therefore it follows that it is He whose color is like gold, who is the Lord of Uma, that is spoken of as the one dwelling within the sun. Here His characteristic marks are: He is Nilagriva or dark-necked, He is the Lord of Uma. These cannot be ascribed to any being other than the Paramesvara. The possession of eyes like lotus is a general mark, applicable to other beings besides Narayana. We speak of a woman or a man having eyes like lotus. When the two marks are mentioned together, the special mark should prevail in our determining of the exact being spoken of here. The passage cited above to show that Narayana should always be meditated upon as the deity dwelling within the sun should be understood in a figurative sense. Wherefore it follows that the Being who has to be meditated upon as dwelling in the sun by seekers of Moksha is none but the Blessed Paramesvara described in the Savitri or Gayatri-Hymn – of golden form, having three eyes, dark-necked the Lord of Uma, the Lord of all regions and all desires, untouched by any evil whatsoever.
[* Maha.Up. 23. † Mahana. Upanishad. 18.]

Adhikaranas 9, 10.

Having mentioned that form of Siva – the Para-Brahman possessed of omniscience and other attributes – which is to be worshipped as the source of supreme good, the Sutrakara introduces the next section with a view to answer a possible objection that the given definition of Brahman is too wide in as much as the same names which are applied to Brahman are by usage applicable to other things as well.

Akasa (is Brahman), because of His characteristic marks. (I. i. 23). For the same reason, Prana (is Brahman). (I. i. 24).

The subject of discussion in this section is a passage in the Chhandogya-Upanishad, which reads as follows:

"All these beings, verily, take their rise from akasa, and return into akasa." *

"All these beings, verily merge into Prana alone, and from Prana they arise." *

[* Chha. Upanishad 1-9-11.]

Here a doubt arises to whether the terms "Prana" and "akasa" – which denote the cause from which all beings take their arise and in which they attain dissolution – point to Paramesvara, or to bhutakasa (akasaas one of the rudimental elements) and to prana (vital air).

The *prima facie* view may be stated as follows: it is prana (vital air) and bhuta-akasa that are treated of here, since they are spoken of as the cause of all beings in the following passages:

"From prana alone, verily, are these beings when, by prana do these born creatures live; into prana they go and enter."

"From akasa is the air-born" etc. ‡ [‡ Tait. Upanishad. 2-1.]

Against the foregoing view we hold as follows It is Paramesvara who is referred to by the terms "prana" and "akasa," because of His characteristic marks, such as His being the cause of all. Now such passages as "From prana alone, verily, are these beings born," only inculcate the proposition that Brahman, who is bliss in essence, is the cause. They do not teach that prana etc., are the cause. On the other hand, they form mere anuvada, *i.e.*, the sruti merely repeats what has been thought by another. Akasa being one of the *bhutas* or rudimental elements, it is included in the term all 'bhutas'; and the rise of "all bhutas" can be from Paramesvara alone, as the sruti says "From Atman is akasa born."* Wherefore it should be concluded that the material akasa (bhutakasa) and prana are not the causes of all beings. [* Tait. Upanishad 2-1.]

(*Question*): What is the use of the qualification "bhuta" (material) in "bhutakasa"?

(*Answer*): The epithet has a purpose to serve, in as much as there exists another akasa viz., the Paramakasa or transcendental Light, the Para-Prakriti or the Great Cause, the cause of all bhutas.

(*Question*): Then how to conclude that akasa is Paramesvara?

(*Answer*): Because there is no distinction between the two, between Paramesvara and Paramakasa.

The Vedanta-Sutras with Srikantha Bhashya

Adhikarana. 11

In a former section it was shown that the solar orb is the abode of Parabrahman, the Lord of Uma, the Lord of the whole universe, free from all taint and from all latent tendencies of evil, the repository of unsurpassed good. Here, then, the, Sutrakara refers to another abode of the Lord:

(Brahman is the) Light, because of the mention of the foot. (I. i. 25).

The subject of discussion here is a passage in the Chhandogya-Upanishad which reads as follows

"Now that Light which shines above this heaven, higher than all, higher than everything, in the highest world, beyond which there are no other worlds, but is the same light which is within man." † [† Chha. Upanishad. 3-13.]

Here a doubt arises as to whether the Supreme Light which is said to be in heaven, pervading in all worlds, is Paramesvara or some other being?

(*Purvapaksha*): The word 'dyu' stands for heaven, and the light which is said to be "above this heaven" may therefore here mean the sun himself. Or, as the words 'the light within man' point to the light being within man, it may be that the digestive fire in the stomach is here referred to."

(*Siddhanta*): The words "the light which shines above this heaven" refer to Paramesvara Himself who is the Supreme Light, higher than all; for, in a former passage, "All creatures form a foot of His"* in all creatures are said to be a part of this light. This cannot apply to the sun and digestive fire in the stomach, whose range of action is limited. [* Chha. Upanishad. 3-12.]

(*Objection*): In a former passage, Gayatri is described to be all-pervading in the words "Gayatri, verily, is all this existence." † As occurring in the same context, the passage "All creatures form a foot of His" teaches only that the universe is a part of Gayatri. [† Chha. Up. 3-12.]

This objection is thus answered:

(If you say it is) not so because of the mention of the metre, (we say) no, because (it is) the meditating (of Brahman) in that way (that is) taught so indeed, there is an instance. (I. i. 26.)

(*Objection*): Because of the mention of the metre in a former passage, "Gayatri, indeed, is all this existence," the same thing is spoken of here, not the Paramesvara.

(*Answer*): It cannot be that Gayatri, a mere metre, is all-pervading. On the other hand, we are taught to contemplate Paramesvara who resembles Gayatri: just as Gayatri is made up of four feet containing six syllables each and is four-footed, so Brahman too is four-footed. Accordingly, elsewhere, a word denoting metre is found applied to a different thing in virtue of some point of resemblance; as for instance, in the Samvarga-Vidya where the sruti beginning with the passage, "These five and the other five make ten, and that is the *krita*" ‡ says "these are again the Viraj." Wherefore in the determining of the subject propounded in the passage in question, the characteristic mark of Paramesvara, *viz.* all-pervadingness, should prevail as against the argument derived from the fact or the passage occurring in the section treating of Gayatri. [‡ Chha. Up. 4-3.]

And because of its congruity with the description of creatures etc. as feet, (it should be) so. (I. i. 27.)

The statement that it is four-footed by creatures, earth, body and the heart, cannot apply to the metre called Gayatri. It applies only to Paramesvara.

The Sutrakara again raises and refutes an objection:

If (you hold it is) not (so) because of a diversity in the teaching, (we answer) no, because there is no inconsistency in either case. (I. i. 28).

(*Objection*): It is not right to hold that, because there is a reference made to a connection with heaven in the passage "All creatures form one foot of His; His immortal three feet being in heaven," * Paramesvara is described in the passage which speaks of 'light'; for, the two being quite distinct from each other as shown by a diversity in their teaching, there can be no reference to the one by the other. In the passages "His immortal three feet are in the heaven," and "The Light which shines *above* the heaven," † the word denoting 'heaven' occurs in two different cases, (i.e., in the locative and the ablative cases), and therefore there is a diversity in the teaching. Hence the mutual opposition of the passages in question. [* Chha. Up. 3-12, 13. † Chha. Up. 3-12, 13.]

(*Answer*): No, for there is no diversity between the two passages, just as there is no different between the following two statements: "There is a hawk *on* the top of the tree;" and "There is a hawk *above* the top of the tree." Wherefore in either case it is intended to declare that the light is above the heaven. By this characteristic mark, it may also be concluded that it is Paramesvara who is the Purusha spoken of in the Purusha-Sukta, in as much as there, too, it is taught that "A foot of His are all the creatures." ‡ Hence the conclusion that the Supreme Light which shines in heaven and of which the whole universe forms only a part is none other than Paramesvara. [‡ Tait. Aranyaka 3-12.]

Adhikarana 12.

In the last adhikarana it has been shown that the Paramesvara, referred to as the main object of worship in the orb of the Blessed Sun, Himself constitutes the whole universe. The present section proceeds to show that other beings form object of worship as ensouled by Him, and not otherwise.

So is prana, because of the occurrence (of His attributes) (I. i. 29)

The passage which has to be discussed here is the Indra's speech occurring in the Kaushitaka-Upanishad:

"I am Prana; do thou meditate on me as the conscious Atman; as life, as immortality."* [* Kaushitaka-Upanishad 8.]

The doubt arises here as to whether the being referred to as an object of worship and put in apposition with the word 'prana' is Indra or Paramesvara.

(*Purvapaksha*): Here in the passage "I am prana, the conscious Atman, and me etc." we see that the word 'prana' is evident put in apposition with 'Indra.' The passage, "worship me," clearly states that the injunction of worship refers to none but Indra. It is but proper to speak of him as prana because he supports all beings by means of rain. As possessed of supreme power, he may also be spoken of as the object to be worshipped by all. Accordingly the sruti says "Indra is the king who rules the world" † and so on. Wherefore Indra himself is here spoken of as the object of worship.

The *Siddhanta* maintains that it is the Paramesvara – Why?- Because His peculiar attributes – such as, He is the Bliss, He is without decay, immortal, He is the conscious Self – are found described when speaking of the being referred to by the word prana:

"He is none other than prana; conscious Atman, the Bliss, without decay, immortal." † [† Tait. Aranyaka 3-11.]

In the passage "Indra is the king" we should by the context understand the word "Indra" to mean Isvara.

Again an objection is raised and refuted:

(If you say it is) not (He), because of the speaker's reference to himself, (we reply that) there is indeed in this (section) a preponderance of attributes of Atman. (I. i. 30.)

(*Objection*): The being here referred to as the object of worship is not Paramesvara; for, in the opening sentence such as "known me alone............. the three-headed son of Tvashtri did I stay." ‡ Indra who is well-known to be a jiva is spoken of as the object of worship. And the concluding passage of the section should be interpreted in accordance with the opening passage. [‡ Kaushitaka Upanishad 2.]

(*Answer*): It is not right to say so in this section, from the very commencement, Paramesvara's characteristic attributes are found in great preponderance. Thus, the opening passage proposes to treat of the most beneficial worship in the words "That which thou thinkest the best for man."* [* Kaushitaka Upanishad 3.] This, indeed, is a characteristic property of Paramesvara, His worship alone being the most beneficial as a means of attaining moksha.

In the middle of the section, too, He is spoken of as the impelling agent of others in all their actions, in the following passage:

"For he makes him, whom he wishes to lead up from these worlds, do a good deed; and the same makes him, whom he wishes to lead down from these worlds, do a bad act." *
[* Kaushitaka Upanishad 3.]

So also he is spoken of in the following passage as the basis of the whole universe made up of both the sentient and insentient existence:

As in a car the circumference of a wheel is placed on the spokes and the spokes on the nave, thus are these external objects placed on the subjective states of consciousness and these states of consciousness are placed on the prana." † [†Kaushitaka Upanishad 3.]

And this too, being a characteristic property of Paramesvara Indra cannot be the being here spoken of as the object of worship.

(*Objection*): - If, as the Jiva, Indra is not the object of worship, then how is it that he inculcates the worship of himself?

The Sutrakara thus answers:

(It is) from the standpoint of the scriptures that he inculcates it, like Vamadeva. (I. i. 31.)

From the standpoint of such passages of the scriptures as "In the form of this Jiva entering, I shall differentiate name and form," ‡ Indra saw that Paramesvara was the being denoted by all words and that therefore Indra himself was His body; and he accordingly refers to Paramesvara by his own name 'Indra' and inculcates Him alone as the object of worship. Hence the reference to Paramesvara by the word 'Indra.' [‡ Chha. Upanishad. 6-3.]

The Sutrakara quotes an example, "like Vamadeva." Vamadeva saw that Paramesvara was none but his own Atma and exclaimed "I have become Manu and Surya." Just so is Indra's declaration. § [§ Brihada. Upanishad 3-4.]

Or thus: When, by the contemplation of the harmonious nature of Brahman and Atman brought about by Vedantic knowledge, Vamadeva attained to the state of Brahman and was freed from all the imaginary limitations due to the identifying of himself with the human body and so on, and his mighty ego expanded so as to embrace the whole universe, he saw that he was present everywhere and accordingly spoke of himself as one with the whole universe including Manu and Surya. So, it may be concluded, it was in the case of Indra. In the passage "I am prana, the conscious Atman," * Prana refers to Para-Brahman, in as much as He, blissful by nature, is the cause of all life, as said in the sruti "Prana is the conscious self, the Bliss, undecaying and immortal." Accordingly it is from the standpoint of Brahman that Indra taught "I am Brahman," "me do thou worship" So, too, Krishna taught to Arjuna, and so several others. [*Kaushitaka Upanishad 6.]

Again an objection is raised and refuted:

(If you say it is) not (so) because of the characteristic marks of Jiva and prana proper, (we reply) no, because, His worship being threefold and He being their basis, it is explicable. (I. i. 32.)

(*Objection*): It is but proper that Indra should speak of himself us the object of worship and as an all-pervading being, when, having attained by the contemplation of Brahmajnana to the condition of Brahman, he was freed from the condition of jiva and spoke from the standpoint of Brahman. Here in the passages "I killed the three-headed son of Tvashtri" † and "till prana dwells in the body, till then there is life,"† the characteristic marks of jiva and prana proper are evident. So this teaching is not explicable.[† Kaushitaka Upanishad 3.]

(*Answer*): You should not say so. It is but proper that Paramesvara is spoken of as a jiva and prana; for there is a threefold worship. Here it is intended to teach a threefold worship of Paramesvara, - in His own form, in the form of Bhokta or jiva, in the form of Bhogya or the object of sense. This may be explained by the fact that He is the basis of Bhokta and Bhogya, the jivas and objects of sense. The worship of Paramesvara in His own form leads to immediate salvation, whereas the other two do so in of Paramesvara who dwells in him as his Atman, Indra forms an object of worship.

Thus ends the commentary of Srikantha-Sivacharya on Para i.e., of the Adhyaya I, of the Brahma-Mimamsa.

SECOND PADA.

Adhikarana. I.

Owing to the endlessness of Vedantic passages treating of Brahman, it is not possible to discuss every one of those passages. By a discussion therefore, of some only of those passages, the meaning of others have to be determined on the same principles of interpretation. Thus, a few only of the passages are dealt with in the Sutras by way of determining that those passages treat of Brahman as shown by a concurrence of the marks which serve to determine the main drift of the passages.

In the first pada have been discussed a few of such passages as contain clear hints showing what that main drift of the passages is. In the second pada will be discussed a few of such passages as contain hints which are not quite so explicit.

(The passage refers to Paramesvara) as teaching of Him who is present everywhere. (I. ii. 1).

The passage which forms the subject of discussion here occurs in the Chhandogya Upanishad and reads thus:

"The *manomaya*, whose body is prana, whose form is thought, whose will is unfailing, whose nature is like Akasa, from whom all desires proceed...He is myself within the heart." * [* Chha. Up. 3-14.]

Here a doubt arises as to whether the being spoken of as *manomaya* and so on is Paramesvara or Jiva.

(Purvapaksha): It is Jiva. – Why so? – Because he is more proximate. In the passage which just precedes the one under discussion, viz.,

"Now man is a creature of will. According to what his will is in this world, so will he be when he has departed this life. Let him therefore have this will and belief;"† [† Chha. Up. 3-14.]

Jiva is spoken of as wandering in this and in the next world under the influence of karma. Then comes the passage commencing with "*manomaya*." Wherefore we conclude that it is Jiva who is referred to as "manomaya." These attributes – that he partakes of the nature of manas and that he has prana for his body – belong to a samsarin; they are not attributes of Paramesvara. When this interpretation is accepted, the epithet "*satiasankalpa*" may be applied to a samsarin or jiva by interpreting to mean "satyasankalpa, he whose thought is not directed to the Real (Sat)," Wherefore it is Jiva that is spoken of as 'manomaya' and so on, not Paramesvara.

As against the foregoing we hold as follows: - It is Paramesvara that is spoken of as 'manomaya' and so on. Why? – Because it is the Para-Brahman, the Paramesvara, that is spoken of as the cause of all and as the object of worship in the opening passage:

"All this is Brahman, as beginning, ending, and breathing in Him; and therefore let a man meditate on Him."

This passage may be explained as follows: The origin, existence and end of all this depends on Brahman. All this, both the sentient and the insentient existence, is verily Brahman, and therefore let a man meditate on Brahman, tranquil in mind. Just as water-bubbles which have their origin, existence and end in the ocean, are found to be only forms of that ocean, so, too, that which depends for its origin etc. on Brahman associated with sakti must be made up of Brahman and nothing else. Nothing distinct from Him is ever perceived. Accordingly in the Atharvasiras it has been declared by Isana as follows:

"Alone I was at first, (alone) I am and shall be; there is none else distinct from Me." ‡

And then was declared by Him in the words "I am Brahman," § that the whole universe is His own form. And in the words "He entered the more hidden from (or *than*) the hidden one" etc.* His entering into the universe is given as a reason for the whole universe being His own form. Thus, this universe having no origin, existence or end outside Brahman, it is not a quite distinct thing from Brahman. Accordingly the learned say –

The Vedanta-Sutras with Srikantha Bhashya

"His saktis or energies (form) the whole world, and the Mahesa or the Great Lord is the energetic (Saktiman). Never can energy exist distinct from the energetic. Unity of these two is eternal, like that of fire and heat, in as much as unseparateness always exists between energy and the energetic. Wherefore the supreme energy belongs to the supreme Atman, since the two are related to each other as substance and attribute. The energy of heat is not conceived to be distinct from fire and so on.

Vayu-Samhita, too says:

"From Sakti up to earth, (the whole world) is born of the principle Siva. By Him alone, it is pervaded, as the jar etc. by clay. His variegated supreme Sakti, whose form is knowledge and bliss, appears as one and many, like the light of the sun."

The following passages of the sruti speak of Para-Brahman as possessed of infinite powers of creating, ruling and maintaining the world, all inherent in Him:

"His supreme Sakti is spoken of as manifold, inherent, endued with the activity of knowledge and life." * [* Sveta. Upanishad. 6-8.]

"One verily is Rudra, - they were not for a second – who rules these worlds with the powers of ruling." † [† Sveta. Upanishad. 3-2.]

In short, on the authority of Sruti, Smriti, Itihasa, Purana, and the sayings of the learned, the Supreme Sakti – whose manifold manifestation this whole universe of chit and achit is, whose being is composed of Supreme Existence, Intelligence and Bliss, and is unlimited by space and time – is inherent in the nature of Siva, the Supreme Brahman, and constitutes His own essential form and quality. Apart from Sakti He cannot be the Omniscient, the Omnipotent, the cause of all, the all-controlling, the all-adorable, the all-gracious, the means of attaining all aspirations, and the omnipresent; and, moreover, such grand designations as '*Mahesvara*' the Supreme Lord, '*Mahadeva*' the supreme deity, and '*Rudra*' the expeller of pain, cannot apply to Him. Thus it is Brahman whose body is the whole sentient and insentient universe, and who is denoted by all words. Just as the word 'blue' denotes not the blue color only, but also the lotus which is of blue color, so does the word 'universe' also denotes Brahman. Therefore, such passages as "All is Rudra verily" teach that Brahman is denoted by all words. Accordingly the passage "All this, verily, is Brahman" refers to Brahman whose body the whole of the sentient and unsentient universe is. The universe being thus a form of Brahman and being therefore not an object of hatred etc., let everyone be peaceful at heart and worship Brahman. This doctrine is clearly expounded even in the puranic texts such as the following: -

"The body of the God of Gods is this universe, moving and immoving. This, the Jivas (Pasus) do not know, owing to the mighty bondage. They say sentiency is Vidya, and insentiency Avidya. The whole universe of Vidya and Avidya, is no doubt the body of the Lord, the Father of all; for the whole universe is subject to Him. The word '*sat*' is used by the wise to denote the real and the good, and '*asat*' is used by Vedic teachers to denote the contrary. The whole universe of the *sat* and the *asat* is the body of Him who is on high. Just as, by the watering of the roots of a tree, its branches are nourished, so by the worship of Siva, the universe which is His body is nourished. Atman is the eighth body of Siva the Paramesvara, pervading all other bodies. Wherefore the whole universe is ensouled by Siva. If any embodied being whatsoever be subjected to constraint, it will be quite repugnant to the eight-bodied lord; as to this there is no doubt. Doing good to all, kindness to all, affording shelter to all, - this, they hold, is the worshipping of Siva." And so on.

Brahman being all-formed, it is but right to say "all is Brahman" and "let everyone be peaceful and worship Brahman." Wherefore it is Brahman who in the opening passage is stated to be the object of worship, that is also spoken of as manomaya, as partaking of the nature of manas, and so on. Neither should it be supposed that the partaking of the nature of manas is a characteristic mark of a samsarin; for Brahman may limit Himself by assuming a shape which can form an object of worship.

As to the contention that because Jiva, is a creature of his own will it is Jiva who is spoken of as 'manomaya.' – we say that such a contention is untenable; for, since the upasana has to be construed as having for its object Brahman who is mentioned as such in the sentence where the upasana is enjoined, it is not possible for that upasana to have again for its object Jiva who is but incidentally mentioned; as in the case of *amiksha*,* which has been proved to appertain to Visvedevas who have already been mentioned in connection with it, not the *vajina* which belongs to *vajins*. Wherefore it is Brahman who is to be worshipped as possessed of attributes mentioned in the passage commencing with '*manomaya*'. [* See Jaimini Mimamsa. 2-2-23.]

(*Objection*): - If it be held that it is Brahman mentioned in the opening passage who is spoken of as manomaya etc., the reference to jiva who is mentioned incidentally would serve no purpose.

(*Answer*): -   The Sutrakara says: -

And because of the appropriateness of the qualities intended to be taught. (I. ii. 2.)

Since the qualities intended to be taught, - namely, that He is of unfailing will, that from Him all desires proceed, - can be applied only to Brahman, He alone is the object to be worshipped. And jiva who is incidentally mentioned is the worshipper, there being a necessity for the supply of that factor to complete the injunction.

Adhikarana 2.

In the last adhikarana it has been shown that jiva in general cannot be an object of worship but that he can be only a worshipper. Now again, the next section proceeds to establish that even Narayana, who is the upadana or material cause of the Hiranyagarbha, the aggregate of all jivas, is only a worshipper of Brahman who is above all universe, but not an object of worship.

The Vedanta-Sutras with Srikantha Bhashya

Owing to incongruity, the embodied is not (meant) (I. ii. 2).

The passage which forms the subject of discussion here occurs in the Mahopanishad:

"The Lord of the universe, the Atman, the Isvara, the Eternal, the Good, the Indestructible, Narayana, the Great one who was to be known," and so on.

Here a doubt arises as to whether it is the embodied entity, or the Paramesvara, or someone else, who is spoken of as Narayana and described as the Lord of the universe and so on.

(*Purvapaksha*): - It is Narayana, the embodied entity, who is spoken of as the Lord of the universe, firstly because Narayana, the embodied entity, is repeated as the subject, of whom thousand-headedness etc., are to be predicated, in the section beginning with, "The thousand-headed Deity," * secondly because of his characteristic marks – such as lying in the ocean – spoken of in the section; thirdly because of the use of the synonymous terms, *Achyuta, Hari* applicable to him alone. [* Mahanarayana Upanishad.]

Siddhanta, however, maintains that it is Mahesvara, the Supreme Lord, the Atman of Narayana – How? Because such attributes of Paramesvara as the lordship of the whole universe cannot be applied to any other being such as Narayana. Lordship of the whole universe is predicated of the Paramesvara alone by repetition in the words "to Him who is the Lord of cattle, the Lord of trees, the Lord of the worlds... I salute." † That no other being than Rudra is the Lord of the universe is declared by the following passage: [† Taittiriya-Samhita 4-6.]

"One verily is Rudra, - they are not for a second, - who rules these worlds by the powers of ruling." ‡ [‡ Svetasvatara Upanishad 3-2.]

And the sruti "Rudra is high above the universe" § teaches that it is Rudra who is high above the universe. Wherefore it is but right to say that the Being spoken of as the Lord of the universe is the Paramesvara, the Atman of Narayana. [§ Maha. Up. 10.]

(*Objection*): - To speak of Him as the Self of Narayana is to imply that Paramesvara is the Antaryamin or the Inner Regulator of Narayana; which is not right. In the words "Narayana is the Supreme Brahman," the sruti declares that Narayana is the Supreme Brahman. Then the passages beginning with "like unto the lotus-bud" speaks of Purusha as located in the heart-lotus; then jiva is described in the passage beginning with "in its midst is the flame of fire", and then in the words "in the middle of that flame is the Paramatman established," Narayana is spoken of as the Paramatman, as the Antaryamin or Inner Regulator of the jiva. Thus, we see that He (Narayana) is the object of worship. The passage "He is Brahma, He is Siva" and so on declares that Brahma, Siva and other beings are His vibhutis or glorious emanations. Wherefore Narayana Himself is the Lord of the universe, the very Supreme Brahman and is to be worshipped as the Antaryamin or Inner Regulator of jivas. It is therefore unjust to hold that the Paramesvara is Narayana's Atman, and that as such He is above Narayana and to be worshipped by him.

In reply the Sutrakara says: -

Because of their mention as the object and the agent. (I. ii. 4.)

There, the Paramesvara and Narayana are mentioned respectively as the worshipped and the worshipper, as the object and the agent. – How? – The passage "like unto the lotus-bud" describes the heart of Narayana who has been just spoken of; and the passage "Paramatman is established" declares that the Paramesvara who is himself the Paramatman is the object of worship as dwelling within Narayana. Thus, Narayana is spoken of as the agent, as the worshipper; and Paramesvara as the object, as worthy of being worshipped. Wherefore the Paramatman who is to be worshipped is some being other than Narayana. The passage "He is Brahma, He is Siva" and so on teaches that Paramesvara manifests His own glory in the form of the universe comprising Brahman, Vishnu, Rudra, Indra and the like. Though Vishnu is not mentioned here (as the Paramesvara's vibhuti), He is mentioned as such in the Kaivalya Upanishad. After speaking of the heart-lotus, the Upanishad says:

"Him whose help-mate is Uma, who is the Supreme Lord, who is Mighty, Three-eyed, Dark-necked and serene; having meditated thus, the sage reaches Him who is the womb of all beings, the witness of all, transcending Tamas. He is Brahma, He is Siva, He is Indra, He the Indestructible, the Supreme, the self-luminous. He Himself is Vishnu, He is Prana, He is Time, "He is Fire, He the Moon," and so on.

The same principle should be applied here. The following passage from the Atharva-upanishad should also be taken into consideration:

"That Lord who is Known as Rudra, He is Bhuh, Bhuvah, Suvah as well as he who is known as Brahma; to Him we bow. That Lord who is known as Rudra, He is Bhuh, Bhuvah, Suvah as well as he who is known as Vishnu to Him we bow. That Lord.... as well as he who is known as Mahesvara,....." and so on

The omission of Vishnu between Rudra and Siva in the passage quoted from Mahopanishad is to be accounted for by the fact that Vishnu has been spoken of as the worshipper. Hence no mutual contradiction among these passages.

(*Objection*): - The Being (Purusha) spoken of in the Purusha-sukta which begin: with "Thousand-headed is Purusha" is said to be endued with a world forming a part of Himself, as declared in the sruti "A foot of His do all these creatures form." The same Being is treated of here – in the passage under discussion – under the name "Narayana." The same Being is designated by the name Brahman in the passage "Narayana is the Supreme Brahman" Indeed it is Brahman who is to be worshipped by all. How can it be that such a Being is the worshipper of another?

The Sutrakara answers the objection as follows:

Owing to the specific word (I. ii. 5).

The specific text "Brahman is above Narayana" declares that Brahman is higher than Narayana. Wherefore the Supreme Brahman who is distinct from Narayana is to be worshiped, in as much as the Para-Brahman Himself puts on the form of the thousand-headed Purusha and forms the upadana or material cause of the universe. In II.23 we shall show that Narayana, having Parabrahman for his Atman or the Impeller, assumes the form of the universe.

The sutrakara adduces another sort of evidence to prove that Narayana is an upasaka or worshipper:

And because of smriti (I. ii. 6).

From the following passage of the smriti,

"Having thus spoken, then, O King, Hari, the great Lord of Yoga, showed to the son of Pritha the Supreme Form of Isvara."* [* Bhagavadgita. 11-9.]

It is evident that Narayana, the great Master of Yoga is engaged in Yoga or samadhi, *i.e.*, in the contemplation of Paramesvara, the Supreme Lord. Bearing on this subject there is the following speech of the Paramesvara addressed to Asvatthaman:

"I am duly worshipped; by Krishna who is unwearied in action; therefore none else exists who is dearer to me than Krishna."

Wherefore the Supreme Brahman who is to be worshipped is different from Narayana.

The sutrakara again raises an objection and refutes it:

If (you hold it is) not (so) because of His having a small abode and being so designated, (we say) no; He is so (designated) because He is to be worshipped; and He is like akasa. (I. ii. 7.)

(*Objection*): - The Being here spoken of cannot be the Paramesvara who is all-pervading, since the former is described in the following passage as dwelling within the small flame of fire and so having a small resting ground and is denoted by terms implying smallness.

"There is (a streak of light) which is as fine as the bristle of a Nivara grain, which is yellow in color, the standard of things that are fine: Within that flame does Paramatman abide."

(*Answer*): - Not so. He is so designated because He is here described as an object of worship. Not that He is small in himself; for it requires no proof that He is infinite in Himself, like the akasa which when conditioned by an Upadhi such as a jar is said to be small, and which is said to be infinite when regarded in itself. Hence no inconsistency.

Again the sutrakara raises an objection and answers it:

If (you say that this) necessitates enjoyment, (we say) no, because there is a difference. (I. ii. 8).

(*Objection*): - It is the same Being spoken of as higher than Narayana and therefore as the object of worship is the Being described as "Honest and True, the Supreme Brahman, the Purusha dark and brown, whose semen is held above, of diverse eyes"[*] and so on. Here the Parabrahman is described as *dark* and *brown* because of His being tinged with Maya, the Supreme Sakti or Power; He is described as one '*whose semen is held above*' because of His having Fire for His semen: He is "*of divers eyes*" because of His having three eyes: He is *Purusha* because He has in the lotus of Dahara, the akasa in the heart; He is "*Honest and True*" because in him there is no inconsistency between speech and thought. Wherefore as possessed of a form containing three eyes, etc. He is subject to enjoyment of pleasures and pains pertaining to the body. [* Mahanarayana Upanishad 11.]

(*Answer*): - No, because there is a difference. There exists, indeed, a difference between Brahman's body and the bodies of jivas, which latter are meant for the enjoyment of pleasure and the suffering of pain; for, He has assumed the body at His own will, whereas their bodies have been brought into existence by their respective *Karma*. Wherefore the sruti describes Paramesvara as "free from sin, free from old age, free from death and grief, from hunger and thirst, desiring nothing but what He ought to desire, and imagining nothing but what He ought to imagine," † [† Chhandogya Upanishad 8-7.] and thus devoid of the attributes pertaining to the body of a samsarin. But not so in jiva, the samsarin. Therefore it is that in the passages like "with perfect limbs, He is many formed and fierce,"[*] [* Rik-Samhita 2-7-17.] the Paramesvara's voluntarily assigned forms of great beauty – the divine forms which are free from sin, old age, death, grief and so on – are declared to be perfect and eternal. Wherefore, the Parabrahman, the Supreme Lord, being different from jiva, He cannot be tinged with any of the defects pertaining to the body. The *Upakrama* and other text passages point to the conclusion that the diverse-eyed Brahman is the highest of all and is the Being who ought to be worshipped. To explain: in the Upakrama or opening passage beginning with "Subtler than the subtle," † [† Mahanarayana Upanishad 10.] the Lord has been described to be a very glorious being, as dwelling in the caves of the hearts of all creatures, as also being cognized by that person who, by the great Grace of the Lord, has been freed from all grief. Again in the passage "the seven pranas arise from Him: the same Being endued with the Supreme Sakti is described as the upadana or material cause of the universe which is composed of prana etc. Then in the passage, "That great sage, Rudra, who was the first, before all gods, above all universe, saw the Hiranyagarbha being born," He is referred to as the cause, as being above all universe, as being omniscient, as being the generator of the Hiranyagarbha, the first of all emanations. The same Being, dwelling in the cave of the Supreme Akasa, is described to be attainable as the Supreme Immortal Being by those aspirants who perform all acts without longing for fruits, who know the drift of the Vedanta, who have subdued their senses. Then as the question arises as to the way by which to reach Him, contemplation in Dahara is recommended. There it has been said – but only in a general way – that the Being who dwells in the lotus of *Dahara* ought to be worshipped. Then the question arising as to who that Being is, the sruti says that it is He who is the Supreme Being called Mahadeva. Then again the question arises as to what His form is; and in answer to this question the sruti concludes by saying that He is possessed of a form containing diverse eyes and so on. Narayana who is incidentally mentioned in the chapter referred to should be construed as the worshipper on the principle explained in the preceding adhikarana. Though all have to worship Paramesvara, Narayana is specially mentioned here, because he is the highest of the worshipper. We can justify the description of Narayana here by Brahman's attributes, - regarding Narayana the worshipper as not distinct from the diverse-eyed Brahman, the object of worship, - on the ground that it is a description of Narayana who is the upadana or material cause of the universe and who is ensouled by Him the Supreme Brahman.

Adhikarana – 3.

(He is) the Devourer, because of the mention of the moving and the unmoving. (I. ii. 9.)

The passage which is to be discussed here occurs in the Kathopanishad and reads as follows: -

"Who then knows where He is, he to whom the Brahmanas and Kshatriyas are (as it were) but food, and death itself a condiment?"* [* Kathopanishad. 2-25.]

Here a doubt arises as to whether the Being who is described as the devourer of the whole universe of sentient and insentient existence – which is referred to by the mention of Brahmanas and Kshatriyas and which forms as it were a morsel of food mixed with the condiment of death – is the Paramesvara or some other being.

(*Purvapaksha*): - The highly Merciful and all-Gracious Being cannot be the devourer of all. It is cruel to put an end to other's lives. Anger is the sprout from which springs up the act of cruelty. The root of anger which is an evil passion is none other than Moha or delusion. The cause of delusion which is the source of all destruction is *Tamas*. Wherefore the devourer of all is a Tamasic Being. Tamasic nature consists in being devoid of all light, the light of knowledge etc. being enshrouded by Tamas, the darkness of ignorance. To speak of Brahman as the destroyer of all is to attribute ignorance, darkness, delusion, anger and other evil qualities to Him who is ever pure, who is the repository of unmixed good, who is free from all taint of samsara. Then such attributes, as omniscience and ever-contentedness, which have been conclusively shown to form the characteristic marks of His essential nature, would be meaningless. Therefore some other being distinct from Brahma and possessed of the attributes referred to must be the destroyer.

(*Siddhanta*): - It is Brahman who is spoken of as the all-destroyer. – Why? – Because of the mention of the moving and the unmoving. As for the contention that it is not right to regard Brahman as the devourer of the whole universe of moving and unmoving objects, we say that that very description marks the characteristic nature of Brahman, in as much as a Jiva who is of limited powers has not got the power of destroying all the moving and unmoving objects. "To that Destroyer, to that great Devourer, I bow," thus is Paramesvara described in the Atharvasiras as the all-destroyer never is a Jiva so spoken of. "Who all these worlds sacrificed," * [* Rik-Samhita. 8-3-16.] Thus Brahman, is described as offering all the worlds as an oblation in the fire of His own Light. A Jiva who is classed as an oblation can never possess this power. When the Supreme Lord remains alone, having absorbed into Himself the whole universe, everything other than Himself, moving or unmoving, sentient or insentient, then all luminaries such as the sun and the moon being absent, all divisions of time into day and night being done away with, all forms and names having disappeared, all this universe remains as mere Tamas (darkness), there being no perception of gross and subtle objects, of men, Devas, or other beings. Even then remains He alone, the Supreme Lord, of infinite Light, the Witness of all. Accordingly the sruti says,

"When the light has risen, there is no day, no night neither existence nor non-existence; Siva alone is there," † [† Sveta. Up. 4-18.]

Here the words, neither existence nor non-existence" do not prelude even the bare existence of Jiva and bondage – of *pasu* and *pasa* spoken of as *existence* and *non-existence*, - but they only indicate that these are not gross enough to be invested with distinct forms and spoken of by distinct names.

(*Objection*): - Despite the existence of the ever-luminous Siva, the Supreme Brahman, how can the universe be mere darkness?

(*Answer*): - No, How can it detract from the self-luminous Siva, the all-witness. There can be no perception of the universe by Jivas whose body and senses are powerless with regard to sense-objects which, as having then no forms nor names, are beyond perception, while their faculty of spiritual wisdom (Jnana) is overpowered by original sin (*mala*). Even the sel-luminous Siva does not perceive (the universe) as before. Wherefore this grand state of Supreme Sushupti or Sleep, when there is no cognizing whatever of created existence in any particular aspect of its manifestation is spoken of as Tamas. Accordingly the smriti says:

"This was mere Darkness, unknown, without any characteristic marks."* [* Manu-Smriti. 1-5.]

Siva is said to have existed *alone*, possessed of the potency of the universe, of sentient and insentient existence in its subtlest form, undistinguishable by name or form. Again, at the time of creation He manifests His Primal Sakti or Energy and then creates from out of Himself and brings into manifestation all sentient and insentient beings, - each with its own form and name – by His own mere thought, without having recourse to an external material cause. Hence the saying of the learned:

"The Deity, the self-conscious Atman, brings, like a Yogin, the whole existence which lies within, into manifestation without, by means of His will (Ichchha), without an upadana or material cause."

(*Objection*): - Maya and Purusha are spoken of as the upadana or material cause in the following passages of the sruti:

"Let him know Maya to be Prakriti and the Possessor of Maya to be the Mahesvara."
† [† Svetasvatara-Up. 4-10.]

"From Him Viraj was born." ‡ [‡ Purusha-Sukta.]

How can it be said that no upadana or material cause existed?

(*Answer*): - True. In the production of a jar by a potter, the clod of earth is found to be distinct from the body of the potter and is the material cause of the jar; not so, however, is Maya and the like – which are held to be the upadana of the universe – found to exist distinct from the Paramesvara, in as much as it is from out of the Paramesvara Himself who puts on the form of Maya that the universe is evolved. Hence no incongruity. Wherefore the Supreme Purusha Himself whose subtle Maya has no independent existence apart from Himself, is said to be also the upadana or material cause of the universe. Accordingly the Atharvasikha says:

"Whatever has to be contemplated, let him contemplate it as the Lord. Brahma, Vishnu, Rudra, Indra, - all these are born as well as all the sense organs and the elements of matter. The Cause of causes is not a contemplator. On the other hand, the cause is ever to be contemplated; He who is endued with every kind of power, the Lord of all, the source of all - Good abiding in the middle of Light."

Thus, where all beings undergo dissolution, thence only is the origin of all beings, and therefore so long as these beings which are infinite in number are held in dissolution, they abide there alone, in Siva, of infinite potencies (Saktis). So it is Siva, the all-destroyer is the Being denoted by the word 'Brahman.'

As to the contention that, because destruction is an act of cruelty, Brahman becomes tinged with anger the cause of the cruel act, and other evil qualities, we merely answer that this contention arises from absence of enquiry; the quality of Tamas, which is the root of anger and other evil passions, being an attribute of Prakriti. As to the Paramesvara being above all darkness, the divine sruti itself is the authority which says,

"Uma being His help-mate, the Supreme Lord,......the Witness of all, above Tamas (darkness)." * [* Kaivalya-Upanishad.]

The Puranic saying given below also declares that the Paramesvara is ever possessed of Jnana etc. which prevent delusion and other like sources of evil.

"Knowledge, indifference to worldly objects, lordly power, austerity, truth, forgiveness, fortitude, creative power, spiritual wisdom, and mastery – these ten ever exist undiminished in Sankara."

The Purana says also:

"He whose pure unfailing intelligence comprehends all objects of knowledge; He is a youth who delight in the joy arising from the tasting of the nectar or His own Sakti."

It is indeed the Paramesvara of infinite glory who, desirous to create, resorts to His own Sakti, - to His Maya, to His Will (Ichchha), - with a view to become the manifold universe, as said in the sruti, "He desired, may I become many" Then as the sruti says "He brooded over Himself," * [* Taittiriya-Upanishad 2.6.] He thinks of the materials, by which to bring into existence bodies suited to the different Jivas according to their respective Karma, by His power of knowledge (Jnanasakti) spoken of as *tapas* (penance) in the sruti. And having thus brooded, He rouses into being the whole panorama of the universe on the wall of Maya or Ichchhasakti by resorting to his Kriyasakti which is quite capable of accomplishing all that He has thought of, as declared in the following passage, "He created all this."* [* Taittiriya Upanishad. 2-6.] Then, as the sruti says, "Having created it, he entered into the same," * [* Taittiriya Upanishad. 2-6.] He enters the whole creation, and in association with these three Saktis He becomes the whole universe including the three Murtis – the three embodied manifestations of the Lord as caused by the three gunas *satva, rajas* and *tamas* – and other beings. So, who here can gauge the greatness of the omnipotent and omniscient Siva." Wherefore we may conclude that the all-destroyer is the Paramesvara.

And because of the context (I. ii. 10.)

The passage under discussion occurs in a section devoted to Paramesvara, as the following texts in the same section show:

"The wise who knows the Atman, as great and omnipresent does never grieve." * [* Taittiriya Upanishad. 2-6.]

"That Atman cannot be gained by the Veda." † [† Katha-Upanishad 2-22, 23.]

For the foregoing reason also it is evident that the all-destroyer is the Supreme Brahman, the Paramesvara, and none else.

Adhikarana – 4.

The next adhikarana proceeds to show that the Paramesvara, who has been proved to be the all-destroyer in the adhikarana just closed, is ever associated with Jivas, the manifestation of His own glory, as declared in the following passage:

"Two birds, inseparable friends, cling to the same tree. One of them eats the sweet fruit, the other looks on without eating." & [Svetasvatara-Upanishad 4-6.]

Those who entered into the cave are verily the two Atmans, because so it seen. (I. ii. 11).

The passage to be discussed in this adhikarana runs as follows:

"There are the two, drinking their rewards in the world of their own works, entered into the cave (of the heart), dwelling on the highest summit (the other in the heart). Those who know Brahman call them shade and light, likewise those householders who perform the Trinachiketa sacrifice." * [* Katha-Upanishad 3-1.]

Here two beings are spoken of, as distinct from each other as shade and light, those two have entered into the cave of the heart in the body of a Brahman or other person, - which is spoken of as 'the world of their own works' and as 'the highest summit' – and who are the eaters of the fruits of works. A doubt arises as to whether these two are Buddhi and Jiva, or Jiva and Paramesvara.

(*Purvapaksha*): - The two are none other than Buddhi and Jiva. – Why? – Because the words "drinking the rewards" show that the two are enjoyers. Paramesvara is not an enjoyer, because we find it said that "the other looks on without eating." It is a well-known fact that Buddhi and Jiva are enjoyers. Moreover, there exists no such thorough distinction between Jiva and Isvara who are both sentient, as between shade and light. Buddhi being insentient there is a distinction between Buddhi and Jiva. Thus Buddhi and Jiva are the two beings spoken of here.

As against the foregoing we hold as follows: the two beings who lie in the cave are none other than Jiva and Paramesvara, because we find it said that they have entered into the cave in the following passage:

"Him who is difficult to be seen, who has entered into the dark, who is hidden in the cave, who dwells in the abyss, who is the ancient." * [* Katha-Upanishad, 2. 12.]

As to the contention that Isvara is not an enjoyer, it is wrong to say so; for, the words "whose delight is in prana, whose bliss is in manas" show that even Brahman who delights in Atman is in the enjoyment of His own inherent bliss which is accessible to manas alone. The Purana also says.

"He is a youth who delights in the joy arising from the tasting of the nectar of His own Sakti; who as a rule tastes only the sweet honey of the supreme infinite bliss."

Every one knows that Jiva is the eater of the fruits of his own Karma. Though we are thus told that the two are alike enjoyers, a distinction has to be made in accordance with the nature of the two enjoyers. When, for instance, we say 'the king and his servant eat food' we mean that each eats that kind of food which is suited to his rank.

As to the contention that there is no distinction between them, we cannot assent to it; for, though the passage "the eternal of the eternal ones, and the sentient of the sentient ones" † declares the equality of Jiva and Isvara in so far as they are eternal and sentient, there still exists a distinction between them caused by the existence of beginningless *mala* (original sin) is Jiva and its absence in the other. The Sruti "there are two, one knowing and the other unknowing, both unborn, one strong and the other weak" ‡ declares that there is a distinction caused by knowledge and ignorance, by independence and dependence and such other attributes. [† Katha-Upanishad 5-13. ‡ Svetasvatara-Upanishad 1-9.]

(*Objection*): - While both of them are alike associated with a body, how is it that one of them is afflicted with ignorance and other evils while the other is untouched by any evil?

(*Answer*): - There is no room for any such objection. Their occupation of the same body has nothing to do with the blissful condition of the one or the miserable condition of the other. On the other hand it is the independence of the Isvara that makes Him blissful, and it is the dependence of Jiva that makes him miserable. Accordingly the Sruti says:

"On the same tree man sits grieving, immersed, bewildered, by his own impotence. But when he sees the other, the Lord, contented, and knows His glory, then his grief passes away."

The traditional interpretation of this passage is given as follows: The Jiva bound by the shackles of beginningless Karma, having entered into many a body made of Maya – each suited to the enjoying of a particular fruit – is subjected to a lot of incurable misery; and unable to ward it off on account of his impotence, he does not know what to do and grieves. He is thus immersed in the ocean of grief caused by his great delusion. When, however, by the Lord's Grace he intuitively sees Him who as the Impeller dwells with himself, who is gracious to all, who is ever associated with Uma, then he attains to the unsurpassed greatness of the Lord, free from all grief. Wherefore though Siva, who is independent and who has been free from samsara from time without a beginning, is in contact with the body, he is not subject to its evils as the Jiva is. Wherefore it is Jiva and Paramesvara that are said to lie in the cave of the heart.

The Sutrakara again explains:

And because of the specific attribute (I. ii. 12).

Moreover, in this section of the Upanishads, Jiva and Paramesvara are specifically described. Jiva is described as follows: "The knower is not born, nor does he die,"† and so on. The Paramesvara is described as "smaller than small, greater than great." ‡ How can this specific description apply to Jiva and Buddhi? Hence the conclusion that it is Jiva and the Paramesvara that have entered into the cave of the heart and dwell therein as the impelled and the Impeller, as the body and the Embodied. [† Katha-Upanishad. 2-18. ‡ Ibid. 2-20.]

Adhikarana 5.

Here will be mentioned another place for worshipping Paramesvara who has been shown to be the object of worship dwelling in the cave of the heart.

(Paramesvara is the Being) who is within (the eye) because (to Him the attributes are) applicable. (I. ii. 13).

The subject-matter of discussion in this section occurs in a passage of the Chhandogya-Upanishad, which reads as follows:

"The person that is seen in the eye, that is the Atman. This is the immortal, the fearless, this is Brahman." * [* Op. Cit. 4-16.]

Now, who is the person within the eye spoken of as 'the immortal' etc? Is he the Isvara or some other being?

(*Purvapaksha*): - Such a doubt arising, we hold that he is being other than the Paramesvara; for, in the Mahanarayanopanishad 10, 11 etc., the Paramesvara is spoken of as dwelling only in the heart-lotus. On the other hand, Jiva enters into the organ of sight when perceiving color etc., in virtue of his connection with the manas. He is the person in the eye. Or, it may be the reflected person.

(*Siddhanta*): - As against the foregoing *prima facie* view we explain as follows: It is the Paramesvara Himself who is spoken of as the person in the eye; for, to Him alone are applicable such attributes as immortality and fearlessness in their absolute sense.

As to the contention that the Isvara is nowhere spoken of as dwelling in the eye, the Sutrakara says:

And because He is declared to be seated and so on. (I. ii. 14.)

Isvara is declared to be seated in the eye and to rule it within, in such passages as the following:

"He who dwells in the eye, and within the eye, whom the eye does not know, whose body the eye is, and who rules the eye within, he is thy Atman, the ruler within, the immortal." † [† Brih. Up. 5-7.]

Wherefore it is verily the Supreme Isvara.

The Sutrakara now proceeds to show an incongruity in case it is held that the reflected image of the person is spoken of in the passage referred to:

And verily because of the declaration that he is endued with bliss. (I. ii. 15.)

The person referred to is the Isvara for the very reason that he is declared to be endued with bliss in a former passage which runs as follows:

"Bliss is Brahman, akasa is Brahman." ‡ [‡ Chhandogya Upanishad. 4-10.]

Indeed no bliss can exist in the reflected image of a person.

As to the contention that the person in the eye is the Jiva, the Sutrakara says:

And for that very reason he is Brahman. (I. ii. 16.)

Because to Upakosala who was afraid of samsara, and sought to know Brahman the sruti beginning with the passage "Bliss is Brahman, akasa is Brahman," teaches that "what verily is bliss, that verily is the akasa and what verily is the akasa that verily is bliss," * therefore the akasa spoken of as "Kha" is none other than Brahman. Is there any such appropriateness in the case of Jiva? Indeed in Jiva there cannot exist the absolute bliss. Wherefore, the very Brahman who has been spoken of in the opening passage as the infinite bliss being afterwards declared to be the person seated in the eye, Paramesvara is the being spoken of as the person in the eye. [* Chhandogya Upanishad 4-10, 15.]

In the Purvapaksha there is, moreover, an incongruity, as the Sutrakara says:

And because of the mention of the path of those who have learned the Divine Wisdom. (I. ii. 17.)

Because the sruti which begins with the words "He goes to light, from light to day" and ends with the words "there is a person not human; he leads them to Brahman; this is the path of the Devas, the path that leads to Brahman; those who proceed on that path do not return to the life of man, yea, they do not return;" * teaches, in connection with him who has known of the 'person in the eye,' the path of light etc., - the path which has to be learnt by those who have known of the nature of Brahman, - therefore, the person spoken of is neither Jiva nor the reflected image in the eye; on the other hand, he is none other than the Isvara.

Adhikarana 6.

Owing to looseness and impossibility, not the other. (I. ii. 18.)

The passage which has to be discussed here occurs, in the Mahopanishad and reads as follows:

"The thumb-sized Purusha, seated in the thumb, the Lord, the Master of the whole world, the eater of the whole, is pleased. † [† Op. Cit. 35.]

Here a doubt arises as to whether the being spoken of as 'thumb-sized' and so on is the Paramesvara or someone else.

(*Purvapaksha*): - In as much as this passage occurs in the section of *Pranagnihotra*, and because the Purusha is spoken of as small – by the epithet 'thumb-sized' – we have to understand that it is Prana or the Vital air which is the eater of the five oblations. And it cannot be urged that Prana cannot be the eater; for, even the air is spoken of as an eater in such passages as the following:

"The waters and the earth are the food, and the fire and the air are the eaters."

From all points of view the passage refers to the vital air.

(*Siddhanta*): - It is none other than Paramesvara who is spoken of here; for, if the attribute of lordship over the whole universe and that of being the eater of the whole be (somehow) applied to the other (Prana), then these attributes are too loosely applied.* [* That is, they become applicable to many other entities.] These attributes cannot be strictly applied to it (prana). Wherefore none but Isvara can be such a being. He is declared to be an object of worship even in the form of prana, as the sruti speaks of Him as the seat of prana in the following words:

> "Then art the knot of all pranas (senses),
> Thou art Rudra, the destroyer (of pain); do
> Then enter into me." † [† Mahanarayana Upanishad 37.]

As to His being spoken of as "thumb-sized," there can be no inconsistency, in as much as He is so described only for the purpose of meditation. Though the vital air is found described in several places as the eater, it cannot be 'the eater of the *whole.*' Accordingly we should understand that the Isvara is here described to be of the form of prana and has to be worshipped by Pranagnihotra.

Adhikarana. 7.

For the purpose of contemplative worship, it has been shown that Siva, the Supreme Brahman, is seated in the orb of the sun, in man's heart-lotus, and so on, though He is all-knowing, all-powerful, all-benign, and all-pervading. This section proceeds to show that He is seated everywhere.

(He is) the Inner Ruler abiding in the Devas, in the worlds and so on, because of the mention of His attributes. (I. ii. 19.)

The text which forms the subject of discussion in this section occurs in the Antaryami-Brahmana and runs as follows:

"He who dwells in the earth, within the earth, whom the earth does not know, whose body the earth is, and who rules the earth within, he is thy Atman, the ruler within, the immortal." ‡ [‡ Brihadaranyaka-Upanishad 5-7.]

A doubt arises as to whether he who is thus spoken of as the Inner Ruler in all beings, - in all things mentioned in the series extending from earth up to Atman, - is the Paramesvara, or Jiva, or the Virat-Purusha, or the Pradhana.

(*Purvapaksha*): - It becomes only Jiva to enter into the sense-organs of all beings for the enjoying of the variegated fruits which he has earned. It becomes the Virat-Purusha to enter into all beings, as he is the upadana (material cause) of all sentient existence. Or, it is right to maintain that it is the Pradhana which pervades all, as it becomes transformed in the form of the *mahat* and so on. It cannot be that the Paramesvara who, as superior to the universe, is declared in the sruti to have crossed beyond all phenomenal existence (vikara) has entered into the universe of phenomenal forms. Wherefore the *Antaryamin*, the Inner Ruler, must be one of the three mentioned above, - Jiva, Virat-Purusha, or Pradhana, - but not the Paramesvara.

(*Siddhanta*): - As against the foregoing we hold as follows: He who is described to be the Antaryamin, the Inner Ruler in the earth and so on, is none but Paramesvara, because of the mention of the attributes of being within all and the like. In the Atharvasiras also the

Paramesvara is found described to have entered into all beings as their Atman. In the words "He is thy Atman, the ruler within, the immortal," Siva alone is described as immortal and liberated from time without beginning, it being said in the Jabala-Upanishad that "these are verily the designations of the Immortal." Just as the Paramesvara is described in the sruti as superior to the universe, He is also described as all-formed in the words "all verily is Rudra," and so on. In every subsequent passage of the section (following the one quoted in the opening part of the adhikarana from the Brihadaranyaka-Upanishad) the word 'immortal' is used evidently to show that He is not in the least tinged with the phenomenal change though he is present in all changing phenomena. In that section of the Atharvasiras which begins with the passage "He verily who is Rudra is the Blessed Lord; He is Bhuh, Bhuvah, Suvah, as well as he who is known as Brahma; to Him, verily, we bow, we bow," the Paramesvara is described as Brahman, Vishnu, Rudra, Uma, Lakshmi, Saraswati, Ganesa, Skanda, Indra, and other guardian spirits of the world, the seven worlds comprising the earth etc., the five material elements comprising earth etc., the sun, the moon, the planets, the stars, time and so on, - in each case repeating in its turn(all that has been said when describing Him as Brahma in the opening passage of the section here quoted.) And even here, with a view to prevent the notion that owing to His entrance into all sentient and insentient existence He may become tainted with evil, the word "Bhagavat" (blessed Lord) has been used in each case, thus showing that He is always endued with the excellent divine attributes of lordship and so on. Wherefore it is but right to hold that Siva, the Supreme Lord, is superior to all and is the Atman of all.

As to the contention that Pradhana etc. may be spoken of as the Antaryamin, the sutrakara refutes it as follows:

And not what the smriti speaks of, there being no mention of its attributes; nor is it the embodied. (I. ii. 20).

And we cannot hold that what the sruti speaks of as Antaryamin, the Inner Ruler, is the Pradhana mentioned in the smriti (of the Sankhyas), there being no mention of its attribute, such as changeability, inertness and so on. Nor can the embodied Virat-Purusha be the being here referred to, in as much as he cannot be the ruler of all.

And it is not Jiva either:

Both alike, verily, declare Him as different. (I. ii. 21).

Both the schools, the Kanvas as well as the Madhyandinas, declare the Antaryamin as different from the Jiva, in the words "He who abides in the Vijnana," and "He who abides in the Atman," and so on. Wherefore it may be concluded that Paramesvara is alone the Inner Ruler of all, not the Pradhana, not Virat-Purusha, nor Jiva.

Adhikarana 8.

This adhikarana is introduced with a view to show that the Paramesvara, who has been declared to be embodied in the visible forms of the earth etc., is not Himself visible like them.

(Paramesvara is the being) possessed of the attributes of invisibility and so on, because of the mention of (His) attributes. (I. ii. 22).

The passage which forms the subject of discussion in this adhikarana runs as follows:

"But the higher knowledge is that by which the indestructible (Akshara) is apprehended; that which cannot be seen, nor seized, which has no family and no caste, no eyes nor ears, no hands nor feet, the eternal, the omnipresent, infinitesimal, that which is imperishable, - it is that which the wise regard as the source of all beings.* [* Mundaka-Upanishad I-1-5, 3.]

Here a doubt arises as to whether the indestructible (Akshara) refers to Pradhana, Jiva, or Paramesvara.

(*Purvapaksha*): - Here Akshara refers to Pradhana, in as much as it can be the source of all beings, transforming itself into mahat and so on. Or, Akshara may refer to jiva. He, can indeed, be rightly spoken of as Akshara, as said in the following passage of the sruti:

"That which is perishable (Kshara), the Pradhana, the immortal (amrita), the indestructible (Akshara)." † [† Svetasvatara-Upanishad I-10.]

He can be the source of all beings through his Karma. Wherefore Akshara may refer to one of the two.

(*Siddhanta*): - As against the foregoing we hold as follows: The Akshara is none other than Paramesvara, His attributes being spoken of in the words "From Him who perceives all, and who knows all, whose penance (tapas) consists of knowledge"‡ and so on. [‡ Mundaka-Upanishad I-1. 9.] Indeed, such attributes as omniscience can pertain to none other than Paramesvara. As to the contention that Pradhana and Jiva can be the source of all beings, we say it is wrong to say so, in as much as they are (respectively) insentient and possessed of limited knowledge, and are therefore incapable of the act of (creating all beings).

Again, the Sutrakara proceeds to show that 'Akshara' cannot properly refer to Jiva and Pradhana:

And because of the mention of qualifications and a distinction, (it is) not the two others. (I. ii. 23).

Here the Upanishad opens with the enunciation of the proposition that, one being known, all is known, in the words "Which one, O blessed Lord, being known, all this becomes known?"§ [§ Ibid. 1-1-3.] Besides this, there are other qualifications. Owing to a mention of such qualifications 'Akshara' cannot here mean Pradhana. Neither does 'Akshara' refer to Jiva, in as much as the Akshara is described to be different from Jiva in the words "higher than the high, (higher), than the imperishable.¶ [Ibid. 2-1-2.]

And because of the description of (His) form (I. ii. 24).

The Akshara is described to be of the form of the three worlds in the following passage:

> "Fire is his head, his eyes the sun and the moon, the quarters his ears, his speech the Veda disclosed, the wind his breath, his heart the universe; from his feet came the earth, he is indeed the inner Atman of all beings." * [* Ibid 2-1-1.]

And for this reason, Paramesvara, the Atman of all, is alone referred to by the word '*Akshara.*'

Adhikarana 9.

It was shown in a former section that Paramesvara is to be worshipped as the seat of prana. This section proceeds to show that He is to be worshipped as the fire in the stomach.

The fire (Vaisvanara is Paramesvara), because of the specification of the general designation. (I. ii. 25).

The following scriptural text forms the subject of discussion in this adhikarana:

> "But he who worships the space-limited Vaisvanara Atman as identical with himself, he eats food in all worlds, in all beings, in all Atmans."† [† Chhandogya-Upanishad 5-18.]

Here a doubt arises as to whether the Vaisvanara here presented as an object of worship refers to Paramesvara, or to some other being.

(*Purvapaksha*): - The word 'Vaisvanara' denotes the fire in the stomach; for we find the word used to denote the fire in the stomach in the following passage:

> "Agni Vaisvanara is the fire within man, by which the food that is eaten is cooked, *i.e.*, digested. Its noise is that which one hears, if one covers one's ears. When he is on the point of departing this life, he does not hear that noise." ‡ [‡ Brihadaranyaka-Upanishad 7-9.]

Or it may refer to 'fire' the third of the five 'great elements' the word 'Vaisvanara' being applied to fire in such passages as the following:

> "This fire, verily, is the Vaisvanara." § [§ Taittiriya-Samhita 3-3-8.]

Or, the word may denote the god known by that name, in as much as he, as the god to be worshipped, is declared to be the giver of the reward in such passages as the following:

"When a son is born, oblations should be offered to the Vaisvanara in twelve cups." ¶
[¶ Ibid 2-2-5.]

It can never refer to Paramesvara, since the sruti teaches us that Vaisvanara is a finite being, in the words "space-limited."

(*Siddhanta*): - As against the foregoing we hold as follows: Paramesvara Himself is referred to by the word 'Vaisvanara.' – How? – Though the word Vaisvanara is a common designation, yet in this section of the Upanishad it is defined by such specific designations as 'Brahman' – which are peculiarly applicable to Paramesvara, - in the following passages:

"Who is our Atman? What is Brahman?" * [* Chhandogya-Upanishad 5-11.]

"You know at present that Vaisvanara Atman; tell us that."

This specific designation cannot be applied to the fire in the stomach etc. Wherefore Vaisvanara is none but Paramesvara.

The Sutrakara adduces another piece of evidence to show that Paramesvara is meant here:

In as much as what is repeated may form a mark by which to infer. (I. ii. 26).

In such passages as "Fire is his head, his eyes the sun and the moon," † Paramesvara is declared to be embodied in the form made up of the regions extending from heaven to earth. Such a form is spoken of in the section of the Upanishad we are here discussing in the following words:

"Of that Vaisvanara Atman, the head is Sutejas (having good light), the eye Visvarupa (multiform), the breath Prithagvartman (having various courses), the truth Bahula (full), the bladder Rayi (wealth), the feet, the earth." ‡ [‡ Chhandogya-Upanishad 5-19.]

The form here spoken of forms the mark by which we may infer that Paramesvara is meant here.

If (you hold it is) not (so) because by word etc. It is said to be established within, we cannot (grant it) because of its being so taught for the sake of contemplation, and on account of its incongruity; and moreover, they declare him to be Purusha. (I. ii. 27.)

(*Objection*): - This Vaisvanara fire is none other than the fire in the stomach, because of its being spoken of as the three fires and as the receptacle of the oblations offered to the pranas, in such passages as the following:

"The heart is the Garhapatya fire, the mind the Anvaharya fire, the mouth the Ahavaniya fire. Therefore the first food which a man may take is in the place of homa;* [* Chhandogya-Upanishad 5-18, 19.]

and also because of its being declared to be established within man in the following passage:

"He who knows this Vaisvanara fire to be of the human form and established within man." † [† Satapathabrahmana 10-6-1-11.]

The Vaisvanara fire is not Paramesvara.

(*Answer*): - Not so; because it is taught that He has to be worshipped in the form of the fire in the stomach, and that it is impossible to hold that the fire in the stomach is of the form of the three worlds and so off. Moreover, in the words "this Vaisvanara fire is he who is known as Purusha," the Vajasaneyins declare this Vaisvanara to be the Purusha. Moreover, none but Paramesvara can be strictly spoken of as Purusha, as the sruti says:

"By that Purusha all this is filled." ‡ [‡ Mahanarayana Upanishad 1.]

Wherefore it is right to hold that Paramesvara is meant here.

Hence only, neither the God nor the element. (I. ii. 28.)

Because this Vaisvanara has the three worlds for his body and is known by the name of Purusha, therefore neither the fire-god nor the third element (of fire) is meant here.

It having been proved that Paramesvara is denoted by the word 'agni' (fire) as having to be worshipped in the form of the fire in the stomach, the Sutrakara now proceeds to show how other teachers (acharyas) have variously explained the application of the word 'agni.'

Jaimini (sees) no incongruity even in literally (applying the word) (I. ii. 29.)

The application of the word 'agni' to Paramesvara is justifiable nor merely on the ground that He has to be worshipped in the form of fire, but also on the ground that the word can be literally applied to Paramesvara himself as 'leading (the devotees) to the front. Thus Jaimini sees no incongruity in applying the word to Paramesvara.

Asmarathya (holds it to be) for manifestation's sake! (I. ii. 30.)

Sage Asmarathya holds that the Unlimited becomes limited in space occupied by the regions from the heaven down to the Earth, with a view to manifest Himself to his devotees.

Badari (holds it to be) for recognition's sake. (I. ii. 31.)

Badari holds that the representation of the regions from the heaven to the earth as the head, feet and other parts of the body is meant for recognition, that is, for the attainment of Brahman.

Jaimini (holds it to be) for exaltation's sake; so, indeed, (the sruti) reveals. (I. ii. 32.)

Jaimini thinks that it is with a view to exalt in thought the oblations to prana etc. – taught in connection with the worship – to the rank of an Agnihotra that the chest etc. of the worshipper are represented as the altar and so on in the following passage:

"The chest is the altar; the hairs, the grass on the altar; the heart, the Garhapatya fire; the mind, the Anvaharya fire; the month, the Ahavaiya fire." * [* Chhandogya-Upanishad. 5-18.]

And accordingly the sruti says: "He who offers this Agnihotra with a full knowledge of its true purpose." † [† Briha-Up. 5-24.]

And they declare Him to be therein. (I. ii. 33.)

The Taittiriyakas declare that the Paramesvara dwells in the devotee's body when oblations are offered to prana etc., as the recipient of those oblations, as the following passages show:

"O oblation! Enter into me as Siva, that there may be no sensation of burning." ‡ [‡ Mahana. Up. 35-36.]

"The Lord is pleased, the eater of all." ‡ [‡ Mahana. Up. 35-36.]

Wherefore in the opinion of all teachers, as also in point of reason, it is right to hold that Paramesvara alone is to be worshipped in the form of the fire in the stomach, by the prana-agnihotra.

End of the Second Pada of the First Adhyaya.

THIRD PADA.

This pada will be concerned with an enquiry into the meaning of such of the Vedantic passages as contain explicit marks of Brahman, as also incidentally with determining as to who is qualified (for the study of this science):

The abode of heaven, earth etc., is the Paramesvara, owing to the word 'self' (I. ii. 1).

The passage referred to here occurs in the Mundaka-Upanishad and reads thus:

"In him the heaven, the earth and the sky are woven, the mind also with all the senses. Know him alone, the Atman, and leave oft other words. He is the bridge of the immortal." * [* Mundaka-Upanishad 2-2-5.]

(Purvapaksha): - It seems that some being other than Paramesvara viz. Vayu, is the abode of the heaven, the earth etc., for he is declared to be the abode of all in the following passage:

"By air, as by a thread, O Gautama, this world and the other world, and all creatures are strung together." * [* Brihadaranyaka-Upanishad 5-7-2.]

As against the foregoing, we hold as follows:

The Paramesvara is the abode of the heaven; the earth etc., because of the word 'Ataman' is the passage "Know him alone, the Atman."

What is the objection to Vayu, the Sutratman, being denoted by the word 'Atman.'

The Sutrakara answers thus

And because of the declaration (that he is) reached by the liberated (I. iii. 2.)

It is none other than Paramesvara, because that Being is to be reached by the liberated souls, - those who are liberated from name and form generated by the meritorious and sinful acts – as declared in the following passages:

"When the seer sees the brilliant maker and lord (of the world) as the person who is the source of Brahman, then he is wise, and shaking off good and evil, he reaches the highest *Samgam* free from passions." * [* Mundaka-Upanishad 3-1-3.]

"As the flowing rivers disappear in the sea, losing their name and their form, thus, a wise man, freed from name and form, goes to the divine Person who is greater than the great." † [† Ibid 3-2-8.]

How can this be possible in Vayu? Vayu becomes the Sutratman only as ensouled by Paramesvara, in as much as Vayu is one of the eight forms of the Paramesvara. Hence the conclusion that it is not Vayu.

Not the subject of inference, for want of its designation; nor the living being (I. iii. 3.)

It cannot be maintained that what is spoken of as the abode of heaven, earth etc., refers to Pradhana as known by inference, in as much as it is the upadana or material cause of all; for, there is no word denoting Pradhana. Neither can it be the Jiva, for, then, it would involve an incongruity.

Because of the mention of a distinction (I. iii. 4.)

Here a distinction is made between Isvara and Jiva in the following passage:

"On the same tree man (Purusha) sits grieving, immersed, bewildered by his own impotence. But when he sees the other Lord contented and knows his glory, then his grief passes away."‡ [‡ Mundaka Upanishad 3-1-2.]

Wherefore He who is the Supreme Lord (Paramesvara) in Himself can alone be the abode of heaven, earth etc.

By the context (I. iii. 5.)

This section, indeed, treats of the Supreme, and begins thus:

"Now the supreme knowledge by which that Indestructible is known." § [§ Mundaka Upanishad 1-1-5.]

Wherefore also, the Paramesvara is here referred to.

And on account of presence and eating (I. iii. 6.)

And also because, after having said that Jiva eats the fruits of his actions, the sruti speaks of Him who shines forth without eating, in the following passage:

"Two birds inseparable friends, cling to the same tree. One of them eats the sweet fruit, the other looks on without eating." * [* Ibid. 3-1-1.]

Hence the conclusion that it is the Paramesvara Himself, distinct from the Jiva, who is spoken of as the abode of heaven, earth etc.

Adhikarana 2.

The Sutrakara proceeds to show that unsurpassed Bliss is the result of reaching Paramesvara who, as has just been described, has to be reached by the liberated souls:

The Infinity (is Paramesvara) because of its mention after serenity (I. iii. 7.)

In the Chandogya-Upanishad, after declaring that "Infinity only is bliss," the Sruti describes the nature of the Infinity as follows:

"Where one sees nothing else, hears nothing else, that is the Infinite." † [† Op. cit. 7-24-1.]

Here arises a doubt as to whether it is the Paramesvara or some other being who is denoted by the word 'Infinite.'

(*Purvapaksha*): - The Infinite is some being other than Paramesvara, namely Prana. When, as regards 'name' and other things mentioned in the previous passages, Narada asked "Is there something better than a name." ‡ [‡ Ibid. 7-1-5.] Sanatkumara mentions "speech" and other things, in such words as "speech is better than a name;" § [§ Ibid. 7-2-1.] but, after Prana, sruti introduces the Infinite without resorting to a question and an answer. Because Paramesvara is thus not the subject of discourse here, therefore Prana is the Infinite.

As against the foregoing we hold as follows: Paramesvara alone is denoted by the word 'Infinite,' as coming after 'serenity.' 'Serenity' means Jiva as spoken of in the sruti "Now that serene being which etc." || [|| Ibid. 8-3-4.] And he is referred to by the word 'Prana.' After him, the Infinite is declared as something different from him in the words. "But in reality he declares what is beyond who declares the Highest Being to be the true," ¶ and so on. [¶ Ibid 7-17-1.] Here, after declaring that He who understands Prana declares that which is beyond in the words, "He who sees this, perceives this, and understands this, declares 'but,' that he who declares the Highest Being to be the True is superior to him who is mentioned above, - to him who declares that Prana is the Being who is beyond all. Therefore it is to be concluded that the being who is called the True and is the subject subsequently spoken of as the Highest Being is superior to Prana previously spoken of as the Highest Being. It is that Being who is described in a succeeding passage as possessed of the attribute of infinitude. He is even spoken of as Atman in a passage next succeeding it, in the words "Next follows the explanation of the Infinite as the Atman." † [† Ibid. 7-25-7.] Wherefore the Infinite is the Atman, none other than the Paramesvara, who is Superior to Jiva spoken of by the word 'Prana.'

And owing to the appropriateness of the attributes (I. iii. 8).

The attributes that He rests in His own greatness, that He is the Atman of all, that He is the cause of all, and so on, are taught in the following passages:

"O Lord, wherein does He rest? In His own greatness." ‡ [‡ Chh. Up. 7-24-1.]

"Atman is all this." § [§ Ibid. 7-25-2.]

"From the Atman comes Prana; from the Atman, hope." || [|| Ibid. 7-26-1.]

These are appropriate only when applied to Paramesvara, not to Jiva denoted by the word 'Prana.' Wherefore, it may be concluded that Paramesvara alone is the Infinite, not the other.

(*Objection*): - In the preceding adhikarana it was shown that the liberated souls attain equality with Brahman, as said by the sruti. "He reaches the highest equality free from passions." ¶ [¶ Mundaka-Upanishad. 3-1-3.] Accordingly it is to be concluded that the liberated souls who have attained union with Brahman remain separate from Him. In the passage "where one sees nothing else, hears nothing else, understands nothing else, that is the Infinite," ** it is declared that, when Brahman denoted by the word 'Infinite' is seen, there can be no perception of the universe as opposed to Brahman. How to reconcile this?

(*Answer*): - The meaning of the assertion that "one sees nothing else" when the Infinite is immediately perceived, may be explained as follows: He whose nature is unsurpassed bliss, in whom – when immediately seen – merged, a man does not seek to perceive color and other sense-objects with a longing for any more pleasures, He is the Infinite, He is Brahman. Indeed, the various kinds of sensuous pleasures are only the infinitesimally small fractions of Brahman's bliss. Accordingly the Sruti says, "All other creatures lives on a small portion of this bliss."* [* Bri. Up. 6-3-32.] Wherefore here, as regards Brahman, there can be no denial of duality. We need not specially investigate as to how the perception of the universe which is alien to the highest end of man can be avoided so long as the universe exists. For, in the case of liberated souls, it is not the material (Prakrita) universe which is perceived by them. On the other hand, it is Brahman Himself, whose essential nature is unsurpassed bliss, that forms the object of perception in the form of universe. Accordingly the Sruti says:

> "That, then, he becomes; Brahman whose body is Light (akasa), whose nature is true, whose delight is in Prana (Supreme Sakti), whose bliss is in Manas." † [† Tait. Up. 1-6.]

There, the liberated soul is introduced in the words "He attains to the state of self-effulgence, he attains to the mastery over manas," and so on. In "he is the master of speech" and so on, he is said to be endued with speech and other sense-organs which are under his own control, which are non-material (aprakrita) and perfectly pure. To him, then, on attaining to that condition, this visible array of the material (Prakrita) universe becomes the very Brahman whose body is akasa, i.e., whose body is the Light of spiritual consciousness. This is the hidden meaning of the passage. Wherefore equality of the liberated souls with Brahman consists in their perceiving the universe as one with Brahman in essence. Hence the propriety of the whole doctrine.

Adhikarana 3.

The Akshara (is Paramesvara) because of the supporting of (the universe) including akasa. (I. ii. 9.)

The passage which forms the subject of discussion here occurs in the Brihadaranyaka, and runs thus:

> "O Gargi, the Brahmana call this the Indestructible (Akshara). It is neither coarse nor fine, neither short nor long, neither red nor fluid; it is without shadow;"* and so on. [* Bri. Up. 5-8-8.]

Here a threefold doubt arises as to the meaning of the word 'Akshara': does it refer to Pranava, Jiva or Paramesvara?

(*Purvapaksha*): - One of the two, Pranava or Jiva, is denoted by the word 'akshara.'- How? – It is but right that it should refer to Pranava in as much as the word 'akshara' is synonymous with 'letter.' It is also right that 'akshara' should refer to Purusha or Jiva, as said in the scriptural passage 'Purusha is termed akshara."† [† Bhagavad Gita. XV.16.] Wherefore they alone are referred to by the word 'akshara.'

As against the foregoing we hold as follows: Here, it is Brahman who is denoted by the word 'akshara.' Why? Because the Akshara is said to support everything including akasa. When Gargi asked "In what then is the akasa woven like warp and woof;" ‡ - that akasa which is described as the basis of all phenomena in the passage, "That of which they say that it is above the heavens, beneath the earth, embracing heaven and earth, past, present, and future, that is woven, like warp and woof, in the akasa," § - Yajnavalkya said, "O Gargi, the Brahmanas call this the Akshara....In that Akshara then, O Gargi, the akasa, is woven, like warp and woof." || We are taught that the Akshara so described supports the universe including akasa. Where else is this possible except in the Paramatman? Wherefore Paramesvara alone is the being denoted by the word 'Akshara.' [‡ Bri. Up. 5-8-7. § Ibid 5-8-7. || Bri. Up. 5=8=11.]

And that, by the command. (I. iii. 20).

And we are taught that this support is owing to the high command, as the Sruti says, "By the command of that Akshara, O Gargi, Sun and Moon stand apart"¶ [¶ Ibid. 5-8-9.] Jiva cannot exercise such a command over the world, as the Sruti says that there cannot be a second in the command of the world, in the passage, "One alone is Rudra: they are not for a second" **. [**Atharvasiras.] Wherefore Paramesvara alone is denoted by the word '*Akshara.*'

And because of the exclusion of distinction (I. iii. 11.)

"Distinction" means being a separate entity. The concluding portion of the passage, - namely, "This Akshara, O Gargi, is unseen, but seeing; unheard, but hearing; unperceived, but perceiving; unknown, but knowing." – excludes the idea of the Akshara being distinct from Paramesvara, in as much as neither Jiva nor Pranava can be spoken of as seeing and being at the same time unseen. Hence the conclusion that Paramesvara alone is the Akshara.

Adhikarana. -4

This Adhikarana is intended to show that the Paramesvara, though beyond the reach of sensuous perception, yet becomes immediately perceptible to His devotees, as a result of His Supreme Mercy:

He is the object of perception, because of the mention (of His attributes). (I. iii. 12.)

The passage which forms the subject of discussion here occurs in the Prasna Upanishad and reads as follows:

"Again he who meditates with this syllable '*Aum*' of three matras, on the Highest Purusha, he comes to light and to the sun. And as a snake is freed from its skin, so is he freed from evil. He is led up by the Saman verses to the Brahma-world, and than Him who is superior to the Jiva-mass he sees the Higher Purusha lying in the body." * [* Op. Cit. 5-5.]

Here a doubt arises as to whether the entity spoken of as the object of perception is the Paramesvara or some other being.

(*Purvapaksha*): - He is not the Paramesvara. He is none other than the Hiranyagarbha, as the sruti speaks of the attainment of his regions, in the words, 'by the Saman verses, he is led up to the Brahma world.' And the world 'Highest' too is applicable to him who is the highest of the Jiva. Or, it may be Narayana; for he is the being denoted by the word 'Purusha'. He can also be spoken of as higher than the Hiranyagarbha who is the aggregate of the Jivas He alone is known to be designated by Pranava His abode alone is declared in the Sruti to be intuited by the wise, in the words, "That supreme abode of Vishnu do the wise over see;" † and in the concluding verse this fact is thus referred to: [† Taittiriya-Samhita 4-2-9.]

"Through the Rik-verses he arrives at this world, through the Yajus-verses at the sky, through the Saman-verses at that which the wise teach." * [* Prasna-Upanishad 5-7.]

As against the foregoing we hold as follows: Here the object of the act of perception is the Paramesvara, because of the mention of His distinguishing attributes such as tranquility in the following passage:

"The wise arrives at that which is tranquil, free from decay, from death, from fear, - the Highest" † [† Ibid 5-7.]

Indeed, in the Hiranyagarbha who is a creature of the Paramesvara, no such attributes as tranquility can exist. The term 'Brahma-world' means the region of Siva – the Para-Brahman – which is worthy of attainment. He, indeed, who is 'higher than him who is superior' to the Hiranyagarbha, the aggregate of Jivas spoken of as 'Jiva-mass'- is declared as the object of meditation. Hence the untenability of the view that the Hiranyagarbha is meant here (to be the object of perception).

As to the assertion that Narayana is meant here, it needs investigation. How can he be spoken of as eternally free, as the cause of fearlessness, as the supreme, beyond all universe, as taught in the words "free from death, from fear, and highest"? He is, indeed, of the form of the universe. And how then to explain the statement that the devotee directly sees Him who is higher than Narayana-than him who is superior even to Hiranyagarbha the 'jiva-mass,'- Him who lies in the body as the Antaryamin and is therefore called Purusha, Him who is Para-Brahman? Indeed, the sruti declares as follows:

"Superior to Narayana is Brahman." ‡ [‡ Mahana. Upanishad.]

"True, real, the Supreme Brahman, the spirit (Purusha), dark and yellowish, celebrate, diverse-eyed" § [§ Ibid.]

Wherefore it is but right to maintain that the sruti – "he sees the Purusha lying in the body, Greater than the Great," – declares as the object of perception Him who is called Purusha as dwelling in the Dahara-lotus in the body; who is denoted by the Pranava, as declared in the sruti, "Designated by that (Pranava) which is merged in its root (the syllable a) is He who is the Highest, the Mahesvara (Great Lord);" who, as said in the sruti "Brahman who is greater than Narayana," is greater than Narayana who is the form of universe; who is true and real, as devoid of all divergence in speech and thought; who, as possessed of three eyes, is said to be diverse-eyed; who, as colored by the Supreme Energy (Para-sakti) called Uma – a word formed of the constituent sounds of the Pranava in their reversed order, - is described as dark and yellowish; who is the supreme all-transcending Brahman. Now as to the assertion based on the sruti "That Supreme abode of Vishnu": there is no incongruity whatever, in as much as that very supreme form of Vishnu which, when looked apart from the universe, is made of unsurpassed bliss, is itself the Supreme Brahman called Siva. That is to say, there is no essential distinction between Vishnu and Siva, the material and efficient causes of the universe, except what is due to a difference of state.

Adhikarana 5.

Thus, it has been shown here that the Sakshatkara or direct perception of Parabrahman, the diverse-eyed, - who is above the universe including Vishnu, Brahma and so on, who, lying in the body as an act of Grace to the devotee, is called Purusha, whom is associated with Uma, the Supreme Energy (Parama-Sakti), - enables His devotees who are always intent on His name, Pranava, to attain Him, by way of bringing about the cessation of all samsara. This adhikarana proceeds to speak of His residence in the body and of His worship:

Dahara (is Paramesvara), because of the next-mentioned (attributes) (I. iii. 13).

The passage which forms the subject of discussion here occurs in the Chhandogya-Upanishad and reads as follows:

"There is this city of Brahman, and in it the palace, the small (Dahara) lotus and in it that Dahara (small) akasa. Now what exists in that Dahara-akasa, that is to be sought for, that is to be understood." * [* Op. Cit. 8-1-1.]

Here a doubt arises as to whether it is the material ether (Bhutakasa), or Jiva or Paramesvara that is denoted by the word 'dahara.'

(*Puruvapaksha*): - The application of the word 'akasa being restricted to the material ether, 'Dahara-akasa' denotes bhutakasa or material ether. Or, the word 'dahara' refers to Jiva, because the word means 'small in size' and is therefore applicable to Jiva who is anu, of atomic size. 'Dahara' cannot denote the all-pervading Paramesvara.

As against the foregoing we hold as follows: 'Dahara-akasa' is none other than the Paramesvara. Why? Because of the attributes next mentioned, such as the attributes of being free from sin and so on, thus declared in a subsequent passage of the section:

"This Atman is free from sin, free from old age, free from death and grief, free from hunger and thirst, of unfailing desires, of unfailing will." * [* Ibid. 8-1-5.]

How can these exist in Jiva who is a samsarin, a being of the world? Wherefore Dahara-akasa is none other than the Isvara, possessed of the attribute of being free from sin, and so on.

And because of going of the word. So indeed it is found; and there is an indicating mark (I. iii. 14.)

'Dahara-akasa' denotes Paramesvara, also because it is declared that the creatures daily go into this Dahara-akasa, and because it is spoken of as 'Brahmaloka' in the following passage in the same context:

> "As people who do not know the country walk again and again over a gold treasure that has been hidden somewhere in the earth and do not discover it, thus do all these creatures day after day go into the Brahma-loka, and yet do not discover it, because they are carried away by untruth." † [† Ibid. 8-3-2.]

So, indeed elsewhere the sruti speaks of the creatures thus going to the Paramesvara, as found in the following passage:

> "In the same manner, my son, all these creatures, when they have become merged in the True, know not that they are merged in the True." ‡ [‡ Ibid. 6-9-2.]

We also find the word Brahma-loka applied to the same in the following passage:

> "This is Brahma-loka, O King." § [§ Ibid. 6-9-2.]

Moreover, even leaving out of consideration the fact that the sruti speaks *elsewhere* of the creatures daily going to Brahman and refers to the Dahara-akasa by the word 'Brahma-loka,' we find ample evidence, showing that Dahara-akasa is Paramesvara, in the section under discussion which speaks of all creatures going daily to Brahman and contains the word 'Brahma-loka' referring to Dahara-akasa.

Because of His greatness- the supporting (of the universe) – being found in this (Dahara-akasa). (I. iii. 15).

The act of supporting the universe, which constitutes the Paramesvara greatness, is predicated of this Dahara-akasa, in the following passage:

> "Now that Atman is the limit the support, so that these worlds may not become jumbled up." * [* Chha. Up. 8-4-1.]

And this supporting of the universe forms the greatness of Paramesvara, as the following sruti declares.

> "He is the lord of all, the master of all beings, the protector of all beings. He is the limit, the support, so that these worlds may not become jumbled up." † [† Bri.Up. 6-4-22.]

Wherefore also, Dahara-akasa is Paramesvara.

And it being well-known (that He is to be worshipped there). (I. iii. 16).

The Mahopanishad says:

> There is that small lotus situated in the body's midst, free from sin, the abode of the great; and therein is the Dahara (small) akasa, free from grief; and that which is there within has to be worshipped." ‡ [‡ Mahana. Up. 10.]

The Kaivalya-Upanishad says:

> "Having regarded the heart-lotus as free from all stain, ... and having contemplated the Lord Paramesvara, with His helpmate Uma, as the Trilochana (three-eyed) as Nilakantha (dark-necked) as serene...."

From such passages as these it is clear that Paramesvara associated with Uma is to be contemplated as dwelling within the small lotus. For this reason also, Dahara-akasa is Paramesvara.

(*Objection*): - From such passages in another Upanishad as "In that akasa within the heart, there reposes the ruler of all, the lord of all, the king of all,"§ it is clear that the Paramesvara is to be contemplated as dwelling in the Dahara-akasa within the small lotus. Here He is to be contemplated as the Dahara-akasa itself. There is thus a self-contradiction in the Upanishads.

(*Answer*): - Even here it is the Paramesvara dwelling within the Dahara-akasa that has to be contemplated. But, in as much as sinlessness and other attributes of Paramesvara are found predicted of Dahara-akasa, Paramesvara may also be spoken of as Dahara-akasa when conceived as *Chid-ambara*, as enrobed in the Spiritual Light.

(If you say that) – owing a reference to the other – that (other) is meant here, (we reply) no, owing to impossibility (I. iii. 17).

(*Objection*): - The other, namely jiva, is referred to in the following passage:

> "Now that serene being who, after having risen from out this earthly body, and having reached the highest Light, appears in his true form, that is the Atman: thus he spoke."
> * [* Chha. Upanishad 8-3-4.]

Therefore the akasa under discussion can be no other than the Jiva.

(*Answer*): - No; because the attributes mentioned above, such as freedom from sin, cannot pertain to him. Wherefore akasa properly refers here to none other than Paramesvara to whom those attributes belong.

(If you say that it is jiva) because of the subsequent (passage), (we hold that it speaks of jiva) whose true nature has manifested itself (I. iii. 18.)

(*Objection*): - In the sequel, in Prajapati's words, the sruti declares that Jiva is devoid of all sin and so on, thus:

> "The Atman who is free from sin, free from old age, from death, and grief, from hunger and thirst, whose desires never fail, whose will is ever true, He it is whom we must search out; He it is whom we must try to know. He who has searched out that Atman and understands Him obtains all worlds and all desires."

The sruti also speaks of the characteristic mark of Jiva – namely his association with the three avasthas or states – in the following passages:

> "That person who is seen in the eye, he is Atman; thus he said." † [† Chha. Upanishad 1-15]

> "He who moves about happy in dreams, he is the Atman." * [* Ibid 8-10-1.]

> "When a man being asleep, reposing, and at perfect rest, sees no dreams, that is the Atman." † [† Ibid 8-11-1.]

Therefore it is right to say that Jiva is here referred to.

(*Answer*): - There is no force in this contention. Here the sruti describes Jiva whose attributes, such as sinlessness, had been veiled by the body generated by his own beginningless sin and karma, but who, when afterwards become united to the Supreme Light, has his own true nature manifested, as well as the attribute of freedom from sin and the like, it is not the Jiva who is of samsara.

But the Dahara-akasa denotes the Being whose several blessed inherent attributes are never hidden. Thus, the Dahara-akasa here spoken of is neither bound nor liberated.

The reference serves a different purpose. (I. iii. 19).

The manifestation of Jiva's true nature on reaching the Supreme Being denoted by the word Dahara-akasa is spoken of in the following passage:

> "Having risen from out this earthly body, and having reached the highest light, he appears in his true form." ‡ [‡ Ibid. 8-3-4.]

Here the reference to Jiva serves to show that such is his greatness. Hence no contradiction.

(If you hold that Jiva is here referred to) because of the sruti speaking of smallness, this has been answered. (I. iii. 20).

As to the objection that, as dwelling in a small place, the Dahara-akasa must be a limited being, and that it is therefore not the Supreme Being here referred to, - it has already been answered in the sutra I. ii. 7.

And because of his resemblance. (I. iii. 21).

The Jiva's resemblance to the Supreme Light referred to by the word 'Dahara-akasa' is spoken of in the sequel:

"That limit day and night do not pass, nor old age, death and grief; neither good nor evil deeds. All evil-doers turn back from it; for the world of Brahman is free from all evil. Therefore he who has crossed that limit, if blind, ceases to be blind; if wounded, ceases to be wounded; if afflicted, ceases to be afflicted. Therefore, when that limit has been crossed, night becomes day indeed; for the world of Brahman is lighted once for all." * [* Chha. Up. 8-4-1, 2.]

Here, indeed the sinlessness and constant luminosity of the Dahara-akasa which has to be reached are given out as the reason why, like the old age etc. which are the result of sin, the evil of blindness etc. ceases to be on reaching the Dahara-akasa, and why then there is a constant light. That the former is the cause of the latter is clearly seen in another passage which reads as follows:

"Free from all taint, he attains to highest equality." * [* Mundaka. Up. 3-1.]

Thus we have that he who has reached the Dahara-akasa attains the result mentioned above, namely, the resemblance there to by way of attaining equality. This will hold good only when the Jiva is distinct from the Dahara-akasa. And therefore it may be concluded that Jiva is not the being spoken of here.

Again, the sutrakara cites yet another authority on the subject:

And, moreover, (It is so) said in the Smriti. (I. iii. 22).

It is said in the Smriti that Brahman dwells within the small lotus and is the object of worship:

"Or, from the teaching of a Guru let him know Paramatman whose body is the Supreme Bliss, who is Purusha, dark and yellow. By practice, O Gargi, the righteous perceive Brahman in the city of Brahman, in mid-akasa of the small lotus, and do thou also proceed in the same way."

Accordingly it may be concluded that the Para-Brahman whose nature is the Supreme Light, who has to be reached by the liberated, who is associated with Uma as His Supreme Energy, should be contemplated as dwelling within the akasa in the small lotus, as possessed of sinlessness and other attributes inherent in his own nature.

Adhikarana – 6.

Now the Sutrakara proceeds to treat of another form in which Paramesvara may be worshipped:

By the text itself He is declared. (I. iii. 23).

The passage which forms the subject of discussion here occurs in the Katha-Valli:

"The Purusha, of the size of a thumb, stands in the middle of the body, the Lord of what was and what is yet to be; thenceforward he fears none." * [* Op. Cit. 4-22.]

Here a doubt arises as to whether the Purusha, said to be 'of the size of a thumb,' is Jiva or Paramesvara.

(Purvapaksha): - It is but right to say that Jiva is here spoken of; for, Jiva is declared to be of the size of a thumb, in the following passage

"He assumes all forms; he is led by the three gunas, following the three paths. He is the lord of life and migrates through his own works. He is of the size of a thumb, brilliant like the sun, endowed with thoughts and egoism." † [† Svetasvatara-Upanishad 5-8-9.]

And the words "stands in the middle of the body," show that the Purusha here spoken of dwells in the middle of the body. The all-pervading Paramesvara cannot be the Purusha here spoken of.

As against the foregoing we hold as follows: It is well to say that it is Paramesvara who is spoken of as thumb-sized Purusha; for the passage under discussion describes the characteristic marks of Paramesvara, in the words "He is the lord of what has been and what is yet to be;" and so on. The Sruti declares (elsewhere) that He alone is the lord of all, in the words "endued with all power, the lord of all, Sambhu dwells in the Akasa's midst."

How, then, to explain the finitude frequently predicated of the Paramesvara? As regards this, the Sutrakara says:

But (it is said) because of (His being) in the heart, while teaching what man has to do. (I. iii. 24).

It is with reference to the heart of the devotees that Paramesvara though infinite, is said to be thumb-sized; and the injunctions of the science of Upasana (contemplation) are to human beings. The Paramesvara who is supremely merciful assumes the form of the same size as the heart of the human devotee, thus rendering contemplation possible. Hence the conclusion that the Paramesvara who is full of light, dwells within the heart of the devotees in the form of *linga* or the subtle form.

Adhikarana. – 7.

In the adhikarana just closed, it has been shown that the worship of Paramesvara is intended for man alone. How is it that the Atharvasiras speaks of Devas worshipping the Paramesvara, in the words, "Then the Devas saw not Rudra, and those Devas (began to) contemplate Rudra."?

In reply to this question, the next adhikarana proceeds as follows:

Even above them, as Badarayana holds; because it is possible. (I. iii. 25).

The passage which forms the subject of discussion occurs in the Atharvasiras and reads as follows:

"Those Devas contemplate Rudra."

Here a doubt arises as to whether it is possible or not for Devas to engage in the worship of Paramesvara.

(Purvapaksha): - It is not possible. He alone is qualified for Vedic ritual who is possessed of an aspiration, who is able, wise, and not excluded by the Sastra. They have not the requisite ability, for want of a body. Indeed it is the embodied ones that can engage in the act of adoring, contemplating, and the like. It cannot be maintained that they do possess bodies, on the authority of such passages as "Indra raised his thunderbolt (*vajra*) against Vritra"; for those passages which are subservient to the inculcation of an injunction cannot point to anything other than that injunction. Even supposing that they do possess bodies, they have nothing to aspire after, in as much as their abode and that of Paramesvara are one and the same. From the passage "Devas went to the region of savage, and these Devas asked Rudra 'who art Thou?'", w understand that the region of Svarga is itself the abode of Rudra, the Parabrahman; and that is also the region of Devas. We also learn that even the Mukta or liberated soul has ultimately to attain to the region of Svarga, from such passages as the following:

"He attains to the region of svar." * [* Taittiriya. Up. 1-6.]

Nor do they possess requisite knowledge, since, in the absence of Vedic study preceded by the sacramental process of Upanayana, no Vedantic enquiry is possible and they cannot therefore acquire a knowledge of Brahman. Hence, too, their exclusion (from worship) by the Sastra. Wherefore the Devas are not qualified for the worship of Brahman.

(*Siddhanta*): - Even the Devas are competent for the worship of Brahman. – Why? – Because there is room for aspiration in their case. And it cannot be said that the abode of the Devas and the abode of the Paramesvara are same; for, the word 'Svarga,' though signifying bliss in general, denotes a particular kind of bliss according to the context. The word 'Isvara,' for instance, signifying 'master' in general, applies to a king who is the ruler of a country, in virtue of the context, as in the following passage:

"And one should also visit the king (Isvara) for the sake of acquisition and security."

But the same word occurring in a section treating of Brahman signifies unsurpassed power and applies to Brahman. So also, in virtue of the context of knowledge concerning the subject, the word 'Svarga' signifying 'bliss' in general denotes the abode of Devas which affords a (comparatively) small amount of bliss, tainted as it is with the defect of being liable to decay and of being less exalted than some other kind of bliss. On the other hand, it denotes Siva the Para-Brahman's abode as being unsurpassed bliss itself, and as the place from which there is no return. Thus it is quite possible that the Devas who dwell in a place where happiness is tainted with the evil of being less exalted than some other kind of happiness, aspire to attain to Brahman's abode which is marked with unsurpassed bliss. On the authority of passages speaking of subjects subsidiary to an injunction, it may also be seen that the Devas are embodied entities, and, as such, are efficient agents of action. Though some passages as "the sun is the sacrificial post," and "Fire is the antidote to the frost," which figuratively speak of things subsidiary to the main injunction, are not intended to inculcate what they literally convey, still, such subsidiary statements as "Indra raised the thunderbolt against Vritra," which are neither contradicted by other authorities nor vouchsafed by any other sources of knowledge, may justly inculcate what they speak of as a truth to be accepted. It is also possible that, - either because, in virtue of their exalted power, the Vedic doctrine reveals itself to them, or because they have not forgotten what they had learnt before, - they possess requisite knowledge. The Sastra having enjoined divine worship on all in general, it cannot but be intended for the Devas, so that there is not the slightest ground for the exclusion of Devas. Wherefore Devas are competent for Brahmavidya.

The Sutrakara supposes an incongruity resulting from the Devas being embodied and refutes it as follows:

If you urge an incongruity in ritual (Karma), (we answer), as, the assumption of more than one (body) being revealed. (I. iii. 26.)

(*Objection*): - While the Devas are embodied entities, it should at the same time be supposed that, being invoked in the several sacrificial rituals performed in various places, they are simultaneously present in all those places. This does not hold good. Thus arises an incongruity in the matter of ritual.

(*Answer*): - No such incongruity can be urged here. It is declared that, though embodied, Saubhari and others have assumed more than one body. Hence no incongruity whatever.

Let there be no incongruity in the matter of ritual; but an incongruity does arise in the matter of Vedic Revelations. As against this objection the Sutrakara proceeds as follows:

If (you urge an incongruity as to) Revelation, (we answer) no, because of the origin thence, (as may be seen) from the direct (revelation) as well as (the indirect revelation or) inference. (I. iii. 27.)

(*Objection*): - Though there may arise no incongruity in the matter of ritual, an incongruity does arise in the matter of Vedic Revelation. – How? – Being made up of parts, the Devas are naturally impermanent. From this it necessarily follows that Indra and other Devas had also a birth. Then it is necessarily either that, previous to their birth and subsequent to their death, such Vedic words as 'Indra' have no meaning, or that the words are impermanent. If impermanent, they must have proceeded from an individual person; and then the injunctions and prohibitions lose their authority, and the rituals therein enjoined have no ground to rest upon. Thus many are the evil logical consequence of the doctrine. Accordingly, to avoid incongruity as to the Vedic Revelation, the doctrine that the Devas are embodied should not be assented to.

(*Answer*): - Not so; for, *thence i.e.*, from the very Vedic words such as 'Indra,' Indra and other beings were created. If 'Indra' and other words denote particular individuals, then, indeed, it would follow either that on the extinction of the beings denoted by those words they will have no objects to denote, or that they are impermanent. We maintain that, like the word 'cow,' such words as Indra' merely denote a general form. Accordingly, a potter thinks of a general form suggested to his mind by the word 'pot,' and then produces a pot; so too, on the disappearance of a former Indra, Brahma thinks of the particular form of that Indra suggested by the Vedic word 'Indra' and produces another Indra of the same form, and so on. Wherefore, though Indra and other individuals may disappear, the several general forms do not cease, and the words are accordingly eternal. Hence no incongruity whatever. If you ask for authority on this point we appeal to *Sruti* (direct revelation) and *Smriti* (indirect revelation). Thus says the Sruti:

"By Veda, Prajapati projected the forms, existent (or sensuous) and non-existent (or super-sensuous)." * [* Taittiriya-Brahmana. 2-6-2.]

"He uttered "Bhuh," and he created the earth." † [† Ibid. 2-2-4.]

"The names and acts of all, severally, and the various forms. He created at first from the Vedic words themselves." ‡ [‡ Manu. I. 21.]

And hence, indeed, (its) eternality, (I. iii. 26.)

Hence alone, though Visvamitra and others are the authors of mantras – as may be seen from such passages as

"He should invoke the authors of mantras." * [* Apastambha-Pravarasutras 1-7.]

"This is Visvamitra's Sukta (hymn)." † [† Taittiriya-Samhita 5-2-3.]

Still, such words having reference only to general forms of things, the eternality of the Veda which is made of *mantra* and *brahmana* becomes explicable. For, Brahma recollects by Vedic Word what things are to be created and then creates them. He being endued with the power of seeing the mantras without learning them from a teacher. Accordingly, on the expiry of the *Naimittika-Pralaya-i.e.*, the deluge of the three worlds taking place at the end of a day of Brahma – Brahma recollects, by the Vedic word, the several forms, such as that of

Visvamitra, belonging to preceding cycle, and creates others possessed of the same form and endued with the same powers, and these give out all the mantras without having studied them at all. Thus they are the authors of the mantras, while at the same time the Veda is eternal.

(*Objection*): - It may be so in the case of the Naimittika-Pralaya. But how to explain the eternality of the Veda in the case of the Prakrita-pralaya or Kosmic Dissolution when Brahma and the word called the Veda disappear altogether?

In answer, the Sutrakara says:

They being of same names and forms, no incongruity in the return (of the Kosmos) either, as shown by Revelation and smriti. (I. iii. 29).

Because the things to be created are of same names and forms, there is no incongruity in the Kosmos coming again into being after the Prakrita-pralaya. To explain: - The Paramesvara, the original Creator, who is Omniscient and Omnipotent, and who is beyond the whole universe, recollects the form of the preceding Kosmos and creates again a Kosmos of the same form, and He also recollects the Vedas as they were arranged before and gives them to Brahma, His son – How is this known? – By Sruti and Smriti. Sruti says:

"The sun and the moon, the Creator made as before, as also heaven and the Earth, the Mid-Air and Svarga." ‡ [‡ Mahanarayana-Up.]

"Who creates Brahma first, and who gives Him the Vedas." § [§ Sveta-Up. 6-12.]

Smriti also says.

"He first created water alone, in that He cast seed. That became a golden egg, like in splendor to the thousand rayed (sun); in that was born spontaneously Brahma, the ground parent of all the worlds." * [* Manu, I, 8, 9.]

"He first created Brahma and gave Him the Vedas."

Wherefore, even though the whole Kosmos has to come afresh into being after the Prakrita or Kosmic Pralaya, the Vedas are eternal.

The Sutrakara proceeds to state another view:

Owing to impossibility in Madhu etc., Jaimini holds that they are not qualified (I. iii. 30).

In Madhu-Vidya † (Vide Brihadaranyaka-Upanishad. 4-5) and other such Upasanas, the Vasus and other Devas are themselves the objects of contemplation and form the goal of the worship. Now it is impossible that the Vasus should form the objects of their own worship, owing to the impossibility of one and the same entity being the agent and object of the same act. Moreover, as they are themselves Vasus, the state of the Vasus has been attained already and cannot form an object yet to be attained. Jaimini, therefore, thinks that the Vasus and other Devas are not qualified for them (*i.e.*, for the Madhu-Vidya and other Upasanas).

And because they are (qualified) for the Light. (I. iii. 31).

Though Parabrahman, the Light, has as a matter of course to be worshipped by the Devas in common with men, the Sruti (specially) declares that they should worship Him, in the following words:

"Him, the Light of lights, Devas (should) worship as life, as immortal."

From this, it seems quite reasonable that they are not qualified for the worship enjoined in the Madhu-brahmana.

The Sutrakara now declares his own view:

But Badarayana (holds that they) do possess (the qualification), because there is (a possibility) (I. iii. 32).

Badarayana thinks that the Vasus and other Devas are qualified even for Madhu-Vidya and the like; for, though they are Vasus etc., they may worship Brahman in the form of the Vasus, and they may also seek to attain to the state of the Vasus etc. in the next cycle (Kalpa). Here Brahman has to be worshipped both as the cause and as the effect. In the passage beginning with the words "The sun is indeed the honey of the Devas" ‡ [‡ Chha. Up. 3-1-1.] Brahman to be worshipped is presented as the effect, endued with the names, forms, and functions of the Adityas, the Vasus, and so on, and in the passage beginning with the words "When from thence he has risen upwards he neither rises nor sets" * [* Ibid. 3-11-1.] Brahman to be worshipped is presented as the Cause, dwelling as the Antaratman or the Inner Ruler of the subtle sun devoid of all names, forms, and functions. The result of the worship of Brahman in both the aspects consists in the statement of the position of Vasus etc., in the next cycle (kalpa), and the attainment of Brahman on the expiry of the terms of both the effects. The passage "He who thus knows this nectar becomes one of the Vasus, and with Agni at their head, he sees the nectar and rejoices"† [Ibid. 3-6-2.] speaks of the result which consists in the attainment of the position of the Vasus etc; and the passage "to him who thus known the secret of Brahman, the sun does not rise and does not set; for him there is day once and for all," ‡ [‡ Ibid. 3-11-3.] speaks of the result consisting in the attainment of Brahman. Thus the Devas are qualified for the Madhu-Vidya and the like. Wherefore the Devas are in every way qualified for Brahma-Vidya.

Adhikarana – 8.

Now, from the sutra I. iii. 24 it would appear that men in general are all qualified. As against this supposition, the sutrakara says:

Because his grief is shown by the hearing of the taunt and by his running up (to the teacher). I. iii. 33).

The passage which forms subject of discussion here occurs in the Chhandogya-Upanishad and reads as follows:

"You have brought these, O Sudra; but only by that mouth did you make me speak." §
[§ Op. Cit. 4-2-5.]

Here the teacher addresses the pupil as Sudra. So, a doubt arises as to whether Sudras also are qualified for Brahma-Vidya or not.

(*Purvapaksha*): They do possess the qualification, because of the possibility of their aspiring for it. It cannot be restricted to the three castes, in as much as it has been shown that, though coming under none of the three castes, the Devas are yet qualified for it. To this one may object as follows: Though Devas are not formally initiated by *upanayana* and do not learn the Vedas from a teacher, yet it is possible for them to attain knowledge in as much as the Vedic doctrine reveals itself to their minds; how is this possible in the case of these (the Sudras)? This objection is untenable; for, even in the case of these, knowledge can be attained by listening to the Puranas etc., and it is even possible that they are qualified for initiation into the grand truths (Mahavakyas), on the principle of *nishada-sthapati* (vide Jaiminiya-Mimamsa 6-1-51, 52) Wherefore it is but proper to say that they are qualified for Brahmavidya.

As against the foregoing we hold as follows: Sudras have no right to Brahmavidya; for, in the absence of Vedic study, it is not possible for them to attain that knowledge of the Deity to be worshipped and of His attributes, to which such a study forms an essential means. The Itihasas and Puranas form a means only as expatiating on the teaching of the Veda, but not independently of it. And the permission accorded to the Sudras listening to the Itihasas and Puranas is merely intended to bring about the extinction of their sins. Vidura, the Dharma-Vyadha and the like were devotees of Brahman because of the knowledge they had acquired in the previous births not having vanished. If you ask how, when teaching Brahma-vidya, the master addressed the disciple as Sudra, we reply as follows: He was addressed here as Sudra, not because he belonged to that class, but because he was found to be overpowered with grief for not having attained Brahma-jnana. That he was overpowered with grief is indicated by the fact of his having heard the swan's taunting reference to him for not being possessed of Brahmavidya, and by the fact of his running up immediately to the master. He having been addressed as Sudra not because he belonged to that class, the Sudra has no right to worship Brahman.

For the following reason also, the disciple is addressed as Sudra, not as belonging to that class:

And it being known that he is a Kshatriya (I. iii. 34.)

It being known that Janasruti, the disciple, is a Kshatriya, he is addressed as Sudra not because he belongs to that caste. At the commencement of the episode, Janasruti is described as the master of the wealthy, and as the giver of an abundant quantity of prepared food, thus:

"There lived once upon a time Janasruti-Pautrayana (the great grandson of Janasruti), who was a pious giver, bestowing much wealth upon the people, and always keeping open house. He built places of refuge everywhere, wishing that people should everywhere eat of his food." * [* Chhand.Up. 4-1-1.]

In the middle, he is spoken of as directing a charioteer, in the following words:

"As soon as he had risen in the morning he said to his charioteer." † [† Ibid. 4-1-5.]

At the end he is spoken of as offering many towns in the following words:

"There is this wife and this village in which thou dewllest." ‡ [‡ Ibid. 4-2-4.]

"These are the Raikva-parna villages in the country of the Mahavrishas where Raikva dwelt under him." § [§ Ibid. 4-2-6.]

From these characteristic marks, Janasruti appears to be a Kshatriya.

And because of the indicatory mark in the sequel in connection with Chaitraratha. (I. iii. 35.)

In the sequel of this Samvaga-Vidya, we find references to the Brahman and Kshatriya castes alone, in such passages as the following:

"Once while Saunaka-Kapeya and Abhipratarin Kakshaseni were being waited on at their meal, a religious student begged of them." ‖ [‖ Ibid. 4-3-5.]

Abhipratarin, a descendant of Chitraratha, appears to be a Kshatriya, because of his connection with a priest belonging to the family of the Kapeyas. The Sruti does speak of Chaitaratha's connection with a Kapeya priest, in the following words.

"The Kapeyas caused Chaitraratha to perform the sacrifice; him alone they made a master of food."

Thus, though, on account of a difference in the name, he is not identical with Chitraratha, it is certain that he belongs to the same family for generally, members of one and the same family become priests of the others who are members of one and the same family. As a member of Chitraratha's family, he must be Kshatriya, as evident from a complimentary passage occurring elsewhere: "From him, one Chaitraratha is born, a Kshatriya nobleman." Accordingly, it is concluded that Abhipratarin who is mentioned as connected with a Brahman of the family of the Kapeyas is a Kshatriya. Similarly, it may also be inferred that Janasruti who is connected with the Brahman Raikva is a Kshatriya. Wherefore, he is addressed as Sudra while in fact he is a Kshatriya.

As to the allegation that, on the principle of *Nishada-Sthapati*, the sudra is merely entitled to initiation into the Grand Truths (Mahavakyas), the Sutrakara says:

Because of a reference to the sacrament and of the mention of its absence. (I. iii. 36).

At the commencement of Brahma-Vidya, in such passages as "I shall initiate thee;" Him did he initiate;" * reference has been made to the sacrament of upanayana. And in some passages such as. "There is no sin in a Sudra, and he is not fit for a sacrament;" † and "the Sudra, the fourth caste, has one birth alone;" ‡ - the smriti speaks of its absence in the case of a Sudra, for both these reasons, he is not entitled to Brahma-vidya, Because of the injunction "Let him cause a *Nishada-sthapati* to perform a sacrifice," there is no objection in that particular case. There is no scriptural injunction anywhere permitting the initiation of a Sudra into the Grand Truths (Mahavakyas), in spite of the absence of Upanayana. [†Manu. 10-126. ‡ Gautama 10-50.]

And because he proceeds (to initiate) on ascertaining its absence (I. iii. 37).

A Sudra is not entitled to it, in as much as master proceeded (to initiate), to ordain and to teach the Vidya only after ascertaining that Jabala was not a Sudra because he told the truth, as the Sruti says:

"No one but a true Brahmana would thus speak out. Go and fetch fuel, friend, I shall initiate you. You have not swerved from truth." § [§ Chhand. Up. 4-4-5.]

(*Objection*): - Does the prohibition of the uttering of the Veda in the absence of Upanayana apply to some cases only or to all cases? It does not apply to all cases, for notwithstanding the absence of Upanayana in the case of a child, there is an injunction to the effect that the child should recite the Veda while making an offering to the manes, as declared in the following passage:

"Let him not be made to utter the Veda except when making an offering to the manes." * [* Gautama 2-5.]

It is therefore proper to hold that the prohibition applies only to a few cases. Wherefore the uninitiated Sudra is prohibited from uttering the Veda while performing the pakayajnas (small sacrificial rituals), but not when learning the Brahma-Vidya.

As against the foregoing objection, the Sutrakara says:

Because of the prohibition of the hearing, studying, and (knowing the) meaning (of the Vedas). (I. iii. 36).

The hearing of the Vedic texts by a Sudra is prohibited in such passages as the following:

"Therefore, Vedas should not be recited near a Sudra."

To one who should not hear the Veda, whence comes the study etc. thereof.

And on account of the Smriti. (I. iii. 39).

The Smriti lays down punishments in the case of a Sudra hearing the Veda and so on, in the following words:

"Now, when hearing the Vedas, his ears should be filled with (molten) lead and wax; when uttering the Vedas, the tongue should be cut asunder; when keeping the Vedas in mind, his body should be torn." † [† Gautama 12-4-6.]

In the face of this prohibition of the recitation of the Vedas in the Sruti and the Smriti, how is an enquiry into the teaching of the Vedas possible in the case of a Sudra? It is therefore to be concluded that, except after the sacrament of Upanayana, such as is performed on a Brahman eight years old (and so on), no study of the Vedas is anywhere possible to anyone under any circumstances. Therefore, the Sudras are not entitled to Brahmavidya.

Adhikarana 9.

Having thus incidentally shown what sort of a person is qualified for Brahmavidya, the Sutrakara now proceeds with the main subject.

Because of trembling. (I. iii. 40).

In the Katha-Vallis, in the section treating of the thumb-sized Purusha, it is said as follows:

"Whatever there is, the whole world, when gone forth (from the Brahman) trembles in the breath; (it is) a great terror, the thunderbolt uplifted; those who know it become immortal." * [* Of Cit. 6-2.]

Here a doubt arises as to whether the cause of trembling is the Paramesvara or some other being.

(Purvapaksha): - Here the sruti speaks of the trembling of the whole universe by fear caused by the entity denoted by the word "breath". It is not right to say that the Paramesvara, who is so sweet-natured as to afford refuge to the whole universe and who is supremely gracious, is the cause of the trembling of the whole universe. Therefore, as the word 'thunderbolt' occurs here, it is the thunderbolt that is the cause of the trembling. Or, it is the vital air which is the cause of the trembling, because the word 'breath' occurs here. Since the vital air causes the motion of the body, this whole world which is the body as it were moves on account of the vital air. Then we can explain the passage "Whatever there is, the whole world, when gone forth (From the Brahman), trembles in the breath." Then, we can also explain the statement that "it is a great terror, the thunderbolt uplifted," in as much as, like lightning, cloud and rain; the thunderbolt which is the source of great terror is produced by action of the air itself. It is also possible to attain immortality by a knowledge of the air, as the following sruti says:

"Air is everything itself, and air is all things together; he who knows this conquers death." * [* Bri. Up. 5-3-2.]

(*Siddhanta*): – As against the foregoing, we say that Paramesvara himself is the cause of the trembling. It is possible that, as the Ruler, Paramesvara is the cause of the trembling of the whole universe; and by the fear of Hi command all of us abstain from prohibited actions and engage in the prescribed duties; and it is by the fear of His command that Vayu and others perform their respective duties, as may be learned from such passages as the following: -

"By fear of Him, Vayu (the wind) blows." * [* Tait.up. 2-8.]

Though gracious in appearance, Paramesvara becomes awful as the Ruler (of all. Hence the Sruti:

"Hence the King's face has to be awful"! † [† Taitt. Bra. 3-8-23.]

Wherefore as the Master, Isvara Himself is the cause of the trembling of the whole universe.

Adhikarana 10.

This Adhikarana proceeds to show that the Paramesvara, who has been mentioned as the object to be worshipped in the Dahara and so on, is the Being to be reached (by the liberated):

The Light (is Parabrahman) because we find (it so). (I. iii. 41).

The passage which forms the subject of discussion here occurs in the Chhandogya-Upanishad:

"That serene being, arising from this body, appears in its own form, as soon as it has approached the highest light. He is the highest person (Uttama-purusha)."

Here, a doubt arises as to whether the highest light said to be reached by the liberated is Paramesvara, or Narayana the Embodied.

(*Purvapaksha*): - It being found that the highest light to be reached by the liberated is spoken of as the highest person, the *Uttama Purusha*, and the designation "*Uttama Purusha*" being a specific designation of Narayana, Narayana is the highest light to which the epithet Uttama-Purusha is here applied.

(*Siddhanta*): - As against the foregoing, we hold as follows: The highest light, here said to be reached by the liberated, is the Supreme Brahman called Paramasiva, it being found that those alone do not return who have reached Him. How can it be right that those who reach any other being than the Para-Brahman have no return? Though specifically applied to Narayana, the epithet *Purushottama* is used to denote Brahman, who is above all Purushas, - all Jivas. In the ritual of Brahmamedha, the word Purushottama is used as a synonym for Para-Brahma who has to be reached. Wherefore the highest light here refers to Para-Brahman Himself.

Adhikarana 11.

Akasa (refers to Paramesvara), because of the mention of His being a distinct being, and so on. (I. iii. 12.)

The passage which forms the subject of discussion here occurs in the Chhandogya-Upanishads and reads as follows:

"He who is called Akasa is the creator of name and form. That within which these are contained is Brahman, the Immortal. He is Atman." * [* Op-Cit. 8-14-1.]

Here a doubt arises as to whether the "Akasa" spoken of as the creator of name and form is Paramesvara, or the Ether, or Jiva.

(*Purvapaksha*): - Here "Akasa," refers to the Ether, since, by affording space for all beings to exist in, the Ether can be said to be the creator of name and form. Or, it may refer to Jiva, in as much as Jiva is declared to have some connection with the manifesting of name and form, in the following passage:

"In the form of this Jiva, I will enter and make name and form manifest." † [† Chha 6-3-2.]

As against the foregoing, we hold as follows: - Here, by the word, "Akasa," it is the Paramesvara who is declared as the creator of name and form, because of the mention of immortality and other attributes of His. Indeed neither of Jiva nor of the ether can immortality and the like be predicated. Wherefore, "Akasa" refers to Paramesvara Himself.

(*Objection*): - Because of the unity declared in the passage "That thou art," Paramesvara is not a being distinct from the Pratyagatman.

In answer, the Sutrakara says:

(Because of His being declared) as distinct in sleep and death (I. iii. 13).

Paramesvara is a being distinct from Jiva, because as conscious during sleep and death, He is declared to be distinct from Jiva who, in those states, is devoid of all consciousness, both subjective and objective, in the following passages:

"Embraced by the intelligent" Atman, (the Jiva) knows nothing that is without, nothing that is within." * [* Bri.Up. 6-3-21.]

"Mounted by the intelligent Atman, the Jiva moves along groaning." † [† Ibid. 6-3-35.]

It is He who is here spoken of as akasa.

And because of the words such as "Master." (I. iii. 44.)

From the words such as "master" applied to the Intelligent embracing the Jiva, it may be seen that He is distinct from the Jiva. For, in the sequel, the scripture has the following:

"He is the ruler of all, the lord of all, the king of all. He does not become greater by good works, nor smaller by evil works. He is the lord of all, the King of all beings, the protector of all things." ‡ [‡ Bri. Up. 6-4-22.]

From such passages as the following:

"Bow to the Lord of Cattle, to the Lord of trees," § it is clear that the Paramesvara is the Lord of the world; and nowhere do we find it said that Jiva is the Lord of the universe. Wherefore, the being here spoken of as akasa is the Paramesvara, distinct from Jiva. § [§Taittiriya-Samhita 4-5-2.]

End of the Third Pada.

Fourth Pada.

Adhikarana. 1.

In the preceding Pada were discussed such passages as contained clear and vague indications of Brahman. This Pada proceeds to discuss certain passages which contain vague indications of Brahman.

If (you hold that) with some the inferential (is meant), (we say) no, because of reference to that which is included in the figure; and so the sruti says. (I. iv. 1).

The passage which forms the subject of discussion here is read by a school of the Kathas as follows:

"Beyond the senses (Indriyas) there are the objects (arthas); beyond the objects there is the mind (manas); beyond the mind there is the intellect (Buddhi); the Great (Mahat) Atman is beyond the intellect."

"Beyond the Great, there is the Avyakta; beyond the Avyaka there is Purusha, the supreme; beyond Purusha here is nothing; this is the limit, the supreme Goal." * [* Katha-Upa. 3-10, 11.]

Here a doubt arises as to whether that which is spoken of as Avyakta beyond the Mahat is the Pradhana of Kapila, or the body.

(*Purvapaksha*): - It is the Pradhana. – How? – For, Mahat, Avyakta, and Purusha are only known to us as treated of in the Sankhya system of philosophy. As these are referred to herein the sruti, there is no occasion whatever to treat of the body. Therefore it is the Pradhana of the Sankhyas that is here spoken of.

Siddhanta maintains that the body is here spoken of; for in a preceding passage, - namely,

"Know Atman to be sitting in the chariot, the body to be the chariot, the intellect (buddhi) the charioteer, and the mind (manas) the reins.

"The senses (indriyas) they call the horses, the objects of the senses their roads." † [† Ibid. 3-3, 4.]

Atman, the body, etc., which are the means of upasana (worship), are represented as the chariot, and the driver in the chariot, with a view to show that they are to be brought under control; and it is the body included in this figurative representation, still remaining unnoticed (after all else has been noticed), - that is referred to by the word Avyakta. Indeed in the verse quoted above, - beginning with "beyond the senses there are the objects," and ending with "this is the goal, the highest road," – one thing is spoken of as superior to another with a view to show that each should be brought in subjection to the one that follows. This the sruti declares in the sequel as follows:

"A wise man should restrain speech in manas; he should restrain that (manas) in the Atman which is knowledge; he should restrain the knowledge in Atman, the Mahat; he should restrain that (mahat) in Atman, the tranquil." ‡ [‡ Ibid 3-13.]

Therefore Avyakta here refers to the body.

(*Objection*): - By Avyakta, everybody understands Pradhana. How can it refer here to the body?

In answer, the sutrakara says:

The subtle, verily, (in the body) because of the capability for it. (I. ii. 2.)

"The subtle" means Avyakta or Unmanifested. – Being capable of manifesting itself as the body, the Unmanifested or subtle form of the body, it may be rightly held, is spoken of as "Avyakta,"

The sutrakara adduces another reason.

As subject to Him, everything serves its purposes. (I. iv. 3).

Atman, the body, and all, serve their purpose, *i.e.*, conduce to the fulfillment of worship, when subjected to Paramesvara. Paramesvara, the Inner Ruler, impels all including Atman. As such, as thus forming an accessory of worship, He is spoken of as the finality of the principles to be brought under control; and as the Being to be ultimately reached. He is spoken of as "the supreme Goa;." Therefore Avyakta here means the body itself.

Because of the absence of all mention that it has to be known. (I. iv. 4).

If the Pradhana of the Sankhyas be here referred to by the word ("Avyakta," then It would have been mentioned as a thing worth knowing; and there is nothing of the sort. Hence no reference to Kapila's Avyakta.

Now the Sutrakara proceeds to refute the objection that there is a mention made of the Pradhana as worth knowing:

If (you urge that the sruti) speaks of (it as such) (we say) no; for, by context, it is the Intelligent (I. iv. 5.)

Objection: - The Pradhana, too, is spoken of as a thing worth knowing in a subsequent passage, which reads as follows:

"Having perceived that which is without sound, without touch, without form, without decay, without taste, eternal without end, beyond the Mahat, and unchangeable, one is freed from the jaws of death." * [* Katha-Up. 3-5.]

Answer: - No, for, it is the Prajna or the Intelligent that forms the subject of discourse, as may be seen from the following:

"One should restrain speech in the mind" † etc. [† Ibid. 3-15.]

Hence the "Avyakta" refers to the body.

The Sutrakara says that there is no occasion to speak of the Pradhana:

And of three alone is this exposition and this question (I. iv. 6).

In this section, the question and the exposition are concerned with three things alone as worth knowing namely, the being to be worshipped, the worship, and the worshipper, - not with the Pradhana. Their exposition is contained in the section beginning with the following passage:

"The wise who, by means of meditation on his Atman, recognizes the Ancient who is difficult to be seen, who has entered into the dark, who is hidden in the cave, who dwells in the abyss – as God, he indeed leaves joy and sorrow far behind." * [* Ibid. 2-23.]

The question is contained in the following passages:

"There is that doubt, when a man is dead, - some saying, he is; others, he is not. This I should like to know, taught by thee; this is the third of my boons." † [† Ibid. 1-20.]

"That which thou seest beyond Dharma, and beyond Adharma, neither cause nor effect, neither past nor future, tell me that." ‡

Wherefore, "Avyakta" is the body, not the Pradhana, as it is a thing with which the present section is not concerned.

Moreover, there is yet another thing pointing to this conclusion, as the Sutrakara says:

And like the Mahat (I. iv. 7).

Just as, on account of the word "Atman" in the passage "beyond Buddhi is Mahat, the Atman," "mahat" cannot refer to the mahat technically so-called, so too, it may be concluded here that the word "Avyakta" cannot mean the Pradhana.

Adhikarana – 2.

(*Objection*): - Granted that there is no occasion here to speak of the Pradhana, as the present section is not concerned with it. Elsewhere the Pradhana itself is spoken of as the cause.

In answer, the sutrakara proceeds with this adhikarana:

For want of a distinguishing mark, unlike "Ghamasa." (I. iv. 8).

The passage which forms the subject of discussion here occurs in the Svetasvatara-Upanishad:

> "There is one unborn being (female), red, white and black, uniform, but producing manifold offspring. There is one unborn being (male) who loves her and lies by her; there is another unborn being who leaves her, having enjoyed all pleasures." * [* Svetasvatara-Up. 4-5.]

Here a doubt arises as to whether the Prakriti which is spoken of as the cause of the whole universe and therefore as devoid of birth, is the one which the Sankyas have assumed, or the Supreme Prakriti (of the Paramesvara).

(*Purvapaksha*): - It is but right to say that it is the Prakriti assumed by the Sankyas; for, it is declared to be 'unborn,' devoid of birth, to be the cause of all creatures; and we also find a reference to the three gunas indicated by the three colors, "red, white and black." We cannot hold that anything else can be of this nature.

(*Siddhanta*): - It is not the Prakriti technically so called that is here declared to be the cause. Indeed, by the mere mention of absence of birth, we cannot understand that that (Prakriti) alone is meant; for there is no differentiating mark in the section, unlike the case of "Chamasa" in the passage "A vessel (chamasa) with aperture downwards"† which is followed by another sentence, - namely, "this (*chamasa*) is the head"; - which indicates what particular kind of vessel is meant. For a word understood in its (generic) etymological sense to convey an idea of a particular thing requires some other word supplying a differentiating mark. Therefore it is not the Prakriti technically so called that is here meant.

The Sutrakara proceeds to show what that Prakriti is which is distinct from the one technically so called:

Accordingly, indeed some read by commencing with Light. (I. iv. 9).

"The Light" means Paramesvara. This 'unborn' Prakriti is rooted in the Paramesvara as the cause. Accordingly, some, namely the Taittiriyas, read the verse treating of the nature of the Prakriti, so as to declare that which is rooted in the Paramesvara as its cause. Having started with a description of Paramesvara in the words "subtler than the subtle, greater than the great," the Upanishad speaks of the origin of the universe from Paramesvara in the words "From him emanate the seven pranas," and so on; and it is while thus describing the universe as made up of him, that they read the verse (quoted above) beginning with "There is one unborn being." Because of this reference to him, it may be concluded that the unborn (Prakriti) is the one rooted in Paramesvara. Hence the untenability of the contention that the Prakriti technically so called is meant here.

(*Objection*): - As caused by the Paramesvara, this Parakriti is declared to be an effect. How can each a thing be also described as unborn?

In answer, the Sutrakara says:

And because of the construction being taught there is no incongruity, as in the case of 'honey.' (I. iv. 10).

"Construction" means creation or emanation. – There is no incongruity whatever in the divine Prakriti being described both as unborn and as the effect caused by Paramesvara because of the creation taught in the following passage:

"That from which the maker (Mayin) sends forth all this – the sacred verses, the offerings, the sacrifices, the penances, the past, the future, and all that the Vedas declare – in that the other is bound up through that Maya. Know then Prakriti is Maya, and the great Lord the Mayin." * [* Svctasvatara-Up. 4-9, 10.]

To explain: During the time of Pralaya, even the Maya which is insentient (achit), though devoid of name and form, yet exists in a subtle form as the body of the Mahesvara, and it may therefore be described as unborn; and it is the effect caused Paramesvara, because it is invested with name and form at the time of creation. For instance, at the time of creation, Aditya is the 'honey,' as the repository of the essence which the Vasus and other gods live upon; he is, however, not an effect, in as much as he exists in such a very subtle form that he cannot be designated by any such word as 'honey,' as declared in the following passages in the *Madhuvidya*:

"The sun is indeed the honey of the Devas." † [† Chha. Up. 3-1.]

"When from thence he has risen upwards, he neither rises nor sets. He is alone, standing in the centre." ‡ [‡ Ibid. 3-11.]

The Vedanta-Sutras with Srikantha Bhashya

Accordingly there is no incongruity whatever in the Divine Prakriti being described both as unborn and as caused by Paramesvara. Wherefore the 'unborn' is not the Prakriti technically so called (by the Sankhyas).

Adhikarana – 3.

(*Objection*): - Elsewhere, again, the twenty-five principles (*tattvas*), established by the science (of Sankhya), are spoken of in the Sruti.

To prevent this supposition, the Sutrakara introduces a fresh Adhikarana:

No, despite the mention of the number; because of (their) being distinct and of excess. (I. iv. 11).

The following passage forms the subject of discussion here:

"Him in whom the five five-beings are established as well as the akasa, do I think to be Atman; knowing the immortal Brahman, I am the immortal." * [* Bri. Up. 6-4-17.]

Here a doubt arises as to whether the things referred to as the "five five-beings" denote the Tattvas of the Sankhya system, or those spoken of in the sruti.

(*Purvapaksha*): - The number twenty-five being prominent in the Sankhya system, and that number being mentioned here, the "five five-beings" undoubtedly refer to *tattvas* of the Sankhya system, and to none else.

As against the foregoing we hold as follows: Despite the mention of the number twenty-five- obtained by multiplying five by five, the technically so called tattvas are not meant here. We are given to understand that the things mentioned here are rooted in the Paramesvara who is referred to by the words "Him in whom." As such, they are distinct from the tattvas (of the Sankhya system); and there is a mention of too many tattvas, owing to the separate mention if akasa. 'Mention of too many tattvas' means that the tattvas (here mentioned) are more than twenty five in number. Wherefore it does not follow that the twenty-five tattvas are here referred to. Neither can it be held that is here any reference to the number twenty-five. The compound "five-beings" – pancha-jana – is a *sanjna* or specific designation, meaning that there are some beings (each of whom is) known as a Pancha-jana; and five such beings are here referred to, just as there are seven *saptarshis*. Wherefore there is no room for the supposition that the *tattvas* of the Sankhya system are here mentioned.

What, then, are they? The sutrakara says:

Prana and others, from the remaining portion of the section. (I. iv. 12).

The "pancha-janas" refer to the five indriyas (including prana) as may be seen from what follows:

"Those who know the life (prana) of life, the eye of the eye, the ear of the ear, the food of the food, the mind of the mind," etc.

From this also it follows that the *tattvas* of the Sankhya system are not meant here.

Again an explanation is given as follows:

By 'light,' according to some, in the absence of 'food.' (I. iv. 13).

'Some' refers to the Kanvas. In spite of the absence of the words "the food of the food" (in the Kanva recension), we may still understand that the five *pancha-janas* refer to the *indriyas*, because of the word 'light' occurring in the opening passage which reads as follows:

"Him the gods worship as the light of lights." † [† Ibid. 6-4-16.]

Having thus said that the Brahman is the light of lights, the illuminator of the illuminators, the sruti then speaks of the five "*pancha-janas*." By this we are given to understand that those lights refer to the five *indriyas*.

And because of the mention, as the cause in akasa etc., of what is specifically declared (I. iv. 14).

All such Vedantic passages as "the non-existent, verily, this at first was;" ‡ and "This verily was then undifferentiated," § not declaring specifically of what nature the cause is which underlies such emanations as the akasa, we understand that the cause (referred to) is what is declared specifically in the passage "Atman alone, verily, this at first was;" ‖ but not the *Avyakrita* or the *Undifferentiated* of the Sankhyas. So, too, we are to understand that the five *indriyas* specifically declared in other passages are here meant, but not the *tattvas* of the Sankhyas. [‡ Taitti.Up 2-2-7. § Bri. Up. 2-4-7. ‖ Aitarey Upanishad 1-1.]

The Sutrakara proceeds to show why the *tattvas* of the Sankhya cannot be meant here:

By backward reference. (I. iv. 15).

Because of the backward reference, in the passage "non-existent, verily, this at first was," to the Omniscient spoken of in a previous passage" He desired 'may I become many'," and because of the backward reference in the passage "He who has penetrated here up to the tips of the nails," to the Avyakrita described before, we understand that He alone is meant; so, too, here, by backward reference, we are to understand that the five "*pancha-janas*" mean the five *indriyas*. Hence no incongruity whatever.

The discussion of the question is to whether the Sankhya's Principle (Pradhana) is referred to (in the Upanishads) is over. Again the sutrakara proceeds to explain how Paramesvara is distinct from Jiva:

Because it denotes the universe (I. iv. 16.)

The passage which forms the subject of discussion here occurs in the Kaushitaki-Brahmana-Upanishad. Commencing with the words "I shall teach these Brahman," the Upanishad goes on thus:

"He who, O Balaki, is verily the creator of all these beings, and whose deed this is, he verily should be known," and so on.* [* Op. cit. 4-1.]

Here a doubt arises as to whether it is Paramesvara or Jiva who is spoken of as the being that should be known

(*Purvapaksha*): - In the previous passages, such as "That being who is in the sun, him do I worship;...him who is in the moon....;......him who is in the lightning...."† it is seen that Jiva too can be the cause of all such beings as the sun here spoken of. The word "deed" denotes something newly produced (apurva); and this new effect (apurva) can only pertain to Jiva, in as much as it can never affect Paramesvara who is derived of all connection with any deed whatsoever. So the being spoken of here is Jiva and no other. [† Ibid. 4-1.]

The Siddhanta: As the word "deed" is put in apposition with word "this," and is capable of being interpreted to mean 'what is done,' it means 'the universe' So that it is Paramesvara, whose deed is the whole universe, that is spoken of here. Jiva, indeed, can never be the creator of the universe.

Again an objection is raised and answered:

If (you hold it is not the case) because of the characteristic marks of Jiva and the Prana proper, (we answer) no; that has been explained. (I. iv. 17).

It cannot be urged that Paramesvara is not referred to because of the characteristic marks of Jiva and the Prana proper found in the following passages:

"As the master feeds with his people, nay, as his people feed on the master, so does this conscious Atman feed with each other Atmans, and so the other Atmans follow this Atman." * [* Kaushitaki. Up. 4-20.]

"When sleeping he sees no dream, then he becomes one with the Prana alone." *

For, in the Pratardana-Vidya, the matter was clearly discussed. Here, too, when the preceding and the succeeding portions of the section are taken into consideration, it will be seen that the section treats of Brahman, so that the other characteristic marks should be interpreted accordingly. To explain: At first, in the opening section, Brahman has been introduced in the words "I shall teach thee Brahman;" in the middle, the passage "whose deed this is" speaks of a being who is the creator of the whole universe; and subsequently in the words "he who knows this conquers all sins and obtains preeminence among all beings, sovereignty, supremacy;" the sruti speaks of sovereignty – accompanied with the destruction of all sins – being the result; a thing which necessarily results from nothing but the worship of Brahman. It being thus shown that the section is devoted to Brahman, those attributes which seem to pertain to Jiva and Prana proper should be so interpreted as to refer to Him alone.

Another view is now set forth:

It is verily, as Jaimini holds, for the sake of the other, (as may be seen) from the question and the answer; and, moreover, even so do some (declare). (I. iv. 18.)

It is with a view to declare the existence of Paramesvara distinct from Jiva that the existence of Jiva as a separate entity from the vital airs etc. is expounded – by way of showing that the vital air does not respond though called by its name and that the person rises when afterwards struck by means of a stick – in the following passage:

"The two together came to a person who was asleep. And Ajatasatru called him saying: 'Thou great one, clad in white raiment, Soma, king. But he remained lying. Then he pushed him with a stick, and he rose at once." * [* Kaushitaki. Up. 4-19.]

That such is the case is shown by the following question and answer:

Question: "Balaki, where did this person here sleep? Where was he? Whence came he thus back?" † [† Ibid.]

Answer: "When sleeping he sees no dream, then he becomes one with that prana;" ‡ [‡ Ibid 4-20.]

This answer being of the same meaning as the following passage occurring elsewhere:

"With the Existent, my dear son, he then becomes united" § [§ Chhandogya.Up. 6-8-1.]

Some, that is, the Vajasaneyins, have a section in which the same thing is very clearly set forth in the form of a dialogue between Balaki and Ajatasatru, as follows:

Question: "When this man was thus asleep, where was then the person, the intelligent? And from whence did he thus come back?" ¶ [¶ Bri-Up. 4-1-16.]

Answer: "When this man was thus asleep, then the intelligence of the senses absorbed within himself all intelligence, lies in the ether which is in the heart." ‖ [‖ Ibid. 4-1-17.]

Wherefore it may be concluded that it is Paramesvara Himself whose work is this whole universe.

Adhikarana 5.

This adhikarana proceeds to show how it is that, while Jiva and Isvara are everywhere spoken of as one, they are treated as distinct entities occupying one abode.

The passages pointing (all to him) (I. iv. 19.)

The passage which forms the subject of discussion occurs in the Brihadaranyaka and reads as follows:

"Verily, a husband is not dear for the husband's enjoyment; but for the Atman's enjoyment the husband is dear..."...." Verily the Atman is to be seen, to be heard, to be reflected upon, to be contemplated." * [* Bri-Up. 4-4-5.]

(*Purvapaksha*): - It is Jiva that is spoken of here, in as much as by such words as "but for the Atman's enjoyment" we are given to understand that the Atman is a samsarin as endued with desire to enjoy.

As against the foregoing we hold that it is Paramesvara who is spoken of here. – Why? – The whole section opening with the statements such as

"But there is no hope of immortality by wealth,"

"When we see, hear, reflect upon, and know the Atman, then all this is known;"

"All this is that which we call Atman;" † [† Ibid.]

And ending with the passage "How should he know Him by whom he knows all this?" points to Paramesvara; and accordingly Paramesvara is propounded here by first speaking incidentally of the jiva who is endued with an attachment for pleasures, Hence no inconsistency whatever.

How, in all these places, may Paramesvara be spoken of by the word denoting the jiva? – This the sutrakara explains according to an alien system:

A mark as to the proof of the proposition, as Asmarathya holds. (I. iv. 20).

Asmarathya thinks that the designating of Paramesvara by a term denoting the jiva serves to show that the jiva, as an emanation of the Paramesvara, is not quite independent of him, so that the proposition may be held as proved that by knowing one the whole is known, as said by the sruti, "when we see Atman all this is known."

Because of the emancipated becoming so, as Audulomi holds. (I. iv. 22).

Audulomi thinks that it is because the liberated soul attains to the state of Paramesvara that Paramesvara is designated by the word Atman.

Because of His dwelling; thus holds Kasakritsna. (I. iv. 22).

Kasakritsna thinks that it is because of Paramesvara dwelling as Atman in the jiva-Atman that the Paramesvara is designated by the word denoting the jiva.

It may be concluded that this is also the sutrakara's view, because of its being mentioned in opposition to two other views already expounded, and because of the absence of a mention of any other. There is, moreover, here a strong affinity to the teaching of the sruti. To explain. In the first section of the Atharvasiras, it is declared that Paramesvara is the being denoted by all words, as due to His having entered into all beings, *chit* and *achit*, sentient and insentient, in the following passage.

"Devas verily went to the Svargaloka and asked Rudra, "Who art thou?" He said, "Alone I was at first, I am and shall be; none else distinct from Me. From the inner into the innermost I have entered; into the four quarters and their very midst. Such a being am I; I am the eternal and non-eternal; I am Brahma; I am the Eastern and the Western, I am the Southern and the Northern; I am up and down, the (four main) quarters and the various (intermediate quarters; I am; I am man, I am woman, Gayatri I am; Savitri I am; I am Trishtubh, Jagati, and anushtubh; the metre I am; I am Garhapatya; I am Dakshinagni and Ahavaniya; I am the true; I am the cow; and I am Gauri; I am the oldest, I am the best, I am the highest. I am the waters, I am light. I am the Rik, the Yajus, the Saman, and the Atharvangiras. The perishable am I, and I am the imperishable, I am the secret, I am the forest. The sacred lake am I, as well as the holy one. I am the beginning and the end, and beyond and the front. I am verily the Light. He that knows Me all knows all."

In the second section also, as due to the very fact of His having entered into everything, it is declared that He is denoted by the words Brahma, Vishnu, Mahesvara, Vinayaka, Uma, and the whole universe of things, in the passage beginning with the following words:

"To that Lord who is called Rudra, to Him who is also called Brahma, to Him I bow."

Accordingly by an investigation into the harmonious teaching of the Sruti, it is found that Siva, the Paramesvara, is the Being denoted by all words, as embodied in all, having entered into all beings, sentient and insentient as their Antaryamin, the Inner Regulator. Wherefore, it is well to conclude that Kasakristsna's view alone agrees with the teaching of the Sruti, of the Sutra, and of the great adepts.

Adhikarana 6.

In a former adhikarana, I. i. 2. It was briefly indicated that Paramesvara is the upadana or material cause of the universe by quoting a passage which speaks of him by means of word in the *ablative* case.* [* Tatti.Up, 3-1.]

"From whom all these beings are born."

This adhikarana proceeds to establish it at full length.

And He is Prakriti also in accordance with the proposition and the illustration (I. iv. 23)

The passages to be discussed here are such as the following:

"From Him, verily, the Atman, was born the akasa." * [* Tait. Up. 2-1.]

"The one God, producing heaven and earth." † [† Tait. Sam. 4-6-2.]

Here a doubt arises as to whether it is right or not to hold that Brahman is the twofold cause. Because the *nimitta* or efficient cause such as the potter is not found to from also the material cause such as clay, and that neither the material cause such as clay forms also the *nimitta* or the efficient cause such as the potter, how can we understand that he can form both the material and the efficient cause with the universe as the effect?

(*Purvapaksha*): - He is only the *nimitta* or efficient cause of the universe, not the *upadana* or material cause – Why? – Because it is impossible. Indeed, the potter who is engaged in making a pot does not make the pot by becoming clay himself, nor does a weaver making a cloth do so. If he would try to do so, it would be quite impossible. Wherefore it is impossible for Brahman, the *nimitta* or efficient cause, to be the *upadana* or material cause as well. And it is useless to suppose that the efficient cause is also the material cause as well, in as much as the production of the required effect can be accounted for without such a supposition. For, we find the pot produced not withstanding that the potter is distinct from clay. Wherefore Brahman is only the efficient cause, but not the material cause as well.

Against this we say as follows: The material as well as the efficient cause is Brahman himself. It is stated that by knowing the Commander all becomes known, that the Commander, the efficient cause, being known, the whole of the sentient and insentient universe becomes known, as the following passage shows:

"You are so conceited; have you ever asked for that Command by which we hear what has not been heard, we think what has not been brought, we know what has not been known." ‡ [‡ Chha. Up. 6-1-3.]

And in explanation of this, the illustration of clay has also been adduced in the following passage:

"As when clay is known, all this which is made of clay becomes known." * [* Ibid 6-1-4.]

If Brahman were the efficient cause merely, knowledge of the whole universe would not be possible when He is known. By knowing the potter, we cannot, indeed, know the pot etc., the effect; but we can do so by knowing clay, the material cause of the pot. Wherefore seeing that this becomes possible when Brahman, the efficient cause, is also the material cause, we must conclude that Brahman Himself is the material cause.

The Vedanta-Sutras with Srikantha Bhashya

"Command" (in the sruti) is put for Him who commands, namely, Brahman. To show that the upadana or material cause is not a thing distinct from Him, the Sutrakara adduces another reason:

And by the declaration of (His) desire (I. iv. 24.)

"He desired, may I become manifold;"† in these words the Sruti declares the desire of the intelligent and all knowing Brahman Himself who is the *nimitta* or efficient cause to become the manifold existence in the form of the variegated universe. Wherefore the material cause is not a distinct entity from the efficient cause. [† Ibid 5-2-3.]

(*Objection*): - From the sruti – such as "Above the universe is Rudra the Great Sage and He saw the Golden-wombed (Hiranyagarbha) being born;"‡ we understand that the Paramesvara himself who is above the universe and is the efficient cause thereof casts his gracious glance upon the Hiranyagarbha, the first of all gods, being born by His (Paramesvara's) will from out of the Prakriti distinct from Him (the efficient cause). How can He ever become the Prakriti or material cause and assume the form of the universe. It is Maya that is declared by the sruti as Prakriti, in the following words: "Let it be known that Maya is Prakriti." § The sruti declares also that Purusha is Prakriti in the words "From Him was born, Viraj, and above Viraj is Purusha" ‖ Thus it is proper that those two alone are the Prakriti, and as such assume the form of the universe. [‡ Mahanarayana Upanishad. 10. § Svet. Up. 4-1. ‖ Purusha Sukta.]

(*Answer*): - The Sutrakara answers as follows:

And He being directly declared as both (I. iv. 25).

In some sections of the Vedantas, the Paramesvara is directly declared to be of the form of the universe as its material cause, and to be the Lord of the universe as it efficient cause, To explain: just as the passages such as "Rudra is above the universe" indicate His being the Lord of the universe, in the same way such passages as "All verily is Rudra"* declare that, as the material cause of the universe, He is also of the form of the universe. In the sata-rudriya, He is declared to be the Lord of the universe, in the section beginning with "Bow to the Golden-armed" and closing with "Bow to the Lord of robbers", † and from there up to "Bow to the leaf born and to the one born in the cluster of leaves" He is declared to be of the form of the universe. Elsewhere, too, the sruti declares Him in both the aspects:

"Brahman was the forest. Brahman became that tree;......Brahman governed the worlds, holding them in their place."‡ [Mahanarayana-Up. 16. † Satarudraya 5. ‡ Taitt. Brahman 2-8-9.]

In the Atharvasiras, he is described to be of the form of the universe in the subsequent portion. Wherefore He being directly declared to be both, it is but right that the Supreme Brahman, Siva, who is Paramesvara, is both the universe and the Lord of the universe, as the material and the efficient cause thereof.

The sutrakara says that there is yet another authority:

Because of His creating (it out of) Himself (I. iv. 26)

"He made it out of himself by himself." § Thus, it is seen that Paramesvara made Himself to be of the form of the universe. Wherefore He is the material as well as the efficient cause. [§ Taitt. Up. 2-7.]

(*Objection*): - Paramasiva is quite free from all trace of evil; He is the unlimited ocean of all excellent attributes; His glory is infinite and eternal, and He is above the universe. How can such a being ever become the Prakriti, the universe which is the basis of all illusion and change, and which has to be avoided as an evil.

By transformation (I. iv. 27)

It is quite explicable how Paramasiva, the efficient cause, who is the Bliss, ever pure, and who by nature is the unsurpassed Good, should assume the form of the universe as the material cause thereof, by transforming Himself into the *chit* and *achit*, or sentient and insentient, forms of existence.

(*Objection*): - Ah! Transformation (*parinama*) means change in the form of the cause, in as much as *parinama* is defined to consist in a change from one form to another form. How is Paramesvara thus subject to what is regarded as an evil?

(*Answer*): - True; but transformation (*parinama*) can take place in such a way that the Efficient Cause is not affected by the change, notwithstanding that He is the Prakriti or material cause.

(Question): - What is this unique transformation? We are curious to know what it is. Please explain.

(Answer): - Listen; we shall explain.

"When it was dark, when there was no day, no night, no existence nor non-existence, then was Siva alone by himself. That is the Imperishable; the Adorable (Light) of the sun; and from Him, Wisdom Ancient went forth." * [* Sveta. Up. 4-18]

At the time when all this was darkness, without the light of the sun and the moon, without the division of day and night, devoid of the individual names and forms, undifferentiated into gross and subtle forms of the sentient and the insentient, into existence and non-existence, then there was Siva alone left by himself, without a second, self-luminous, with the potentialities of the sentient and the insentient existence inseparable from His being. That was then the Imperishable, Supreme Being; that too the Adorable light, as in dwelling in the sun, the primary source of the sun's light. From such a Being, wherein was latent the whole external universe of the sentient and the insentient existence went forth the ancient supreme wisdom, the spiritual energy (jnanasakti), secondless, eternally existent, - the Great Flash of light dispelling all the then darkness. Then "He desired, 'may I become many'; † [† Taitt. Up. 2-6.] then, Paramesvara the Cause, embodied in the subtle form of the sentient and the insentient being which was undifferentiated yet in name and form, willed that He should become embodied in the sentient and the insentient existence differentiated in name and form. And then "all this did He create, and whatever else there is; ‡ [‡ Ibid.] - He differentiated from himself His body, the sentient and the insentient being in its subtle form. Then "having created it He entered into it,"* [* Ibid.] He entered of himself as their Atman into the sentient and the insentient which had been differentiated from him. Then "He became the manifest and the unmanifest," † [† Ibid.] he became variously transformed into the universe, manifest and unmanifest. Thus as man is a child and then a youth, Brahman whose body is the universe, is the cause and the effect. The sruti says.

"Know verily Maya as Prakriti, and Maya (the possessor of Maya) the Mahesvara.

By that which forms His limb is all this universe pervaded." ‡ [‡ Sveta-Up. 4-10.]

From this we learn that Maya is the Prakriti (material cause) of all, that Mahesvara is the being endued with It, and that the whole universe is pervaded by His limb, by a portion of Himself, by a piece of his sentient energy (Chit-Sakti) which, when regarded as the enjoyer, is known by the name of Purusha. Just as the hair and nails and the like are not born of the body alone or of Atman alone, so the universe is not born of Maya alone or of Mahesvara alone. On the other hand, - like the hair and nails being born of the embodied mortals, Purusha, the Prakriti (material cause) of the sentient and the insentient existence comes into manifestation from out of the Paramesvara united with Maya. From Isvara in this form, are born the Avyakta (the Unmanifested, the four-faced (Brahma), and so on. And accordingly Sruti describes Isvara to be Purusha Himself in the following words:

"Purusha verily is Rudra." § [§ Mahanarayanopanishad.]

Wherefore it becomes quite explicable how Paramesvara, who is endued with the sentient and the insentient nature, forms the cause as well as the effect, according to the several stages through which He passes.

And it is indeed that He is the Prakrithi (I. iv. 28.)

It is directly declared that Paramesvara Himself is the Prakriti of all beings.

"Him whose helpmate is Uma; who is the supreme Lord (Paramesvara), mighty, three-eyed, dark-necked, and serene, having mediated thus, the sage reaches him who is the womb of all creatures, the witness of all, transcending darkness." * [* Kaivalya-Upanishad 7.]

Thus the Sruti declares that the Prakriti of all creatures is the Paramesvara himself, who is the witness of all, the omniscient; transcending all darkness, above all universe; associated with Uma, the supreme energy (*Parama Sakti*). Therefore the Supreme Brahman Himself is the Upadana (material cause) as well as the *nimitta* or efficient cause.

Adhikarana 7.

By this, all have been explained; all have been explained (I. iv. 29.)

This exposition of Vedantic passages, carried on from I. i. 2 till now, forms also the exposition of those portions of the *Mantra* and *Brahmana* which, as speaking of the characteristic marks of Brahman, are of the form of the Vedanta, such as the Purusha-sukta and the Satarudriya which form integral portions of Karma-kanda; as also of the Smritis, Itihasas, Puranas, and the sayings of the adepts. Repetition of the words "all have been explained" is intended to show that the adhyaya is over.

Here a doubt arises as to whether the Satarudriya and the Purushasukta which occur in the ritualistic portion (Karmakanda), as also the Smriti, Itihasa, and Puranas, - whether they do or do not point to Brahman, when we take into account the various marks by which to ascertain the purport of a scriptural text; this doubt arising from the sections being of a different character (as devoted to karma).

(*Purvapaksha*): - It is proper to maintain that the Purusha-sukta and the like which occur in the ritualistic portion of Karmakanda) are devoted to an exposition of jiva, the performer of actions; and that they do not point to Brahman, because there is no purpose served (by treating of Brahma). Even the Smritis, Itihasas, Puranas, and the like do not treat of the oneness of Atman; for some of them speak of Brahma as the Parabrahman; some, of Vishnu; some of Rudra; some of Sakti; Some, of Agni; some of Surya; some of Vayu; some of another. As thus, no definite conclusion can be arrived at, these cannot be held to treat of Brahman.

(*Siddhanta*): - As against the foregoing, we hold as follows:

The Purushasukta and the like do teach Brahman, because of His characteristic marks being described therein. We find here described the characteristic attributes of Brahman, that he is the cause of all, that He is beyond darkness, that He is the cause of immortality, - as the following passages show:

"From him Viraj was born." * [* Purusha sukta.]

"Of the color of the sun, beyond darkness." * [* Purusha sukta.]

"Him thus knowing, one becomes immortal here." * [* Purusha sukta.]

Wherefore Isvara Himself is here described as Purusha. And in Satarudriya we find Paramesvara described as the Lord of the universe, as the Atman of the universe, as darknecked and so on. It is therefore but right to hold that He is treated of in the section.

(*Objection*): - It would seem unreasonable that the Paramesvara who is the repository of the finest of the attributes should be the being treated of in the Satarudriya. For, in the very beginning, we find the Being associated with wrath – which is a despicable quality, - as the following words show: "Bow to Thy wrath (*manyu*) O Rudra." † [† Satarudriya. 1.]

(*Answer*): - We should not proceed thus. For here, the word "manyu" means 'knowledge.' Or, it does not matter even if we understand the word in the sense of 'wrath'; for 'wrath' being a quality inhering in the Prakriti which has been voluntarily put on by Him, it has nothing to do with Paramesvara.

The marks which serve to indicate the main drift of the Puranas etc. point of the inevitable conclusion that they, treat of Siva, the Paramesvara associated with Uma, who, as the Atman of all, is the being denoted by the several designations such as Brahma and Vishnu; who is Omniscient and Omnipotent; who is above all; whose glory is unequalled; the being to whom the name Brahman can be fully applied and who forms the final import of all the Vedantic texts interpreted in harmony with each other.

As to the contention that these occur in the ritualistic portion, we have only to say in reply that it is but right that 'section' must be made to yield to characteristic marks' in determining the main drift of the teaching. On the same principle, wherever in the Vedas and other authoritative texts a sentient or an insentient being is declared as the cause of the universe and so on, we are to understand that it is Siva, the Atman thereof, who is there referred to. Wherever we find such attributes as mutability and nescience are predicated, it is a sentient or an insentient being forming the body of Para-Brahman that is meant. Thus everything becomes explicable when properly understood.

End of the first Adhyaya.

SECOND ADHYAYA.

Adhikarana - 1.

If (you urge that) it would lead to the fallacy of making no room for the smriti, (we reply) no because (otherwise) it would lead to the fallacy of making no room for the other smritis. (II. i. 1).

It has been shown that all Vedantic texts as well as the smritis which are common with their teaching, point, as the main drift of their teaching, to the most highly merciful Siva, the Para-Brahman, who is Existence, Intelligence, and Bliss in His essential nature; who by nature is omniscient, omnipotent, and so on; who has been defined by His occasional attributes, that He is the Being from whom the universe is born, and so on; who is distinct from all, the Atman of all; who voluntarily assumes the beautiful form, diverse-eyed; dark and yellow, dark-necked, and so on; and who is known by such specific designations as *Bhava, Siva, Mahadeva, Paramesvara*. Now, this adhyaya is intended to answer objections on the ground of the said construction being opposed to the smritis and arguments which point to a different conclusion from that of the Vedanta.

The main subject of discussion in the whole of this adhyaya is the construction of the Vedanta made out in the preceding adhyaya.

Firs a doubt arises here as to whether the Vedic teaching thus made out has to be modified or not in accordance with the teaching of the Sankhya-smriti – How? – The Veda teaches that Brahman is the cause of the universe, while Kapila's smriti declares Pradhana to be the cause of the universe. Kapila is indeed, one of great wisdom (*tapas*), and, therefore, his word, too, is an authority. And the Blessed Veda is the Sovereign authority of all and cannot so much as smell of untruth. Accordingly a doubt arises as to which of them should prevail against the other.

(*Purvapaksha*): - Now, the Sankhya-smriti serving no other purpose, is stronger in its claim to be considered as an authority in this matter; whereas, the Veda serves its purpose as teaching Dharma (ritual) and is therefore weaker in its claim. Thus it is but right to modify the Vedic teaching in the light of the smriti.

(*Siddhanta*): - We say, no – Why? – Because, other smritis, such as that of Manu, which are unopposed to the Veda, would then receive no recognition. To the Sankhya-smriti whose foundation lie in a sruti of which the very existence has to be inferred from the existence of the said smriti, the orthodox, enquirer should prefer that smriti which says "waters alone did He create in the beginning, and in them did He cast His energy," * [* Manu 1.8.] and thus declares that Brahman is the cause, as taught in the now extant srutis such as the following:

"He saw the Hiranyagarbha being born." † [† Mahanarayana Up. 10.]

And because it is not found (in the Smritis) of others. (II. i. 2.)

Since Kapila's doctrine that the Pradhana is the cause of the universe etc., is not recognized in the smritis of the omniscient teachers such as Manu, it is but right to say that the doctrine of the Pradhana has no foundation in the sruti. Hence no necessity for modifying, in the light of the Sankhya-smriti, the given construction of the Vedic teaching.

Adhikarana - 2.

Thereby has Yoga been answered. (II. i. 3.)

The Smriti of Hiranyagarbha, too, which treats of the means of attaining yoga speaks of the Pradhana as the cause; so that a doubt arises as to whether the construction of the Vedic teaching has to be modified or not in the light of that smriti, though it has to undergo no modification such as may be caused by its opposition to the Sankhya-smriti declaring that the Pradhana is the cause.

(*Purvapaksha*): - We say that modification is necessary. – Why? – In the Svetasvatara – Upanishad Yoga-Vidya is elaborately described as a means to the *sakshatkara* or intuitive perception of Brahman. So that, though the Sankhya-smriti is founded only on a sruti whose very existence is a matter of mere inference, it would seem proper to modify the construction upholding the doctrine that Brahman is the cause, in the light of Hiranyagarbha's smriti which declares that Pradhana is the cause and which is founded on an extant sruti.

(*Siddhanta*): - As against the foregoing we hold as follows. The given construction of the Vedic teaching has to undergo no modification in the light of the yoga-smriti. From the sutra "yoga is the restraint of the thinking principle," onwards, it is devoted to the exposition of the Vedic yoga with its eight *angas* or subsidiary stages, as the main point of its teaching, but not also the non-vedic doctrine that Pradhana is the cause. If it should lay stress on this doctrine also it is but right to reject it as we have rejected the Sankhya smriti. Wherefore, it quite stands to reason that the construction of the Vedic teaching as tending to the inculcation of the doctrine that Brahman is the cause should undergo no modification in the light of Hiranyagarbha's smriti which teaches that Pradhana is the cause.

Adhikarana - 3.

Again the sutrakara first sets forth and then refutes an objection on the ground that the given construction of the Vedantic teaching should be modified in the light of the Sankhya's course of reasoning.

(The universe is) not (an emanation of Brahman); being quite distinct. And that it is so (is known) from the Word. (II. i. 4.)

A doubt arises as to whether the given construction of the Vedanta has, or has not, to undergo a modification in the light of the Sankhya's reasoning, while it need not undergo any modification in the light of his smriti.

(*Purvapaksha*): - From all points of view, the doctrine that Brahman is the cause has to be modified in the light of reasoning – How? – The universe being of a quite distinct nature from Brahman, it cannot be an emanation of Brahman. If you ask how this distinction has come to be known, we reply, it is from the Sruti itself. For, the sruti "Intelligence as well as non-intelligence," * and so on, describes the universe as subject to change, as unintelligent, as something not to be sought for by man. It is, therefore, distinct from Brahman who is Existence, Intelligence and Bliss. How can they be related as cause and effect, any more than the cow and the buffalo? [* Tait. Up. 2-6.]

Because of the specific mention and of association it is only a mention of the presiding Intelligence (II. i. 5.)

Objection against the Purvapaksha: - If this universe be insentient and, as such, distinct from the intelligent Brahman, then how is it that the created objects are spoken of as sentient, in the following passages:

"Him, the earth addressed." * [* Tait. Samhita, 5-5-2.]

"The waters, verily, desired." † [† Tait. Brahmana, 3-1-5.]

"Listen, O wise stones." ‡ [‡ Tait. Samhita, 1-3-13.]

Wherefore, the whole of this universe is sentient. Hence no distinction between Brahman and the universe as sentient and insentient.

Purvapakshin's answer: - Not so. For we are to understand such a mention of an intelligent procedure in every such case as referring to the Devata or Intelligence associated with the object, the word 'Devata' being specifically mentioned in such passages as the following:

"Ah! I shall enter into these three Devatas and differentiate name and form." § [§ Chha. Up. 6-3.]

And the constant association, with the material object, of the presiding Devata or Intelligence being expressly stated in the following passage:

"Agni became speech and entered the mouth." || [|| Aitareya-upanishad, 1-2-4.]

Wherefore, owing to its insentiency etc., the universe is quite distinct from Brahman. Thus the construction that makes Brahman the cause, and this universe the effect, should be given up in the light of reason.

It is, however, seen. (II. i. 6.)

(*Siddhanta*): - Though distinct in their nature, Brahman and the universe can be related as cause and effect, because the sentient scorpion is seen to take its birth in the insentient cow-dung, and that the insentient hair is found growing out of sentient man. Hence the conclusion that mere unaided reasoning cannot prevail against the exegetical interpretation of the sruti.

Again an objection is raised answered:

(If you urge that the effect would be) non-existent, (we reply) no, because it is a mere denial. (II. i. 7.)

(*Objection*): - The cause and the effect being distinct from each other the effect does not exist in the cause; and so the Sruti, says "Non-existent, verily, this in the beginning was."

(*Answer*): - You should not say so. For, the sruti merely declares that the cause and the effect are not necessarily of the same nature. It does not, therefore, detract from the theory that the cause and the effect are one thing essentially.

Adhikarana - 4.

Because of His being subject to them like it in dissolution. It is not right. (II. i. 3.)

If, in accordance with the doctrine that the effect exists in the cause before manifestation and after disappearance, it be held that the universe and Brahman are one thing essentially, then a doubt arises as to whether the harmonious teaching of the Upanishads as to Brahman has to be rejected or not in the light of reasoning.

(*Purvapaksha*): - It has to be set aside. – Why? – Because it has been said that the universe and Brahman are essentially one thing. Then indeed it is an inevitable conclusion that, like the universe, Brahman is subject to all such evils as change and ignorance. Accordingly what is taught by one accordant voice in all the Vedantic texts become incongruous. Thus, the given interpretation of the Vedantic teaching must be rejected.

But as, because there is an analogous case (II. i. 9.)

The word "no" shows that the Purvapaksha has to be rejected. Such passages in the sruti as "Whose body is Atman," "whose body is Avyakta," and such sayings in the Puranas as "The body of the God of gods in this universe, moving and unmoving; this thing, the *pasus* (jivas) know not in virtue of the bond (*pasa*);" such passages show that *chit* and *achit*, the sentient and the insentient, are the body of Siva, the Parabrahman. Though He exists as both the cause and the effect, there is no incongruity whatever in the doctrine taught in one harmonious voice in all the Vedantic texts, since there is an analogous case as to the proper distribution of good and evil. – How? – Just as when the human body and the like pass through the states of childhood, youth, and dotage, childhood and other changes of condition pertain only to the body, and pleasure etc., pertain only to the Atman; so, here, such evils as ignorance and change which are found in the sentient and the insentient beings forming the body of Brahman pertain only to the sentient and the insentient being forming the body; and such attributes as faultlessness, immutability, omniscience, and unfailing will pertain only to the Paramesvara, the Atman. Because of this analogy, there is no incongruity whatever in the teaching of the Sruti concerning Brahman.

And because of inconsistency on his own side. (II. i. 10).

By trusting to reasoning alone the Pradhana-vadin will find the mutual confusion of the attributes of Prakriti and Purusha difficult to explain according to his theory which folds that Prakriti acts in the mere presence of Purusha who is immutable. Purusha, immutable as he is, is not capable of this act of confusion which consists in attributing in thought the properties of one thing to another; and Prakriti which is insentient is altogether incapable of thought. Therefore, the theory which holds that Pradhana is the cause should itself be set aside in the light of reasoning.

Because of the infinality of inference. (II. i. 11.)

Inference being not a final test in itself, and the doctrine of Pradhana being founded thereon, and it being possible to infer even to the contrary, it is the doctrine of Pradhana, not the doctrine of Brahman, that has to be rejected.

(If you say that It) has to be inferred otherwise, (we say) even then there can be no deliverance. (II. i. 12).

It is not right to maintain that the Pradhana should be so inferred in another way that there can be no room for an inference to the contrary. For, even then, it is possible to suppose a contrary inference to this inference; and therefore there can be no release of the test of inference from the defect of being not a final test. Wherefore properly speaking, it is the doctrine of Pradhana, based as it is on bare inference which has to be rejected, but not the doctrine of Brahman based on the strong authority of the sruti.

Adhikarana – 5.

By this, even the heterodox doctrines have been explained. (II. i. 13.)

Just as the Sankhya system has been rejected as being founded on inference, as not being final, and so on, so also, and on the same ground, it may be held that the heterodox systems of Kanada, Akshapada, etc., have to be rejected. That is to say, even the atomic doctrine of Kanada and others has here been refuted.

Adhikarana – 6.

(If you say that) as He would become an enjoyer, there will be no distinction, (we reply) there can be (a distinction) as in the word. (II. i. 14.)

As to the declaration in the preceding adhyaya of the Visishta Sivadvaita or the unity of the conditioned Siva as based on the ground that Siva without a second, associated with sentient and insentient universe, is Himself cause and effect, a doubt arises as to whether this idea of unity derived by an exegetical interpretation of the Vedantic texts will have to be set aside as opposed to reason.

Now the *purvapakshin* says: If it be admitted that Paramesvara has for His body the sentient and the insentient universe, then he becomes an embodied being. Being thus embodied, like the jiva He too may become subject to pain and pleasure attendant upon contact with the body. Then there will be no distinction between Paramesvara and the jiva who is in a state of bondage. Thus since nothing serves to distinguish the one from the other, it cannot be proved, on the theory of Paramesvara's being intimately associated with the universe, that He is by nature free from all evil.

Siddhanta: - There is no incongruity whatever. A distinction can be made between Jiva and Paramesvara in as much as His form is free from all taint and blessed in every way. One becomes subject to evil not because one is embodied, but because one is subject to the control of another. For example, in the human world, the king who is an embodied being is not subject to punishment consequent upon the disobedience of his own command, simply because he is not subject to the control of another. Thus He is not an enjoyer in the same way that the other is. The independence of Iswara and the dependence of Jiva are self-evident, as the Sruti says:

"Knowing and unknowing are the two, the powerful and the powerless." * [* Sveta. Up. 1-9]

Hence no absence of a distinction between Paramesvara who is independent and Jiva who is a dependent being though they are alike embodied.

Adhikarana – 7.

Although a distinction can be made between jiva and Paramesvara on account of their mutually opposed attributes of independence and dependence and the like, still, it may be shown that, as cause and effect, they are one, not distinct from each other.

They are not distinct because of the word 'creation' and so on. (21. i. 15.)

A doubt arises here as to whether it is reasonable or not to maintain that Brahman and the universe, the cause and the effect, are not distinct, as the Srutis declare in one voice. This doubt arises because they are marked off from each other by the mutually opposed attributes of sentiency and insentiency.

(*Purvapaksha*): - How can their unity be explained? In the preceding adhikarana, Paramesvara and jiva have been distinguished from each other, the one being possessed of omniscience etc., the other being ignorant and subject to enjoyment and suffering. As so the insentient beings, they being of a quite different nature, there is no shadow of reason to hold that it is not distinct from Brahman. The fact of their being related to each other as cause and effect cannot prove that they are not distinct from each other; for we hold that the cow-dung and the scorpion are distinct from each other notwithstanding that they are related as cause and effect. Even in the case of clay and the pot, we find that they are quite distinct from each other because they are found in experience to serve quite distinct purpose, and so on. Or thus: if the cause and effect are quite identified, the universe and Brahman must be quite homogeneous, so that we should not experience any distinction among things, such as we daily make between an act, its agent, and the object sought to be attained.

As against the foregoing we hold as follows: The universe, as an effect, is not distinct from Brahman, its cause. – How do you know it? – From the word 'creation,' and so on, in the following passages:

"A creation by speech is change as well as name; what is called clay is alone real." *
[* Chhandogya Upanishad 6-1.]

"Existent alone, my dear, this at first was, one only without a second…

It willed 'may I be many, and be produced'…..All this is ensouled by It; That is real; That is Atman; That thou art, O Svetaketu." † [† Ibid.]

"The whole being, the variegated world, what has become in many forms, and what is becoming, all this is Rudra." ‡ [‡ Mahanarayana Up. 16.]

As to the contention that the relation of cause and effect cannot prove unity, the Sutrakara says:

And because of the perception (of the cause) during the existence (of the effect). (II. i. 16.)

During the existence of the effect as the pot, we perceive that the very substance of clay is the pot. Therefore, the effect is not distinct from the cause. The same thing is taught also in the following passage:

"A creation by speech is change as well as name. What we call clay is alone real." § [§ Chha. Up. 6-1.]

That is to say, change of state as well as name merely enable us to speak of a thing and to use it for certain actual purposes. The very substance of clay, when assuming the form of a pot and named as 'pot,' serves certain actual purposes and enables us to speak of it in that form. In point of fact, the pot is real only as clay, so far as logical proof is concerned; for apart from clay, we find that no pot exists. Or, the above passage may be explained as follows: The effect, namely the pot, exists in so far only as we speak of it. It is the very substance of clay, and it is not a distinct substance, - only undergoing a change in state to serve certain purposes in our actual life. It is because the pot is mere clay – but not a distinct substance – that the term "clay" applied to the pot refers to a real substance, a substance whose existence can be proved by proper evidence. Because a pot is nothing but clay, therefore the effect is not distinct from the cause. As to the difference in the purposes they serve in actual life, it can be explained as due to their being different states of the same substances, while they (clay and pot) are in fact one in substance. Wherefore, like clay and pot, Brahman and the universe are one in substance, the one pervading the whole of the other. Hence the Puranic saying:

"From the Sakti down to earth, everything comes from the principle of Siva. By Him alone is it pervaded, as the pot etc., are pervaded by clay."

(*Objection*): - We hold that the pot is pervaded by clay because we cognize that the pot is mere clay. Not so do we cognize that this universe is Brahman; and therefore the universe cannot be said to be pervaded by Brahman.

(*Answer*): - We do find that Brahman as the existent pervades the universe, as we cognize that a pot exists, that a cloth exists, and so on everywhere. If the universe were not pervaded by Siva in His aspects as the existent and the conscious, then how could we cognize that a thing exists and becomes an object of consciousness, detached as it is from existence and consciousness? It cannot be a reality at all. Wherefore, it may be concluded that as the pot etc. are pervaded by clay, so this universe, as the effect, is pervaded by Siva, the cause, and is one with Him.

And because of the existence of the other. (II. i. 17.)

Because the effect exists in the cause, the effect is not distinct from the cause. It is because the pot etc. were clay itself before, that we now perceive the pot etc. to be mere clay.

The Vedanta-Sutras with Srikantha Bhashya

(If you hold that it is not so) because of its being mentioned as non-existent, (we say) no; because it is due to a different condition, as shown by the sequel by analogy, and by other passages. (II. i. 18.)

(*Objection*): - The effect does not exist in the cause, because the Sruti says that the effect was non-existent:

"Nothing whatever of this (universe) existed at first." * [* Tait. Brahmana 2-2-9.]

(*Answer*): - No. The universe is mentioned to have been non-existent because it was in a different condition, *i.e.* in a subtle form as opposed to its present gross form. – How do you know? – Because in the sequel the Sruti says "While non-existent, it though 'may I be.'" Even thinking is possible only in an existent thing. There is also an analogy pointing to the conclusion that the mention of the universe as non-existent is due only to a change of state. It is only in reference to the clay's mutually opposed, but positive, states of being as lump, as pot, and as potsherd, that we say that the pot did not exist before, that it now exists, and that it will not exist at a certain time in the future. When we thus see how clay itself which exists in all these states may be spoken of as a pot non-existent, it is unnecessary to assume a state of 'abhava' or "nullity," a different state of being altogether, corresponding to a pot non-existent. Accordingly the Sruti says elsewhere:

"This, verily, existed then undifferentiated: it was (since) differentiated in name and form." † [† Bri. Up. 3-4-7.]

The main conclusion may be stated as follows: At first Siva is pure, endued with the Parasakti, the Supreme Energy inseparable from Himself, and composed of the sentient and the insentient existence in so subtle a form that they cannot be differentiated in name and form. Then He projects out of himself and evolves that Sakti, which is Himself, in a gross form as opposed to the previous state, in the form of the sentient and the insentient existence capable of being differentiated in name and form. When the Energy is withdrawn from manifestation, then takes place *pralaya* or dissolution; when it is manifested, creation takes place. Accordingly, the authorities say:

"It is, verily, the Divine Being Himself; the Chidatman who manifests the whole objective existence out of Himself from within like a yogin, by His will, without resorting to an upadana."

That is to say, without resorting to an upadana external to Himself, by Himself becoming the upadana or material cause. Wherefore, the created universe is one with the Supreme cause, Siva the Parabrahman.

Another example is given as follows:

And like a cloth (II. i. 19.)

Small when folded, a cloth becomes when extended a large one, and in the form of a hut becomes an effect. So, too, Brahman is the cause when contracted, and when extended in form He becomes the effect.

And like prana and the like (II. i. 20.)

Just as the Vayu, one in itself, assumes different forms as prana or upward breath and so on, according to its several activities, so too, Brahman, in virtue of the various activities of Sakti assumes manifold form such as Sadasiva and so on. Wherefore it is but right to maintain that the universe as the effect is one with Brahman, the cause.

Adhikarana 8.

The Sutrakara raises and refutes an objection to the foregoing theory:-

(Jiva) being mentioned (to be one with) the other, there follows an incongruity such as neglecting what is good. (II. i. 21.)

(*Objection*): - Because in the words "That thou art,"*[* Chha. Up. 6-8.] and "This Atman is Brahman,"† [†Mandukya. Up. 1] Jiva, the effect, is mentioned as one with Brahman, the cause, it has been shown that they are not distinct from each other. In that case it would follow that the all-knowing and all-pervading Paramesvara undoes the universe for His own good and creates it for His own evil. Then it may be asked, how is it that Isvara, who is all-knowing and of unfailing will, and who knows that the pain of Jiva who is no other than Himself is His own pain, engages in the creation of the universe, which as leading to samsara is an evil, and does not abstain from creation for His own good. Accordingly once it is proved that Jiva and Paramesvara are one, there follows this incongruity, that Paramesvara, though all-knowing, is guilty of a want of sense in so far as He abstains from what is good to Himself and engages in what conduces to His own evil. Wherefore it does not stand to reason that Jiva and Isvara, the cause and effect, are one.

(*Answer*): - In reply we say as follows:

But (the Cause is) superior, because of the mention of a distinction. (II. i. 22).

Though the cause and effect are one, the Cause is declared in the Sruti to be superior to the effect, to the sentient and insentient universe, in such passages as the following:

"Superior to the universe is Rudra the Mighty Sage." * [* Mahana. 10.]

So, a distinction is also made between Jiva and Paramesvara in the following passages:

"But he who controls both, knowledge and ignorance, is another." * [* Sveta. Up. 5-1.]

The Vedanta-Sutras with Srikantha Bhashya

"The one God rules the perishable (Pradhana) and Atman." † [† Ibid. 1-10.]

"Thinking that Atman is different from the Mover (the Lord)." ‡ [‡ Ibid. 1-6.]

"Two birds, inseparable friends, cling to the same tree." § [§ Ibid. 4-6.]

"Two Brahmans ought to be known, the superior and the inferior." ‖ [‖ Maitrayani Up. 6-22.]

"There are two, one knowing, the other not-knowing; both unborn, one strong, the other weak." ¶ [¶ Sve. Up. 1-9.]

"He is the eternal among eternals, the sentient among the sentient." ** [** Ibid. 6-13.]

"Having entered within, He is the Ruler of the creatures." †† [†† Tait. Ara. 3-11.]

"Know then Prakriti is Maya, and the great Lord the Mayin." ‡‡ [‡‡ Sveta. Up. 4-10.]

"From that the Mayin sends forth all this; in that the other is bound up through that Maya." §§ [§§ Ibid. 4-9.]

"When he sees the other, the Lord, contented...then his grief passes away." ‖ ‖ [‖ ‖ Ibid. 4-7.]

"He is the master of nature and of man, the Lord of the three qualities." ¶¶ [¶¶ Ibid. 6-16.]

"Of these creatures (pasus), the Pasupati is the Lord." *** [*** Tait. Samhita, 3-1-1.]

Wherefore quite superior to the universe is Brahman, otherwise called Siva.

(*Objection*): - By establishing non-duality in II. i. 15, and duality in II. i. 22, you have only proved duality and non-duality of Brahman and the universe.

(*Answer*): - No; we do not establish that sort of Visishtadvaita which takes the form of duality and non-duality. We are not the advocates of an absolute distinction between Brahman and the universe as between a pot and a cloth, because of its opposition to the sruti declaring that they are not quite distinct from each other. Neither are we the advocate of an absolute identity as of the mother-p'-pearl and silver, one of them being illusory; for, it is opposed to the sruti which points to a difference in the inherent attributes of Brahman and the universe. Nor do we hold to duality and non-duality, which is opposed to the nature of things. On the other hand, we maintain that the unity of the conditions Brahman – as the cause and the effect – is like that of the body and the embodied, or like that of the substance and its attribute. By unity of Brahman and the universe, we mean their inseparability like that of clay and the pot as cause and effect, or like that of the substance and its attribute. A pot, indeed, is not seen apart from clay nor is the blue-lotus seen apart from the color blue. Similarly, apart from Brahman, no potentiality of the universe can exist; nor is Brahman ever known apart from His potentiality of the universe just as fire is not seen apart from its heat. Whatever is not known apart from something else, the former must ever be conditioned by the latter, and this latter is naturally one with the former.

Wherefore Brahman who is in no way separable from the universe is said to be one with the other. And there is a natural distinction between the two; so that the supreme Brahman is ever higher than the universe. As to their distinction as the cause and effect, it has been already explained in II. i. 9. Wherefore this theory is quite unopposed to the Srutis declaring as well as non-distinction.

And as in the cause of stone etc; it is incongruous. (II. i. 23.)

(*Objection*): - Under all conditions, Jiva and Isvara are one, because of the srutis declaring non-duality.

(*Answer*): - No, because of an incongruity. Jiva and Isvara cannot be identical, because, like the insentient stone, timber, grass, etc, the jiva also is, on account of ignorance etc, said to belong to quite a distinct class from the Isvara who is possessed of such attributes as omniscience. Therefore Isvara is a distinct entity from Jiva. Thus even the Jiva, sentient as he is, cannot be identical with Isvara owing to this difference, that that latter is superior. Much less can the insentient existence which is essentially different be identical with Isvara. From all standpoint of view, by Sruti, Smriti and reasoning, we see that the omniscient and omnipotent Paramesvara is quite superior to the whole universe, sentient and insentient though, as His own emanation, it is not altogether distinct from Him.

Adhikarana 9.

(If you urge that) it is not so, because we see an assemblage, (we say) no; as in the case of milk, indeed. (II. i. 24.)

In such passages as "One alone, without a second;" and "The one God, producing heaven and earth"; we are told that one alone, Paramesvara, is the cause of the world. Is it reasonable or not that He, one alone as He is, is the cause of the variegated world?

Such a doubt arising, the *Purvapakshin* says: It is not reasonable, as involving an incongruity. This creation, made up as it is of ether, air, fire and water, is various. How can this be without the causes being variegated? Indeed, we find an assemblage of many factors in producing such things as car. Wherefore it cannot be that the cause is one.

Siddhantin says: Such a view cannot be maintained. It is possible for even a single cause to be transformed into an effect, as, for example, in the case of milk which, alone, becomes transformed into curd. Wherefore the universe is the effect of the single cause, Brahman.

As to the contention that variety in the effect presupposes a variety in the cause, we say it is wrong, because we see the formation of a variegated effect such as hair, nail, etc., out of the one sentient man. Wherefore in producing the variegated effect of the universe,

Brahman requires no other cause. Now, the sutrakara says that everything is possible for the mighty.

And also, as in the case of Devas etc., in the world. (II. i. 25).

Just as the Devas, of whose powers we are told in the Sastras, can put on as many forms as they like, so also, in the case of Paramesvara, of whose powers we are told in the Sastras, everything is possible. The sruti declares that the power of Paramesvara is infinite, in the following words:

"He who rules these worlds by His highest creative and ruling powers." What is impossible for Him?

Adhikarana 10.

Either it leads to the whole (becoming the effect), or there will be contradiction of the teaching as to partlessness (II. i. 26).

Now, there arises a doubt as to whether the aforesaid doctrine that Brahman becomes transformed into the universe, is consistent or not with reason?

(*Purvapaksha*): - How can we reconcile with reason the doctrine that the One alone is transformed into the universe? In case that He becomes entirely transformed into the universe, as milk is transformed in its entirety into curd, then it would follow that Brahman as a whole becomes the effect, that no Brahman is left as such. Or, if it be only in part, it will contradict the Sruti which declares that Brahman has no parts. Wherefore Brahman's transformation is not consistent with reason.

(*Siddhanta*): - As against the foregoing we hold as follows:

But (it is so) by Sruti, revelation being the only source. (II. i. 27).

The doctrine that the universe is a transformation of Brahman is quite explicable, because the sruti says so Sruti is the sole authority on the matter, there being no other authority. Because it is taught in the sruti, the doctrine is not stultified by Brahman's possession of uncommon powers. He being quite different from all the things we know of from other sources of knowledge. Thus it is quite possible for Him who is quite full to be Himself the cause as well as the effect. The doctrine of genus, for instance, holds that the one genus is present as a whole in each of the individuals of infinite number and utmost variety; no objection being allowed in the matter on the analogy of other things. Hence no incongruity whatever. Revelation being the only source of knowledge regarding the nature of Brahman.

And so in Atman. They are, indeed, various (II. i. 28)

Simply because Jivatman belongs to a distinct class, we find him possessed of the attributes of the sentient as opposed to the attributes of the insentient existence. Even the individual objects of the insentient class such as fire, water, etc., are found to be possessed each of a distinct class of attributes, and are therefore quite various. Accordingly Brahman, too, of whom our knowledge is based solely on the authority of the Revelation, is possessed of various and infinite potentialities. Hence no contradiction whatever.

And because of an incongruity in his own theory. (II. i. 29).

As to the incongruities, such as the whole cause having to become the effect, they can vitiate the theories of Pradhana and other such causes, which are said to be without parts and which are brought under the category of the insentient existence, but not the theory of Brahman based solely on the authority of Revelation.

The Sutrakara proceeds to declare that everything is explicable because Brahman is omnipotent.

And His Sakti is all-embracing as declared in the sruti. (II. i. 30)

We are given to understand that all potentiality is centered in Brahman, in the following passages:

"His Supreme Energy (Para-Sakti) is declared to be various, His inherent energy of knowledge and strength."

"Let it be known that Maya is the Prakriti, and that the Maya is the Mahesvara. By His limb, as it were, is all this universe pervaded."

Wherefore, possessed as He is of all powers, what is not possible for Him?

If you say He cannot be (the cause) as having no sense-organs, (we reply) it has been answered. (II. i. 31)

(*Objection*): - Brahman is said to be without sense, organs in the following passage.

"For Him there exists neither body nor the senses." Wherefore He cannot be the cause.

(*Answer*): - No; this objection has already been answered by saying that Brahman should be known as declared in the Sruti which is the sole authority in the matter. The Holy Divine Sruti – such as "Let it be Known that Maya is the Prakriti, and that the Maya is the Mahesvara; by His limb, as it were, is all this universe pervaded;" – is the sole authority as to Paramesvara, endued with the Supreme Sakti of Maya possessed of various and infinite potentialities, - assuming the form of the universe by a piece of His Sakti, while in Himself He is beyond the universe. On this subject the Purana also has the following:

"Bow to Him, whose thoughts are various and rise higher and higher above the universe; in a piece of whose power the whole is comprehended; whom, as the Master of all paths, the path-knowers declare as the Path; who is distinct from the whole universe."

Thus there is no room whatever for any discussion as to what is possible or what is impossible in Siva, the Paramesvara, the Parabrahman, who is devoid of all taints, and whose omnipotency is based on the sole authority of Revelation.

Adhikarana 11.

Again, the Sutrakara raises an objection and answers as follows:

No because of every action having a purpose (II. i. 32)

It has been decided that Brahman who, as the Sastra says, possesses all powers can be the cause of all effects. Still, all activity having some purpose in view, a doubt raises as to whether it is consistent or not to hold that Paramesvara who has attained all desires engages in the creation of the universe and other such acts.

(*Purvapaksha*): - How is that possible? Indeed, Siva is said to be the unsurpassed Bliss itself and is contended, in such passages as the following:

"Bliss is Brahman."

"All-pervading Consciousness and Bliss; formless and wonderful; associated with Uma."

How can He engage in creation and other activities without any purpose in view? If His activity should have a purpose in view, then he could not be ever contented; if not, He would be doing something out of the way like a senseless being.

(*Siddhanta*): - As against the foregoing we hold as follows:

Still, as in the world, it is a mere sport (II. i. 33)

It cannot be urged that the Ever contented Brahman cannot consistently engage in the creation of the universe and other such acts, which, having no purpose to serve, must be purposeless. Even purposeless activity is consistent on the part of Paramesvara, as a mere matter of sport. Just as, in the world, such activity as the beating of a ball goes on as a matter of mere sport without any purpose in view, so also Paramesvara, though He has attained all desires, engages in creation etc., as a matter of mere sport. Hence no incongruity whatever.

Adhikarana 12.

No partiality nor mercilessness, because of reference to an external standard. So indeed the Sruti declares. (II. i. 34).

It has been shown that, notwithstanding the absence of all purpose, Paramesvara engages in the creation of the universe etc., as a mere matter of sport. Here again a doubt arises whether this is possible or not.

(*Purvapaksha*): - The act of creation, even as a matter of sport, is not consistent on the part of Paramesvara, who, as all – full, is devoid of likes and dislikes.

As equal to all, Paramesvara must be quite indifferent. Creating happy bodies, like those of the Devas etc., for some beings, and painful bodies like the human for some others, He cannot but be guilty of partiality. Moreover, creation being preceded by destruction, Paramesvara who instantaneously destroys the whole, is also guilty of mercilessness. Therefore of what avail to Paramesvara is the act of creating the universe which brings on what is undesirable?

(*Siddhanta*): - As against the foregoing we hold as follows: All things considered, Paramesvara cannot be charged with partiality and mercilessness when He creates the universe, in as much as variety in the creation is determined by Karma. So the sruti says:

"Those of good conduct attain good birth, and those of evil conduct attain evil birth."

If you urge that no Karma exists because of the absence of differentiation, (we reply), no, because it is beginningless. It is quite consistent and found in experience. (II. i. 35).

(*Objection*): - Before creation there is no karma, because of the absence of kshetrajnas (jivas); and the absence of these is indicated by the state of non-differentiation, declared with a determinateness in the words, "Existent alone, my dear, this at first was."

(*Answer*): - No; just the Jivas are beginningless as declared in the sruti, "one knowing and the other unknowing are the two, the unborn, one strong, and the other weak," so also their Karmas are beginningless. Indeed, we do see that Samsara is the result of a continuous stream of Karma. Paramesvara, indeed, omniscient as He is, sees the various Karma of the jivas; and by means of Sakti He creates the seat of enjoyment, the body of a Deva or the like, just suited to their respective Karma. Thus, variety in creation is due to Karma. And the destruction of the universe cannot render Paramesvara guilty of mercilessness, in as much as, like sleep it is a source of rest to those jivas who are oppressed with the mundane life.

(*Objection*): - If Karma alone is to decide the happiness and misery of the jivas, of what avail is Paramesvara, useless being?

(*Answer*): - Even Karma being subject to His control, it does not detract from His independence. Against this it should not be urged that, like a thief who wants to evade payment of toll arriving at dawn at the very toll station after wandering the whole night with a view to get beyond the city limits by an uncommon route, this contention again makes the Paramesvara guilty of partiality and mercilessness, in as much as Karma is not independent of Him. For, Paramesvara merely assorts the infinite Karmic potentialities latent in Maya. Karma being, thus, by its own power, the cause of variety in creation, there can be no partiality on the part of Him who merely assigns to each Jiva his respective Karma.

(*Objection*): - The insentient Karma being unable to create the bodies of jivas when uncontrolled by the sentient, it should be admitted that Paramesvara who is a sentient being, is the sole efficient cause. How can it be that Paramesvara, so merciful, again unites the jivas with the body which is the cause of samsara, though they have been free from all pain of Samsara with all the organs of enjoyment destroyed?

(*Answer*): - Without Karma becoming ripe no knowledge can arise in the jivas; without knowledge, there can be no Moksha, the unsurpassed bliss; and Karma cannot become ripe without enjoyment of fruits. With a view to the enjoyment of the fruits of Karma, the all-benign Paramesvara again creates the body etc., for the jivas. When Karma thus becomes gradually ripe, He enables the pure-minded jivas to attain to a knowledge of Himself, and manifests to them the wealth of Moksha, the unsurpassed bliss.

(*Objection*): - Paramesvara being thus mighty and extremely merciful, why should He not instantaneously cause the Karma of all Jivas to ripen and manifest bliss of Moksha to all alike?

(*Answer*): - Yes, Paramesvara is equally benign to all. But those of ripe *mala* (sin) are alone liberated, while those of unripe one have still to bide their time. Though, for instance the rays of the sun are equally distributed, it is only the ripe lotus that open, but not the unripe ones. Thus, Paramesvara, blessed in Himself, does everything for the sole benefit of others. Accordingly the Purana clearly sets forth the whole of the foregoing doctrine by way of showing that Paramesvara is all-benign:

> "As without the sun all this world would be dark, so would this whole world be dark without Siva. As without a physician unhappy patients would suffer, so without Siva, the world would be unhappy and suffer much. As medicine is by nature an antidote to diseases, so, it is in the nature of Siva to be an antidote to all evil of Samsara. As this terrible sphere of samsara has been in time without a beginning, so Siva, the Deliverer from samsara, has been in time without a beginning."

Wherefore it is possible that Paramesvara, who acts only for the benefit of all, engages in the creation of the world and other activities.

And because of the applicability of all attributes. (II. i. 36)

In short, whatever attributes cannot be applied to Pradhana, to the atoms, to Karma, to Time or the like, are all of them applicable to Brahman. Wherefore it is but right to say that Brahman, who is above all, is the cause of the creation of the world, and so on.

End of the first *Pada* in the second *Adhyaya*.

SECOND PADA

Adhikarana 1.

The inferred (Pradhana) cannot be (the cause), because then there can be no creation; and because of its possibility (in the presence of a sentient agent.) (II. ii. 1)

In the preceding Pada, the Vedantin's own theory has been established by answering the objections raised by the Sankhya and others on the strength of reasoning. Now, again, on the strength of reasoning the Sankhya and other opposed schools are criticized. First, an inquiry is started as to whether the Sankhya doctrine of Pradhana is reasonable or not.

The cause of doubt in all these cases is clear and may be easily made out.

(*Purvapaksha*): - We see that the doctrine that Pradhana is the cause of the universe is alone reasonable. For, Pradhana is made up of *sattva*, *rajas*, and *tamas*. This alone is fit to be the cause of the universe, in as much as we find everywhere its effects namely, pleasure, pain, and delusion. Such things as cloth are pleasurable when found, as serving us to cover our bodies with. When taken away by others, they are sources of pain. When neglected as serving no purpose they are committed to oblivion. As pleasure etc., are thus constant in all things, the cause of the universe must be Pradhana, made up of the three *gunas* or constituents.

As against the foregoing we hold as follows: Pradhana is not the cause of the universe, because it is insentient. To explain: We see that a piece of wood or the like, when not acted upon by a conscious agent, can be effectual in building a car or a palace; and we see that when acted on by a conscious agent, some effect is produced. Wherefore Pradhana, not governed by a conscious agent, cannot be the cause of the universe. As to the allegation that pleasure etc., is constant in all effects, we say that it cannot be, because pleasure, and the like are internal *i.e.*, subjective, whereas the cloth etc., are external, *i.e.*, objective. Wherefore the theory that Pradhana is the cause is not consistent with reason.

A question is raised and answered:

(If you say it can be the cause) as milk and water (we say) even there (it is not so). (II. ii. 2)

(*Objection*): - Just as milk and water become curd and hailstone without being acted on by a conscious agent, so Pradhana can become the universe.

(*Answer*): - No, even there, the reason cannot hold good; for milk and water, being insentient objects, fall within the sweep of our inference. Moreover,

And because, when it is independent, the opposite state can never come about (II. ii. 3)

If the insentient being can evolve effects without being acted on by a conscious agent, then creation will be constant, and there can be no *pralaya* or dissolution, the opposite of creation. Wherefore, the insentient cannot be the cause of the universe.

It cannot even be as in the case of grass (eaten by a cow), because of failure elsewhere (II. ii. 4)

It does not stand to reason to contend that, like the grass eaten by a cow becoming milk, Pradhana, though insentient, can be the cause; for, since we find no transformation into milk in the case of grass eaten by a bull or not eaten by any being, even grass must be acted on by a conscious agent.

(If you say it is possible) as in the case of man and loadstone, (we reply) even then (it cannot be). (II. ii. 5)

(*Objection*): - The Purusha causes Pradhana to act by his mere presence, though the letter is insentient, like a lame man leading another who is blind, or like a loadstone causing iron to move. Thus there is no necessity for a conscious entity.

(*Answer*): -   Even then, it is not possible for Pradhana to act, since Purusha remains unaffected. The lame man and the loadstone do undergo a certain change by way of teaching the way or by way of being taken to the proximity of iron, and so on. Wherefore, mere presence of the immutable Purusha cannot account for Pradhana's activity.

Also because of the inexplicability of (the relation) as the main (and the subordinate) (II. ii. 6)

The Sankhyas say that the universe comes out of the Gunas which become related to each other as the main and the subordinate, when one of them gets an ascendency over the others. This relation, as the main and the subordinate, assumed to come into being at the time of creation, cannot be explained, in as much as the Gunas which attain to a state of balance during dissolution, undergo no disturbance whatever. For this reason also, the creation of the universe cannot be properly accounted for according to the theory of Pradhana.

Even when inferring to the contrary, (it is inexplicable) because of the absence of the power of intelligence (II. ii. 7)

Even if you infer that Pradhana acts otherwise than in the manner referred to, the theory will still be open to objection, in as much as, in the absence of intelligence, Pradhana is not capable of the intelligence plan (we find in the creation of the universe).

Because, even when assumed, it serves no purpose (II. ii. 8)

If any purpose has to be served by assuming Pradhana, we may assume it somehow or other. There is no purpose whatever served by the assumption. For Purusha being immutable, he cannot be affected by way of perceiving Pradhana or undergoing any other change, and therefore it is not possible to maintain that Purusha becomes subject to enjoyment and suffering by ascribing to himself the properties of Pradhana and that he attains liberation by right discrimination thereof. Wherefore, in the absence of all purpose, there is no need to assume Pradhana.

And owing to contradiction it is unsound. (II. ii. 9)

We see a thousand contradictory attributes assumed, such as that Purusha is the perceiver, the enjoyer, immutable, and so on. For this reason, too, Kapila's theory is quite unsound.

Adhikarana 2

Thus it has been shown that the doctrine of Pradhana being the cause of the universe has no support of a proper authority. Now this adhikarana proceeds to refute the theory which maintains that atoms (*paramanus*) are the cause of the universe.

What is big or possessed of length (comes out of) the short and infinitesimal ones (II. ii. 10)

Here a doubt arises as to whether the theory which maintains that the atoms are the cause of the universe is consistent with reason or not.

(*Purvapaksha*): - The doctrine of Pradhana not admitting a supreme Lord (Paramesvara) governing the universe, it is no doubt opposed to reason to maintain that Pradhana is the cause of the universe. But, the theory that atoms are the cause of the universe is supported by reason. To explain: When the universe is in a state of dissolution, on Paramesvara conceiving a desire to create, by Karma of the sentient beings is induced first activity in the motionless atoms. In virtue of this activity one atom conjoins with another atom, and from that conjunction a *dvyanuka*, *i.e.*, a molecule composed of two atoms, comes into being. Three *dvyanukas* form one *tryanuka*, and so on. In this way the whole universe is created. Thus there is no objection to the theory that atoms are the cause of the universe.

(*Siddhanta*): - As against the foregoing we hold as follows: According to the theory of Kanada, from out of short and extremely small atoms (called paramanus) are produced *tryanukas* which possess length and appreciable size, and *dvyanukas* which are short and possess the size of an atom. How is this possible? To explain: *Paramanus* are endued with the size called *parimandalya*, with the size which is smaller even than an *anu* or atom. Out of two such *paramanus* which have not the size even of an *anu* or atom is produced, as the Vaiseshika say a *dvyanuka* (two-atomed molecule) which has the size of an *anu*. So also, out of the paramanus which are short, a dvyanuka is said to be produced which has no length.

From out of three such dvyanukas, they say, is born a tryanuka which possesses length, but not the size of an atom (anu). All this is inconsistent, because it is opposed to their theory as to what takes place in the qualities of the cause. Parts of a whole, having each six sides, combine with one another and produce that whole which is bigger in size than any one of the parts. Since paramanus have no sides, they cannot combine together to produce a bigger substance. Wherefore the doctrine of paramanus is unsound.

The Sutrakara points out another inconsistency:

In either way, no activity; hence its absence. (II. ii. 11)

Because of the absence of first activity in atoms, there can be no conjunction of atoms, caused by that first activity. If the activity be independent of the ripeness of the *adrishtas* (Karmas) of the jivas, then activity may arise in the atoms even before the Jivas adrishtas become ripe. If, on the other hand, it should depend on the adrishtas of the Jivas, then it cannot be that those adrishtas produce activity in the atoms only on certain occasions. No such quality as ripeness residing in the adrishtas is ever perceived by us. On the other hand, we can say that an act becomes ripe only when and where according to the sruti enjoining the act, the act is destined to produce its effect. Those acts as to which no specific time is mentioned, become ripe in the absence of all other acts which are stronger than the act and obstruct its natural course. Adrishtas by nature, such as tend to produce effects in accordance with the acts of which they are results. Wherefore it is not possible to suppose that acts, done by the infinite number of souls, as productive of fruits of different sorts and at different times, become ripe all at one time and in one form. Hence the untenability of the doctrine of atoms as the cause of the universe.

There is again another inconsistency, as the sutrakara says:

And because it likewise (involve the fallacy of) infinality owing to the postulate of samavaya. (II. ii. 12)

A relation called *samavaya* or intimate relation is postulated. Hence an inconsistency – How? – Even in the case of samavaya, as in the case of jati (genus) and gunas (qualities) – the postulate being that these are supposed to become related to the substance by the relation of samavaya – we will have to postulate a separate relation by which samavaya may become related to the substance, and so on, infinitely. This involves the fallacy of anavastha or infinite regress. Hence another inconsistency in Kanada's doctrine.

(The members conjoined must also be) quite eternal, because, (Samavaya is constantly) present. (II. ii. 13)

It is postulated that samavaya is an eternal relation; and this is not possible unless the members related to each other by samavaya are also eternal. Thus, it would follow that the parts and the whole made up of those parts are also eternal. Wherefore the theory is unsound.

And as endued with color etc., the reverse, must be the case as we find it in experience. (II. ii. 24)

It is here postulated that paramanus possess color etc. Then they cannot be eternal; for we find that pots etc., which are possessed of color etc., are perishable. Wherefore also, the theory is unsound.

And because of inconsistency in either way (II. ii. 15)

If, to avoid the conclusion that paramanus are perishable, it be postulated that they are devoid of color etc, then it cannot be maintained that all qualities in an effect are produced by those inhering in the cause. If, again, with a view to maintain this, it be postulated that the paramanus are endued with color etc., this postulate would lead to the undesirable conclusion that they are perishable, and so on. Thus, in either case, Kanada's theory is open to objection and is therefore unsound.

Having no following it has to be aside altogether (II. ii. 16)

The Sankhya theory, though opposed to Sruti and reason, is accepted by the orthodox followers of the Vedic doctrine in some points, such as satkaryavada, the doctrine which maintains that the effect exists in the cause even before the manifestation. Kanada's theory being, on the other hand, not accepted in any of its parts, those who seek Moksha should neglect it altogether.

Adhikarana 3

In both the causal aggregate, it (the aggregation) cannot take place. (II. ii. 17)

The theory of the so called Vedic systems has been refuted. Now, the theory of the non-Vedic systems will be refuted. First the question is started as to whether the doctrine of aggregates, as propounded in the Buddhistic systems, can be upheld by reason or not.

Purvapaksha: - It is reasonable. They propound the doctrine as follows:

There are two aggregates, external and internal. The eternal aggregate comprises earth etc. The internal one comprises the mind and its functions. The whole universe consists of the two aggregates. To explain: Paramanus are the cause of the external aggregate. They are of four sorts, those of earth, of water, of light and of air. Out of these simultaneously combining together, the external aggregate is born. Of the internal aggregate the cause is the five skandhas or bodies. These Skandhas are respectively composed of forms (rupa), feelings (Vedana), ideas (Vijnana), names (sanjna) and tendencies (samskara) as perceived by the mind. The Rupa-skandha, the body of forms, is composed of sound, touch, color and the like. When manifested in thought they constitute the Vijnana-skandha, the body of ideas. The pain caused by this last forms the Vedana-skandha, the body of feelings. Devadatta and other names compose the Sanjna-skandha, the body of names. The latent impressions of these make up the Samskara-skandha, the body of tendencies. Out of these combining together, the internal aggregate is formed. Thus in the doctrine of aggregates there is no inconsistency whatever.

As against the foregoing we explain as follows: The theory that the two aggregates are the cause of the universe is untenable. They (the Buddhists) hold that everything is momentary. How is it possible for momentary things to form an aggregate? The causes existing only for one moment, they vanish as they come into being and are therefore incapable of producing any effect.

If you say that it is possible because (avidya and attachment) are the cause of each other, (we say) no, because (avidya) cannot cause aggregation (II. ii. 18)

(The Buddhist): - The avidya which regards the impermanent as permanent, and such feelings as attachment, are the cause of each other, and thus aggregation becomes possible.

(Vedantin): - No, for avidya cannot cause aggregation. The mother-o'pearl cannot actually solve the purpose of silver, by mere avidya, i.e., when the mother-o'pearl is only mistaken for silver. To one who knows the truth, the avidya vanishes then and there, and then no attachment or anything of the sort caused by avidya can possibly wise. Wherefore the theory that the aggregates are the cause of the universe cannot stand.

The sutrakara adduces another argument:

And because of the disappearance of the first at the birth of the second (II. ii. 19)

Because when the second moment of a pot comes, the first moment thereof has disappeared, and because abhava exists ever the same as the cause, everything may be produced everywhere and at all times.

If not existent, there is a contradiction of the hypothesis, if otherwise, there is a simultaneity. (II. ii. 20)

If the cause does not exist when the effect arises, then it will be contrary to the hypothesis that the sense-organs, light and such other auxiliary circumstances produce cognition. Now, if the cause were to abide till the effect is produced, then two pots* would be simultaneously seen in one. If the cause were not to abide till the effect is produced, then the contact of senses with objects will be simultaneous with the (resultant) cognition.

[* It being held that a pot as it existed at the previous moment and its idea are necessary causes for a pot and its idea to arise at a given moment.]

Cessation accompanied with an act of thought and cessation unaccompanied with an act of thought cannot be established, because there is no interruption complete.

Cessation means destruction without leaving any residue. This is not possible in either of its two alleged forms gross or subtle. For, the destruction of a pot, for instance, consists in its being reduced to the state of fragments; and thus something continues to exist when the pot is said to be destroyed. Wherefore momentariness of things cannot be established.

Because of its being objectionable in either way (II. ii. 22)

Whether it be that what has come into being is reduced to nothing, or that something comes out of nothing, in either case the theory is open to objection. For, it is not possible for anything to come out of nothing; and what comes out of nothing must itself be nothing. As the theory is open to these objections, it is untenable.

Not even as to Akasa, there being no difference whatever. (II. ii. 23)

Even akasa cannot be regarded as a nonentity, in as much as our uncontradicted experience testifies to its reality as the element where the hawk and other birds can fly.

And because of recognition (II. ii. 24)

Also because of recognition, momentariness cannot be established. "This is (the same as) that"; thus, by the relation of opposition between the two words, 'this' and 'that' we come to understand that one and the same thing can exist in the past as well as in the present. It is the contact of the objects with the senses of the man, who retains the impressions of a former experience, which has given rise to this recognition. Wherefore, as propounding such doctrines as that all things are momentary, the theory which maintains that the aggregates are the cause of the universe is quite incoherent.

Adhikarana 4

Of those who hold that external objects have an independent existence, the theory of those Buddhists who hold that the cow and the pot and the like are perceived by the senses has been refuted. Now the sutrakara proceeds to refute the theory that the existence of external objects has only to be inferred from our cognitions thereof:

Not (an attribute) of the non-existent, because it is never seen. (II. ii. 25)

Here a doubt arises as to whether the contention of some of the Buddhists that the existence of an external world is to be inferred from our cognition is consistent with reason or not.

The Vedanta-Sutras with Srikantha Bhashya

Purvapaksha: - From a variety found in the cognitions, the cogniser has only to infer a corresponding variety in the external world which impresses its form on the cognition and then disappears.

Siddhanta: - This does not hold good; for, an external object is admitted to exist but for a moment; and we have seen nowhere any attribute of a non-existent object which has vanished out of sight attaching itself to something else.

Then even the indifferent would attain the end (II. ii. 26)

It being admitted that everything is momentary, it would follow that one performs an act while another reaps the fruit thereof; so that even to those who make no effort at all everything will accrue. Thus this theory is very hard to explain.

Adhikarana 5.

(The external object cannot be) non-existent, because we perceive it. (II. ii. 27)

Here a doubt arises as to whether the pure Vijnanavada is consistent with reason or not.

Purvapaksha: - It is reasonable. For Vijnana (cognition) in its various forms is alone real. External objects are not real, in as much as, in svapna, we find all experience brought about by the mind alone in the absence of external objects. Similarly, the Jagrat experience can be explained. Wherefore Vijnana alone is real.

As against the foregoing we hold as follows: It is not possible to maintain that external objects do not exist; for the external object enters into consciousness as its object which the perceiver has to take note of as expressed in the words "I know it." When consciousness is spoken of a putting on the form of an object, it simply means that the person is thereby enabled to know the particular object as it is and act upon that knowledge.

As to the contention that, on the analogy of svapna, the Jagrat experience is void, the Sutrakara says:

On account of a difference, it is not like Svapna etc. (II. ii. 28)

Unlike svapna and the like, the Jagrat consciousness is not illusory, in as much as the latter differs from the former in so far as there is no defect in the sense-organ and the Jagrat consciousness is never falsified by subsequent experience. Wherefore it cannot be that Vijnana alone is real.

The Sutrakara adduces another argument:

There can be (no cognition without an object) as it has never been so found. (II. ii. 29)

No cognition can possibly exist without a corresponding object, since such cognition is never met with in experience. It is quite possible that even the Svapnic cognition has an object corresponding to it.

Hence the incongruity of the theory that cognitions alone are real.

Adhikarana 6

And because of its incongruity in every way (II. ii. 30)

The question raised in this adhikarana for settlement is whether the doctrine that everything is void is reasonable or not.

Purvapaksha: - It is reasonable. It may be explained as follows. The universe as a whole is not existent, because it is falsified by other experience. Neither is it non-existent, because we are conscious of it. Neither is it both existent and non-existent, as such a connection involves a contradiction. We cannot say it is neither existent nor non-existent, since such a conception is impossible. On the other hand all is a mere void, not coming under any one of the four alternatives. Its appearance as an object of sensuous perception is due to *samvriti*, avidya or illusion. Hence the soundness of the theory of Nihilism.

Siddhanta: - The doctrine that everything is void is untenable – Why? – For, as when we speak of the universe being existent, so when we speak of it as non-existent or something else, the subject spoken of cannot be a non-entity; and accordingly the words *sat* and *asat*, existent and non-existent, as well as the ideas corresponding to them, all refer to a really existing entity spoken of as subject to the mutually opposed conditions of existence and non-existence.

As to the contention that the fact of the universe becoming an object of sensuous perception is a creation of *samvriti* or illusion, it is ridiculous to advance any such statement. If all is void, who is subject to the illusion? To whom does the illusion present itself? Therefore the theory that all is void is opposed to all experience.

Adhikarana 7

We have done with the Buddhists. The doctrine of the Jainas is refuted as follows: -

It cannot be because of its impossibility in one. (II. ii. 31)

The Jainas, indeed, explain contradictory states in one and the same thing by the logic called *Saptabhangi-naya*, or "the system of the seven paralogisms." The questioned is whether this doctrine of theirs is reasonable or not.

Their theory runs as follows: There are two *padarthas* or predicaments, *Jiva* and *Ajiva*, soul and non-soul. Jiva is sentient, of the size of the body, and composed of parts. Ajiva again is of six classes: one class comprises such things as trees, mountains, and the like; the remaining five classes are *Asrana, Samvara, Nirjara, Bandha* and *Moksha*. Asrava is the aggregate of the senses, so called because it is by their means that jiva moves towards external objects. Samvara comprises *aviveka*, non-discrimination, etc., so called because *viveka* or discrimination is thereby concealed. Nirjara is the self-mortification, such as the plucking out of the hair and the getting on a hot stone, so called because desire, anger and the like is there by completely brought to decay. *Bandha* or bondage is the series of births brought about by the eight forms of *Karman* or action, - the four sinful acts of injury and the four virtuous acts of non-injury. Moksha is the incessant upward march of the Jiva when liberated from those acts. These seven predicaments should be determined by the logic of *Saptabhangi-naya* which is stated as follows: "May be, it is," "May be, it is not," "May be, it is and it is not," "May be, it is not explicable," "May be, it is and yet not explicable," "May be, it is not, and not explicable," "May be, it is and it is not, and not explicable." "May be" here means somewhat. Accordingly, the seven predicaments are established on the logic of *Sapta-bhangi-naya*. This is unreasonable; for it is impossible for one and the same thing both to be and not to be, to be both eternal and non-eternal, to be both different and not different. Such mutually opposed conditions of being and non-being, of clay-hump, of pot, and pot-shreds, which come into being one after another, can never co-exist simultaneously in a substance. The Jain doctrine, therefore, is full of contradictions.

So also is the Non-universality of Atman. (II. ii. 32)

So also, the non-universality of Atman is incongruous. If Atman be of the size of the body, it will follow that he will be wanting in some parts when passing from a big body to a smaller one. It is, therefore, quite unreasonable to maintain that Atman is of the same size as the body.

Nor can the incongruity be averted by supporting a fresh condition, because of change etc. (II. ii. 33)

The foregoing incongruity cannot be explained away by supposing that Atman assumes a smaller form afresh; for, then, it would lead to the undesirable conclusion that Atman is subject to change etc.

Both being eternal is the persistency of the final (size), there is no difference. (II. ii. 34)

The final size, the size in the state of moksha, persisting the same, it is the natural size of Atman. Thus Atman as well as his size being alike eternal, the size must be the same in the preceding state also. When Atman assumes the sizes of the different bodies, imperfectness is inevitable. Wherefore, by the theory that one and the same thing both is and is not and so on, and by the theory that Atman is of the size of the body, the Jain system is quite full of contradictions.

Adhikarana 8

The Lord (Pati) (cannot be a mere efficient cause), because of an incongruity. (II. ii. 35)

The Tantrikas, the so called orthodox, those who profess to follow the Paramesvara's Agamas, without knowing the real import of their teaching, hold that Pati, the Paramesvara, is a mere efficient cause, though, according to Sruti, He is both the (material and the efficient) cause of the universe. Now, a doubt arises whether this theory is reasonable or not.

Now, the *Purvapaksha* may be stated as follows: The potter and others, who are, not of course, the material cause, becomes the agent as merely wielding the stick etc. So, too, the Isvara, a by-stander, is the mere *Nimitta* or efficient cause. Maya is the Upadana or material cause; Saktis are the instruments. Otherwise, if Isvara be the *Upadana* or material cause like clay etc., it will follow that He is likewise subject to change. Wherefore, Paramesvara is merely an efficient cause.

As against the foregoing we hold as follows: It is not reasonable to maintain even that Isvara, the Lord (Pati), is a mere efficient cause, because the theory is incongruous as opposed to Sruti and reasoning.

The Sutrakara proceeds to show how it is opposed to reasoning.

And because of the incongruity of rulership (II. ii. 36)

It cannot be explained how the Paramesvara who has no body can act upon Maya, the material cause. In ordinary experience it is found that an embodied being alone such as the potter can operate on a material cause such as clay-lump. The analogy therefore, of the potter does not hold good. When Maya is not operated upon, there can be no such Isvara as has been contended for, and thus we are led to the Sankhya theory, there being no use of supposing the existence of Isvara. Wherefore, it cannot be that the Paramesvara is a mere Efficient cause.

An objection is raised and answered as follows:

If you hold (that He is without a body) like the sense-organs, (we say) no, because He would be subject to enjoyment etc. (II. ii. 37)

(*Objection*): - Nobody is necessary for Him in operating upon the material cause. Just as a sense-organ, though having no body, yet operates upon the physical body, so does Isvara operate upon Pradhana.

(*Answer*): - No; for, He would be subject to enjoyment of pleasure and pain pertaining to Pradhana Just as Atman, who has no body, becomes subject to pleasure and pain pertaining to the body, while operating upon the body, so, too, Paramesvara will become subject to pleasure and pain pertaining to Pradhana while operating upon Pradhana. Wherefore, Isvara is no mere efficient cause.

Finitude and limited knowledge, too. (II. ii. 38)

(*Objection*): - Like the potter, Paramesvara has a body; and as the potter operates upon a lump of clay standing a part, so does He operates upon the material cause, standing apart from it.

(*Answer*): - No. If so, like the samsarin, Isvara, the Lord, would be a finite being and would not be an omniscient Being. As He would thus be subject to pleasure and pain, and so on, Isvara cannot be one who operates on Pradhana.

(*Objection*): - Though operating upon Pradhana, Paramesvara would not be subject to pleasure and pain, in as much as the Sruti declares that "the other, not eating, merely witnesses." * [* Mund. Up. 3-1]

(*Answer*): - If so, we should not rely on the strength of reasoning; we should, on the other hand, look to Sruti alone. Accordingly it should be admitted that Paramesvara is also the upadana or material cause of the universe, as declared in the following passages: "that Atman made Himself (into the universe), of Himself." † [† Tait. Up. 2-7] "May I be born many." ‡ [‡ Chha. Up. 6-2] "All is verily Rudra." § [§ Mahana. Up. 16] Though Paramesvara is thus both the efficient and the material cause of the universe, yet He is not subject to change as we may understand from the sruti which declares that He is "without parts, without action." || [|| Svc. Up. 6-19.] In the Vayu Samhita, we are told that, in the universe comprising Maya and so on, Siva Himself with His Sakti or potentialities forms the material cause in the following words:

"Sakti was the first-born, followed by the Santyatitapada. Thence came Maya; thence Avyakta. From the Lord Siva endued with Sakti, the Santyatitapada was born, and thence the Santipada, in succession."

Again it says:

"From Sakti to the Earth, all is born from the Siva-tattva. By him alone is all pervaded, just as a pot is pervaded by clay."

From this we understand that the universe is pervaded by Siva, the material cause, as the pot is pervaded by clay. And on the authority of the Agamas it may be held without fear of contradiction that Paramesvara is both the efficient and the material cause of the universe, as declared in the following passage:

"It is the Divine Being Himself, the self-conscious Atman, who, like a Yogin, by His will manifests externally all the things which existed within himself, without resorting to any material cause."

Former Acharyas (teachers) maintain that this Adhikarana is intended to set aside the theory, advanced in parts of Siva-Agamas, that Siva, the Parabrahman, is a mere efficient cause. On the contrary, we see no difference between the Veda and the Sivagama. Even the Vedas may properly be called Sivagama, Siva being the author thereof. Accordingly

Sivagama is twofold, one being intended for the three (higher castes), the other being intended for all. The Vedas are intended for people of the three castes, and the other for all. Siva alone is the author of both. That He is the author of the Veda is declared in the following passages of Sruti and Smriti:

"He is the Lord of all Vidyas." * [* Mahana-Up. 44.]

"(The Veda) is the breath of the Mighty Being." † [† Bri. Up. 6-5-11.]

"Of these eighteen Vidyas of various paths, the original author is the wise Sulapani Himself. So says the Sruti."

Elsewhere also the Paramesvara Himself is thus spoken of. Wherefore, the author being the same, both teach the same thing and are alike authoritative.

Or, the question may be viewed thus: - The Vedas and the Agamas are both authoritative in as much as we find, in both alike, Brahman, Pranava, the Panchakshari, Prasada and other mantras; mention of Pasu, Pati, Pasa and other things; such lofty Dharmas as the smearing of ashes, the wearing of tripundra, worship of Linga, the wearing of rudraksha, and all other such things. The author being the same, and both expounding the same thing, they are not opposed to one another. Wherefore we maintain that this adhikarana refers to the Yoga-Smriti of Hiranyagarbha which speaks of Isvara as the mere efficient cause. Therefore this adhikarana is properly intended to overthrow the Hiranyagarbhagama.

Or, as someone says, there is nothing objectionable (in this adhikarana being made to refer to Sivagama) in as much as it is intended to remove an incidental doubt arising with reference to the teaching of the Sivagama itself, just as the doubt concerning the origin of akasa will be removed (Vide. II. iii. 1) Anyhow, our conclusion is that Isvara is not a mere efficient cause.

Adhikarana 9

Because of the impossibility of birth. (II. ii. 39)

The Pancharatra system was revealed b Vasudeva. It speaks of Jiva as being born, and so on. A doubt arises as to whether such a thing is possible or not.

Purvapaksha: - It is possible. For, what has been revealed by the Blessed Lord, Vasudeva, must be an authority. The theory therein expounded may be stated as follows: The Blessed Lord, Vasudeva, is one alone, and is Paramatman, the Supreme Spirit. From him is born Jiva, known by the name of Sankarshana. From Jiva comes Manas, called Pradyumna, and from Manas comes Ahankara or Egoism called Aniruddha. These four groups form the essence of everything. Wherefore, Vasudeva being superior to Hiranyagarbha and all the rest, his revelation must be authoritative, and all that is thus taught therein must be true.

(*Siddhanta*): - As against the foregoing we hold as follows: This Sastra, which speaks of Jiva being born and so on, is not authoritative; for, the birth of Jiva is an impossibility, since then it would follow that deeds go for nothing and that something accrues from what is not done. When someone who has done acts of virtue and sin dies away at the time of *pralaya*, then, (at the time of creation), some other jiva reaps the fruit. Thus something accrues to a jiva from what he has not done; and what the other has done is lost to him. Wherefore the Sastra which speaks of the birth of jivas is no authority.

The Sutrakara proceeds to point out another incongruity.

Neither can the sense-organ come out of the agent. (II. ii. 40)

It is said that from Jiva called Sankarshana, manas called Pradyumna was born. It is impossible that a sense-organ should be born from Jiva, the agent, in as much as the sense-organ, which is evolved out of Prakriti or matter, cannot have been evolved out of consciousness.

(Suppose the opponent explains as follows):

Or, no denial thereof, as they become consciousness etc. (II. ii. 41)

'Consciousness' means jiva. Here jivas etc., are not spoken of as having birth. On the other hand, Sankarshana etc., are said to become jivas etc. To become jivas etc., to govern them from within. Accordingly the authority of the Sastra should not be denied. Thus explains the opponent. (This objection is answered as follows):

And because of its rejection. (II. ii. 42)

Though the mention of the birth of Jivas is thus explained away, the system of Pancharatra cannot be accepted, because it is rejected as teaching that the doctrine of Isvara which is opposed to the teaching of Sruti conduces to moksha, and as inculcating the duty of having certain symbols branded on the body. Wherefore, the system of Pancharatra is inconsistent. And it is specially prohibited in passages such as the following:

"In Pancharatra or in Buddhism, or in Kalamukha, by Ye initiated with faith, O dregs of the Brahmanas."

Being thus rejected, the system of Pancharatra is no authority.

(*Objection*): - In such passages as "Purusha is verily Rudra," Paramesvara Himself is spoken of as Purusha, as Vasudeva; and by knowing and worshipping Him, one will gradually attain to the goal to Paramesvara, as the Sruti says. If the Pancharatra, which treats of His worship, be no authority, then it would follow that He should not be worshipped.

(*Answer*): - Though, as contradicting the Sruti, the Pancharatra is no authority, how does it affect Him? For, it is possible to worship Him in the way pointed out by the Sruti. Hence no inconsistency whatever.

End of the Second *Pada*.

THIRD PADA

Adhikarana 1.

All the course of reasoning which has been adopted by the rival systems of thought has been set aside. Again, in the remaining part of the adhyaya, the Sutrakara proceeds to explain apparent contradictions in the Siddhanta itself:

Akasa is not (born), there being no sruti. (II. iii. 1)

As having no parts, akasa may seem to be unborn; and therefore a doubt arises as to whether the birth of akasa is reasonable or not.

(*Purvapaksha*): It seems that akasa is not born. For, it is not so declared in the Sruti. To explain: In the Chhandogya-Upanishad, creation of elements commencing with light is declared in the words. "Existent alone. My dear, this at first was ... It created light." There no mention is made of the birth of akasa.

As to the passage "from Atman, akasa was born," occurring in the Taittiriya, it must be understood only in a figurative sense; for it is difficult to trace the material cause etc., which could give rise to akasa. Wherefore, akasa is not born any more than Jiva.

As against the foregoing, we hold as follows:

But there is (II. iii. 2)

Akasa has a birth, because the Sruti says "Thence, from the Atman, is akasa born," and so on. But Atman has no birth, because it is denied in the words. "The knower is not born, He does not die." There is no Sruti which denies the birth of akasa. Wherefore akasa is born.

As to the assertion that the passage speaking of the birth of akasa should be understood in a figurative sense, the Sutrakara explains the opponent's position as follows:

It is figurative, because of the impossibility and the Sruti (II. iii. 3)

Because the Sruti declares that light was first created in the words, "It created light," * the passage "Akasa was born" † should be understood in a figurative sense, in as much as it is impossible that the akasa which has no parts can ever be born, and that the sruti declares it to be eternal in the words, "the air and the ether, both these are imperishable." ‡ [* Chha. Up. 6-2; † Taitt. Up. 2-1; ‡ Bri. Up. 4-3]

And like word 'Brahma' it is possible for one word to be used both ways.

It is possible for one word 'born' to be used in a figurative sense when predicated of akasa, and in its primary meaning when predicated of others, though used in one and the same context, as it is possible when a word is repeated in two different passages in the sruti.

The word 'Brahman', for instance is used in a figurative sense when spoken of as Prakriti or the material cause, in the following passage:

"Thence, this Brahman (the Prakriti) is born as name, form and food." § [§ Mundaka Up. 1-1]

And the same word is used in its primary sense when repeated in the following passage.

"By meditation Brahman grows." § [§ Mundaka Up. 1-1]

So also here. Wherefore it does not stand to reason to hold that akasa is born.

Now follows the refutation of the opponent's position.

The original proposition can be upheld by non-distinctness (II. iii. 5)

"Whereby what is not heard becomes heard." || [|| Mund. Up. 1-1] This proposition that from a knowledge of the one comes a knowledge of the whole can be maintained only when the akasa etc. are not distinct from Brahman as being produced out of Brahman. Therefore it cannot be that the word "born" is used in a figurative sense, since it would lead to the giving up of the original proposition. The passage should be so construed as not to militate against the original proposition.

From texts (II. iii. 6)

Light is regarded as the first object of creation simply because akasa is not mentioned in the Sruti "It created light." This cannot prevent one from holding that akasa has a birth as declared in the passage, "from Atman akasa was born."

The division, however, is meant for the whole creation, as in ordinary speech. (II. iii. 7)

"All this is made up of this Atman." From these words, we may understand that even akasa etc., are to be regarded as created; and therefore we are to conclude that the mention of objects of creation from light onwards points to the whole created existence. In ordinary speech, for example, a man says that he has ten children and then speaks of the birth of a few only of them. So, too, here. Wherefore it is quite reasonable to maintain that akasa had a birth.

Adhikarana 2

Thereby the air has been explained. (II. iii. 9)

In the Sutra II. iii. 10, the Sutrakara is going to speak of light; and accordingly, the air is separately considered here.

A doubt arises as to whether, like akasa, the air has a birth or not.

(*Purvapaksha*): - The air has no birth; for, in the Chhandogya-Upanishad, creation commences with light, and no creation of the air is spoken of; and in the Brihadaranyaka-Upanishad it is said to have no birth in the words. "The air is a being which never disappears." * On all accounts, the air is not born. [* Br. Up. 3-5-22]

(*Siddhanta*): - As against the foregoing we hold as follows: Though, in the Chhandogya-Upanishad, the air is not said to have been born, yet on the principle that we may understand in one place what has been declared in another place on the same subject; the birth of the air which has been spoken of in the Taittiriya-Upanishad may be taken to have been declared in the Chhandogya-Upanishad as well. The words that "this being never disappears" used with reference to the air are meant as a mere praise, as it occurs in a section treating of the contemplation (upasana) of the air. Wherefore, the air, too, has a birth.

Adhikarana 3

The existent has no birth indeed, because it cannot be explained. (II. iii. 9)

It has been shown that from Brahman, the Existent, akasa etc. have been born, as the sruti says: "The Existent alone, my dear, this at first was." * [* Chha. Up. 6-2.] Now a doubt arises as to whether Brahman, the Existent, the cause of all, Himself takes His birth from some cause, or not.

(*Purvapaksha*): - Now, it is maintained that Brahman, too, has a birth, just as the akasa, which is a cause, has a birth. Only it being declared that "the Existent at first was," it had its birth before all objects of creation. If you ask what its cause is, we say it is the non-existent, because the sruti says "Non-existent this at first was; thence verily was born the Existent." * [* Chha. Up. 6-2.] Therefore, Brahman, too, the Existent is born.

(*Siddhanta*): - Brahman is not born; for it is emphatically declared that Siva, Brahman, alone was in the following passages:

"The Existent alone, my dear, this at first was, one alone without a second." * [* Chha. Up. 6-2.]

"When there was no darkness, no day nor night, no existence and non-existence, Siva alone was, isolated from all." § [§ Svet. Up. 4-18.]

He has therefore no birth, as the existence of all else is thus denied. All else has a birth, since the contrary is impossible.

(*Objection*): - Just as Brahman is declared to be the cause of all, so the sruti speaks of something else as the cause of Brahman in the following words:

"Non-existent alone this at first was; thence verily the existent was born." † [† Tai. Up. 2-7.]

Thus the non-existent is the cause of the existent.

(*Answer*): - It is wrong to say so, because it is denied in the words "How can the existent be, born from the non-existent." ‡ [‡ Chha. Up. 6-2] If the existent should be born out of the existent, it would involve the fallacious view that a thing is based in itself. Wherefore Brahman alone the Existent has no birth; while all else has a birth, because, otherwise, the proposition that all becomes known when the One has been known becomes untenable.

Adhikarana 4

Hence (comes) light, so indeed, it says. (II. iii. 10)

Here a doubt arises as to whether the air and other objects of creation are born of Brahman directly, or of the causes which immediately precede them.

(*Purvapaksha*): - Each of them is born of the cause immediately preceding it. To explain: From the scriptural passage. "From akasa is the air born." * [* Taitt. Up. 2-1.] It is seen that the air is born of akasa, not of Brahman directly. So, also, light is born of the air. Accordingly, the Sruti says "Light is born of the air."

Waters. (II. Iii. 11)

"From fire comes waters:" † in these words the Sruti says that waters, too, come from fire. [† Ibid.]

Earth (II. Iii. 12)

"From waters comes earth:" * this Sruti declares that earth comes from waters alone. Wherefore the elements (bhutas) are not born of Brahman directly. [* Ibid.]

Because of the section, color, and other passages (II. iii. 13)

In the Chhandogya also, it is earth that is spoken of as 'food' in the passage "they created food;" for, the section treats of creation of elements (bhutas), and the Sruti speaks of the color in the words, "The black color pertains to the food;" † and there is a distinct Sruti, "from waters (was born) earth." Wherefore it is earth that is born of waters. On this principle, Brahman is not directly the cause of all, but it is only indirectly that He is their cause.

Siddhanta is stated as follows:

He (is the cause) verily because of His characteristic mark, namely, His act of willing (II. iii. 14)

It is indeed from Brahman alone that all the elements take their birth. Accordingly in the passage beginning with the words "From him, from this Atman verily, was akasa born," ‡ [‡ Taitt. Up. 2-1] it is not declared that the elements beginning with air and ending with earth are each born of that which just precedes it; on the other hand, it is declared that it is from Brahman, the cause, assuming the form of akasa etc, that all the succeeding effects such as air are produced, each in its turn. Thus it is Siva alone, the Paramatman, who is the direct generator of all elements; for, as in the passage "It (the Existent) willed 'may I become many'", so in the passages "That light willed 'may I become many,'", and "those waters willed" 'May I become many,"* [* Chha. Up. 6-2] there is His characteristic mark, namely, the act of willing. It is from Brahman assuming the form of Sadasiva, etc., from the Atman dwelling in sound etc., that air are born, as declared in the following passage:

> "Sadasiva is of the form of sound, Isvara is of the form of touch; Rudra is of the form of light; Janardana is of the form of sapidity itself; the Four-faced (Brahma) is of the form of smell; these are the five forms."

These, verily, Sadasiva etc., designated as the five Brahmans, the Atmans dwelling in the five elements, constitute the body of the Parabrahman. From Parabrahman, verily, embodied in the five Brahmans, proceed the creation etc., of the universe. These, Sadasiva etc., having become the five elements, are born of Paramatman.

(*Objection*): - The passages such as "akasa was born," speak of the birth of the elements alone; creation of Sadasiva etc., is not directly spoken of.

(*Answer*): - It is in fact declared. It has to be understood from other Srutis. Accordingly, the birth of Brahma etc., as well as of the sense-organs is declared along with that of the elements in the Atharvasikha as follows:

> "One should contemplate Isana; all this should be contemplated (as Isana). From Him they are born, Brahma, Vishnu, Rudra and Indra, and all the sense-organs, along with the elements. The Cause of causes is not the contemplator; the Cause is ever to be contemplated, He who is endued with all powers, the Lord of all, Sambhu who dwells in the midst of akasa (of the heart)."

It is thus declared that Sambhu should be contemplated in the middle of the supreme akasa as the cause of causes. Hence the conclusion that the birth of all effects proceeds directly from Brahman assuming the forms of the various causes.

Adhikarana 5

And the order contrary to this (order of creation) can also be explained. (II. iii. 15)

Here a doubt arises as to whether the order of creation indicated in the preceding adhikarana is reasonable or not.

Purvapaksha: It is not so indeed. For, in the Mundaka-Upanishad, it is declared that prana etc., are born before akasa etc., in the following words:

> "Hence is born prana, manas, and all the sense-organs; akasa, air, light water, and earth which maintains all." * [* Mundaka-Up. 2-3]

And in the Atharvasikha, a simultaneous birth of Brahma etc., as well as of elements and sense-organs is declared in the words, "They are born, Brahma, Vishnu, Rudra and Indra, and all the sense sense-organs, along with the elements." Wherefore it is held that the foregoing order of creation of akasa etc., is not reasonable.

Siddhanta: - The foregoing factor of creation is quite reasonable. In the words "Manas, indeed, my dear, is made up of food (earth), prana is made up of water, and speech is made up of light," † [† Chhandogya-Up. 6-8] the Upanishad teaches that prana etc., is made up of elements, so that they are comprehended in the elements and therefore no separate order of creation need be mentioned in their case. Brahma etc. are said to be born simultaneously with the elements because the former are embodied in the latter and are therefore comprehended in them. Wherefore there is no inconsistency whatever in the foregoing order.

If you say that the intellect and manas come between them in order, (we say) no, because they are all alike. (II. iii. 16)

(Objection): - The Mundaka sruti declares, indeed, that the sense-organs and manas are successively born midway between prana and the elements; and this is pointed to by the sruti describing the elements – such as "ether, air. Light" – as have been created in the same order in which they are said to be created in another sruti. Wherefore the Mundaka-sruti also points to a definite order of creation.

(*Answer*): - No, for the words "Hence is born," have to be construed alike separately along with all entities beginning with akasa and ending with earth. Therefore, Isvara alone is the cause of all. Hence the puranic saying:

"All things beginning with Sakti and ending with earth are born from the principle of Siva. The whole is pervaded by that one Being, just as a pot is pervaded by clay."

The existence of a definite order, too, points to the birth of all from the principle of Siva. Wherefore it is proper to maintain that Brahman is the cause of all.

Adhikarana 6

The designation of Brahman by words denoting the moving and the unmoving objects is not secondary, because of His having cherished the idea of becoming those objects (II. iii. 17)

In a former section it was shown that Brahman is spoken of as akasa etc. This forms the subject of discussion here.

A doubt arises as to whether the words designating things animate and inanimate, moving and unmoving, is directly applicable to Brahman or not.

(Purvapaksha): - It cannot be directly applied to Brahman, in as much as a word designation one thing cannot be directly applied to another. To explain: in the expressions such as "The sun is the sacrificial post" * [* Taitt. Brahmana 2-1-5.] and "the sacrificer is the stone" † [† Taitt. Brahmana 3-3-9.] The sacrificial post etc., are spoken of as the sun etc., merely because of some resemblance such as similarity in form, but not directly. Here also, in such expressions as "That light willed," Brahman, the sentient Being dwelling in light etc., is merely indicated indirectly by the words 'light' etc., in as much as the insentient light cannot possess the power of willing; just as it is in the case of the expression "the sofas (*i.e.*, people occupying the sofas) are crying." Therefore, it is only by a figure of speech that Brahman dwelling in akasa is spoken of as akasa etc.

Against the foregoing we hold as follows: The designation of Brahman by words applicable to moving and unmoving objects of creation is not secondary; on the other hand, they are directly applicable to Brahman; for, for the differentiation of names and forms of all things, Brahman is said to have cherished the idea of entering into them as their respective Atman, as their indwelling soul, as the following sruti declares:

> "Of these beings there are three germs, and three only, the egg-born, the womb-born, and the earth-born. That Divine Being willed, "Ah! I will myself enter these three Divine entities in the form of this live, as their Atman, and differentiate name and form." * [* Chhandogya-Up. 6-3.]

The sacrificial post and the like cannot be spoken of as the sun etc., directly, in as much as there is no reason for it. In the case of the sofas, the people lying therein cannot be directly spoken of as the sofas because they merely abide in them. But here, in as much as Brahman has entered into the universe as its very Atman, He can be directly spoken of by the word denoting it. Atman for instance, who has entered into the body of a Brahmin and so on is directly spoken of as a Brahmin and so on; otherwise, the sacraments of *upanayana* and the like enjoined in the words "one should initiate a Brahmin of eight years"† [† Gautama-Dharmasutras 8-23] would apply to the body alone, and it would follow that Atman is not regenerated by the sacrament, and then the text, - namely, "He who has undergone these forty sacraments and who is endued with the eight attributes of Atman will attain unity with Brahman;" ‡ [‡ Ibid.] – which holds out a certain result to the Atman who has passed through the sacraments, would be meaningless. Moreover, such injunctions as "let the Brahmin sacrifice," would be vain. Therefore Brahman is directly designated by the words denoting all moving and unmoving objects of creation into whose bodies He has entered.

Adhikarana 7

Atman is not (born), as the Sruti says, and because of his eternality as declared by them (Srutis) (II. iii. 18)

In a former section, Akasa etc., are said to have been born directly from Brahman, Here a doubt arises as to whether, on the same principle, jiva also is born to Brahman or not.

(*Purvapaksha*): - Jiva is born of Brahman; for the sruti declares emphatically that Brahman alone existed prior to creation and that there was neither the existent nor the non-existent, in the following words:

"When there was no darkness, neither day nor night, neither the existent nor the non-existent, then was Siva alone." § [§ Svetasvatara-Up. 4-18.]

"One alone, secondless." * [* Chha.-Up. 6-2.]

Therefore jiva is born of Brahman at the time of creation. The illustration by sparks of fire is also consonant with the birth of jivas, the sruti declaring as follows:

"Just as from fire, small sparks proceed in a number, just so from this Atman, all lives, all worlds, all Devas, all beings, all Atmans proceed in a number." † [† Bri-Up. 4-1-10.]

Wherefore as sparks are born of fire, so are Atmans born of Brahman.

(*Siddhanta*): - As against the foregoing we hold as follows: Atman is not born; for the sruti declares, "the Intelligent has neither birth nor death;" ‡ [‡ Katha-Up. 2-18.] and he is also declared to be eternal in the following srutis:

"The eternal among the eternals, the sentient among the sentients." § [§ Katha-Up. 5-13.]

"Knowing and unknowing are the two, the unborn, the Mighty and the weak." ‖ [‖ Sveta-Up. 1-9.]s

"The emphatic declaration of the unity of Brahman prior to creation is due to the Jiva as well as the insentient matter having been resolved into Brahman, and to their names and forms having been consequently undifferentiated, but not the non-existence of jivas in their essential nature. The Sruti illustrating creation by sparks of fire only points to their manifestation in name and form, but not to their birth; otherwise it would involve the fallacy of one's deeds being destroyed without yielding their fruits, and to other such fallacies. Wherefore jiva is not born of Brahman.

Adhikarana 8

Hence is he a knower. (II. iii. 19)

In the preceding section it has been shown that Jiva is eternal. Again, a doubt arises as to whether he has knowledge inherent in him or not.

(*Purvapaksha*): - Jiva is not endued with knowledge inherent in his nature. For, in the sruti "The two, the one knowing and other unknowing," it is declared that jiva is ignorant. Therefore quite unknowing is jiva who is mere consciousness (chaitanya) in essence. But in virtue of the power of Maya, he is endued with the body and sense-organs and is bound by egoism, which makes him regard himself to be a man or a god and perceive such objects as a cloth and a pot to be external to himself. Thus he passes from world to world. As possessing knowledge only in the state of samsara, jiva is not a knower in his essential nature. Otherwise, how can he attain salvation?

(*Siddhanta*): - As against the foregoing we hold as follows. This Atman (jiva) is a knower. Manas is the knowledge constituting his essential attribute, as may be seen from the following srutis:

"He who feels 'I smell this,' he is Atman,...he sees by manas those objects of desire which are in the region of Brahman and is delighted." * [* Chha-Up. 8-12.]

"Manas is his divine eye." * [*Chha-Up. 8-12.]

Wherefore he is a knower in himself.

As to the contention that the virtue of the power of Maya, he is a knower in the state of samsara, we admit that it is true. By association with material manas, jiva indeed transmigrates as the enjoyer of pleasure and pain, as the knower identifying himself with the body and the egoism, while his inherent power of intelligence is overpowered by the power of Maya. But, when he shakes off the connection with the triple dirt by knowledge and constant contemplation of Brahman, then he becomes equal to Brahman, and, with his inherent unsurpassed attribute to knowledge then manifesting itself, he is said to be liberated.

Moreover, 'the sruti,' "Delighting in prana and enjoying in manas," * [* Taitt-Up. 1-6] gives us to understood that Brahman has a natural sense-organ in the form of manas by which He perceives His own unsurpassed bliss. From this we may understand that the liberated jiva, as possessed of similar attributes, is endued with manas, an internal sense-organ quite independent of the external organs of sensation, and which is a means of enjoying his own inherent bliss. The sruti which speaks of the two as "the knowing and the unknowing" implies only that jiva is of limited knowledge. It declares that Paramesvara who is not a samsarin is omniscient. Wherefore, while in samsara, Atman is of limited knowledge and when liberated he is omniscience. Thus Atman is a knower.

Adhikarana 9

(As the sruti speaks of his) departure, going and returning, (Atman is very small). (II. iii. 20)

As the Atman, who has been proved to be a knower in the preceding section, is declared to have a departure and so on, he must be very small (*anu*) in size. Here a doubt arises as to whether this holds good or not.

(*Purvapaksha*): - He cannot be very small (anu), As the Sruti "This Atman is, indeed, great and unborn" † [† Bri-Up. 6-4.] shows that jiva is all-pervading, and as the sruti "I have surpassed the whole universe" ‡ [‡ Taitt-Up. 3-20.] shows that, by pervading all, he has surpassed the whole universe; this Atman must be all-pervading from all standpoint of view.

(*Siddhanta*): - As against the foregoing we hold as follows: This Atman is anu, *i.e.*, extremely small, because the sruti speaks of his departures, his going and returning. His departure is thus declared: "With the flash, that Atman departs." § [§ Bri-Up. 6-4.] "His going is declared in the following words; those who depart from this world go to the moon." ‖ [‖

Kaushitaki-Upanishad. 1-2] His return is thus spoken of: "From that world they come back to this world of action." ¶ [¶ Bri-Up. 5-4.] If jiva be all-pervading, his departure, going and returning cannot be explained.

It is true that Atman, though all-pervading, may be said to depart when separated from the body; but going and returning cannot thus be explained as the sutrakara says:

And (because) the last two (can be accomplished) by himself (II. iii. 21)

Atman must be extremely small, in as much as the last two, namely, going and returning, can be accomplished only by himself. As to the sruti "Atman is great and unborn," it occurs in a section treating of Isvara, and does not therefore refer to jiva. As to his surpassing the whole universe by his all pervasiveness; it has to be explained as referring to the liberated jiva whose sakti or intelligence coming into manifestation on the removal of the veil of dirt, sends out its rays everywhere. Therefore Atman is quite small.

Sutrakara raises an objection and answers:

(If you say that He is) not small because of the sruti teaching the contrary, (we say) no, because it is a different section. (II. iii. 22)

(*Objection*): - The sruti "That Atman is indeed great and unborn" shows that jiva is not small.

(Answer): - No; because this sruti occurs in a section treating of Paramesvara, commencing thus:

"He who knows and contemplates Atman, etc." * [* Bri-Up. 6-4-13.]

And because of the very word and measure (II. iii. 23)

He is spoken of as *anu*, as extremely small, in the following sruti:

"This extremely small Atman can be known by the mind he in whom prana has entered five-fold." † [† Mundaka-Up. 3-1-9.]

And his measure is also given in the following sruti:

"The lower one is indeed known to be in size like the point of the iron thong at the end of a whip." ‡ [‡ Sveta-Up. 5-8.]

Thus Atman is extremely small. *Measuring* consists in citing a thing which is like an atom and declaring that Atman is of that size.

If jiva be very small, whence then is the experience of a feeling all over the body? The Sutrakara says:

There is no incongruity as in the case of sandal (II. iii. 24)

Just as a drop of sandal ointment, though remaining in one place, yet produces extending over the whole body, so too, here there is nothing incongruous.

Again, the sutrakara raises an objection and answers:

If you say (that the two cases are not similar) because there is a special abode (in the case of sandal) (we say) no, because we admit it (in the case of jiva) indeed (jiva is said to abide) in the heart. (II. iii. 25)

(*Objection*): - The sandal ointment abides in a special abode.

(*Answer*): - This objection cannot apply to us; for we admit that Atman also has a special abode, as the sruti says:

"In the heart, indeed, is this Atman." * [* Prasna-Up. 3-6.]

"He who is within the heart, in the pranas, full of consciousness, that light which pervades, full of consciousness, that light which pervades all." † [† Bri-Up. 6-3-7.]

So (*i.e.*, by the illustration of sandal-ointment) do some Vedantins explain (how a small thing can produce a feeling extending all over the body.)

The Sutrakara states his own view as follows:

Or by his attributes as in the case of light. (II. iii. 26)

Atman experiences – by pervading the whole body – by means of intelligence which constitutes his inherent quality; just as a gem illumines an adjacent object, by way of pervading it by means of its own light. Therefore, there is no incongruity whatever light. Therefore, there is no incongruity whatever.

As to the contention that intelligence and Atman are not distinct, the sutrakara says:

There is a distinction as in case of odour; so in indeed, the sruti declares (II. iii. 27)

Just as we say that earth is that which has odour so when we say 'I know' we perceive intelligence to be an attribute of Atman. Accordingly there is a distinction between intelligence and Atman. The sruti declares the distinction in the following words:

"This person does know."

Because of its being mentioned separately. (II. iii. 28)

Intelligence is mentioned separately from Atman in the following sruti:

"There is no failure of the intelligence of the intelligent one." ‡ [‡ Bri-Up. 3-3-30.]

Thus it has been shown that Atman has the attribute of intelligence which is eternal. Then, how is it that, while Atman has intelligence for his attribute, he is spoken of as intelligence itself? The sutrakara answers as follows:

Indeed because that is his chief attribute, he is given that designation, like the Wise. (II. iii. 29)

Because Atman's chief attribute is intelligence, the designation of intelligence is given to him – not because he is mere intelligence itself, - just as the Wise (Prajna, Brahma) is spoken of as "Truth, Intelligence," though He is one possessed of intelligence. Therefore there is nothing wrong in designating Atman as mere intelligence.

Again he explains as follows:

Because it is co-extensive with Atman, there is nothing wrong, as we do see it (elsewhere). (II. iii. 30)

As intelligence inheres in the nature of Atman, it is not wrong to designate him by it. We do find an individual cow designated as cow in virtue of the attribute of cow-ness, merely because that attribute inheres in her. Accordingly in as much as the attribute of intelligence inheres in Atman, he is designated as intelligence.

How can intelligence which does not exist in sleep (Sushupti) and other states, be said to be co-extensive with Atman? The Sutrakara says:

As in the case of virility, it may exist (in Sushupti) and come into manifestation (thereafter). (II. iii. 31)

Intelligence does inhere in the essential nature of Atman, because, while existing Unmanifested in Sushupti and the like, intelligence springs into manifestation in Jagrat or the waking state and so on; just as the seventh principle, (namely, the semen), which constitutes the characteristic ingredient of a human, body of the male sex, though present even in childhood manifests itself only in youth. Wherefore, it is not wrong to maintain that intelligence is intimately associated with Atman's nature.

The sutrakara now speaks of the purpose served by maintaining that Atman is a knower and is infinitesimally small.

Otherwise, there would be an eternal perception and non-perception, or, either of them exclusively. (II. iii. 32)

Otherwise, *i.e.*, if Atman were omnipresent and mere consciousness, then because he is eternal and subject to no limitations, there would be a constant perception, of him; and Atman being ever in the same condition his non-perception too, must be constant. The same objection applies to the theory that Atman is all-pervading and that his intelligence is only accidental; for, all Atmans being alike present everywhere, the causes of perception, such as conjunction with manas, are common to all. If the cause of perception be *adrishta*, something unseen (such as past karma), even this cause is common to all, and there is nothing which goes to restrict it. Or perception and non-perception being quite opposed to each other, the causes (referred to) may either give rise to perception exclusively, or to non-perception exclusively. Then, there would be either the one or the other exclusively.

Wherefore, what was declared above alone holds good.

Adhikarana 10

(Atman is the) doer as the Sastra must have a purpose (II. iii. 33)

It has been shown that Atman is a knower and is infinitesimally small. A doubt arises as to whether or not he is a doer.

(*Purvapaksha*): - Atman, who is immutable, cannot be a doer. Properly speaking, either the buddhi (intellect) or Prakriti (the root of all matter) must be the doer. Atman appears to be the doer by falsely assuming to himself the agency of the other. Therefore it is not right to say that Atman is the doer.

(*Siddhanta*): - Atman is no doubt the doer; for the Sastra must have a purpose. Otherwise the Sastra which enjoins and prohibits would serve no purpose.

And because of the declaration of his taking and wandering (II. iii. 34)

He is the doer, undoubtedly; for it is declared that he takes and wanders, as in the following sruti:

"Thus, verily, does he take these pranas and wanders as he likes in the body." * [* Bri-Up. 4-1-18.]

As to the contention that agency pertains to the buddhi and the Prakriti, the sutrakara argues against the agency of the buddhi in the following words:

And because of its declaration in reference to the ritual. If not, there would be a difference in declaration. (II. iii. 35)

"Consciousness achieves sacrifice": † [† Taitti-Up. 2-5] in such words as these, Atman is spoken of as the agent, and therefore he is certainly the doer.

(*Objection*): - The word 'consciousness' denotes the *buddhi*, not the *Atman*.

(*Answer*): - No. If so, the wording would be different, in the form "with the consciousness" Elsewhere when the buddhi has to be spoken of, we find the word 'consciousness' used in the instrumental case, as in the sruti "Having taken, with the consciousness, the consciousness of these pranas (senses)." ‡ [‡ Bri-Up. 4-1-17.] Hence the conclusion that buddhi, being an instrument, cannot be an agent.

The sutrakara objects to the view that Prakriti is the agent:

As in perception, there could be no restrictive (II. iii. 37)

If Prakriti were the agent, then, as it is common to all, there would be nothing to restrict the result (of an act to an individual), any more than in the case of perception already discussed.

And because of a reversal of the potentiality (II. iii. 38)

If Prakriti were the agent, then, in as much as the agent of an act should also be the enjoyer of its fruits, Prakriti would itself be the enjoyer. Thus, then, Atman would cease to be the enjoyer.

And because of the absence of the contemplation. (II. iii. 39)

Moreover, if Prakriti were itself the agent, there would be no room for the contemplation that "I am distinct from Prakriti." Wherefore, Atman is the agent.

And like a carpenter he (proceeds) in both ways. (II. iii. 39)

If Atman is the agent, he acts when he wills to act and he ceases to act when he does not will to act; and thus there is here a defined order of procedure, as in the case of a carpenter's procedure in his own calling.

(*Objection*): - Possibly, the will to act also pertains to buddhi; and thus here alike, the definite procedure can be explained.

(*Answer*): - No; for, will is the attribute of a sentient being. Wherefore, it may be concluded that Atman is the agent, but not the buddhi nor Prakriti.

Adhikarana 11

From the Supreme indeed because of the declaration. (II. iii. 40)

I has been shown that Atman is the knower and the agent. Now, a doubt arises as to whether this agency abides in himself or is dependent on the Isvara.

(*Purvapaksha*): - It abides in himself. Otherwise, as impelling jiva to good and evil acts, Isvara would be guilty of partiality and so on. Moreover, if the activity of jiva be dependent on Isvara, then, jiva would no longer be the agent; and thus all scriptural injunctions and prohibitions would be vain. Wherefore Jiva's activity is dependent on jiva himself.

(*Siddhanta*): - Jiva's agency is dependent on Paramesvara, upon himself, because of the sruti, "He who being within, controls Atman."

Now, as to the contention that Isvara, as impelling jiva to action, would be guilty of partiality and the like, and that all scriptural injunctions and prohibitions addressed to him would be vain, the sutrakara says:

But with a view to the efforts made (by jiva), in order that the injunctions and prohibitions may not be purposeless, and so on (II. iii. 41)

Jiva, of his own accord, makes an effort towards activity or cessation of activity, in virtue of his karma having become ripe. With reference to this effort made by Jiva which lends to activity or cessation from activity, the Supreme Being impels jiva to action by giving His consent, as may be seen from injunctions and prohibitions having a purpose to serve and from the grace and punishment meted out by him. Just as a boy who, with the help of a stronger person, manages to convey a very heavy beam of wood, is still amenable to injunctions and prohibitions so far as his own efforts is concerned, so, though Jiva engages in activity with the help of the Paramesvara, he is himself amenable to injunctions and prohibitions. Accordingly, as acting solely with reference to the efforts made by jiva, Isvara, who impels jiva to acts, is not guilty of partiality; and in as much as, even in the case of jiva, there exists as activity for which he has to rely on himself, it cannot be, we may conclude, that injunctions and prohibitions are purposeless.

Adhikarana 12

(Jiva is) an integral part (of Brahman), because of the declaration of a distinction. And it is even otherwise; that (Brahman) is one with fishermen and so on, some to declare (II. iii. 42)

It has been shown in the foregoing sections that Jiva is eternal, intelligent, and extremely small; that he is an agent engaging in action with the help of Paramesvara. Here, a doubt arises as to whether jiva is Paramesvara Himself, or His integral part.

(*Purvapaksha*): - Jiva is Paramesvara Himself. Paramesvara Himself is manifested in the form of jiva on account of the multifarious upadhis or media of manifestation, just as the one akasa manifests itself in various forms and is limited in space owing to the upadhis such as a pot. Accordingly the sruti says "This Atman is Brahman." * [* Bri-Up. 4-5-19.] Therefore, Isvara Himself has become jiva owing to ajnana or nescience.

(*Siddhanta*): - The Jivatman is indeed an *amsa* of Paramesvara, an integral part of His body, as the sruti declares a distinction between them in the following passages:

"Entering into them in the form of this jiva, i shall differentiate name and form." † [† Chha. Up. 6-3-2]

"He who dwelling in the Atman...." ‡ [‡ Bri. Up. 5-7-22.]

"Thinking of the Atman and the Impeller as separate...." § [§ Svetasvatara-Up. 1-6.]

"Know then Prakriti is Maya, and the Mahesvara the possessor of Maya. This whole world is filled with what constitutes a member of His." || [|| Ibid. 4-10.]

As to the contention that Brahman Himself is jiva because of the sruti teaching "This Atman is Brahman," the sutrakara says as follows: The oneness has to be explained otherwise. From such passages as "That thou art," "this Atman is Brahman," we are to understand that jiva and Brahman are a unity because one pervades the other. Moreover, some clearly declare a unity of this sort in the following words. "The fishermen are Brahman, the servants are Brahman, these rogues are Brahman." Thus though jiva is an integral part of Brahman, he may be spoken of as Brahman, as pervaded by the latter, just as a faggot or the like, pervaded by fire, is spoken of as fire itself. Still, fire and faggot are not, indeed, one and the same. Therefore an integral of Brahman in himself, jiva attains to the form of Brahman. If we assume that Brahman Himself becomes jiva by ajnana or nescience, it is impossible to avoid contradicting many a passage in the sruti.

Because of the mantra. (II. iii. 43)

"A foot Thereof are all beings:" this Mantra gives us to understand that jiva is only a part (amsa) of Brahman. The sruti, - namely,

"Know then Prakriti is Maya, and Mahesvara the possessor of Maya. This whole world is filled with what constitutes a member of His." –

Declares that Maya is the *prakriti* or material cause, that Mahesvara is endued with that Maya, and that the whole universe constitutes His member. Wherefore, Purusha or Jiva is only a small portion of Paramesvara who is endued with Maya.

It is even declared in the smriti. (II. iii. 44)

"Atman is the eighth form of Siva, the Paramatman, which penetrates other forms; the universe, therefore, is Siva Himself."

From this passage in the smriti, Atman is only one portion of Siva's body.

But as in the case of lustre etc., not thus is the Supreme. (II. iii. 45)

Though jiva is a portion of Brahman, yet the Paramesvara is not of the same nature and form as jiva. On the other hand, He is indeed endued with omniscience etc – How? – Like lustre etc. Just as the lustre of gems etc., which possess it as their attribute constitutes a part thereof an, integral part of the composite whole, so, as embodied in Jiva, Brahman has jiva as an attribute of His, and the jiva forms a portion of Brahman. – The word "etc." (in the phrase "lustre etc." is intended to bring under the same category *jati* (genus) and *guna* (quality) which always constitute attributes of substance, - Though attributes, as integral parts of the substances, constitute part and parcel of these substances, yet it involves no contradiction to maintain that they are distinct things, as shown by such passages of the sruti as the following:

"He who abides in Atman."

And so the smriti also declares. (II. iii. 46)

"The body of the God of Gods is this universe, moving and unmoving. This thing the souls (pasus) knows not, owing to the strong bond (pasa)." And so on the smriti says. Wherefore, jiva is only a portion (amsa) of Brahman. Brahman being the possessor of the portion, there is an essential distinction between them.

Permission and prohibition is due to connection with the body, as in the case of light etc. (II. iii. 47)

(*Objection*): - Though all jivas are alike portions of Brahman, how is it that permission to study the Vedas etc., is accorded to some, while it is prohibited in the case of others?

(*Answer*): - This may be explained as due to the connection with the Brahman body and so on, just as a distinction is made in the case of fire according as it is found in the house of a pious man or in the cremation ground.

As limited in space, they are all alike. (II. iii. 48)

As different in the different bodies, as limited here and there in their atomic size, and thus not pervading everywhere, knowledge, pleasure and the like are of one sort in the case of those who identify themselves with the bodies feeling thus: 'I am stout' 'I am lean;' 'I am happy;' 'I am miserable;' 'I am a Brahmin;' 'I am a Kshatriya;' – What is this tantamount to saying? – Because those who identify themselves with the body are alike limited in extent, their limited knowledge, pleasure etc., which are peculiar to samsara, are of one and the same sort and do not get intermixed. From this it follows that in the case of those liberated souls who cease to identify themselves with the body, and who, by their all-pervasive nature, have risen to universal egoism, the samsaric knowledge etc., given place to the inherent knowledge etc., which are eternal and infinite.

As to the contention that Brahman Himself becomes associated with ajnana and upadhi, the sutrakara replies that, in all that case, there would be no definite order of things:

And it is a mere semblance. (II. iii. 49)

The arguments adduced on behalf of both the theories, - namely that Brahman Himself becomes jiva when bound by an upadhi, be it real or unreal, - are only semblances of reasoning.

To explain:

Because it cannot be defined by adrishta. (II. iii. 50)

If Atmans or jivas be the creatures of real or unreal upadhis, then, since *ajnana* and *upadhi* pertain to Brahman Himself, the relative positions (of Brahman and jiva, or of jivas among themselves) cannot be defined even by adrishta (the unseen effect of actions) generated by them.

And so too, in the case of purposes etc. (II. iii. 51)

So, too, even as regards purposes which are the causes of *adrishta* (the unseen effects of actions) the definite relations cannot be explained.

(If it be said that it is) due to (difference in space) (we reply) no, because of comprehension. (II. iii. 52)

(*Objection*): - The distinction is due to the distinction in the parts of Brahman associated with different upadhis.

(*Answer*): - No; for, when the upadhis are gone, all parts are comprehended in Brahman. Wherefore, according to either of the theories that Brahman is jiva when limited by upadhi, be it real or unreal, the distinction cannot be explained. Wherefore it is quite reasonable to maintain that jiva is a part of Brahman and that jiva is of the nature of an attribute of Brahman.

THE FOURTH PADA.

Adhikarana 1.

So, the pranas. (II. iv. 1)

It has been shown before that *bhutas* or elements of matter are born of Brahman, and that jiva is eternal. Now we have to enquire whether the sense-organs (*indriyas*) have a birth like the elements of matter, or they are eternal like jivas. Just as, being eternal, the jiva is not born, so also are the sense-organs not born; for, there is the Sruti which says that they also, like the jiva, are eternal. Accordingly, the Sruti declares the continuance of sense-organs (pranas) at the time of pralaya or cosmic dissolution, in the following passages:

> "Non-existent this at first was. They asked what that non-existent was. Rishis indeed were the non-existent at first. Then they asked who are those Rishis? Pranas are verily the *Rishis*." * [* Saatapathabrahmana. 6-1-1.]

Wherefore the sense-organs (prana) are not born of Brahman.

As against the foregoing we hold as follows:

It is said in a secondary sense, because of an impossibility; and because the sruti declares that (to have existed) first. (II. iv. 2)

The sense-organs did not exist prior to creation. On the other hand, it is Paramesvara that then existed, as the sruti declares "Existent alone, My dear, this at first was." † [† Chha. Up. 6-2-1] The words *rishi* and the word *prana* apply only to Paramesvara. As He cannot be many, the use of the plural is only secondary. Hence the existence of Brahman alone prior to creation, not of the sense-organs.

The Sutrakara adduces another argument:

Speech being preceded by it. (II. iv. 3)

All other receive their names and forms only after Paramesvara's creation. The word *prana* used with reference to the time (prior to creation) cannot denote the sense-organs. Therefore, Brahman alone is the prior.

Adhiakarana 2.

Because seven are taught and specifically enumerated. (II. iv. 4)

Now, a doubt arises as to how many in numbers are the sense-organs which have been shown before to have been born of Brahman.

Purvapaksha: - Sven. – Why? – Because seven only are enumerated in the following passages:

"When the five instruments of knowledge stand still together with the mind, and when the intellect does not move, that is called the highest state."

And also because the number seven is specifically mentioned in the following passage:

"Seven pranas are born of Him."

As against the foregoing, the sutrakara says:

But there are hands etc., when (jiva) abides (in the body); wherefore it is not so. (II. iv. 5)

The sense-organs are not seven only. Hands etc., too, are sense-organs, in as much as they are alike instruments of the jiva so long as he abides in the body. The sense-organs are, on the other hand, eleven in number, because of the sruti and the smriti.

"These ten are the pranas (sense-organs) in the person; and manas (atman) is the eleventh." † [† Mahanarayana. Up. 12]

"The sense-organs, ten and one." ‡ [‡ Bri. Up. 5-9-4.]

Buddhi etc., are not separate senses; but they are only different functions of manas. § [§ Bhagavad-Gita 13-5] As to the speaking of the steadiness of seven sense-organs and their specific enumeration of seven sense-organs and their specific enumeration as seven it is due to their importance. Wherefore, sense-organs are not seven, but they are eleven in number.

Adhiakarana 3

And (they are) small (II. iv. 6)

A doubt arising as to whether those senses are all-pervading or very small, it may at first be thought that they are all-pervading, because of the eye and other sense-organs having the power of perceiving things at a distance. In reply we say that they are very small; for, the sruti says, "The prana departing, all pranas (sense-organs) depart after it." * [* Bri. Up. 6-4-2] They are not all-pervading. If they were all-pervading their departure is not possible. The eye and other sense-organs have the power of perceiving things at a distance, not because they are all-pervading, but because they are luminous and very small and therefore pass very quickly. Wherefore the sense-organs are very small.

Adhikarana 4

And the chief. (II. iv. 7)

Here a doubt arises as to whether the vital air, with its fivefold function – spoken of in the sruti as the chief of all pranas or vital activities in the words "The prana departing, all pranas depart after it." – is born of Brahman or not.

(*Purvapaksha*): - The vital air is not born, because of the activity of the vital breath being declared to have existed, even prior to creation, in the words "It breathed windless." * [* Bri. Up. 6-4-2]

(*Siddhanta*): - As against the foregoing we hold as follows: Even the prana-vayu, the vital air, is born. The word 'breathed' does not refer to the activity of vital air, in as much as the word 'windless' points to its absence. It denotes only the existence of Brahman. Wherefore the prana or vital air cannot be beginningless.

(*Objection*): - Granted that this vital air has a birth; but it is not distinct from the activities of sense-organs, as said in another science in the words "A general function of the sense-organs are the five vital airs such as prana or upward breath;" † [† Taitt. Brahmana. 2-8-9] or, it is not distinct from the material air as declared in the sruti "This vitality is the air." * [*Bri. Up. 6-4-2]

(*Answer*): - As against the foregoing, the Sutrakara says:

It is neither the air nor the activity, because of its separate mention. (II. iv. 8)

This vitality with its fivefold function is not the air; nor is it the general function of the sense-organs, as it is separately mentioned in the Sruti:

"Hence is prana born, manas and all sense-organs, akasa, air, light, waters, the earth which maintains the whole universe." * [* Mundaka-Up. 2-1-3]

Wherefore prana is quite distinct from the air and from the function of the senses.

Though distinct from the air, still it does not constitute a distinct element of matter by itself, as the Sutrakara says:

Like the eye etc., indeed, because of its being mentioned along with them, and so on. (II. iv. 9)

Though distinct from the air, it is not a distinct element of matter like fire etc. On the other hand, the air itself, acquires the power of keeping up the body, because it is rooted in the Paramesvara, as the following passages show:

"Himself the supporter, being supported by Paramesvara he supports, the one Deva who dwells in many a form."

"Thou art one, having entered many." * [* Taitt. Aranyaka 3-14.]

"Thou art the knot of the vitalities. O Rudra. Enter not as destroyer." † [† Mahanarayana-Upanishad. 35.]

Moreover, prana is the jiva's instrument like the eye and other organs, in as much as in the dialogues among pranas or vital organs, prana or the vital breath is mentioned along with the eye, etc., as subserving the jiva's purposes in the same way as the sense-organs do, as being the chief of them all, and so on.

And there can be no objection on the ground of its inactivity. Accordingly, indeed, the sruti says there is no objection. (II. iv. 10)

No objection can be raised against the foregoing on the ground that prana does no service to jiva. For, the sruti itself declares that the vital breath is the cause of the body and the sense-organs not being unloosed. When Prajapati said (in the dialogue among pranas) "Whosoever departing, this body looks very wretched, he is the chief among you," * [* Chha. Up 5-1-7] the sense-organs such as speech departed one by one at a time; but, on each occasion, the body and the other sense-organs did remain in their places. When, however, prana or vital body left the body, the body and the sense-organs are said to have been unloosed.

It is declared to be of fivefold function, like manas. (II. iv. 11)

The one prana or vital breath is designated differently as prana or upward breath, as apana or downward breath, and so on, after its own five different functions, just as the one manas is spoken of as desire (kama) etc. Wherefore, it has to be concluded that the one prana, which is distinct both from the element of matter called air and from the function of the sense-organs, subserves jiva's purposes.

Adhikarana 5

And it is minute. (II. iv. 12)

A doubt arises as to whether this prana in its fivefold function is minute like the senses, or all-pervading.

(*Purvapaksha*): - It is not minute, Prana is all-pervading, being the support of all, as the sruti says:

"He is equal to a grub, equal to a gnat, equal to an elephant, equal to these three worlds, nay equal to this universe." † [† Bri. Up. 3-3-22.]

"In prana all is established." ‡ [‡ Pra. Up. 2-6.]

"All this, verily, is enveloped by prana."

(*Siddhanta*): - As against the foregoing view, we hold as follows: The vital air is minute, because of its passage declared in the Sruti "Prana departing." § [§ Bri. Up. 6-4-2.] The prana of the plane of cosmic intelligence, known as the Hiranyagarbha, - the prana in the aggregate – is all-pervading while the prana of the individual organism is not. Thus there is no self-contradiction. Wherefore, minute is the prana in its fivefold function.

Adhikarana 6

The dominion over the eye, etc., is verily dependent on Paramesvara, because of its being so declared; as also of the living soul, on account of the word. (II. iv. 13)

The sruti declares that the sun, etc., are the lords of sight etc., in the following words:

"The sun became sight and entered the eyes." ‖ [‖ Aita-Up. 1-2-3.]

Jiva, too, is said to be the lord of the eye, etc., with the object of perceiving color etc., in the following words:

"Thus does that soul take these various senses and moves about, according to his pleasure, within his own body." * [* Bri. Up. 4-1-18.]

Now a doubt arises as to whether the lordship of the sun etc., as well as of jiva, over the sense-organs is dependent on Paramesvara, or quite independent.

(*Purvapaksha*): - In the passages such as "The sun became sight and entered the eyes," the sin etc., are said to be independent, and their dominion is therefore not dependent on Paramesvara.

(*Siddhanta*): - The dominion of the sun etc., over the sense-organs etc., is dependent on Paramesvara. Why? For, the sruti declares as follows:

"Who, dwelling within, controls the sun." * [* Bri. Up. 4-1-18.]

"Who, dwelling within, controls the Atman;" *[* Bri. Up. 4-1-18.]

and all activities proceed from the will of Paramesvara. Wherefore, the dominion of Jiva and of the sun etc., over sense-organs etc., is quite dependent on Paramesvara.

And because of its eternality. (II. iv. 14)

Paramesvara's control over everything is eternal. For this reason also is their dominion quite dependent on Paramesvara's will.

Adhikarana 7

They are the senses, because of the designation being applied to other than the chief. (II. iv. 15)

Now, a doubt arises as to whether speech and other sense-organs mentioned before are distinct from the functions of prana or not.

(*Purvapaksha*): - They are the functions of the chief prana or vital breath, because of their being declared to be forms of prana in the words "of him alone did all become the form," † [† Bri. Up. 3-5-21.] and because, at death when speech etc., are quiescent, it is generally held that life is gone. Wherefore the senses are not distinct from prana or vital breath.

(*Siddhanta*): - As against the foregoing we hold as follows: The senses are distinct from the chief prana or vital breath; for, in words "the senses, ten and one," ‡ [‡ Bha. Gita. 13-5.] it is sight and others that are designated as the senses, thus showing that those vital activities (pranas) which are distinct from the chief prana are the senses.

Because of their separate mention and of a distinction in their nature. (II. iv. 16)

"Hence is born prana, manas and all senses;" § [§ Mundaka. Up. 2-1-3.] in these words the sruti speaks of the birth of prana and the senses separately. We also see a distinction in their nature, which consists in the functions of prana not ceasing during the quiescence of the senses. Wherefore, too, the senses are distinct from the functions of prana.

Adhikarana 8

Creation of names and forms verily belongs to Him who triples, because it is so taught. (II. iv. 17)

In a former section, it has been said that the Akasa and other elements of matter with their presiding deities such as Sadasiva, are born of Paramesvara. A doubt arises as to whether, when they are thus born, the subsequent creation of names and forms of Devas etc., proceeds from Him alone, the First Cause, or from someone else.

(*Purvapaksha*): - From the passage "That light willed, may I be born as many, and It created waters," we learn that Rudra, the Intelligence identifying Himself with light, creates waters and casts therein His own seeds that in them arises Vishnu endued with *sattva*. Vishnu is called Narayana because the principle of water which is born of Rudra is His abode, as the sruti says "Waters are born of Nara, and Nara is Rudra," Narayana, the Intelligence identifying himself with the water, creates earth spoken of as food in the sruti "The waters willed ...and they created food." * [* Chha. Up. 6-2-3.] There, in the egg made up of the earth-principle, arises Hiranyagarbha. Accordingly the sruti says: "The Golden Egg in the midst of the ocean was first born of Rudra's seed. Therein Vishnu was born as Brahma, with his wisdom manifest."

Manu says:

"He created the waters alone first and placed his seed in them. That seed became a golden egg, in brilliancy equal to the sun; in that egg he himself was born as Brahma, the progenitor of the whole world. The waters are called Nara; as they were his first residence (ayana), he then is named Narayana. Narayana transcends Avyakta; from Avyakta is the birth of the egg; within the egg are these worlds, as well as the earth with its seven islands." † [† Op. Cit. 1-8...11.]

Purana, too, says,

"The form of the Deva called Rudra becomes tangible body. By Him identifying Himself with the body was the seed cast in water. That seed became an egg, in brilliancy equal to the sun. Vishnu entered into it directly, by My great power, indeed. Again, by My command, he obtained the designation of Narayana. In this connection they quote the following verse regarding Narayana: "Water, it should be known, is the subtle essence, and water is called Nara as born of Nara. Thence came Brahma. Nara is declared to be Siva Himself. Nara is said to be His residence and therefore He is called Narayana. Brahma also, O best of men, entered the body of odour."

Thus, in accordance with the sruti "by Veda Prajapati developed the forms, manifested and Unmanifested," * [* Taitt. Bra. 2-6-2.] either the Hiranyagarbha dwelling within the egg must have created the names and forms of Devas etc., dwelling within the egg, or their creator may be Narayana, as declared in the sruti, "the egg was born of waters and of the essence of earth;" † [† Taitt. Aranyaka. 3-13.] but the Paramesvara who is beyond the Brahmanda cannot be their creator.

(*Siddhanta*): - The order of creation explained above is not sound. On the other hand, it is Brahman, designated the Existent, that is the cause of the five elements of matter, as the following passage shows:

> The Existent alone, my dear, this at first was, one alone without a second....It willed, may I become many, and created light." ‡ [‡ Chha. Up. 6-2.]

It was already shown that light was not the first thing created. Accordingly, Brahman assuming the form of elements from Akasa down to earth under the designations of Sadasiva and so on, every preceding element is the cause of that which immediately succeeds it, as may be learned from the sruti "It willed....the light willed....the water willed...." From the passage "I shall enter these three elements in the form of this Jiva and differentiate name and form; I shall make each one of them threefold," § [§ Chha. Up. 6-3.] we learn that it is Paramesvara Himself -- who triples the elements – that, assuming the form of the air, etc., enters the three elements of light, water and earth through the jivas, *viz.*, Brahma, Vishnu, and Rudra, and creates name and form. Therefore it is reasonable to hold that He alone, who triples the elements and who ensouls the Four-faced Brahma and others, creates all names and forms. The tripling of elements is not possible for the four-faced Brahma alone, in as much as the Egg is born of the tripled elements of light, water and earth. After this comes the four-faced Brahma's creation, as said in the following sruti:

> "The golden egg in the midst of the ocean was first born of Rudra' seed. There Vishnu was born as Brahma, with wisdom manifest."

(*Objection*): - It is possible that the four-faced Brahma himself is the author of the tripling of elements. The process of tripling that takes place among jivas created by the four-faced Brahma subsequent to the creation of the egg is taught in the sruti as follows:

> "Do thou, my dear, learn from me how indeed these three elements, entering the creatures, become each threefold. The food eaten is resolved into three. The grossest ingredient of it becomes the dung, the middling one becomes flesh, the subtlest becomes manas." * [* Chha. Up. 6-4-7.]

(*Answer*): - The Sutrakara refutes the objection as follows:

Flesh etc, is earthen; and as to the other two, according to the word. (II. iv. 18)

In the passage "the food eaten is resolved into three," something other than the tripling process previously declared, - namely, the process of transformation that takes place in the food etc., eaten by persons dwelling in the egg – has been described; but not the tripling process. Otherwise, flesh and manas, being subtler than the dung, would have been respectively composed of water and light. So that, the commencement of the tripling process of the earth alone as started in the words "The food eaten is resolved into three," would be inconsistent with the declaration that manas is made up of earth as stated in the passage "made up of food, verily, is manas, my dear." Similarly the threefold division of the other two, viz., water and light, would involve a contradiction. Therefore the sutrakara says, "Flesh etc., are earthen; and as to the other two, according to the word." Like the dung, flesh and manas also are earthen; so, like the urine, blood and vitality are watery; and so too, like the bone, marrow and speech are made up of light.

(*Objection*): - If the elements have been tripled already, then everything must be made up of the three elements. How then, can we speak of food (earth), water, light?

(*Answer*): - The sutrakara says:

Owing to preponderance, verily, are they spoken of as such. (II. iv. 19)

Owing to the preponderance of food (i.e., earth) we speak of a thing as food (earth). Wherefore it is quite reasonable to maintain that Paramesvara who triples the elements also creates all names and forms, by ensouling the four-faced Brahma etc.

END OF THE FOURTH PADA IN THE SECOND ADHYAYA.

THIRD ADHYAYA

FIRST PADA.

Adhikarana 1

In attaining to another (body), (the jiva) runs embraced (by subtle elements), as the question and the answer show. (III. i. 1)

In the second adhyaya have been answered all objections against the theory which was established in the first adhyaya as the one taught by the Upanishads in one voice, the theory, namely, that Brahman is the cause of the universe. To go into further details: in the first pada of the second Adhyaya, all objections brought against the theory on the strength of the Sankhya and other modes of reasoning were answered; in the second pada was shown how the doctrine that the Pradhana was the cause, and other such doctrines were opposed to reasoning; in the third pada, it was first shown how the passages speaking of the creation of elements of matter are not contradictory, and then jiva was defined as eternal, and so on; in the fourth, after describing the nature of prana or vital breath as well as senses and declaring that they were all born of Brahman, it was shown how the names and forms of all things were differentiated. Now, the first pada of the third adhyaya will treat of the departure and the return of the eternal jiva; the second pada will treat of the essential nature of Isvara, after first explaining the Jiva's avasthas or states of consciousness; the third will show how we are to gather together the various details of the prescribed modes of worshipping the Isvara as given in different places in the Veda; and the fourth pada will treat of the duties of the Asramas or religious orders, and so on.

Now in the first adhikarana of the first pada, a doubt arises as to whether the jiva, in going to and returning from the other world, does or does not carry with him the subtle elements of matter wherewith to create another body.

(*Purvapaksha*): - When departing from the body, the jiva does not carry with him any subtle elements of matter which may form the seeds of the future body, in as much as all the trouble goes in vain, the elements of matter being easily found everywhere.

(*Siddhanta*): - As against the foregoing we hold as follows: That the jiva leaves this world embraced by the subtle elements of matter whereby to obtain another body is shown by the question and the answer occurring in the *Panchagni-Vidya*, the contemplation of the five fires – How? – There the question was, "Do you know how in the fifth oblation, the waters come to be spoken of as Purusha?" The answer was, "Thus verily in the fifth oblation the waters come to be spoken of as Purusha." Their meaning may be briefly explained thus: the jivas dwelling in the body of a brahmana or the like offers oblations and does other acts. Leaving this body with a view to enjoy their fruits, he departs, embraced by the subtle element of water combined with other elements existing in the present body, and reaches heaven represented as a fire. Embraced by the same waters which become transformed into a body full of nectar, he becomes subservient to the Gods (Devas), and in their company he enjoys the peculiar pleasures of the region. With the residual Karma which will give him the body of a brahmana or the like, he again comes to this world to do works, and embraced by the same waters he reaches the clouds which are represented as a fire. Then, with the rain drops, he descends to the earth also represented as a fire. Thence, with paddy and other grains, attaining the form of food, he reaches the body of a man who is represented as another fire. Then, embraced by the same waters converted into the semen in man, he reaches a woman represented as yet another fire. Embraced by the waters converted there into a body which may be called a human being, he is born with the body of a brahmana or the like according to karma. All this will become clear later on. Wherefore when jiva has to attain to the next body, he goes embraced by the subtle elements.

(Water includes other elements) because of the triple character (of everything), (but they are referred to by water) because of its predominance. (III. i. 2)

Everything is of a threefold nature, because everything was tripled; and therefore it is only water combined with other elements that is referred to by the word "waters." They are so designated because of the predominance of water among them. There is, therefore, nothing wrong in speaking of water alone in the passage "In the fifth oblation, waters come to be spoken of as man." * [* Chha. Up. 5-9]

And because of the departure of the senses. (III. i. 3)

"When prana departs, all the senses depart after it." † [† Bri. Up. 6-4-2] This passage speaks of the departure of the senses along with the jiva, and we are therefore to understand that the body also, which is the seat of the sense-organs, departs. Wherefore, when the jiva departs, he is certainly embraced by the body of the body of the subtle elements.

The Sutrakara raises an objection and answers:

(If you say that it is not so) because of the Sruti speaking of them as going to Agni and so on. (We say) no, because it is a figurative language. (III. i. 4)

(*Objection*): - The Sruti says:

"When the speech of this dying man goes to Agni, his vital breath goes to the air, the eye to the sun," ‡ [‡ Bri. Up. 5-2-13.] and so on.

In this passage the Sruti speaks of the senses going to Agni and so on. Therefore the senses do not go with the jiva.

(*Answer*): - No, because of the words 'speech' and the like being figuratively applied to the Gods who identify themselves with the senses of speech & c. They are indeed spoken of along with the hair & c., which do not certainly go to the Gods who identify themselves with them. The Sruti says. "The small hairs go to the plants the big hairs to the trees."

(If you object to this) because of the absence of their mention in the first, (we answer) no, for they alone (are referred to) as may be explained. (III. i. 5)

(*Objection*): - In the first, *i.e.*, when speaking of the first fire, namely, the region of heaven, waters are not mentioned and therefore they do not depart. There the Sruti says "In this fire, the gods pour the oblation of faith." || speaks only of faith (Sraddha). [|| Chha. Up. 5-4]

(*Answer*): - No; it is only waters that are spoken of as 'faith.' Why? For, what follows can be explained only when the oblations of Sraddha means that of waters. And the word 'faith may be used to denote waters, because the Sruti says "faith, verily, is the waters." * [* Taitt. Brah. 3-2-4]

The Sutrakara again raises an objection and answers:

(If you say that Jiva is not meant) because he is not mentioned. (We say) no, because of the doers of sacrificial rites and the like being referred to. (III. i. 6)

(*Objection*): - Here, in the question and in the answers, waters alone are mentioned, not the jiva embraced by them.

(*Answer*): - No, for, in the sequel the Sruti says: "But they who living in a village practise (a life of) sacrifices, works of public utility and alms, they go to the smoke, from smoke to night, from night to the dark half of the moon, from the dark half of the moon to the six months when the sun goes to the south. But they do not reach the year. From the months they go to the world of the fathers, from the world of the fathers to the ether, from the ether to the moon. That is Soma, the King. Here they are loved (eaten) by the Devas, yes, the Devas love (eat) them. Having dwelt there till their (good) works are consumed, they return again that way as they came, to the ether, from the ether to the air. Then the sacrificer, having become air, becomes smoke, having become smoke, he becomes mist, having become mist he becomes a cloud, having become a cloud, he rains down. Then he is born as rice and corn, herbs and trees, sesamum and beans. From thence the escape is beset with most difficulties. For whoever the persons may be that eat the food and beget offspring, he henceforth becomes like unto them." † [† Chha. Up. 5-10.]

This passage speaks of the performers of sacrifices who enjoy the fruits of their good Karma in heaven with the body of the nectar here spoken of as the King Soma, and who, on the exhaustion of their good Karma, again come here and enter into the womb; and the same individuals are again referred to as King Soma, in the following passage.

"On that alter the Devas offer the Sraddha libation. From that oblation rises Soma, the King." ‡ [‡ Ibid. 5-4]

Therefore, even in the question and the answer, it is found that it is jiva, embraced by waters and having those waters for his body, that is spoken of as waters. Hence no contradiction.

It is only a figure of speech, because of his ignorance of Atman, so indeed the Sruti shows. (III. i. 7)

(*Objection*):- The water cannot stand for jiva, because it is spoken of as being eaten b the Devas when it attains to the state of Soma, the King, in the words, "That is Soma, the Kind. Here they are eaten by the Devas, yes the Devas eat them." * [* Chha. Up. 5-10]

(*Answer*): - It is only by a figure of speech that they are said to be eaten; and it simply means that they, as not knowing Atman, are mere instruments of enjoyments for the Devas. Accordingly, indeed, does the Sruti declare that those who do not know Atman are like cattle mere instruments of enjoyment for the Devas, in the words "Like an animal, he is to the Devas." † [† Bri. Up. 3-4-10]It should therefore be understood that as the knowers of Atman are the instruments of Paramesvara, so are those who are ignorant of Atman the instruments of the Devas. It may thus be concluded that when jiva departs from here to take another body, he goes there embraced by subtle elements.

Adhikarana 2

On the exhaustion of works (the soul returns) with a residual karma – as the Sruti and the Smriti says, - as he had gone and otherwise. (III. i. 8)

In the preceding section, it has been shown how Jiva is endued with a body of subtle elements of matter, when he goes to Svarga and other regions and there enjoys fruits consonant with his own karma in the body of a Deva and so on. Now, then, a doubt arises as to whether, when that jiva descends to this world again after enjoyment, he is accompanied with any residual portion of karma, or he returns to the earth after having enjoyed the whole of his karma.

(*Purvapaksha*): - Now it is but proper to maintain that the soul descends to this world from Svarga without *anusaya*, without any residual karma at all. *Anusaya* means residual karma, so called because it remains (*sete*) with (*anu*) jiva. No residual karma can exist in him who descends from Svarga, the fruits of that karma having been enjoyed in Svarga. Accordingly on this subject the sruti says: "Having dwelt there till their karma (*sampata*) is consumed, they return again that way as they came."‡ [‡ Chha. Up. 5-10-5] Here *sampata* means the aggregate karma. They remain there in Svarga till their whole karma is exhausted. Wherefore, after enjoying all the fruits of their karma, the jiva descends from Svarga without any karma at all.

(*Siddhanta*): - When, on the exhaustion of good works, the jiva descends again to this world, he comes accompanied with a residual Karma – Where is it so said? – Of course, in the sruti and in the Smriti. The Sruti says:

"Those, whose conduct has been good, will quickly attain some good birth, the birth of a Brahmana, or a Kshatriya, or a Vaisya. But those whose conduct has been evil will quickly attain an evil birth, the birth of a dog, or a hog, or a chandala." * [* Ibid 5-10-7]

The Smriti says "they are born so and so by good karma." Otherwise, there can be no enjoyment of pleasure and pain for an infant just born, in the absence of Dharma and Adharma, etc. Therefore, when returning the way he went up and otherwise also, the soul is certainly accompanied with a residual karma. To explain on his return he descends to the akasa on his way to the air, and so far follows the way he went up; but he does not pass through the region of the Pitris and so on, and so far the order of ascent is violated.

Again the Sutrakara raises an objection and refute it first according to another's view:

If you say (that the existence of residual Karma cannot be proved) because of the word 'conduct,' Karshnajini replies that the word indirectly points to it. (III. i. 9)

(*Objection*): - It is the word 'conduct (charana)' which occurs in the Sruti quoted above. That does not prove the existence of residual karma. The word 'charana' denotes the moral conduct spoken of in the Smritis.

(*Answer*): - No. Here, the word 'conduct (charana), stands indeed for residual karma (anusaya), in as much as the latter alone can produce happiness and the like.

If you say that conduct would (then) be of no use, (we say) no because the other stands in need of it. (III. i. 10)

(*Objection*): - If so, the moral conduct inculcated in the religious institutes (Smritis) would be of no purpose and therefore taught in vain.

(*Answer*): - No, merely because all good work stands in need of it, as said in the scriptural passages like the following: "Whoso is without Sandhya (morning and evening devotion); is impure, and, as such, is unfit for all works, whatever other work he does, he attains not its fruit." Such is the view of Karshnajini.

But Badari holds that the word means good deed and evil deeds. (III. i. 11)

But Badari maintains that the word 'conduct (charana)' in the Sruti quoted above denotes the good and evil deeds themselves, as the common usage shows. This is also the view of the Sutrakara. If Badari holds that the word 'conduct' denotes the good and evil deeds primarily, but not by a mere figure, then it is tantamount to his admitting that karma (work), to be effective, stands in need of moral conduct inculcated in the smriti.

Wherefore it may be concluded that, when jiva descends from Svarga, he comes accompanied with the residual traces of good and evil works he had done.

Adhikarana 3

It is declared even for those who have done no works of utility and the like. (III. i. 12)

Here a doubt arises as to whether, just as those who do works of public utility and sacrificial acts go to the moon, others also go to the moon or not.

(*Purvapaksha*): - Certainly, even those who have not done any acts of public utility or sacrificial acts go to the moon. The Sruti declares that all alike go to the moon in the words "Whoever departs from this world, all of them go to the moon." * [* Kaushitaki-Upanishad. 1-2.]

No doubt the sinners have no enjoyment there; still, it must be admitted that they do go to the Svarga, so that the fifth oblation is accompanied and the body formed which is assumed on return to the earth. It therefore stands to reason that even those who have not done acts of public utility and sacrificial acts go to the moon.

(*Siddhanta*): - As against the foregoing we hold as follows:

But others ascend and descend by experiencing in Samyamana, as the Sruti shows their passages. (III. i. 13)

Those who have done no acts of public utility and sacrificial acts or the like do not go to the moon. On the other hand they enjoy the fruits of their karma in the world of Yama and then return to earth. Such only are their ascent and descent as declared in the Sruti. "The son of Vivasvat is the goal of the born creatures." † [† Taittiriya-Aranyaka 4-1.]

One goes to Svarga to enjoy, but not to make up the fifth oblation, because in the case of Drona and the like, the principle of five oblations fails, the oblation of woman being absent. Wherefore it is but right to maintain that sinners go to the world of Yama.

And the Smriti says so (III. i. 14)

This thing is declared in the smriti as follows: "And these, O Lord, verily come under the control of Yama." * [* Vishnupurana.]

And also seven (narakas) (III. i. 15)

The Smriti speaks of sinners going to the seven great hells (narakas) such as Raurava.

And because of his influence even there, there is no contradiction. (III. i. 16)

Even there in the hells which are ruled by Chitragupta and others, Yama their leader is active by way of guiding them. It does not therefore contradict the statement that they are under the control of Yama.

Vidya and Karma being verily the things spoken of (III. 1. 17)

One goes to Brahman or to the moon for the enjoyment of the fruits of Vidya (Upasana) and Karma respectively. It is Vidya and Karma that are spoken of as leading to Brahman and to the moon in the following passage:

"Those who know this, and those who in the forest follow faith and austerities go to light... But they who living in a village practise sacrifices, works of public utility and alms, they go to the smoke." † [† Chha. Up. 5-10.]

Wherefore it can never be made out that sinners go to them.

(There is no necessity for going to Svarga) in the third, because of the sruti so declaring. (III. i. 18)

Neither can it be maintained that even the sinners must go to Svarga, on the ground that even in their case the body can be formed only on passing through five oblations. For the sruti expressly declares that they do not go to Svarga, in the following words:

"On neither of these two ways those small creatures (flies, worms. Etc.,) are continually returning of whom it may be said, Live and die. Theirs is a third place. Therefore that world never becomes full." ‡ [‡ *Ibid.*]

The "third place" means men of sinful deeds. Wherefore sinners do not go to heaven.

And it is said in the world. (III. i. 19)

In the world it is said that even in the case of persons of virtuous deeds such as Draupadi, one of the five oblations is dispensed with in the formation of the body.

And because we find (a passage in the Sruti). (III. i. 20)

Moreover, we find it declared in the following passage of the Sruti:

"Of all living things there are indeed three origins only, that which springs from an egg (oviparous), that which springs from a living being (Viviparous), that which springs from a germ." * [* Chha.Up. 6-3-1.]

Here, in the case of the sweat-born and the germ-born, we find one of the five oblations (viz., woman) is dispensed with.

(*Objection*): - In the Sruti quoted above, there is no mention made of the sweat-born.

(*Answer*): - The Sutrakara answers as follows:

The sweat-born is included in the third word. (III. i. 21)

The sweat-born is also included in the mention of the germ-born. Therefore the conclusion is that sinners do not go to heaven.

Adhikarana 4

He attains to a similar form, because it is reasonable. (III. i. 22)

In the preceding adhikarana it has been shown that in his descent from Svarga after the enjoyment of the fruit, the soul is accompanied with a residual Karma. The sruti declares that while descending he becomes ether (Akasa) and so on, in the following words:

"Then they return again that way as they came, to the ether, from the ether to the air. Then the sacrificer, having become air, becomes smoke having become smoke, he becomes mist; having become mist, he becomes a cloud; having become a cloud, he rains down."

Here a doubt arises as to whether the sun becomes embodied in the ether and the like or becomes similar to them.

(*Purvapaksha*): - From the words "having become," it appears that the soul becomes the ether and so on.

(*Siddhanta*):- As against the foregoing we hold as follows: When descending, the soul does not become embodied in the ether and so on; but he becomes similar to them; for, there he experiences no pleasure and pain. It is only for the experiencing of pleasure and pain that the soul assumes the several bodies; and it cannot be that one thing actually becomes another thin. Hence the only rational conclusion that, while descending, the soul attains to a form similar to ether and so on.

Adhikarana 5

Not very long, because of the specific mention. (III. i. 23)

A doubt arises as to whether the descending jiva lingers or not according to circumstances, or he does not as a rule linger at all.

(*Purvapaksha*): - In this connection, the sruti declares that jiva attains to the state of the rice-grain and so on in the following words:

"They are born here rice-grains, barley-grains, plants, trees, sesamum-seeds, and beans." * [* Chha. Up. 5-10-6]

Prior to this attaining to the state of the rice-grain etc., the soul may or may not liger in the akasa etc., according to circumstances, there being no specific rule as to the one or the other.

(*Siddhanta*): - As against the foregoing we hold as follows: Prior to attaining to the state of rice-grain etc., the jiva does not linger long in the akasa and so on. – How? – For, the sruti says that it is difficult to escape from the state of the rice-grain etc., in the following words:

"Thence it is very hard indeed to escape." † [† Ibid.]

Thus, as the jivas are said to linger long in the rice-grain and the like, we have to infer that in other places they pass on swiftly, and we therefore conclude that in akasa etc., the jiva does not linger.

Adhikarana 6

(It is only a contact with the rice-grain etc.) indwelled by another (jiva), because of the mention similar to the above. (III. i. 24)

Now a doubt arises as to whether the jiva comes in mere contact with the rice-grain etc., or he is born as the rice-grain etc.

(*Purvapaksha*): - He is born as the rice-grain etc., because the sruti says that they 'are born' as the rice-grain and so on.

(*Siddhanta*): - As against the foregoing we hold as follows: The jiva comes in mere contact with the rice-grain etc., in which other jivas abide. Because of the sruti not declaring the cause of the birth (in the rice-grain etc.,) of the descending jiva any more than when passing into the akasa, the words of the sruti "are born" should be understood in a secondary sense. Where the jiva is born as a brahmana and so on, there the sruti speaks of the causes if such births in the words "those of good conduct,...those of evil conduct..." Wherefore, because of the sruti declaring that he is born only as a brahmana and so on, the conclusion is that mere contact is meant in other cases.

(If you say that there was) an impure act, (we reply) no, because of the word (III. i. 25)

(*Objection*): - Of the sacrificial rites which had been formerly performed by the descending jiva, such rites as Agnishomiya were impure acts, because they involved cruelty to animal life. To reap the fruits of those acts, he should be born as rice-grain etc.

(*Answer*): - No; for, the sruti declares that such cruelty to animals is no cruelty, in the following words:

"Golden-bodied, to the upper Svarga does it go."

"Not indeed dost thou die, nor wilt thou ruined." * [* Rik-samhita 1-162-21.]

Therefore (the descending jiva) is not born as the rice-grain etc.

The sutrakara gives yet another explanation:

Contact with the semen-shedder (is declared) in the sequel. (III. i. 26)

In the sequel, the sruti speaks of jiva's mere contact with him who sheds semen, in the following passage:

"Whoever, indeed, eats the food and whoever sheds semen, full of that does he verily become." † [† Chha. Up. 5-10-6]

Wherefore, in the preceding case of rice-grain etc., the sruti must mean mere contact.

From the womb (comes) the body (III. i. 27)

When he reaches the womb, then alone is the body produced. Prior to this, there can be a mere contact.

Thus Ends the First Pada of the Third Adhyaya.

SECOND PADA.

Adhikarana 1

In the intervening state is (Jiva's) creation; indeed (the Sruti) says. (III. i. 1)

In the preceding section has treated of the jiva's departure and return. Here his avasthas or states of consciousness will be discussed. In the intervening state, i.e., in svapna or dream, the Sruti speaks of creation in the following words:

"There are no (real) chariots in that state, no horses, no roads; but he himself sends forth (creates) chariots, horses and roads." * [* Bri. Up. 4-3-10.]

A doubt arises as to whether this creation is the jiva's or the Paramesvara's act.

(*Purvapaksha*): - It seems to be an act of the jiva; for the Sruti declares that Jiva himself who is conscious of the dream is the agent, in the following words.

"But he himself sends forth (creates) tanks, lakes, and rivers. He indeed is the maker."† [† Ibid.]

And as the maker, some (declare), (creating the objects of desire such as) sons and so on. (III. ii. 2)

Some Upanishads declare that in Svapna the jiva himself is the creator of the objects of desire in the following words:

"That Purusha who is awake in us while we are asleep, shaping one lovely sight (kama) after another." ‡ [‡ Kaha. Up. 5-8.]

Here the word 'kama' must mean sons and the like, the objects of desire; for, having said at first, "Ask for all objects of desire as you choose," § [§ Ibid 1-25.] the Upanishad says, by way of explanation, "Ask for sons and grandsons who will live a hundred years." ‖ [‖ Ibid 1-23.] For this reason also, the creation of objects is Svapna is only an act of jiva.

(*Siddhanta*): - As against the foregoing, the following is said in reply:

But it is mere Maya, (Jiva's) nature being not fully manifested. (III. i. 3)

All the objects such as chariots created in Svapna are mere Maya, created by Isvara, not created by jiva, intended to be experienced by him who sees the dream, and ending with the end of the dream. They are said to be mayamatra, mere maya, because they are very strange. Jiva can have no power of creating chariots and so on, in as much as his unfailing will is quite obscured. Therefore the 'Purusha,' who is said in the Upanishad to create the objects of desire, does not mean Jiva. On the other hand, the 'Purusha' is the Isvara Himself, as the sequel shows:

"That indeed is the Bright, that is Brahman, that alone is called the Immortal. All worlds are contained in it, and no one goes beyond." * [* Ibid 5-8.]

As pointing to the same Being, the words "He indeed is the maker" † [† Bri. Up. 4-3-10] refers indeed to Isvara. Wherefore the creation of objects in Svapna is an act of the Paramesvara.

The Sutrakara gives the reason why Jiva's true nature is obscured:

By the will of the Supreme, is it obscured; thence, verily, are his bondage and the opposite state. (III. ii. 4)

Owing to the continuous current of Jiva's beginningless transgression, his unfailing will and other (divine) powers are obscured by the will of the Paramesvara. By the same will of the Paramesvara, caused by his transgression and its continuance, jiva is subject to bondage and liberation, bandha and mukti. Accordingly the Sruti says:

"When he finds freedom from fear and rest in that which is invisible, incorporeal, undefined, unsupported, then he has obtained the fearless. For, if he makes but the smallest distinction in it, there is fear for him." ‡ [‡ Taittiriya. Up. 2-7]

Or it may even be on account of contact with the body. (III. ii. 5)

The Jiva's true nature becomes obscured at the time of creation by contact with inert matter in the form of bodies, such as bodies of Devas, men and the like, while during pralaya or dissolution his true nature is obscured by contact with inert matter in a very subtle form, with matter undifferentiated in name and form. Thus, the power of creating strange objects in svapna which last for the time being cannot exist in jiva whose unfailing will and other powers are obscured.

The Sutrakara affords another explanation:

And foreboding indeed it is, as the sruti says. And its proficient also declare. (III. ii. 6)

Svapna is indeed indicative of good or evil, as the sruti declares in the following passages:

"If during sacrifices which are to fulfil certain wishes, he sees in his dreams a woman, let him know success from this vision in a dream year from this vision in a dream." * [* Chha. Up. 5-2-9]

"Next come the dreams. If he sees a black man with black teeth and that man kills him," * and so on. [*Chha. Up. 5-2-9]

The proficients in the science of svapna speak of particular dreams which are indirective of good or evil. The objects seen in the dream are not created by the jiva. If they be jiva's creation, then those objects which may forebode evil would not be created at all. Therefore it stands to reason that creation in svapna is an act of Paramesvara.

Adhikarana 2

Its cessation is in the nadis and in the Atman because of its being declared. (III. ii. 7)

'Its cessation', the cessation of svapna, here points to Sushupti, or dreamless sleep. We are given to understand that during Sushupti jiva sleeps in the nadis (tubes) in the puritat (pericardium), and in Brahman, as the following passages declare:

> "And when a man is asleep, reposing, and at perfect rest, so that he sees no dream, then he has entered into those nadis (tubes)." † [† Aita. Aranyaka. 3-2-4-16, 17.]

> "Next when he is in profound sleep and knows nothing, there are the seventy-two thousand nadis called Hita, which from the heart spread through the body. Through them he moves forth and rests in the surrounding body." ‡ [‡ Chha. Up. 8-6-3]

> "When a man sleeps here, then, my dear son, he becomes united with the Sat, the True." § [§ Bri. Up. 2-1-19]

There arises a doubt as to whether jiva sleeps in any one only of these, or in all of these together.

(*Purvapaksha*): - It is in someone only or other of the places (nadis etc.) that jiva goes to sleep; for, sleep which has to be produced is but a single purpose. Just as, when the Veda enjoins "let him sacrifice with rice," and "let him sacrifice with barley," we understand that they form two alternative courses open, since the cake to be produced is but one purpose, so also, sleep which has to be produced being but a single purpose, it may be served by any one only of the places; the jiva may at one time sleep in the nadis, at another time in the Puritat, at another time again in Brahman. So that it is proper to understand the sruti to mean that they are alternative cases.

(*Siddhanta*): - The Sruti means their conjunction. – Why? – For, more purposes than one have to be served. To explain: Nadis serve as a means, as passages by which jiva goes to Brahman dwelling in the heart. Jiva may sleep in the Puritat and Brahman at the same time, the last two forming as it were a hall and bed therein. Thus, jiva approaches by means of nadis and reposes in Brahman in the Puritat, so that, the different places serving different purposes, a conjunction of them all is meant here.

For this reason also: from Him is the waking. (III. ii. 8)

"When they have come back from the True, they know not that they have come back from the True." In these words the sruti declares that jiva wakes from Brahman. Therefore the conjunction (of all the places) must be meant here. If, indeed, an alternation is meant, then the interpretation is open to eight objections. To hold, in the first place, as one of the alternatives, that jiva lies in the nadis only at one time, is to detract for the time being from the *prima facie* authority of the statement that he lies in the Puritat and Brahman, and to admit that they are false, which no one ever suspects. And then again to hold, as the second of the alternatives that jiva lies in the Puritat and Brahman is to grant to the statement the authority denied to it before and to deny the falsity which was ascribed to it before.

Thus to interpret the passage as pointing to an alternation is to subject the statement that Jiva lies in the Puritat and Brahman to four objections: the abandoning of what is *prima facie* evident, the admitting of what is not evident, the admitting again of what has been abandoned, and the abandoning of what has been admitted. Similarly, it may be shown that the statement that jiva lies in the Nadis is subject to the same four objections. Thus the interpretation of a passage as pointing to alternation involves eight objectionable points. Therefore, when a conjunction is possible, it is improper to resort to alternation.

Adhikarana 3

It is himself indeed, because of the acts, of the memory, of the word, and of the injunction. (III. ii. 9)

Here the passage to be discussed is the following:

"With the True, My dear son, he then becomes united." * [* Chha. Up. 6-8-1]

In the last section, jiva's state of Sushupti has been treated of. Now arises a doubt as to whether he who awakes is the very one that went to sleep in Brahman, or someone else.

(*Purvapaksha*): - It must be someone else, because of the impossibility of the return of one who has attained to Brahman. It is impossible that the jiva who attained equality with Brahman and unsurpassed Bliss should again return to the mundane existence which is full of misery. How can he come out who became one with the True? Where is the distinction between the two?

(*Siddhanta*): - As against the foregoing we hold as follows: Though he became one with the True yet the same jiva who went to sleep rises again on awaking from sleep; for, in the absence of knowledge, he has yet to reap the fruits of the acts done already. He, moreover, remembers what he has experienced before. Further, the following passage declares that the jiva becomes again what he was before:

"Whatever these creatures are here, whether a tiger, or a lion, or a wolf, or a boar, or a worm, or a midge, or a gnat, or a mosquito, that they become again and again." * [* Ibid. 6-10-2.]

Otherwise, all passages that teach of the means of attaining salvation would be of no purpose. In sleep the jiva does not become quite absorbed in Brahman as he does it mukti, because the sruti declares the absence of all knowledge of the bliss of Brahman, in the words

"They come back from the True, and they know it not." † [† Ibid.] Wherefore it is proper to hold that he alone who first went to sleep awakes again.

Adhikarana 4

When stupefied, it becomes half (death), as the only alternative left (III. ii. 10)

We speak of a person being stupefied or unconscious; and this points to the experience of a state (avasthas) called stupefaction (Murchha). A doubt arises as to whether this state is distinct from Sushupti, etc., or not distinct from them.

(*Purvapaksha*): - As no state distinct from the Jagrat, svapna and Sushupti is known to us, it must be one of them.

(*Siddhanta*): - As against the foregoing we hold as follows: The state of a person who has been stupefied is equivalent to half death. Thus, as the only alternative left, it is different from sushupti, etc. It cannot be brought under Jagrat or svapna, because in it is about all consciousness of the universe. And the state of stupefaction must be different from sushupti because of this difference: in sushupti the face, etc., are calm and serene, whereas stupefaction is marked by a distorted face, etc.

Adhikarana 5

Though abiding (in all) no (taint attaches itself) to the Supreme; for, both attributes (are described) everywhere. (III. ii. 11)

In the former sections have been described the essential attributes of jiva – spoken of as 'thou'. – his departure and return, as well as his various states of consciousness (avasthas). Now will be described the essential attributes, etc., of the Paramesvara, spoken of as 'That' (in 'That art thou'). The Sruti speaks of Paramesvara entering into all by becoming one with them, in the following passages:

"He entered within from within; He entered all the quarters within." * [* Atharvasiras.]

"He who dwells in the Earth....." † [† Bri. Up. 3-7-3]

A doubt arises as to whether, when dwelling in all states of being as the Inner Regulator of all, He is or is not subject to the taint of evil of the various sorts.

(*Purvapaksha*): - He is subject to evil. – To explain. The Sruti denies form, etc., to the Paramesvara in such words as the following:

"Not stout, not small, not short." ‡ [‡ Bri. Up. 3-8-8]

"Partless, actionless, tranquil, sinless, taintless." § [§ Sveta. Up. 6-19]

Lest any such evil may be attributed to Him, He is described as mere consciousness, infinite and true, in the following words:

"True, Consciousness, Infinite is Brahman." * [* Taitt. Up. 2-1]

If He be said to have any connection with the material phenomena, He, too, like jiva, should be subject to all the evils of material phenomena.

(*Siddhanta*): - No. Though dwelling in all states of being as the Antaryamin (the Inner Regulator) of all, still, Paramesvara is subject to no taint of evil whatever. – Why? – For, everywhere in the Sruti, as is well known to all, both the attributes are mentioned, - that He is free from all taint of evil, and that He is the repository of unsurpassable excellences, - in such passages as the following:

"It is Atman, free from sin, free from old age, from death and grief, from hunger and thirst, of unfailing desires, of unfailing will." † [† Chha. Up. 8-1-5]

"There is that one who is the seat of excellent qualities which are infinite in extent, who is the creator of all worlds, who is distinct from pasus (jivas) and pasa (bondage, matter)."

Wherefore, though dwelling as the Antaryamin in the Earth, and so on, He is not subject to evil.

(If you say that He is tainted by evil) because of the variety (of being), (we say) no, because of the denial in every case. (III. ii. 12)

(*Objection*): - Just as the jiva, who in himself is free from sin and possessed of such other attributes, is yet subject to evil because of his being connected with the body of a Deva or the like and being thus placed in a variety of state of being, so even the Paramesvara may be subject to evil because of His being connected with a body – as declared in the words "whose body is Earth" – and being thus subject to various states of being.

(*Answer*): - No, because of the declaration, in every case, that He is not subject to evil. In all such passages as "Whose body is Earth...," the Antaryamin, the Inner Regulator, is indeed said to be free from all evil, in the words, "He is thy Atman, the Antaryamin the Immortal." ‡ [‡ Bri. Up. 3-7-3.] As to jiva, on the other hand, it has been said that his essential nature has been obscured by the will of the supreme.

Moreover, so do some (declare). (III. ii. 13)

Moreover, literally to the effect that, between jiva and Isvara, though dwelling in one and the same body as its tenants, there is this difference, namely, that the one is subject to evil while the other is not, - some declare as follows:

"Two beauteous winged companions, ever mates, perch on the self-same tree; one of the twain devours the luscious fruit, fasting its mate looks on."

Wherefore, unlike jiva, Isvara is not subject to evil.

Now, the sutrakara proceeds to show that, though alike dwelling in the body, there is a difference in the mode of their dwelling:

Quite like the formless, indeed, is He, that (differentiation) being His chief (concern) (III. ii. 14)

That Brahman, that Paramesvara, though dwelling in the bodies of Devas and the like as their tenant, remains altogether like a thing that has no form – How? – Because He is chiefly the creator of names and forms. Accordingly the Sruti says:

"He who is called Akasa is the creator of names and forms; That which is contained within these names and forms is the Brahman." * [* Chha. Up. 8-14-1.]

He dwells within names and forms altogether untouched by their effects. It is said that He dwells within them, simply to show that He is independent of them; whereas, indeed, jiva dwells in the body to enjoy the fruits of actions. Hence the difference between the two.

And like light, (He must have divine qualities), since (the scriptures are) not meaningless. (III. ii. 15)

Just as Brahman is said to be Consciousness itself, because He is self-luminous as declared in the scriptural passage – "The True, Consciousness, the Infinite is Brahman." – which must have a meaning, so, too, Brahman must be taintless, the seat of excellent attributes, if the hundred and more passages such as the following should have a meaning at all:

"Partless, actionless, tranquil." † [† Svet. Up. 6-19.]

"Devoid of sins." ‡ [‡ Chha. Up. 8-1-5.]

"Existence itself, with delight in life, and with bliss in manas." ‖ [‖ Taitt. Up. 1-6.]

"Who is omniscient, who knows all." § [§ Mund. Up. 1-1-10.]

"The Lord of Pradhana and Jiva, the Ruler of Gunas." ¶ [¶ Svet. Up. 6-16.]

"He is said to have a Supreme Power (Para Sakti), of various nature." * [* Ibid. 6-16.]

"Now, why is He called Mahadeva? – Because He is the Being who, rising above all states of being, excels in the great power of the knowledge of Atman and of Yoga, therefore He is called Mahadeva." † [† Atharvasiras.]

And (the Sruti) declares (Him to be) that alone. (III. ii. 16)

The Sruti, "the True, Consciousness, the Infinite is Brahman," says merely that Brahman is the Infinite Consciousness. It denies not other (attributes), because thereby no additional meaning is conveyed; nor is there any incompatibility between them. To speak of a crown as made of gold is simply to declare that it is formed of gold; it does not deny that there are no gems and the like set therein. So, too here, the Sruti "the True, Consciousness, the Infinite is Brahman," simply declares that the Parabrahman, as a Mighty Light in Himself, is nothing but Supreme Consciousness in essence. How can it also deny the wisdom, or omniscience of Brahman to be subsequently spoken of. He is wise, because He has consciousness which sees all things of various kinds. Hence no incompatibility.

And the Sruti reveals it, as also the Smriti. (III. ii. 17)

The Blessed Sruti itself reveals everywhere Brahman of both characters, as free from evil qualities, and also as endued with good qualities. The Sruti says:

"Brahman is luminous in body; the existence itself, with delight in life, with bliss in mind; replete with peace, and immortal; thus do thou, O Prachina-Yogya, contemplate." ‡ [‡ Taitt. Up. 1-6.]

Brahman is Akasa, that which shines everywhere, the Light, the all-pervading Intelligence (Chidambaram). He is the Existence. He delights in life, *i.e.*, in Himself, not in external things. His bliss lies in manas, in mind, not in external senses. Here 'manas' means Intelligence, the inner sense (antah-karana); and it is in virtue of His knowledge – which stands in no need of external organs, and by which the whole external universe in manifestation is immediately perceived, and which is ever free from faint, - that Brahman is said to be omniscient. He is said to enjoy bliss in mind because by mind He enjoys the infinite bliss which constitutes His very nature. He is replete with peace, being quite free from attachment, aversion, and other evil qualities; He is quite devoid of all evil taint. He is immortal from time without a beginning; He is the True, Consciousness itself; He is omniscient, manifesting His inherent nature of unsurpassed bliss of Atman; He is free from all evil. The Sruti thus shows that the Supreme Brahman is of a twofold nature. The following passages also declare that Brahman is of this twofold nature:

"Parties, actionless, tranquil" * [* Svcta. Up. 6-19.]

"Who brings good and removes evil, the Lord of bliss." † [† Ibid. 6-6.]

"Him, the Highest the great Lord of lords." ‡ [‡ Ibid. 6-6.]

The smriti also declares that Brahman, designated as Siva, is of the twofold nature:

"The All-pervading Being, whose nature is quite pure particularly because of the absence of all connection with the beginningless sin (mala), is called Siva."

"The Lord, who is infinite bliss itself and possesses excellent qualities, is called Siva by the wise who know the real nature of Siva."

That is to say, Brahman who is devoid of all taint of evil, who is the Supreme Goal of man, is said to be perfect in His qualities as designated by the word 'Siva' which denotes a

The Vedanta-Sutras with Srikantha Bhashya

Being of Supreme purity and excellent attributes. Brahman being thus denoted by the word 'Siva', we conclude that Brahman is endued with the twofold nature.

Hence, indeed, the simile, like the reflected sun, etc. (III. ii. 18)

It is because Paramesvara, though abiding in the earth and everywhere, is free from all taint and is the repository of excellent attributes that He is compared in the scriptures to the sun reflected in water, and so on, in the passages like the following:

"Just as the one Akasa (ether) becomes, indeed, different in the pot and the like, so the one Atman (becomes different) abiding in many, like the sun in the several bodies of water."

The author of this passage cites two illustrations – the Akasa (ether) which really exists (in the different places), and the sun not really existing (in the different reflections) – this idea in mind: Just as the ether, which is one alone, really exists differently in the different objects such as pots, so, the Paramesvara who is one alone exists really in the different things, such as earth, as their Atman. Thus on the analogy of ether we can understand that Paramesvara, though one alone, can actually dwell in many things. Again, just as the sun, who does not actually abide in the various bodies of water wherein he is reflected, is not affected by their changes and other evil aspects, so is the Paramesvara, though actually dwelling in the earth and other objects, unaffected by their changes and other evil aspects. Thus, by the analogy of the sun, we are to understand that the Paramesvara, the Inner Regulator (Antaryamin) within all, is untainted and has all His essential attributes intact. Thus, on the analogy of the ether and the like, the Paramesvara, the Atman of all is, we may conclude, endued with the two fold nature.

Here the following objection is raised:

Not being understood as in the case of water, indeed it cannot be so. (III. ii. 19)

(*Objections*): - The sun in water is regarded as unreal, but not so is the Paramesvara in the earth (unreal). On the other hand, it is regarded that He actually dwells there. So, how can He be free from all taint?

The objection is answered as follows:

(No) liability to growth or decline by dwelling within, because (then alone) the two (similes) will have a consistent meaning, as also because (similes are) found in similar (use). (III. ii. 20)

(*Answer*): - The word 'no' occurring in the preceding Sutra should be understand here. – Notwithstanding the fact of His abiding actually within the earth and the like, the Paramesvara is not liable to the growth and decline to which they are subject. We come to this conclusion, because then alone the two similes will have a due significance. Indeed, it has been already said that the use of the two similes – the sun who does not actually abide (in the reflections) and the ether which actually does abide in all objects – points to the conclusion that the Paramesvara, though abiding in all objects, is unaffected b their evil as though He does not abide in them. We do find similes used, pointing merely to a similarity in some particular attribute, as for example, "the moon-like face." Hence the conclusion that Isvara, though really abiding in the earth and other objects, is endued with the twofold nature.

Or, (to interpret the last reason in another way), - even in the Sruti we find a simile employed, pointing to a similarity only in some particular attribute, as in the passage like the following: -

"Having shaken off sin as the horse shakes off the hair." * [* Chha. Up. 8-13-1.]

Thus, the two similes being reconcilable only on the ground of similarity in some particular attributes, it may be concluded that Brahman in endued with the twofold nature.

Adhikarana 6

The Sutrakara imagines an objection based on the impossibility of the twofold nature, and answers as follows:

(The Sruti) denies, indeed, His being only so much, and so says again. (III. ii. 21)

In the preceding Adhikarana it has been shown that Brahman is of a twofold nature. Now a doubt arises as to whether this conclusion is falsified or not.

(*Purvapaksha*): - Having declared – in the words "there are two forms of Brahman, the material and the immaterial," * [* Bri.Up. 2-1-3.] – that Brahman is in the form of the universe, material and immaterial, as made up of earth, water, light, air and ether, the Sruti says "next follows the teaching: (HE is) not thus, not thus." † [† Ibid 2-3-6.] As the word 'thus' refers back here to what has been said already, what has been said regarding Brahman – viz., that He is in the form of the universe, material and immaterial – is denied.

(*Siddhanta*): - As against the foregoing we hold as follows: The words "not thus, not thus," do not deny what has been already taught, - *viz.*, that Brahman is in the form of the universe, - in as much as it is not proper to deny what has been taught as a new thing, as unknown before. On the other hand, we ought to understand that the words only go to deny that Brahman is not merely what He has been here declared to be; for, subsequently in the following words, the Sruti again speaks of attributes which have not been already declared:

"For there is nothing else higher than He (who has been) declared to be 'not thus." Then comes the name, 'the True of the true'; the lives are verily the true, and He the True of them." * [* Ibid.]

This passage teaches that there exists nothing else higher than Brahman who has been described in the words "not thus, not thus." Then His name is declared in the words "the Tree of the true." The meaning thereof is then explained in the words "The lives are, verily, the true, and He the True of them." Here "lives" mean jivas, the individual souls, and they are true because unlike ether (Akasa) they have no birth. Even of these jivas, the true ones, He is the True, because unlike them, His knowledge is never obscured. Thus the words "not thus, not thus," going only to deny the limitation of His attributes to those which have been already declared, it does not detract from the former conclusion that Brahman is of a twofold nature.

(*Objection*): - The True (Brahman) corresponds to the existence which is present in all things, of which we speak in the terms "the pot existing," "the cloth existing," and so on. Everything else, such as the pot, the cloth, etc., which varies, is denied (*i.e.*, is said to be not Brahman) by the Sruti in the words "not thus, not thus."

(*Answer*): - As against this, the Sutrakara says:

It is Unmanifested, (the Sruti says) indeed. (III. ii. 22)

The essential nature of Brahman is revealed by no other pramana or organ of knowledge such as pratyaksha or sensuous perception. The Sruti says, "His form stands not within the vision's field, with the eye no man beholds Him, by mind...is He revealed; † [† Katha. Up. 6-9.] therefore, the existence which is revealed b sensuous perception cannot be Brahman.

The Sutrakara proceeds to show what the organ of perceiving Brahman is:

But (it is revealed) in ecstasy as (told) by direct and indirect (Revelation). (III. ii. 23)

But the essential nature of Brahman is apprehended in ecstasy by the mind attaining to the state of intense meditation. That to those who contemplate Brahman, regarding themselves as Brahman, the essential nature of Brahman becomes accessible is known from the following passages of the Sruti:

"This Atman is not obtainable by explanation, nor yet by mental grasp, nor by hearing many times; by him whom so he chooses, by him He is obtained. For him, the Atman His proper form reveals." * [* Katha-Up. 2-23.]

"Then does one, in ecstasy, Him free from parts behold." † [† Mund. Up. 3-1-8.]

The following passage of the smriti is also to the same effect:

"He is not in the ken of sensuous perception."

And as in the case of light, etc., so exactly here. And the manifestation (takes place) by constant practice of the act. (III. ii. 24)

They to whom, as a result of constant worship of meditation, Brahman manifests Himself, - they, when seeing by that vision of Brahman, find that like consciousness, bliss, etc., sovereignty over the universe is alike His attribute. To explain: that those who meditate upon Brahman realise in themselves all the attributes of Brahman as a result of the meditation of unity is declared by the Sruti in the following passages:

"I have become Manu as well as the Sun." ‡ [‡ Bri-Up. 1-4-10.]

"Do thou meditate upon me as life, as immortality." § [§ Kaush. Up. 3-2.]

Such passages as "i give thee divine sight, see my divine power," do indeed testify to the manifesting in Krishna and the like of the Divine power as the result of a constant meditation of unity. And by constant meditation of Brahman, Visvamitra, Agastya and others attained the power of creating another Svarga, of drinking the ocean, and the like. In the world of today, those who take to the repetition of mantras (incantations) develop, by meditating upon *Garuda* the peculiar properties of *Garuda*.|| [|| Bh. Gita.11-18.] Thus it is clear that, when the idea of unity with Brahman has attained perfection, the Upasakas attain to the peculiar state in which they find themselves in possession of all the peculiar attributes of Brahman. It is therefore unreasonable to maintain that Brahman is the mere existence revealed by sensuous perception, and formed in association with all objects such as a pot. Thus, because contemplation (nididhyasana) and other means of attaining an intuitive perception would otherwise have no purpose to serve, and because the mere existence (even supposing that it is not apprehended in sensuous perception) is not declared anywhere to be possessed of the attributes of Brahman, it does not at all stand to reason to say that Brahman as mere existence is immediately perceived and that the Sruti, "not thus, not thus," denies all else.

Wherefore (He is endowed) with infinite (attributes). Hence, indeed, His nature. (III. ii. 25)

Because wisdom, bliss, supreme dominion and other characteristic attributes of Brahman manifest themselves even in those who devoutly contemplate Him, therefore it may be concluded that Brahman does possess excellent qualities, infinite in number, as mentioned in the Sruti. "There are two forms of Brahman"* [* Bri.Up. 2-3-1.] Hence the twofold nature of Brahman.

(*Objection*): - The assertion of the sruti – in the words "There are two forms of Brahman" * [* Bri.Up. 2-3-1.] etc, - that the universe is the form of Brahman can be explained only by regarding Brahman and the universe as brought together by illusion, by way of mistaking one for the other; their mutual relation being incapable of any other explanation. Wherefore, it is but right to hold that the passage, "Next follows the teaching: He is not thus, not thus," † points to a denial of the reality of the universe which has been supposed to exist owing to illusion.

(*Answer*): - The sutrakara, before explaining the relation in his own way without resorting to the hypothesis of illusion, first states (two) other theories:

Because of the mention of both, (He is) verily like the serpent and the coil. (III. ii. 26)

(i) Because of the assertion of both unity and diversity of Paramesvara, as made in such passages as "All verily is Rudra;" ‡ [‡ Mahana. 16.] "Heaven and Earth producing the Divine is one", § [§ Ibid. 1-12.] the earth and other forms of being spoken of in the sruti – "There are indeed two forms of Brahman," etc. – pertain to Paramesvara Himself, just as the serpent may be in either form, straight or coiled.

Or, (it is) like (the unity of) light and its above (which are one) because both of them are luminous things. (III. ii. 27)

(ii) Though light, and its abode are substantially different, yet they are regarded as one because both of them pertain to the genus of luminous objects; so also, Brahman and the insentient are regarded as one, both of them coming under the one genus (of Brahman). This forms another explanation of the unity of Brahman and the Earth, etc.

Or as before. (III. ii. 28)

The word 'or' shows that what follows is quite distinct from the two theories above referred to. In a former section it was shown that *chit* or spirit constitutes a portion (of Isvara), in as much as it forms an integral part of the composite whole (Isvara), standing, always in an attributive relation (to Isvara) genus, qualities, and bodies like light. So, too, in the case of *achit* or matter. It is possible to speak of spirit and matter in one word, as is done in the passage "All verily is Rudra," * [* Mahana. 16.] only when they constitute the form of one Entity and are related in the way mentioned above. In the case of the two other theories, it is impossible to avoid the conclusion that Brahman is impure. And we conclude that the *chit* and the *achit*, spirit and matter, constitute the body of the eight formed Brahman, on the authority of the following passages of sruti and smriti:

"Whose body is Earth." † [† Bri. Up. 3-7-3.]

"Whose body is Atman." † [† Bri. Up. 3-7-3.]

"They call sentiency vidya and insentiency avidya. The whole universe made up of vidya and avidya is no doubt the form of the Lord, the Lord of all; for the whole universe is in his control."

And because of the denial. (III. ii. 29)

Though Brahman ensouls chit and achit, spirit and matter, He is said to be devoid of their attributes in such passages as the following:

"Not by the decay of this does It decay." ‡ [‡ Chha. 8-1-5.]

"Not gross, not subtle, not short." § [§ Bri. Up. 3-8-8.]

And for this reason, too, that Brahman, though associated with *chit* and *achit*, is free from evil, and is the repository of all excellent qualities.

That is to say: Though Brahman or (Siva) is the cause of *chit* and *achit* and is associated with them, He is ever free from mutability, ignorance and other undesirable qualities, and is ever endued with such supremely excellent qualities as omniscience, eternal bliss, eternal wisdom, absolute independence, undiminished power, infinite potentialies.

Adhikarana 7

Now the Sutrakara first raises an objection with a view to declare ultimately that there exists nothing higher than he, the odd-eyed Siva, the Supreme Brahman, the one homogeneous essence, with the Supreme Energy (Paramasakti) manifested in the form of the whole sentient and insentient existence, free from passions, thought-impressions, and taints of all kinds the ocean of all auspicious attributes such as omniscience.

(There is something) beyond Him, because He is spoken of as a bridge, while a measure, relation and separateness are predicated of Him. (III. ii. 30)

A doubt arises as to whether there exists or not something even beyond that Paramesvara, who has been described, from I-ii-2 up to III-ii-29, as the Supreme cause.

(*Purvapaksha*): - There does exist something beyond. To explain: This Parabrahman is said to be a bridge, a something to be crossed over, a thing capable of measurement, and a thing leading to something else in such passages as the following:

"Now, this Atman is a bridge, the sustainer." * [* Chaa. 8-4-1.]

"Having crossed this bridge, though blind one is no longer blind." * [* Chaa. 8-4-1.]

"Four-faced is Brahman." † [† Ibid. 3-18-2.]

"To the Immortal He is a bridge." ‡ [‡ Mund. Up. 2-2-5.]

Wherefore, even higher than He, there exists something.

Now, Siddhanta follows:

But (it is) because of a resemblance. (III. ii. 31)

(*Siddhanta*): - The word 'but' shows that Siddhanta follows as opposed to the Purvapaksha. It is not proper to say that there exists anything higher than He, than Siva who is higher than all." "Higher than all, is Rudra, the mighty Sage." * [* Mahana. 10-19.] From these words of the sruti we understand that He is higher than all. And as to His being spoken of as a bridge, it is only because of a resemblance, in so far as He prevents all worlds from getting into confusion. The Sruti says: -

"This Atman is the bridge, the sustainer, that there may be no confusion of these worlds." † [† Chha. 8-4-1.]

It is Brahman, - who is both the material and the efficient cause of the universe as declared in the sruti "All this, verily, in Brahman," ‡ [‡ Ibid. 3-14.] – that is to be reached, as we may understand from the passage "To Him, hence departing, shall I go." Elsewhere, too, the sruti says:

"Him...who is Three-eyed, Dark-necked, and Serene: having meditated Him thus, the sage reaches Him who is the womb of all beings, the witness of all, transcending darkness." § [§ Kaivalya. Up.]

Here it is Brahman – who is beyond darkness, who is the cause of all, the Omniscient, the Three-eyed and so on – that is spoken of as the Goal beyond all. Accordingly to cross here simply means to reach. Otherwise, if there should exist a thing even above the Supreme Cause, above the Supreme Goal higher than all, then it follows that there might exist another thing even beyond that there might exist another thing even beyond that, and so on; and thus the Vedantic texts do not teach anything definitely. Accordingly the Paramasiva is beyond all, and hence the supremacy of Brahman over all.

As to Brahman being capable of measurement, the sutrakara says:

(It is) for the sake of contemplation, as (when speaking) of feet. (III. ii. 32)

It is for the sake of contemplation that the sruti speaks of Brahman as four-footed, as when speaking of speech as a tool of the four-footed Brahman. ‖ [‖ Chha. Up. 3-18-2.]

(It is) on account of the particular place, as in the case of light etc. (III. ii. 33)

It is true that Paramesvara is altogether immeasurable. Still it is proper to think of Him as limited, in virtue of the seat of his manifestation, just as light appears limited with reference to the window or any other place through which it comes.

The sutrakara says that, though he is the Goal, He is also the one who leads the devotee to the Goal:

And because of the propriety. (III. ii. 34)

It is but proper that Brahman who is Himself the Goal is also the one who leads the devotee to the Goal, as the sruti says "He is attainable to him alone whom He chooses." * [*Katha. Up. 2-23.] Wherefore we may conclude that there exists none higher than Paramesvara.

Adhikarana 8

Similarly, (there is none equal to Him), because of the denial. (III. ii. 35)

In the preceding adhikarana it has been shown that there is none higher than the Supreme Brahman, the odd eyed (Virupaksha) Siva. Now, again, a doubt arises as to whether there exists one equal to him.

(*Purvapaksha*): - Though there is no being higher than Paramesvara, there exists a being who is equal to Him in so far as he is the cause of the universe, the lord, and so on. So, indeed, the sruti speaks of a soul (Purusha) as "Thousand-headed Purusha, thousand-eyed, thousand-footed." † [† Tait. Aranyaka. 3-12.] In the words "Thousand-headed Purusha" and so on, the Purusha is represented to have many faces and feet. In the words "A foot of his are all the creatures" † [† Tait. Aranyaka. 3-12.] the sruti shows that he is associated with the universe. "Three feet of his are immortal, in the shining (heaven)" † [† Tait. Aranyaka. 3-12.] in these words the sruti says that he dwells in the Paramakasa the Supreme Light. "From him was the Viraj born, and next to Viraj, the Purusha;" † [† Tait. Aranyaka. 3-12.] in these words he is represented to be the upadana or material cause of the Aryakta and the Hiranyagarbha. In the words "Sun-coloured, (he is) verily beyond the darkness." † [† Tait. Aranyaka. 3-12.] he is said to be above darkness. "Knowing him thus, one becomes immortal here:" from these words we learn that he is then cause of moksha. Again, he is spoken of as the "Thousand-headed God," ‡ [‡ Mahana. 11] as "the Lord of the Universe," as "Narayana and the Supreme Brahman," ‡ [‡ Mahana. 11] and "as Paramatman abiding in the heart" ‡ [‡ Mahana. 11] i.e., as the being who has to be contemplated in the heart. Wherefore this being, Narayana, is equal to Paramesvara in attributes. These, indeed, are the attributes of Paramesvara also. The Mantropanishad says:

> "Whose faces, heads and necks, are those of all, who lieth in the secret place of every soul, spread over the universe is He, the Lord. Therefore the all-pervader is Siva." * [* Svet. Up. 3-11.]

The Mahopanishad says:

> "With eyes on every side, and with faces on every side."

Even in the Siva-Sankalpa, He is declared to have faces on all sides. In the Atharvasiras, the Paramesvara is said to have many faces, feet, and so on. He is said to be associated with the universe as an integral part of His being:

> "(This) Maya, indeed, as Prakriti, man should know and the possessor of Maya as the Mahesvara. All this universe is pervaded by that which forms a limb of His." ‡ [‡ Svet. Up. 4-10.]

He is said to be the causes of the Hiranyagarbha in such passages as "seeing the Hiranyagarbha being born." § [§ Manana. 10-19.] He is said to be beyond Darkness in the words "Who is the witness of all, beyond Darkness." ‖ [‖ Kaivalya. Up.] He is said to be the

The Vedanta-Sutras with Srikantha Bhashya

Being whom we have to contemplate in the Dahara (small bright space in the heart), in the words "who is the small (Dahara), free from sin,"¶ [¶ Mahana. 11.] and in the words "having known Siva one attains limitless peace," ** [** Svet. 4-14.] He is said to be the cause of Moksha. In the words "Endued with lordship overall" †† [†† Atharvasikha.] we are given to understand that He is the Lord of all. Hence the equality in attributes such as that of being of all forms. In the Smritis and other scriptural works, enjoining divine worship, it is declared that either of the two. Paramesvara or Narayana, may be worshipped as alternatives of equal importance; "worship either Siva or Vishnu." And in fact in the words we find places of worship. Puranas and Agamas devoted to both of them alike. Wherefore Purusha or Narayana is equal to Paramesvara.

(*Siddhanta*): - As against the foregoing we hold as follows: Just as there is none higher than Paramesvara so there is none, indeed, equal to Him, because of the declaration that none else can be the cause and the lord of the universe. The following passages declare that none other than Paramesvara can be the cause of the universe:

"There is the One, Rudra alone, - they are not for a second, - who rules these worlds with the powers of ruling and creating." * [* Atharvasiras.]

"Heaven and earth producing, there is one Deva." † [† Mahana. 1-12.]

"The One who is called Rudra." ‡ [‡ Tai. Ara. 1-12.]

"The One Deva, Hara, rules the perishable and the Atman." § [§ Sweta. Up. 1-10.]

"When, like a skin, men shall roll up the sky, then (only, not till then) shall end of sorrow be without men knowing God." ‖ [‖ Ibid. 6-20.]

"Siva alone, the Beneficent one, should be contemplated, abandoning all else." ¶ [¶ Atharvasikhai.]

"When there is no darkness, there is no day, nor night, nor being, nor non-being; Siva alone there is." ** [** Svet. Up. 4-18.]

Wherefore, there is none equal to Paramesvara. As possessed of the Supreme Energy (Paramasakti), Paramesvara alone is the Nimitta or efficient cause. Since Purusha is the upadana or material cause, he is the cause of Hiranyagarbha. He being the material cause, and Paramesvara the efficient cause, both are said to be the cause of the universe. Hence we understand that the sruti "from Him was born Viraj" only declares that Purusha is the upadana or material cause; and Paramesvara is declared to be the efficient cause in such passages as "the heaven and the earth producing, there was the one Deva." From Siva, the omniscient, omnipotent Parabrahman who is above the whole universe, there arises first the Supreme Power (Parasakti) the ultimate Prakriti or Material cause. When the Power is manifested as the Primal Bhoktri or conscious experiencer, we have what is called Purusha, spoken of in the sruti as "the thousand headed Purusha." It is from Siva thus ensouling the Purusha that the whole evolution of the sentient universe takes place. Hence it is that the sruti starts with speaking of Paramesvara as the All, in the words "All verily is Rudra," and then speaks of Purusha or Narayana as the all, because of his being the upadana or material cause. The question arising as to how Purusha can be the All, the sruti declares that even Purusha is but a mighty manifestation of Paramesvara's being and, as such, is in the form of the universe, as witness the following passages:

"Purusha, verily, is Rudra." †† [†† Mahana. Up. 16.]

"Let us contemplate Purusha and let us meditate upon the thousand-eyed Mahadeva." ‡‡ [‡‡ Ibid. 1-21.]

The very Supreme Brahman, who is omniscient, omnipotent, ever contended, independent, higher than the universe, the efficient cause of the universe, wills "May I become manifold" and evolves this Purusha from Himself. By this Purusha who is evolved from, and forms a part of Himself, the Supreme Brahman manifests Himself as the universe, as the following passages in the Sruti clearly show:

"Having created it, He entered into it; and having entered into it, both being and beyond did He become." * [* Taitt.Up. 2-6.]

"(This) Maya, indeed, as Prakriti, man should know, and the possessor of Maya as the Mahesvara. All this universe is pervaded by that which forms a limb of His" † [† Sveta-Up. 4-10.]

The upadana state grows out of the will of the efficient cause, and therefore the efficient cause is superior to the material cause. Because of the inseparability of the upadana from the efficient cause, the attributes of the efficient cause are applied to the upadana. Therefore there exists nothing equal or superior to Paramesvara.

The sutrakara says that, for the following reason also, there exists none whatsoever equal or superior to Paramesvara:

Hence His omnipresence, (as may be learned) from the Sruti speaking of the vast extent and so on. (III. ii. 36)

Through Pursuha, - who is the Upadana, who is the part and parcel of Parabrahman, - the efficient cause, *i.e.*, the Parabrahman, pervades all, as declared in the following passages of the Sruti speaking of His presence throughout the whole universe:

"Whose faces, heads, and necks are those of all." ‡ [‡ Sveta. 3-11.]

"Whose eyes are everywhere, and whose faces are everywhere." § [§ Mahana. Up. 1-12.]

"Smaller than the small....All verily is this Rudra." ‖ [‖ Ibid. 10-16.]

"He who is called Rudra is the Lord...He who, is the True..."¶ [¶ Atharvasiras.]

Wherefore, the whole universe being but a manifestation of Paramesvara there exists none either equal or superior to Him.

Adhikarana 9

The Sutrakara now proceeds to show that, being thus the Lord of all and the all-penetrating Entity, the Paramesvara Himself is the dispenser of the fruits of all actions, either Himself directly or in the form of the respective Gods concerned:

Hence is the fruit, because of the propriety. (III. ii. 37)

Here a doubt arises as to whether the dispenser of the fruits of all actions to those who perform them is the Parabrahman Himself who has been declared in the preceding adhikarana to be the Lord of all, or someone else.

(Purvapaksha): - Karma (action), though vanishing away the moment it is produced, has yet the power of yielding the fruit at some future time through the medium of the apurva (the unseen form which action is said to assume prior to the realisation of its fruit). Thus action itself being capable of yielding its fruit, it seems unnecessary to postulate a distinct unknown entity in the form of the Paramesvara. Therefore, the Paramesvara cannot be the dispenser of the fruits of actions.

(*Siddhanta*): - It is from the Paramesvara duly worshipped that all obtain the fruits of their actions; for, it is reasonable. It stands to reason that devotees should obtain the fruits of their actions from the Paramesvara who is worshipped, as from a king to whom service is rendered. Certainly, neither the insentient action itself nor the insentient apurva (its invisible form) has the power to discriminate and dispense the fruits of several actions just in accordance with their respective nature; for, we do not find any such power possessed by service which is insentient. Here, Paramesvara, as known through the scriptures, is not a mere postulate, and there is therefore no fault of a needless assumption. It is in fact said: -

> "For He makes him, whom He wishes to lead up from these worlds, no good deeds; He makes him, whom he wishes to lead down from these worlds, do a bad deed." *
> [* Kaush. Up. 3-8.]

In these words the Sruti declares that Isvara alone dispenses the fruits of the acts of Dharma and Adharma and impels people to them. On the other hand, it is the postulating of the apurva not taught in the scriptures that involves the fault of needless assumption. Hence the conclusion that Paramesvara Himself worshipped by works dispenses the fruits of actions; not the actions themselves.

And because so He is declared to be. (III. ii. 38)

Indeed the Paramesvara is declared to be the lord of all works, - as worshipped by their means and as the dispenser of their fruits, - in the following passage:

> "...Rudra, the Lord of hymns, the Lord of sacrifices, possessed of medicaments that confer delight." * [* Rig Veda. 1-43-4.]

> "Secure Rudra, the king of sacrifice..." † [† Ibid. 4-3.]

The Smriti, too, based on these passages of the Sruti, declares that the Paramesvara is the lord of all sacrifices:

> "Let everyone worship, by soma, the Divine Being who is associated with Uma and who is adorned with the moon."

And the Ramayana, too, says:

> "There is no sacrifice, higher than the horse-sacrifice (asvamedha), in the matter of Rudra's worship."

And in the Chamakas also (Taittiriya-Samhita IV. Vii. 1-11) – which read "May food (come) to me), may permission (come) to me; ...may Dhatri (come) to me,...may Vishnu (come) to me" – all things such as food, and all Gods such as Vishnu are declared as things to be given, so that, - as the sole alternative left, - the Paramesvara alone is the dispenser of the fruits of all actions. Therefore it is the Paramesvara alone who is to be worshipped by all sacrifices, and who is the dispenser of all fruits.

For the same reason, Jaimini holds that it is Dharma. (III. ii. 39)

Jaimini thinks that Dharma itself is the dispenser of the fruits for the same reasons, *i.e.*, because it stands to reason and because it is so declared in the sruti. It stands to reason, because in the case of tilling, crushing, and so on, we see that the result is produced either directly or indirectly by the action itself. That the act itself in the form of apurva yields its fruits may be taken as declared in the sruti, in as much as we cannot otherwise account for the injunction of an act as the means by which he who seeks a particular result can attain it.

But Badarayana (thinks it is) the former, because He is mentioned as the cause. (III. ii. 40)

The blessed Badarayana thinks that the Paramesvara Himself mentioned before is the dispenser of the fruits of actions, in as much as in the very injunctions of works, - such as "he who seeks prosperity should sacrifice a white animal in honour of Vayu; Vayu indeed is the swiftest God...and he alone leads the sacrificer to prosperity," * - Vayu and other Gods, ensouled as they are by the Paramesvara, are mentioned as the sources of the fruits. [* Tait. Samhita. 2-1-1.] It is only in the absence of a God that we will have to postulate that the transitory act assumes the form of Apurva. On the other hand, when in the sequel of the section enjoining the act the sruti itself explains – with a view to satisfy the natural curiosity that arises close upon the injunction – who it is that dispenses the fruit, that explanation alone must be accepted, just as from the passage "they are very well established, they who perform these rites"† [† Tait. Br. 23-2-1.] the fruit of the act enjoined – without which the injunction is not complete – is accepted as declared in the sequel. From the Atharvasiras, which reads "He who is called Rudra is the Lord," we understand that the Isvara is in the form of all Gods such as Vayu. In the same Upanishad, in the words "He who knows me knows all Gods" it is declared that by knowing Him one gets a knowledge of all Gods who are all ensouled by Himself. Hence the conclusion that it is the Paramesvara, - the Supreme Brahman, Siva,

Uma's Lord Himself – who is in the form of all Gods, who has to be worshipped by all acts, and who is the dispenser of all fruits.

THIRD PADA.

Adhikarana 1

In the preceding portion of the work has been determined the nature of the Pasu, the worshipper (upasaka), spoken of as 'thou' (in "Thou art That"), and endued with the attribute of eternality etc,; as also of Siva, the Lord (Pati), the object of all worship, spoken of as 'That', and endued with omniscience and other attributes. Now a question arising as to how to worship Him, the answer comes in the sequel:

What is enjoined in all Vedas (is the same) because of the absence of all difference in the command etc. (III. iii. 1)

In all the Vedantas (Upanishads) the Dahara-upasana and the like are treated. A doubt arises as to whether the upasana treated in different Upanishads is one and the same or differs with the different recensions.

(*Purvapaksha*): - As context (prakarana) differs with difference in recension (Sakha), the upasana differs with different sakhas. Now, in the Chhandogya and the Taittiriyaka, the Dahara-upasana is treated. In the one, such attributes as sinlessness are described in the passage which begins with the words, "The Atman who is free from sin, free from old age, free from death,"* etc. [* Op. Cit. 8-7-1.] In the other, in the passage "The right, the true," † [† Mahana. 11.] etc., such attributes as dark-brown-ness are mentioned. Here, owing to the difference in the attributes, the upasana differs. In the Chhandogya, again, the Panchagni-Vidya (the contemplation of Five Fires) is designated as Kauthuma, while it is designated as Vajasaneya in the Brihadaranyaka. Here, owing to the difference in the designation, the upasana differs. In the Mundaka-sakha is spoken of a rite called Sirovrata (the ceremony of carrying fire on the head) in the words,

"Let a man tell this Brahma-vidya (science of Brahman) to those only by whom the siro-vrata has been performed according to the rule." † [† Mahana. 11.]

Sirovrata is a special ceremony connected with the study of the Vedas and it is enjoined on the Atharvanikas (the students of the Atharva-Veda), not on others. Owing to this difference in the rite, the upasana differs. Thus, the upasana differs owing to the difference in the sakha etc.

(*Siddhanta*): - The Dahara-upasana and the like, taught in all the different Upanishads, are one and the same; for, as in the case of injunctions of sacrificial works, so here, the words of injunction (chodana), the results to be attained, the form of the Devata, and the designations (of the upasanas) are all same. In the first place, the terms of injunction – such as "let him know", "let him contemplate" – are same in the different sakhas. Even the results to be attained, - such as the attaining of Brahman, - are same. The objects of worship, too, are same, such as the Vaisvanara-Brahman. And even the designations are same, such as the Vaisvanara-Vidya and so on. Therefore the Upasana is one and the same. Notwithstanding the use of different verbs – such as 'let him *know*', 'let him *contemplate*', - the upasana does not differ. In the Chhandogya, the Dahara-Vidya is enjoined in the words, "What exists within that small ether, that should be *sought* for;" * [* Op. Cit. 8-1-1.] and the Taittiriya enjoins it in the words "What is there within, that should be *contemplated*." † [† Mahana. 10-23.] In this case, since the seat of contemplation etc., are same, since Brahman, the object of contemplation, is the same, and since the attributes mentioned in the two Upanishads are not opposed to one another, the Vidya (upasana) is the same. The Brihadaranyaka and the Chhandogya-Upanishad described the nature of the five fires to be contemplated, - namely, heaven, rain, earth, man and woman; and the nature of these fires is described in the same way in both. Hence no distinction in the vidya (upasana).

If (you say it is not so) because of the distinction (implied), (we reply that the distinction is possible) even (when the upasana is) one. (III. iii. 2)

(*Objection*): - Repetition of the same thing, combined with difference in the context (prakarana) or sakha, points to a difference in the upasana. Therefore the upasana taught in different sakhas is not one and the same.

(*Answer*): - Though the upasana is one and the same, repetition of the same upasana in a different context (prakarana) or sakha can be accounted for by the fact of the people who learn the vidya from that other sakha being different. Therefore, the fact does not point to a distinction in the upasana.

(The siro-vrata) pertains to the recitation of the text, because as such, indeed, it is treated of in the ritualistic section. And as in the case of sava, it is restricted to them. (III. iii. 3)

The siro-vrata enjoined in the Atharva-Veda in the words "To them alone let him tell this Brahma-Vidya" ‡ [‡ Munda.Up. 3-2-10.] is intended as an appendage to the recitation of that Veda (svadhyaya), not as an appendage to the Vidya or Upasana; for, the passage "He shall not study it who has not performed the rite" § [§ Ibid. 3-2-11.] shows that the rite pertains to the recitation of the Vedic text, and in the samachara-grantha, *i.e.*, in the work called Samachara (ritual) it is declared to be a Veda-Vrata – a ritual pertaining to the Vedic recitation – in the words "This, too, has been treated by the treatment of the Veda-Vrata." In the phrase 'Brahma-Vidya', the word 'Brahman' means Veda. Therefore just as the Sava-homa is confined to the followers of the Atharva-Veda, so is the siro-vrata confined to them alone, so that it does not point to any distinction in the Vidya or Upasana itself.

The (Sruti) also declares. (III. iii. 4)

The Sruti itself shows the unity of upasana. In the section of the Dahara-Vidya, the Mahopanishad and the Kaivalya-Upanishad described the form of the Isvara as follows:

The Vedanta-Sutras with Srikantha Bhashya

"The Right, the True, the Supreme Brahman, in person dark-brown, chaste, divers eyed." * [* Mahana. 12.]

"Associated with Uma, the Paramesvara, the Lord, Three-eyed, Nilakantha (dark-necked, tranquil." † [† Kaivalya. Up.]

From this one may think that, as a corporeal being, the Isvara is subject to sin, decay, death and the like. It is to prevent this supposition that the Chhandogya-Upanishad declares that He is possessed of the eight attributes mentioned in the passage beginning with the words "Now, as to the small lotus in the city of Brahman" etc." ‡ [‡ Op. Cit. 8-1-1.] In these cases repetition can be accounted for by different attributes being spoken of in different sakhas. So, there is no room for the supposition that it points to a difference in the Vidya itself. Accordingly, since the terms of the injunction are identical, *i.e.*, owing to the absence of a difference in the terms of injunction, etc., pointing to a difference in the Upasana, the Upasana taught in all the Upanishads is one and the same.

Adhikarana 2

The sutrakara now proceeds to state what is aimed at in showing the unity of the Upasanas enjoined in all the Upanishads:

A collection (should be made of attributes) owing to identity of the purpose. As in the case of the appendages of an injunction, so, too, in the case of (an Upasana which is) similar (in kind). (III. iii. 5)

Here, though oneness of Upasana has been established, a doubt arises as to whether the attributes mentioned in one sakha should be gathered in another sakha or not.

(*Purvapaksha*): - They should not be gathered. To explain: in the Chhandogya are mentioned in the Dahara-Vidya the attributes such as sinlessness, but not in the Taittiriya-Upanishad. The attributes mentioned in the Chhandogya-Upanishad should not be gathered in the Taittiriya, because they are not mentioned in the latter. As to the purpose of the Upasana, they are served by the attributes mentioned there, namely 'dark-brown' etc. What need is there for the gathering of attributes mentioned elsewhere, for which there is no direction in the sruti?

(*Siddhanta*): - As against the foregoing we hold as follow: In all cases, where the Upasana is one, such attributes as sinlessness mentioned in the Chhandogya in connection with the Dahara-Vidya etc., should be gathered together elsewhere in connection with the Daharavidya etc., taught in the Taittiriyaka and other Upanishads, in as much as the purpose of these attributes is the same, namely, to subserve the upasana. Just as the subsidiary acts (angas) enjoined (in different sakhas) as parts of one main act enjoined are gathered together in the case of the Agnihotra and the like, so in the case of the Dahara-Upasana or the like, where the terms of injunction etc., are same, the attributes (mentioned in different sakhas) should be gathered together. Wherefore, it stands to reason that the attribute mentioned in different sakhas in connection with the same Upasanas should be gathered together.

The Vedanta-Sutras with Srikantha Bhashya

Adhikarana 3

(If you maintain) that they are different because of the scripture, (we reply) no, because of the non-distinction. (III. iii. 6)

In the Brihadaranyaka-Upanishad and in the Chhandogya-Upanishad, the contemplation of the Udgitha song as Prana, leading to the enemy's defeat, is enjoined. A doubt arises as to whether there is, or there is not, a unity of upasana in this case.

(*Purvapaksha*): - Since the terms of injunction etc., are same, there is a unity of upasana.

(*Objection*): - The object of the upasana as Prana enjoined in the Brihadaranyaka is the agent in the act of singing, *i.e.*, the one that sings the Udgita, as may be known from the following passage:

"Then they said to the breath in the mouth: 'Do thou sing for us.' 'Yes,' said the breath, and sang." * [* Bri. Up. 1-3-7.]

But in the case of the Chhandogas the object of contemplation is the Udgitha, itself which is sung, i.e., which is the object of the act of singing, as may be seen from the following passage:\

"Then comes this breath (of life) in the mouth. They meditated upon the Udgitha as that breath." † [† Chha. Up. 1-2-7.]

Therefore, the upasanas are different.

(*Answer*): The opening statements in both are the same. The Brihadaranyaka opens the section with the following words:

"There were two kinds of descendants of Prajapati, the Devas and the Asuras. Now the Devas were indeed the younger, the Asuras the elder ones. The Devas who were struggling in these worlds, said 'Well, let us overcome the Asuras at the sacrifices by means of the Udgitha." ‡ [‡ Op. Cit. 1-3-1.]

The Chhandogya opens the section with the following words: -

"When the Devas and Asuras struggled together, both of the races of Prajapati, the Devas took the udgitha thinking they would vanquish the Asuras by it." § [§ Op. Cit. 1-2-1.]

Therefore as the opening statements are same, the upasanas are identical.

(Siddhanta): - The sutrakara states the conclusion as follows:

Or (they are) not (one) owing to a difference in the context, as (in the contemplations of the udgitha) as greater than the great, etc. (III. iii. 7)

The Vidyas taught in the Upanishads are not one and the same, because of a distinction in the context (prakarana). Now, the contemplation taught by the chhandogas refers to the Pranava which is a part of the udgitha as declared in the passage "Let a man meditate upon the syllable Om, (a part of) the Udgitha." * [* Chha. Up. 1-1-1.]

But the contemplation taught by the Vajins refers to the whole udgitha. Thus owing to a distinction in the way they begin, the forms contemplated upon are different, and the upasanas, therefore, are also different. Just as among the Udgitha-upasanas taught in one and the same sakha, the contemplation of the udgitha as 'greater than the great' differs from the contemplation of the same as 'golden,' so, too, here the upasanas differ.

The Sutrakara raises an objection and answers:

If (you think they are same) owing to (an identity in) the designation, that (is answered by what) has been said (above). This (identity in designation) is possible indeed. (III. iii. 3)

It should not be contended that the upasanas taught in the two sakhas are same because of the identity in the designation 'Udgitha Vidya.' For, though the things enjoined are different, the identity of designation is possible. For instance, in the case of the daily Agnihotra and the Agnihotra pertaining to the Kundapayin's sacrifice, though the names are same, the rites are different. So here also. Hence no discordance.

Adhikarana 4

And because (of the Pranava being mentioned as the object of contemplation) throughout, it is but right (to say that Pranava is the object of contemplation). (III. iii. 9)

In the Chhandogya it is said "Let a man contemplate the syllable 'Om' the Udgitha." * [* Op. Cit. 1-1-1.] Now, a doubt arises as to whether the contemplation here enjoined refers to Udgitha and Pranava as two distinct objects of contemplation comprehended for facility's sake in one act of contemplation, or it refers to one of them only.

(*Purvapaksha*): - It is true that Pranava and Udgitha are grammatically in the same case, put in apposition to each other and thus referring to one and the same thing; and this is possible when one of them is the substantive and the other an attributive qualifying it. Still, there is nothing to show either that the Pranava is the substantive qualified by the Udgitha, or that the Udgitha is the substantive qualified by the Pranava. The contemplative therefore relates to them as two distinct things comprehended in one act of contemplation.

(*Siddhanta*): - As against the foregoing we hold as follows: the contemplation does not relate to the Pranava and the Udgitha as two distinct things comprehended in one single act of contemplation. In the first prapathaka of Chhandogya, the upakrama or the opening words of the section are, "let a man contemplate the syllable 'Om' the Udgitha; for, with 'Om' * [* This shows that 'Om' is the thing to be contemplated upon.] people begin to sing the Udgitha."† [† Op. Cit. 1-1-10.] As in the opening words, so, even in the sequel, the Pranava is pointed to as the object of worship here intended; "Such indeed is the full account of this very syllable." Thus the Pranava is here the substantive qualified by Udgitha, ‡ [‡ This is to say that Pranava which occurs in the Udgitha song should be contemplated here.] and it is therefore right to hold that the Upasana refers to Pranava alone. Accordingly, Pranava alone is the object of contemplation here enjoined.

Adhikarana 5

Owing to identity in all respects, these (should be understood) elsewhere. (III. iii. 10)

"He who knows the oldest and the best becomes himself the oldest and the best. Prana (breath) indeed is the oldest and the best;"* [* Chha.Up. 5-1-1. and Bri. Up. 8-1-1.] in these words do the Chhandogas and the Vajins, when enjoining the contemplation of Prana, speak of Prana as the oldest and so on, as also the Kaushitakins. By all the three, the seniority of Prana has been explained in one way, namely, on the ground that the stay of speech and all other sense-organs as well as their functions depend entirely on Prana. That Prana partakes of the richness of the sense-organ of speech and so on is declared in the Chhandogya and Brihadaranyaka in the following words:

"Then the tongue said to him: 'If I am the richest, thou art the richest' The eye said to him: 'If I am the firm rest, thou art the firm rest.' The ear said to him 'If I am success, thou art success.' The mind said to him: 'If I am the home, thou art the home." † [† Chha. Up. 5-1-13.]

Now, a doubt arises as to whether the Kaushitakins should or should not include in their contemplation attributes such as richness and so on which are not taught in their Upanishad.

(*Purvapaksha*): - Those attributes should not be included, in as much as such attributes alone as are spoken of in the Kaushitaki-Upanishad are emphatically prescribed for contemplation, in the words "He who contemplates *thus*," etc. ‡ [‡ Op. Cit. 4-20.]

(*Siddhanta*): - As against the foregoing we hold as follows: Though not mentioned in their Upanishad, richness and other attributes should be included by the Kaushitakins in their contemplation of Prana; for, by the word 'thus' even those attributes which are not mentioned in their Upanishad are referred to as well as those mentioned therein; and Prana, - of which all these attributes are predicated – being one and the same, all its attributes are naturally present in the mind. Just as Devadatta who was once seen to teach the Vedas in the city of

Madhura is recognised as a teacher of the Vedas when afterwards seen in the city of Mahismati though here he does not actually teach the Vedas, so also, Prana, described in the Chhandogya and other Upanishads as rich and so on, comes up again elsewhere to the mind as possessed of the same attributes though not there described as possessed of those attributes. Therefore, as they are referred to by the word 'thus', richness and other attributes should be included by the Kaushitakins in their contemplation of Prana.

Adhikarana 6

Bliss and other (attributes should be gathered together, owing to the identity) of the main thing. (III. iii. 11)

"Owing to identity": these words should be understood here. In treating of the contemplation of the Supreme, bliss and other attributes are spoken of in connection with Brahman, - 'the main thing,' the chief object of contemplation, - in the following passages:

"Real, consciousness, infinite is Brahman." * [* Taitt. Up. 2-1.]

"Bliss is Brahman." † [† Ibid. 3-6.]

"Right, real, the supreme Brahman, is Purusha, dark and brown." ‡ [‡ Mahana. 12.]

"Brahman whose body is akasa, whose nature is true, whose delight is life, whose manas is bliss, who is replete with peace, who is immortal." § [§ Tai. Up. 1-6.]

A doubt arises as to whether it is necessary or not necessary to think of all of them in all contemplations of the Supreme.

(*Purvapaksha*): - It is not necessary to gather them all together in all cases; for, Brahman is one, and if many different attributes are predicated of Him, He becomes many different attributes making different substantives. – Or thus: It is not necessary to gather all attributes together because the contemplation of the Supreme as taught in one Upanishad is perfect in itself on embracing the attributes mentioned therein.

(*Siddhanta*): - As against the foregoing we hold as follows: Brahman, the object of contemplation, and of whom these attributes are predicated, is one and the same, and therefore bliss and other attributes should be gathered together in thought in all contemplations of the Supreme, wherever taught. Black, white, red; broken-horned and full-hearted: it is only such sets of opposite attributes as these that make the substantive different; but not such sets of attributes as 'black, sweet-smelling, big lily.' Therefore the several attributes of Brahman being not opposed to one another, they do not make Him different. Accordingly, owing to the identity of Brahman, of whom these attributes are predicated in all the several Upanishads, bliss and other attributes occurring here and there should all be brought together.

Adhikarana 7

No room for such (attributes) as joy-headedness; for, increase and decrease result from differentiation. (III. iii. 12)

"Joy, verily, is His head", * [* Ibid. 2-5.] in such passages as these, joy-headedness and the like are spoken of as these, joy-headedness and the like are spoken of as the attributes of Brahman. A doubt arises as to whether even these should be included in the contemplation of the Supreme, like bliss and other attributes.

(*Purvapaksha*): - What objection is there to including these also, along with the attributes such as "of unfailing will?"

(*Siddhanta*): - We reply as follows: Joy-headedness and the like should not be gathered together in the contemplation of the Supreme; for, they cannot be regarded as attributes of Brahman, in the same way as we can regard the attribute, "of unfailing will." To class them among the attributes of Brahman is to regard Him as composed of parts; and this will subject Him to increase and decrease. If joy-headedness and the like be the inherent attributes of Brahman, He will be differentiated. These attributes cannot therefore be taken into account in connection with the contemplation of the Supreme.

There is no such objection in the case of omniscience and the like attributes, in as much as they are inherent in the very nature of Brahman. So, the Sutrakara says:

But the others (should be gathered together in thought), because of the similarity in the nature of things. (III. iii. 13)

The others, - namely, omniscience, ever-contentedness and so on – are inherent in the very nature of Brahman. As such, they are all similar (to bliss and the like) in their nature and should therefore be brought together; whereas joy-headedness and the like are not inherent in the nature of Brahman and cannot therefore be included in the contemplation of the Supreme.

Adhikarana 8

(The annamaya and others need not be contemplated) because of the absence of use in the devout contemplation. (III. iii. 14)

Now, a doubt arises as to whether it is absolutely necessary or not necessary to contemplate the annamaya (physical) and other Atmans also, in the same way that we should contemplate the Anandamaya or Blissful Atman above referred to.

(*Purvapaksha*): - Their contemplation is absolutely necessary, because it is impossible to contemplate the Innermost Anandamaya or Blissful Atman as the Innermost Being dwelling in the annamaya and other Atmans, without contemplating at the same time the annamaya and other Atmans themselves.

(*Siddhanta*): - As against the foregoing we hold as follows: The contemplation of the annamaya and the like is not quite necessary, because it is of no use. The purpose of their exposition is only to show clearly the nature of Brahman, the Blissful (anandamaya). Accordingly it is necessary to reflect upon the annamaya and the like only till Brahman is reached. Their contemplation is therefore not absolutely necessary.

And because of the word Atman. (III. iii. 15)

"Having united with the annamaya-Atman." * [* Tai. Up. 2-8.] etc. In this and the subsequent passages the word 'Atman' is used along with each; and this shows that 'annamaya' and other words denote the intelligences functioning in the physical body and so on. Since all intelligences other than Brahman are excluded as unworthy of contemplation by the seekers of liberation, they should not form objects of contemplation at the time of Meditation (of the Supreme). Accordingly the Atharvasiras says, "Siva the Beneficent alone should be meditated upon, abandoning all the rest." This passage declares that none other than Siva should be meditated upon by the seekers of liberation. Therefore it is not necessary to contemplate the annamaya and others.

Atman is referred to, as in the other case, (as shown) by the sequel. (III. iii. 16)

Here, the passage, "Yet another inner Atman is the blissful," † [† Ibid. 2-5.] refers to the Atman, the Supreme Soul (Atman), not to the Pratyagatman or the individual soul, just as the word 'Atman' refers to the Supreme Soul in the passage "From Atman is the ether born." ‡ [‡ Ibid. 2-1.] This is proved by the sequel, "Having united with the Blissful Soul (Atman)." * [* Ibid. 3-10.] Therefore the contemplation of the Blissful Soul is the paramount one, being the contemplation of Brahman Himself.

If it be urged that because of the constant presence (of Atman the annamaya, etc., also should be contemplated), we reply that we still hold to our view because of the special stress. (III. iii. 17)

(*Objection*): - Since the word 'Atman' is used even along with annamaya and so on, there is nothing wrong in contemplating them also as the Paramatman, as the Supreme Soul.

(*Answer*): - No; for, from the words "yet another inner Atman is the Blissful," we understand that the Blissful, - the Paramatman, Siva, - is distinct from the annamaya and so on; and the passage "Siva, the Beneficent, alone should be meditated upon, abandoning all else," † [† Atharvasikha-Up.] emphatically declares that Siva alone should be contemplated, all others being abandoned. By the word 'Siva' here is denoted the Supreme Brahman as devoid of all taints, as the repository of all beneficent qualities. Indeed, mukti, the attainment of equality with Brahman, accrues from a continuous contemplation of Him who is Divers-eyed (Virupaksha) and Dark-brown (Krishnapingala) So that, since...fruit corresponds to worship, the contemplation of beings other than Siva, and who are therefore not beneficent, cannot lead to the state of Siva. Therefore, the Blissful Siva alone should be meditated upon.

Adhikarana 9

The new one (is intended) here, because that alone is said to be the act enjoined. (III. iii. 18)

"He who knows the first and the best": ‡ [‡ Bri. Up. 6-1-4...14] the section beginning with these words teaches later on, - in answer to the Prana's question "what shall be dress for me?" – that water is the dress for the Prana and then proceeds to say: "therefore the Srotriyas who know this, rinse the mouth with water when they are going to eat, and rinse the mouth with water after they have eaten, thinking thereby they make the breath dressed (with water)." – What is the thing enjoined here? – Is it the rinsing of the mouth with water as well as the contemplation of Prana (breath) as dressed with water? Or is it only the latter?

(*Purvapaksha*): - Both are enjoined here, as there is nothing to show that the one or the other alone is meant.

(*Siddhanta*): - Since the rinsing of the mouth with water is a thing already known to us through current practice based on Smriti, it is only the meditation of Prana as dressed with water that is enjoined here, since it is the thing which we have not as yet known and which we learn here for the first time. What is not known to us otherwise has alone to be learnt from the Sruti. Where the now thing is not expressly enjoined and the Sruti takes the form of anuvada, a restatement of what is already known, we should understand an injunction with references to it. Therefore, we should understand that the meditation of Prana as dressed with water is alone enjoined here, as a thing not known to us before.

Adhikarana 10

(The Vidya is one and the same) as (some of the attributes mentioned in both) are identical, as also because of the absence of any distribution (in others). (III. iii. 19)

In the Agnirahasya and the Brihadaranyaka the Sandilya-Vidya is taught. In the one it is taught as follows:

"Let a man contemplate Atman, formed of thought, embodied in life, luminous in form, of unfailing will, and of the nature of other (akasa)." * [* Madhyandinasakha.]

In the other it is taught as follows:

"That Person (Purusha) formed of thought, being light indeed, is within the heart, like a grain of rice or barley; He is independent, the ruler of all, the lord of all, - He rules all this, whatsoever exists." † [† Bri. Up. 5-6.]

A doubt arises as to whether two different Vidyas are taught in the two places, or one and the same Vidya is taught in both.

(*Purvapaksha*): - In the one place the Purusha, the object of contemplation, is great, being 'of the nature of ether (akasa)'; whereas in the other He is small 'like a grain of rice or barley.' In the one, again, He is said to be 'of unfailing will,' whereas in the other He is said to be 'independent' and so on. Thus the attributes being different, the Vidyas taught in the two places are different.

(*Siddhanta*): - As against the foregoing we hold as follows: In both alike, the Purusha is described as manomaya (formed of thought) and so on; and so far the attributes described in both are identical. As to His being described to be of the nature of ether (akasa), it may be explained as intended to show that He is pure like akasa, or to praise Him by way of showing how glorious He is. The attribute of independence and the like cannot be in any way distinguished from the attribute expressed in the words, "of unfailing will," and are therefore identical. Hence the identity of Vidya.

Adhikarana 11

So also elsewhere, because of (His) relation (to both alike). (III. iii. 20)

In the Brihadaranyaka, in the section beginning with the words "That Person who is in the orb there and He who is in the right eye here," the Sruti declares that the true Brahman embodied in the Vyahritis – the utterances (such as Bhuh, Bhuvah, Suvah), - should be contemplated as dwelling in the solar orb and in the eye; then the Sruti assigns, in the words "His secret name is Ahah" a secret name to him as dwelling in the cosmos as a whole, and assigns in the words "His secret name is Aham" another secret name to Him as dwelling in the individual organism.

A doubt arises as to whether both the names should or should not be thought of in each case.

(*Purvapaksha*): - The object of worship being the same in both, namely Brahman, one and the same vidya is taught in both. Therefore, in each case both the names should be thought of.

(*Siddhanta*): - The Sutrakara says as follows:

Or, not so, because there is a distinction. (III. iii. 21)

Here there is no identity in the Vidya, because the object of worship is in each case different, as related to such different seats as the sun and the eye. Therefore each name is appropriate in its own place.

Adhikarana 12

And (the sruti) reveals (identity) (III. iii. 22)

The Mandala-Vidya or the contemplation of the orb is taught in the Chhandogya and the Brihadaranyaka. Is the Vidya identical or different?

(*Purvapaksha*): - The Chhandogya teaches as follows: -

"Now, that golden Person who is seen within the sun, with golden "beard and golden hair, golden altogether to the very tips of His nails," and so on.

In the other, having – in the words "He that golden Person who dwells in the sun within," – spoken of the golden Person dwelling in that person who dwells within the orb which is made up of the three Vedas, the sruti concludes as follows: -

"All is Rudra...Homage to the Golden-armed, to the Golden Lord, to the Lord of Ambika, to the Lord of Uma; homage to Him again and again." † [† Mahana. 13...18.]

Thus the Taittiriyaka speaks of the Person as golden-armed, and the Lord of Uma. Now, since in the one He is described as golden in all parts of the body and in the other as golden only in the arms, there is a difference in the form. Again, in the one He is described as the All, while in the other He is described as the Lord of all worlds, and thus there is a difference in the attributes. Hence no identity in the vidya.

(*Siddhanta*): - The Vidya is not different. Identity of His place as dwelling 'within the sun'‡ [‡ Chha. Up. 1-6-6.] points to identity in the vidya. As the Taittiriya-Upanishad§ [§ Maha. 13.] speaks of the Person as golden in the opening words of the section, the description in the sequel that He is golden-armed is only a synecdoche, and therefore even in the concluding passage the sruti means that He is golden in all parts of the body. We have shown that Though He is the Lord of the world, it is right that He is one with the world, because of His having entered into it. Therefore as one and the same entity is referred to in both the places, such attributes as being the Lord of Uma and so on should all be included in the contemplation in each case.

Adhikarana 13

And hence too, the accomplishment and the pervasion of heaven. (III. iii. 23)

The Ranayaniyas in their khilas or supplementary texts read as follows:

"Brahman accomplished mighty deeds of valour; Brahman, the Supreme, in the beginning, permeated heaven; even before the souls did Brahman exist; with that Brahman, who is there fit to complete?" * [* Taitt. Bra. 2-4-7.]

The acts known to all people, - namely, the act of burning the three worlds, the act of swallowing the deadly poison, and so on, - unsurpassed by any, and very hard for others to achieve, have been achieved by the Supreme Brahman in the form of Sri-kantha, - that Brahman who is Superior to Hari, Hara, and Hiranyagarbha and so on, and who lay pervading the abode of Supreme Heaven even prior to their creation. The question is, is it necessary or not necessary to think of this accomplishment of mighty deeds of valour and this pervasion over heaven, in all our contemplations of the Supreme Being?

(*Purvapaksha*): - Because these are, like others, attributes of Brahman, and because these are not spoken of with reference to any particular injunction, they should be thought of in all our contemplation of the Supreme.

(*Siddhanta*): - As against the foregoing we hold as follows: The permeation of the Divine Being through the supreme heaven should not be thought of in all our contemplations. By the very nature of the thing, it should be thought of only when we contemplate Brahman in abodes other than the small ones. "The Devas verily went to the region of Svarga, and they asked Rudra who He was:" * [* Atharvasiras.] here the Sruti speaks of the Supreme Abode, which is Superior even to the abodes of Brahman and others, and which, as the seat of unsurpassed bliss, is called Svarga. Therefore, the permeation through heaven should be thought of in contemplating Brahman in abodes other than small ones, i.e., in contemplating the Vaisvanara and the like. As associated with it, even the accomplishment of mighty deeds of valour should be thought of in those cases only.

Adhikarana 14

And so too in the Purusha-vidya, because of the absence of mention of others. (III. iii. 24)

Purusha-Vidya is taught in the Chhandogya and the Taittiriyaka Upanishads. "Purusha (man), verily, is sacrifice. The twenty-four years of his life is the pratas-savana or morning sacrifice," * [* Chha. Up. 3-16.] and so on: in these words the Purusha-Vidya is taught in the one; and in the other it is taught in the following words: "He who thus knows, - his self is the sacrificer in the sacrifice, his faith is the wife, his body is the fuel, his breast is the altar." † [† Mahana. 52.] A doubt arises as to whether the Vidyas taught in the two Upanishads are identical or different.

(*Purvapaksha*): - Because the Vidyas in both Upanishads alike are named Purusha-Vidya, and because the different members of the sacrifices are imagined alike in both, the Vidyas are identical.

(*Siddhanta*): - As against the foregoing we hold as follows: The Purusha-Vidyas taught in the two places are different; for, the members of the sacrifice declared in the Taittiriyaka – namely, the sacrificer, his wife, etc., - as also the three savannas are not mentioned in the Chhandogya, whereas in the latter the three savannas are represented in quite a different way. In the Taittiriyaka the three savannas are represented in the following manner: "What we call evening, morning and noon are the savannas;" while in the Chhandogya man's life-period is divided into three parts and these parts are represented as the savannas. In the Taittiriya, moreover, no specific fruit is declared. "For the Light of Brahman, one should utter 'Om' and contemplate Atman;" ‡ [‡ Ibid. 51.] in these words Brahma-Vidya has been taught, and the fruit thereof has been declared in the words "He attains Brahman's greatness;" and then is taught Purusha-Vidya in the words "He who thus knows, - his self is the sacrificer in the sacrifice." Thus the Purusha-Vidya is only an appendage of Brahma-Vidya, the subject of discourse, and its fruit is therefore the attainment of Brahman. In the Chhandogya, the fruit of the Purusha-Vidya is declared in the words "He lives sixteen hundred years, indeed." * [* Chha. 3-16-6.] Therefore, owing to a different in the fruit and in the representation of the members of the sacrifice, the Vidyas are not identical.

Adhikarana 15

Because the act of piercing and other things are different. (III. iii. 25)

At the commencement of the Taittiriya-Upanishad occur the following Mantras:

"May Mitra be propitious to us, and may Varuna be propitious." † [† Tai. Up. 1-1.]

"May He protect us both." ‡ [‡ Ibid. 2-1.]

A doubt arises as to whether these Mantras form part of the Vidya or not.

(*Purvapaksha*): - Owing to their proximity to the Vidyas, they form part of these Vidyas.

(*Siddhanta*): - As against the foregoing we hold as follows: just as the mantra which is read at the beginning of the Upanishad of the Atharvanikas forms part of the abhichara or magical rite intended to bring about death of the enemy because the mantra speaks of the piercing of the heart etc., - or just as the rites of Mahavrata and Pravargya treated of at the commencement of the Upanishads of the Aitareyins and the Vajasaneyins are, in virtue of express injunctions, parts of sacrificial rites, so, these two mantras form mere appendages of the act of reciting the Veda as shown by the words. "The true shall I utter" "Efficient may our study prove." They are not parts of the Vidyas, because they are intended for a different purpose. Mere proximity (sannidhi) is invalid when compared with sruti (direct declaration), ling (indicative mark), and Vakya (context).

Adhikarana 16

But where the getting rid of (good and evil) is mentioned. (we should understand the obtaining of good and evil by others) because the declaration of the former is subservient to the latter as in the case of the Kusas the metres, the praises and the singing. It has been explained (already) (III. iii. 26)

In one section (Sakha) of the Veda, the sage who attains Brahman is said to be released from merit and demerit. In another section (Sakha) of the Veda it is declared that, of the merit and demerit from which he has been thus released, the former enters into the friends and the latter into the enemies. In a third section (Sakha) again, both the release from them and the places of their entrance are spoken of. All this is no doubt meant for contemplation. Here a doubt arises as to whether in all places both the release and the places of entrance should be contemplated or only one of them at one's option.

The Vedanta-Sutras with Srikantha Bhashya

(*Purvapaksha*): - What is the *prima facie* view that suggest itself to us? – In the Satyayayanaka, it is said that "His sons comes by his property, his friends come by his merit, and his enemies come by his sins." The Tandins say, "shaking off all evil, as a horse shakes his hairs, and as the moon frees herself from the mouth of Rahu" * [* Chha. Up. 8-13.] The Atharvana-upanishad says, "then he is wise, and shaking off good and evil he reaches the highest oneness free from passions." † [† Mund. Up. 3-1-3.] Here, in the sruti which declares release from merit and demerit, we should not understand as declared the places into which the merit and the demerit enter, for the mere reason that the sruti which speaks of the release does not expressly speak of the matter.

(*Siddhanta*): - As against the foregoing we hold as follows: When the release alone is declared, or when the places of entrance alone are mentioned, it stands to reason that we should understand both as declared in conjunction, not one of them alone. The passage which speaks of the entrance is supplementary which speaks of the entrance is supplementary to that which speaks of the release, and should therefore form an appendage to it; for, as declaring where the abandoned merit and demerit enter the former passage necessarily presupposes the latter.

(*Objection*): - How can a passage which occurs in one section of the Veda be an appendage to that which occurs in another section?

(*Answer*): - Just as the passage "you Kusas, the children of the Udumbara-free", is supplemented by the passage which occurs elsewhere and which serves to particularise the Kusas; or just as the passage "by the metres of the Devas and the Asuras" is supplemented by the passage, "the metres of the Devas should come first," which occurs elsewhere; or just as the passage "he should offer the stotra of the *shodasin*-rite" is supplemented by the passage "he should offer the stotra of the *shodasin*-rite when the sun has half risen;" * [* Taitt. Sam. 6-6-11.] or just as the passage "the ritviks should sing" is supplemented by the passage "the Adhvaryu priest should not sing," † [† Ibid. 6-3-1.] which excludes some of the ritviks from the operation of the injunction, - so also, when it is possible to make out the passage speaking of the entrance as one serving to supplement the passage which speaks of release from merit and demerit, it is not reasonable to say that one or the other of them should alone be contemplated.

It has been said in the first or ritualistic section of the Mimamsa as follows: "It should on the contrary form a supplement to the other statement, since the adoption of one alone is unreasonable." Here in the present case the passage speaking of the entrance serves to praise or magnify what is stated in the other.

(*Objection*): - How can one supplementary passage (arthavada) presuppose another supplementary passage occurring in quite a different context?

(*Answer*): - This does not detract from the validity of our contention. For, we find that the supplementary passage, "The twenty-first from here is the sun we see," which is intended to praise the contemplation of Saman, presupposes another supplementary passage, which occurs in the *sattra* section of the Taittiriya-samhita and which serves to determine how the sun is the twenty-first. This latter passage reads as follows:

> "Twelve are the months, five the seasons, three the worlds we see, and the twenty-first is the sun we see before us." ‡ [‡ Taitt.Sam 5-1-10.]

In these words it has been there determined how the sun constitutes the twenty-first in number. Therefore, though an arthavada, the passage speaking of the merit and the demerit of the sage entering into his friends and enemies respectively should be understood as declared. Moreover, both the release and the entrance are mentioned in one passage in the Kaushitaki-Upanishad in the following words:

> "And there he shakes off his good and evil deeds. His beloved relatives obtain the good, his un-beloved relatives the evil he has done." § [§ Kaushi. 1-4.]

Hence the conjunctions of the two.

Adhikarana 17

(It should be thought of) at the time of departure, because of the absence of anything to be reached. So, indeed, others declare. (III. iii. 27)

A doubt arises as to whether the release from good and bad deeds should be thought of as taking place at the time of separation from the body or on the path to Brahman.

(*Purvapaksha*): - In one place, the release from good and bad deeds is said to take place at the time of departure from the body, in the following words:

> "Shaking off all evil as a horse shakes off his hairs...and then shaking off his body..." * [* Chha. 9-13.]

In another place it is said to take place on the path:

> "He comes to the river Viraja, and crosses it by the mind alone, and there shakes off his good and evil deeds." † [† Kaushi. 1-4.]

Though thus there are two passages speaking of the matter in two different ways, the release should be regarded as taking place only at the time of departure from the body, in as much as there exists no enjoyment of pleasure or pain to be brought about by karma at a subsequent period, the attainment of Brahman alone having yet to be achieved. So, indeed, do others declare:

> "For him there is only delay so long as he is not delivered. Then he will be perfect." ‡ [‡ Chha. 14-2.]

Accordingly, soon after departure from the body, Brahman is attained.

(It may be interpreted) according to our will, because there is no contradiction to both. (III. iii. 28)

The Sruti speaks of the release from good and bad deeds as taking place at the time of departure from the body; and it speaks of the attainment of Brahman as taking place after the release. In order that these two srutis may not be contradicted, we should understand the passage, "there he shakes off his good and evil deeds," according to the meaning, as suited to the context. That is to say, we should construe the passage as occurring prior to the passage "having reached this path of gods." § [§ Kaushi. 1-3.]

|| (The journey on the path of gods is still) justifiable because we find a similar thing (taking place even after the attainment of Brahman), as in ordinary life. (III. iii. 29)

[|| This sutra is intended to explain how the liberated soul's journey on the path of Gods is possible if he has been liberated from all Karma at death and therefore freed from body and the senses.]

Despite the exhaustion of all Karma at the time of departure from the body, the journey on the path is quite justifiable in the case of the worshippers of Brahman. For we do find it said that (even after attaining Brahman) the liberated soul walks about enjoying. It has been said:

"He becomes an autocrat (svaraj), he walks about at will in all worlds." *
[* Chha. 7-25-2.]

It is like what takes place in ordinary life. In ordinary life, the protégés of kings obtain all things which are beyond the reach of others. † [† That is to say, in virtue of the Brahmavidya and by the Divine Grace all the things mentioned here are possible as the liberated soul is then invested with a spiritual body and with spiritual senses.] Similarly the passage which speaks of the path can also be explained. Though the whole karma has been exhausted at the time of departure from the body, still, in virtue of the Vidya, the linga-sarira or subtle body remains, and therewith the journey on the path and the attendant acts may be effected, since then it is possible to walk about in the places located on the path, to converse with the Moon, and to do the other things spoken of in this connection.

(*Siddhanta*): - As against the foregoing we hold as follows:

The passage serves a purpose when the release takes place on both occasions; otherwise, indeed, there is a contradiction. (III. iii. 30)

The passage of the soul on the path of the Gods (Devayana) serves a purpose only when the exhaustion of Karma is held as taking place on both the occasions, - on the occasions of departing from the body as well as on the occasion of crossing over the river Viraja. Otherwise, *i.e*, if the whole karma has been exhausted only at the time of departure from the body, the soul would be immediately liberated and the passage on the path of the Gods would serve no purpose at all; and this is inconsistent with the sruti which speaks of the passage on the path of Gods as well as with the sruti which, in the words "he unites with the supreme Light and attains to his own true being," ‡ [‡ Chha. 8-3-4.] declares that the soul attains, to his true nature by way of attaining the illumination of intellect only after attaining to Brahman by the path of Gods. Therefore, though the soul's wandering in the several places, his conversation with the moon, and his passage on the path of Gods are all possible in virtue of the Vidya or wisdom, just as the subsequent wandering is possible in virtue of the Vidya, still, the samsara, taking the form of intellectual narrowness, and containing till Brahman is attained, cannot be explained as due to the power of Vidya. Wherefore it is necessary to admit the continuance of a part of Karma as forming the root of the samsara. It cannot be maintained that this continuance of the samsara is due – not to Karma, but – to the will of the Paramesvara or Supreme Lord; for we hold that the very will of the Lord constitutes the soul's Karma. Certainly, according to our theory, there exists no merit or demerit except the will of the Supreme Lord as governed by the doing of acts enjoined or of those prohibited by the sruti.

(*Objection*): - If the manifestation of the soul's true nature in the form of intellectual illuminations should take place after the attainment of Brahman, then the Karma which causes intellectual narrowness should continue till the attainment of Brahman. How can the exhaustion of Karma take place the moment after the crossing of the river Viraja?

(*Answer*): - The very act of crossing over the limits of the boundary line of the material universe constitutes the attainment of the abode of the Paramasiva, which is the Paramakasa, the supreme Light; and this is the attainment of Brahman which is spoken of in the words "having united with the Supreme Light." The river Viraja, connected with the abode of Vishnu, constitutes the boundary line of the material universe. The yogins, who are free from all taint of Karma on entering into the river, pass beyond Vishnu's abode and enter the spiritual abode of Siva which is full of supreme bliss. Accordingly the sruti says:

"He reaches the goal of the path, and it is the supreme abode of Vishnu."

Hence no incongruity whatever.

Adhikarana 18

The stay of the office-holders continues as long as the office lasts.
(III. iii. 31)

It has been said above that the Upasakas or devotees of Brahman obtain release from good and bad deeds and attain to Brahman. Now a doubt arises as to whether those in office do or do not attain to salvation in addition to their enjoying of the office.

(*Purvapaksha*): - It would at first seem that there is no salvation at all to the office-holders such as Vasistha, in as much as the Puranas and other scriptures speak of their birth. Therefore the conclusion is that of the knower of truth, some attain salvation, and others do no.

(*Siddhanta*): - As against the foregoing we hold as follows: The office-holders have to enjoy fruits other than salvation even after the death of their body, till the Karma which has invested them with their respective offices is exhausted. Accordingly, till the termination of the offices, they have to stay there (in the samsara) to enjoy the fruits of the Karma which has invested them with the offices; they cannot till then pass on to the path of Light (archiradi-marga). The Prarabdha-karma of even those who have attained knowledge is exhausted only by the enjoyment of its fruits. Thus, those in office attain salvation on the termination of the office, and therefore the knowers of truth invariably attain salvation.

Adhikarana 19

No restriction as to any Vidya; and hence no contradiction to the Sruti and the Smriti. (III. iii. 32)

The Sruti speaks of the path of Light in connection with the Upakosala-Vidya and the like. A doubt arises as to whether the path is restricted to the devotees of that Vidya alone or is open to all devotees (upasakas).

(*Purvapaksha*): - In the Chhandogya, the Path of Light is mentioned in connection with the Upakosala-Vidya and the Panchagni-Vidya alone; in the Atharvasiras it is slightly hinted at in connection with the Pasupata. It is not mentioned in connection with the Sandilya-Vidya and the like. The Path of Light must be restricted to those Vidyas, in connection with which it has been mentioned; it cannot be extended to others.

(*Siddhanta*): - As against the foregoing we hold as follows: There is no rule that the path is restricted to those Vidyas with reference to which it has been mentioned. On the contrary it extends to all Upasanas. Then alone will the Sruti and the Smriti be contradicted. In the Panchagni-Vidya the Sruti extends the path to all without exception, in the words "And those who in the forest devote themselves to austerity and penance, they proceed towards Light." * [* Chha. 5-10-1.] The Smriti also (Bhagavadgita VIII 24) extends the path to all without exception. Therefore the Path of Light is as a rule open to all Upasakas alike.

Some interpret the Sutra as follows: There is no rule that the Path of Light is trodden by all Upasakas alike. Thus alone can the Sruti and the Smriti be absolved from all contradictions.

This interpretation also is unobjectionable; for, those who contemplate Nirguna Brahman, Brahman devoid of all attributes have nothing to do with the path.

Adhikarana 20

The inclusion of (negative) conceptions concerning the Indestructible is necessary, because Brahman is the same and there is (a purpose served); as for instance in the case of the mantra of the upasad. This has been explained (before). (III. iii. 33)

In the Gargi-Brahmana, while imparting a knowledge of Brahman, certain denials are made in the words "Neither gross, nor line, nor short," * [* Bri. Up. 3-8-8.] and so on. In the Atharvana also they are found in such passages as the following:

"That which cannot be seen nor seized, which has no family and no caste," † and so on. [† Mund. 1-1-6.]

A doubt arises as to whether, like bliss, etc., these should be comprehended or not in contemplation Brahman.

(*Purvapaksha*): - At first sight it would seem that those denials need not be comprehended in all contemplations of the Supreme, in as much as, unlike bliss, etc., they are not attributes.

(*Siddhanta*): - As against the foregoing we hold as follows: It is proper to include in all contemplation of the Supreme the conception of denials relating to the Akshara, the Indestructible, since Brahman, the possessor of the attributes, is the same in all places. It is, indeed, by means of these attributes, and in no other way, that a contemplation of Brahman as distinguished from all else becomes possible. For bliss and other attributes to distinguish Brahman from the pratyagatman, they must be such as are unassociated with any mean qualities. And it is the very nature of attributes to always accompany the main thing of which they are spoken of as attributes. For instance: though the mantra "O Agni, know the Hotri's deed, and the sacrifice," which is enjoined in connection with the upasad of the purodasa in the Jamadagnya sacrifice of four nights, - occurring in the Samaveda, has, as such,* [* The rule is that in sacrificial rites the mantras of the Samaveda should be recited aloud while those of the Yajur-Veda should be recited in a whisper.] to be recited aloud, still, in as much as it should follow the main thing, - namely, the upasad be recited in a whisper. This principle has been declared in the former or ritualistic section III. iii. 9.

From this it does not follow that all attributes will have to be included in the contemplation, as the Sutrakara says:

This much (alone should be comprehended), on account of thorough contemplation. (III. iii. 34)

'Thorough contemplation' means the contemplation to which one takes readily. Those attributes alone are to be comprehended everywhere, by which a contemplation of Brahman as distinguished from all else is possible. Accordingly it is necessary to comprehend in the contemplation of Brahman only those negative attributes, namely, "not gross," etc., which are mentioned in connection with the Akshara-Brahman, because they are attributes which serve to distinguish Brahman from all else; but it is not necessary to include also such attributes as "who does all deeds, who has all desire, who has all smells, who has all tastes." † [† Chha. 3-4-2.]

Adhikarana 21

If you hold that in the (passage speaking of Him who is) within (all) (the sruti refers to) one's own self possessed of the aggregate of the elements, and that otherwise the difference cannot be explained, (we say), no, as in the case of the teaching (of the Sad-Vidya). (III. iii. 35)

In the Brihadaranyaka Upanishad, Ushasta asks: "Yajnavalkya, tell me the Brahman who is visible, not invisible, the Atman, who is within all." The answer is given in the following words: "He who breathes in the up-breathing, he is thy Atman and within all. He who breathes in the down-breathing, he is thy Atman, and within all...Everything else is of evil." ‡ [‡ Bri. Up. 3-4.] Then again Kahola asks "Yajnavalkya, tell me the Brahman who is visible, not invisible, the Atman who is within all." But the answer is given in the following words: "He who overcomes hunger and thirst, sorrow, passion, old age, and death. When Brahmanas know that Atman...they wander about as mendicants...Everything else is of evil."* [* Ibid. 3-5.] Here a doubt arises as to whether the two Vidyas are one ore different.

(*Purvapaksha*): - Now, Ushasta's question refers to the pratyagatman or the individual soul united to the aggregate of elements. Otherwise it would be difficult to explain the difference between the entity spoken of in the answer to that question and described as "He who breathes in the up-breathing, he is thy Atman," and the entity referred to in the answer to the question of Kahola and described as having overcome hunger, etc.

(*Siddhanta*): - As against the foregoing supposition the sutrakara states the Siddhanta or final conclusion as follows: You should not say so. This section is like the teaching (of the Sadvidya): † [† Chha. 6] "That Atman who is within all;" in these words the question was asked in both cases alike; and therefore in both cases, the Paramesvara Himself is the entity referred to in the question. And He alone can be the entity who is absolutely the cause of up-breathing, etc., and who has absolutely overcome hunger, etc., as stated in the answers to the questions. As in the case of the teaching of the Sad-Vidya, contemplation of Brahman as Existence, the repetition of question and answer refers to one and the same subject. A difference in the questioner and in the form does not produce a change in the Vidya. Accordingly the sutrakara says:

An exchange (should take place); for (they both) qualify (Brahman), as in the other case. (III. iii. 36)

Once the identity of the subject has been established, a mutual exchange of ideas should be affected between the two questioners. That is to say, Ushasta also hold contemplate Brahman as one who has overcome hunger, etc., while Kahola also should contemplate Him

The Vedanta-Sutras with Srikantha Bhashya

as the cause of up-breathing, etc. For, the passages occurring in both the sections specify the Paramesvara, as in the other case of Sad-Vidya. Wherefore as one and the same entity is spoken of in the questions and the answers, there is no difference in the Vidya. Repetition is intended to remove doubts, as in the case of "That, thou art."

Adhikarana 22

The same (Deity is spoken of); for 'real' etc., (are repeated). (III. iii. 37)

As to the Sad-Vidya also, which has been cited to illustrate the conclusion arrived at in the preceding adhikarana, there arises doubt as to whether the Vidya is one or different.

(*Purvapaksha*): - As a repetition is found in the questioning, and as a difference is found in the answers, at each turn a different Vidya must have been taught.

(*Siddhanta*): - As against the foregoing we hold as follows: There is no difference in the Sad-Vidya. The same Mighty, Deity, referred to in the words "This Devata," etc., * [* Chha. 6-3-2.] occurs in every question and in every answer. "That is real, That the Atman, That thou art;" in these words, again and again, reality and other attributes are found repeated. Therefore, the Entity being one and the same, the Vidya is one and the same.

Adhikarana 23

(The attributes such as the possession of unfailing) desires should be comprehended in the several cases, because of the abode, etc., (being the same). (III. iii. 38)

The Dahara Vidya, - contemplation of the Divine in the heart – is taught in the Chhandogya, in the Taittiriyaka, in the Brihadaranyaka, and in the Kaivalya Upanishads. Are they all one and the same, or are they different?

(*Purvapaksha*): - In the Chhandogya, the eight chief attributes, including sinlessness, of the Being dwelling in the small lotus of the heart, and spoken of as Dahara-akasa, are declared in the passage which begins with the following words:

"There is this city of Brahman (in the body) and in it the palace, the small lotus (of the heart), and in it that small ether." † [† Op. Cit. 8-1-1.]

In the Taittiriyaka the attributes of the Divine Being dwelling in the small lotus of the heart – as the One designated by the word 'Sound (Nada)' which is the root of the Pranava, as the One denoted by the term the "Mighty Lord (Mahesvara), as the One who is dark-brown, as the One who has divers eyes – are declared in the passage "small, sinless,"‡ [‡ Maha. 10.] etc. In the Brihadaranyaka Upanishad are mentioned the attributes such as lordship, in the following passage "There is ether within the heart. In it there reposes the ruler of all, the lord of all, the king of all." § [§ Bri. Up. 4-4-22]

In the Kaivalya-Upanishad the attributes of the Supreme Being dwelling in the heart-lotus – as the three-eyed, as the dark-necked, as consciousness and bliss, as having Uma for His mate, and so on – are declared in the following passage:

> "Regarding the heart-lotus unstained and quite pure, and in its centre contemplation Him who is ... all-pervading; who is intelligence and bliss, the formless, the wonderful; Him whose help-mate is Uma; who is the supreme Lord, mighty, three-eyed, dark-necked, serene."

Now, since dark-neckedness and the like are the attributes of the body and since reality, etc., are the attributes of the body and since reality, etc., are the attributes of Atman, they are two opposed sets of attributes and caused therefore be included in one contemplation. Therefore they are different Vidyas.

(*Siddhanta*): - As against the foregoing we hold as follows: Because the same abode of the heart-lotus is mentioned in the several places, the vidya is one and the same. Therefore the attributes – such as "whose desires are true" – should be comprehended in all cases. Sinlessness and other attributes mentioned in the Chhandogya, lordship and other attributes mentioned in the Brihadaranyaka, the attributes of being designated by the Pranava and other attributes mentioned in the Taittiriyaka, the attributes of being consciousness and bliss is essence and other attributes mentioned in the Kaivalya-Upanishad, - all these attributes of Brahman should be comprehended in the Dahara-Vidya. The attributes of Brahman, described in the Kaivalya-Upanishad in the words "whose help-mate is Uma," "one who has three eyes," are identical in meaning with those of Brahman which are described elsewhere in the words "one who is dark-brown," and "one who has divers eyes." Repetition here is calculated to produce a high regard. The same construction should be put upon all attributes which are thus repeated. The Brahman is the being of whom all these attributes are predicated, and as such He alone is the object of worship in all cases, so that the Supreme Brahman should be contemplated in the middle of the small heart-lotus as endued with sinlessness and so on, as the lord of all, as the thing denoted by the syllable 'one', as one whose help-mate is Uma, as Three-eyed, as Dark-necked, as Consciousness and Bliss, as Infinite, Immortal, Wonderful. Accordingly this contemplation is the most essential in all contemplations of the Supreme. In the Chhandogya and the Kaivalya-Upanishads, it is said that he who devotes himself to this contemplation is said to attain, as the fruit thereof, to the Supreme Brahman Himself, the subject of all worship, transcending the region of Prakriti or the material universe:

> "Having reached the Highest Light he appears in his true form." * [* Chha. 8-3-4.]

> "Having reached thus, the sage reaches Him who is the womb of all beings, the Witness of all, transcending darkness.' † [† Kaivalya-Up.]

Thus, as the attributes of dark-neckedness and the like as well as the attributes of sinlessness and the like are ever present in Brahman, and as each set of attributes presupposes the other, nothing stands in the way of our comprehending them all in one act of contemplation. The denials would be quite out of place if there were no occasion for them.

On seeing the Supreme Brahman described as possessed of a body having three eyes, one would naturally attribute to Him other attendant attributes of the body, such as sin, old age, death, hunger, thirst, vain desires, vain purposes; and it is to prevent this that the sruti declares that He is devoid of all sin, and so on. Though the Supreme Brahman is endued with a body having three eyes and so on, still, He is free from all sins, free from old age, free from grief, free from hunger, free from thirst, His desires are true, his purposes are true, He is consciousness and Bliss. Hence no incongruity.

Adhikarana 24

(*Objection*): - If in the form of Brahman there should exist such parts of the body as would entitle Him to be described in the words "dark-necked," and so on, as He is described in the words "love is His head," then He would be subject to growth and decay and would therefore cease to be "dark-necked."

(*Answer*): - The sutrakara says:

Because of high regard, there is no failure. (III. iii. 39)

In the preceding sections it has been determined that Brahman has a form described as dark-necked, etc., that He is associated with the Supreme Power (Parama Sakti) designated as Uma, and that He has all the attributes including unfailing will and so on. Now a doubt arises as to whether at any time these attributes cease to exist in the Supreme Brahman, or they never cease.

(*Purvapaksha*): - At first sight it would seem that they cease at some time, in as much as they are merely imagined in the Supreme Brahman for the sake of contemplation.

(*Siddhanta*): - As against the foregoing we hold as follows: They never cease to exist in the Supreme Brahman because of the high regard the sruti shows for them by way of repeating in all cases His association with Uma and other attributes. Hence the description of the Supreme Brahman as one of unfailing potentialities. – Where are they repeated with high regard? – We answer, everywhere. Though it has been declared that He is dark-brown and divers-eyed, still, again, to show indeed its high regard for them, the sruti repeats "Whose help-mate is Uma, who is the Supreme Lord, the Master of all, who has three eyes." * [* Kaivalya-Up.] In the Sruti treating of the contemplation of the Divine Being in the solar orb, He is, again, out of high regard, described as the Lord of Uma, in the words "Homage to the Golden-armed, to the Lord of gold, to the Lord of Ambika, to the Lord of Uma."† [† Mahana. 18.] Elsewhere, again, that the Isvara is dark-necked, is, for the sake of regard again repeated in the word "whose neck is dark, to the black-throated,"‡ [‡ Tait. Sam. 4-5.] and so on. It is only to inspire high regard that the attributes of unfailing will and the like are repeated again although they have been once mentioned. Wherefore, on account of the high regard for them which the sruti shows by way of repeating them again and again, the attribute of being the Lord of Uma and such other attributes never cease to exist in the Supreme Brahman.

The Vedanta-Sutras with Srikantha Bhashya

In this case of Dharma and Brahman, - the subjects that are unknowable from any other source of knowledge, - those who follow the authority of the sruti should accept whatever that Divine sruti says as to their nature. Otherwise, if we follow that line of reasoning which is opposed to the sruti, it can never be established that Brahman is the material cause of the Universe, and so on. Accordingly, after having declared that Brahman is Existence and Consciousness and the Infinite, in the words "Existence, Consciousness and the Infinite, is Brahman," § [§ Tait. Up. 2-1.] the sruti itself again declares with reference to Him.

"The Right, the Real, is the Supreme Brahman, the Person who is dark and brown, whose semen is held above, who has divers eyes...." ‖ [‖ Mahana. 12.]

i.e., the sruti declares Brahman's conditioned form, that He is three-eyed and that He is associated with Uma, the Supreme Power (Paramasakti). And again, in the words "that is the one bliss of Brahman," ¶ [¶ Tait. Up. 2-8.] the sruti says that He is possessed of unsurpassed bliss. With reference to Him again, the sruti says

"Whose body is akasa, whose nature is true, whose delight is life whose manas is bliss, who is replete with peace, who is immortal." ** [** Tait. UP. 1-6.]

This means that Brahman shines forth with consciousness, that He delights in Himself, that He exults in the Supreme Bliss which can be experienced by the antah-karana or inner sense alone divorced from all organs of external sensation, that He is untainted with any kind of evil, and that He is free from all bondage from time without a beginning. By describing Him s "freed from all sins"* [* Chha. 8-1-5.] the sruti wards off all evils that may be supposed to pertain to Him, - as they pertain to a Jiva, - owing to His connection with a body described as diverse-eyed and so on. In the words "who is the omniscient, the all-knower," † [† Mund. 1-1-10.] "He has a Supreme Sakti," ‡ [‡ Sveta. 6-8.] "To the Lord of all," § [§ Tait. Sam. 4-5-2.] and the like, the Sruti speaks of His omniscience, His omnipotence, His independence, and so on. Thus the Sruti itself, which stands at the head of all authorities, proclaims everywhere that Brahman is Existence, Consciousness, and Bliss; that He is infinite, omniscient, ever-satisfied, independent, that His manifestation has had no beginning, that He is possessed of infinite and undecaying powers; that He delights in Himself, that His bliss is enjoyed by the inner consciousness alone, that He is tranquil, immortal, dark-necked, diverse-eyed, associated with Uma; that the Supreme Brahman is the soul of all, and the means of Salvation. Who can stand in the way of the Sruti? Wherefore the essential attributes described above never cease to exist in the Supreme Brahman.

The Vedanta-Sutras with Srikantha Bhashya

Adhikarana 25

(The said Brahman is attained by the liberated) since the latter is said to attain freedom because of the (self-realisation accruing) on the attainment of Brahman. (III. iii. 40)

Now a doubt arises as to whether it is the Brahman described in the last section that is attained by the liberated soul, or something else.

(*Purvapaksha*): - One thing suggests itself to us at first. – The Sruti declares the unconditioned Brahman in the passages such as the following:

"Who is without parts, without actions, tranquil, without fault, without taint." * [* Sveta. 6-12.]

"He who knows Brahman becomes Brahman Himself." † [† Mund. 3-2-9.]

In these words, the Sruti says that liberation consists in the liberated soul attaining to Brahman's state. Wherefore it is the unconditioned Brahman, not anything else, that is attained by the liberated.

(*Conclusion*): - As against the foregoing we hold as follows. It is the state of the Conditioned Brahman that is attained by the liberated soul. For, the Sruti declares that the liberated soul secures his relatives at will and attains equality with the Supreme Brahman – as declared in the passages of the Sruti and the Smriti, such as "he moves about there eating, playing, and rejoicing, be it with women, carriages or relatives;" (1) "he attains prefect equality;"[(1) Chha. 8-12-3.] (2) "the liberated soul shall become equal to Siva – only as a result of his attaining to his own true state on attaining to the Supreme Brahman, "on uniting with the Supreme Light" [(2) Mund. 3-1-3.] (3) as the Sruti says, - the Divers-eyed, contemplated within the small heart-lotus. Wherefore the form of the Supreme Brahman described above as Dark-necked is the very form to which the liberated soul attains; it does not pertain to samsara, to the mundane existence, since that form is said to be free from all conditions of mundane existence in the words "Who is freed from all Sins." [(3) Chha. 8-3-4.] (4) The highest wisdom, therefore, concerning the Supreme is one that comprehends Him as possessed of attributes. When the Sruti describes Brahman as one "who is without parts, who is without actions," it is only the evil attributes that are denied, but not the auspicious qualities. To explain. The words "Who is without parts, who is without actions" and "The Lord of Nature and Souls, the Ruler of Gunas" [(4) Ibid. 8-1-5.] (5) describe Brahman both as unconditioned and conditioned, as *Nirguna* and *Saguna;* but from the passages – such as "Who is the omniscient, the all-knower', "Who is freed from all sins" – which speak of the specific nature of Brahman, we understand that the Sruti speaking of Brahman as devoid of qualities, means only absence of evil qualities, and that of the Sruti speaking of Brahman as possessed of qualities refers to the auspicious qualities that He possesses. [(5) Sveta. 6-16.]

Moreover, there is a passage in the scripture itself which teaches that the Saguna is attained as the result of liberation.

The Vedanta-Sutras with Srikantha Bhashya

"He attains all pleasures with Brahman the Wise." * [* Taitt-Up. 2-1.]

That is to say, the liberated soul attains all pleasures with the omniscient Brahman. The word 'with' shows that the enjoyment of bliss is coeval with Brahman's. Wherefore the fruit attained by the liberated soul is none other than the Saguna Brahman.

Adhikarana 26

No absolute necessity for the observance of directions about such contemplations, because so we find. As a separate fruit indeed is non-obstruction (declared). (III. iii. 41)

A doubt arises as to whether the directions concerning the contemplations taught in connection with the Udgitha and such other angas or constituent parts of sacrificial rites should invariably be attended to or not.

(*Purvapaksha*): - It would seem that those contemplations should, of necessity, be gone through in performing the sacrificial rites, because such contemplations form part and parcel of those rites. Though they are taught outside the section which treats of the sacrificial rites themselves, still, through other things mentioned in connection with them, they may be connected with those rites. Though, for instance, the direction that the ladle (juhu) should be of parna tree † [† Tait. Sam. 3-5-7.] is given without any specific reference to a sacrificial rite, still, in as much as the ladle is invariably associated with a sacrificial rite, the specific direction that the ladle should be of the parna tree refers to a sacrificial rite. Similarly, from the statements "He that sings aloud thus regarding;" ‡ [‡ Chha. Up. 1-1-8.] "He who chants saman, thus regarding," § [§ Ibid. 1-7-9.] speaking of the contemplations as associated with the Udgitha, the Saman, etc., which are invariably associated with sacrificial rites, we understand that the contemplations also are connected with sacrificial rites. Therefore, the contemplation of the Udgitha and son are absolutely necessary in the sacrificial rites.

(*Siddhanta*): - As against the foregoing we hold as follows: These contemplations are not absolutely necessary, any more than the milk-pail, etc. To explain: The scripture says, "Let him convey water in the chamasa vessel, - but in the milk-pail (godohana) in the case of one who seeks cattle." Here the milk-pail is prescribed for conveying water, not in the interests of the sacrificial rite itself, but in the interests of the sacrificer, and the observance of the direction is therefore optional, not absolutely necessary like the act of conveying water. Similarly, the contemplation connected with the sacrificial rites are not prescribed in the interests of the sacrificial rites themselves, in as much as these rites may be performed without the contemplations, as the following passage shows:

"Both he who knows this (the true meaning of the syllable Om) and he who does not know, perform the same sacrifice." * [* Chha. Up. 1-1-10.]

Again, the sruti says:

"The sacrifice which a man performs with knowledge, faith, and meditation of the Devata, is more powerful." † [† Ibid.]

Here, though the verb – 'performs' – is in the present indicative, still we assume that the sruti means an injunction, that he who seeks to make the rite more powerful should observe the directions regarding the contemplations as a means of achieving his object. For a sacrificial rite to become more powerful is to produce its fruit soon without encountering obstruction from other stronger forces in action. Further, these contemplations are said to yield distinct fruits of their own, such as objects of desire and rain; and they cannot therefore be indispensable in the interests of the sacrificial rites themselves.

Adhikarana 27

(The Upasanas are different) exactly as in the case of the offerings. This has been explained. (III. iii. 42)

It has been declared that in all the several upasanas of the Supreme, the one Siva, the Supreme Brahman, should be thought of differently as endued with the different attributes specifically in the several contexts. Now, a doubt arises as to whether this stands to reason or not.

(*Purvapaksha*): - It would appear that, notwithstanding a difference in attributes, Brahman, who is possessed of those attributes, is one and the same, and that therefore there can be no change in His upasanas. No change is perceived in the one prince, whether engaged in business, exercise or eating, whether he is seated or engaged in hunting or fighting, though he may put on different ornaments on different occasions, and though he may be seated on the throne or in any other place. So also, notwithstanding the difference in the abodes such as the heart, and not-withstanding the difference in the attributes with which He is endued, Brahman is one, and His upasana must therefore be one alone.

(*Siddhanta*): - As against the foregoing, we hold as follows: Though there is no change in the essential nature of the one Siva, the Parabrahman, still, there is a difference corresponding to the difference in the qualifying attributes, the Supreme Being being endued with different attributes in the several upasanas; and the manner of His contemplation therefore differs by contemplating Him as endued with different attributes. In the case of offerings to Indra, different purodasas are offered according to the difference in the attributes, as the sruti says, "To Indra, the king, let the purodasas of eleven dishes be offered; as also to Indra, the over-lord, and to Indra the self-lord." * [* Tait. Sam. 2-3-6.] Accordingly, the Samkarsha-Kanda says, "The deities are separate because they are separately conceived" † [† Op. Cit. 14-2-15.] So, here, though the Supreme Brahman is one, the upasana differs with the difference in attributes. As to the illustration of the prince who remains one though his dress and seat may change, even there the manner of service rendered by the servants differs with the change of dress and place, though he remains essentially the same all the while.

Adhikarana 28

(The Supreme Brahman associated with Uma is to be contemplated in all upasanas) because of the predominance of the indicatory marks. That, indeed, is stronger; and it has been explained also. (III. iii. 43)

It has been established in the foregoing articles that, in all Highest Vidyas (or upasanas), Brahman should be contemplated. The purpose of this adhikarana is to determine specifically the nature of the Brahman to be contemplated. The Taittiriya says:

"All verily, is Rudra. To that Rudra be this obeisance. Purusha, indeed, is Rudra, the Existence, the Splendour. I bow to Him, bow to Him."

"All being, the variegated world, that which has been born and is being born in various forms; all this, indeed, is this Rudra; and to that Rudra be this bow."

"To excellent Rudra, to the extremely wise, to Him, who rains all blessings, to the Adorable, to the Heart, we shall address this happiest word: 'All this verily is Rudra, and to that Rudra be this homage'"

"Homage to the Golden-armed, to the Lord of gold, to the Lord of Ambika; to the Lord of Uma be this bow, and again this bow." * [* Mahana. 16-18.]

Now a doubt arises as to whether the Supreme Brahman, - who is here declared to be one with all and so on, and to the Lord of Uma, - should be contemplated only in the upasana relating to the solar orb with which the present section is concerned, or in all contemplations of the Supreme.

(*Purvapaksha*): - At first sight it would appear that such Brahman should be contemplated only in connection with the upasana of the solar orb with which the present section is concerned, in as much as it will not do to do any violence to the main subject of the section.

(Siddhanta): - As against the foregoing we hold as follows: This Brahman, the Supreme, associated with Uma should be contemplated as such in all upasanas of the Supreme, owing to the predominance (in this section) of the passages treating of the indicatory marks or attributes mentioned in the several other upasanas of the Supreme. To explain: The passage "All, verily, is Rudra," evidently refers to the attribute of the Supreme that has to be contemplated in the Sandilya-vidya: "All this is Brahman. Let a man meditate on the (visible world) as beginning, ending, and breathing in that Brahman." † [† Chha. 3-14-1.] "Purusha, verily, is Rudra": these words repeats the characteristic attributes mentioned in the Purusha-Sukta and the Upakosala-vidya. "The existence": this corresponds to the attribute of Brahman to be contemplated in the Sad-Vidya, "Existence, alone, my dear, this at first was." ‡ [‡ Ibid. 6-2-1.] The word 'Mahah (Splendour)" refers to the attribute of Brahman to be contemplated in the Vyahriti-Vidya, which says "'Mahah': this is Brahman, this the Atman; its limbs are other Devatas."* [* Tait-Up. 1-5.] "The most beneficent one in the heart:" these words refer to the heart, and thus allude to the attributes of Brahman to be contemplated in the Dahara-vidya. "The the Golden-armed:" these words refer to the attribute of golden form to be contemplated in connection with the solar orb. – "The Lord of Uma:" this is to show that Brahman described here should be contemplated in all upasanas of the Supreme. As expelling (Sk. Root *dru*) the disease (Sk. *ruj*) of samsara, Siva the Paramatman is called *Rudra*. Thus from the very words of the passages occurring in the section, it may be determined that Siva, the Parabrahman, the Lord of Uma, should be contemplated in all Vidyas or Upasanas of the Supreme. This agreement in the words if passage should certainly prevail as against the general subject matter of the section (which would go to restrict the attributes to the one particular Vidya with which that section is concerned), as has been shown in the Purvamimamsa III. iii. 14. Hence the conclusion that the Supreme Being, the Lord of Uma, the expeller of the disease of samsara, should be contemplated in all upasanas of the Supreme.

Adhikarana 29

As an alternative for the preceding, they should form (parts of) the ritualistic sacrifice, because of the section (in which they occur), as in the case of the mental cup. (III. iii. 44)

In the Agnirahasya-Brahmana it is said,

"It saw thirty-six thousand shining fire-altars, belonging to itself, made of mind, built of mind." † [† Satapatha-Brahman, Agnirahasya, 5-3. Many other passages are quoted in the sequel from the same section.]

Further on the sruti speaks similarly of other fire-altars built of speech, built of breath, built of sight, built of hearing, built of action, built of fire. It man's life-span extending over one hundred years, there are thirty-six thousand days. Computing the whole function of mind in a day as one fire, there are thirty-six thousand fires. These should be regarded as the Pratyagatman, the Inner Self. So too in the case of fire-altars built of speech, etc., Now a doubt arises as to whether they form part of the sacrifice of knowledge or part of the sacrifice of ritual.

(*Purvapaksha*): - These imagined fires – such as those made up of speech, those made up of mind, etc., - enter into the sacrifice of ritual, whereof the fire built of bricks, just spoken of, forms a supplementary part. Accordingly, these fires are only alternatives for the fire built of bricks as in the case of 'mental cup.' The explain. The cup offered on the tenth day, called avivakya, of the Soma sacrifice occupying twelve days, - the earth being regarded as the vessel, Prajapati regarded as the Deity, and the ocean being regarded as the substance (soma), - forms part of a ritualistic sacrificed, though it is a mental cup, because the taking up of it, the putting down in its place, the offering of it the taking of the remaining liquid, the invitation to drink it, and the drinking of it can be achieved only in mind: similarly, though mental, these fires form part of the ritualistic sacrifice.

And because of the extended application. (III. iii. 45)

These fires form part of the ritualistic sacrifice, because the particulars connected with the fire built of bricks are extended to them, in the words of the Sruti, "each one of them is commensurate with the one mentioned above."

(*Siddhanta*): - As against the foregoing we hold as follows:

(They are), indeed, knowledge alone, because of the determination and of the Revelation. (III. iii. 46)

They are knowledge alone; i.e., they form parts of the sacrifice of knowledge. Though it is known that these are fires formed of knowledge because of their being merely imagined as fires, the Sruti determines the same thing in the words "these, verily, are built only of knowledge"; and this determination shows that they form parts of the sacrifice of knowledge. And the Sruti expressly declares that it is only a sacrifice of knowledge, in the following words:

"They were built of mind; in these the offering were taken by mind; they praised in mind, and they extolled in mind. Whatever act was done in the sacrifices and whatever act pertained to the sacrifice, all this was done by mind in mental forms, in the mental fires built of minds."

Wherefore they are parts of the sacrifice of knowledge.

And because of the greater force of the direct declaration, etc., this view cannot be set aside. (III. iii. 47)

Our view cannot be set aside on the mere authority of the 'section (prakarana)', because it is weak when compared with 'indicatory mark (linga)', with the 'wording of the passages (Vakya)' and with the 'direct declaration (Sruti)'. The sruti says:

"These, verily, are only built of knowledge; and by him who regards them thus always, all beings are won. Even though he be asleep, these fires are built up in knowledge in the case of him who regard them in this way."

(*Objection*): - "In these, the offerings were taken up in mind:" in such passages as these there is no particle denoting injunction; and therefore there is no sacrifice of knowledge as distinguished from the ritualistic sacrifice.

(*Answer*): - The Sutrakara says:

From the supplementary (statements), we learn that these are distinct from the ritualistic sacrifice), as the other (sacrifices of) knowledge are distinct. It is also seen (elsewhere). This has been explained. (III. iii. 48)

"The offerings were taken by mind": from this and other such supplementary statements in connection with the sacrifice, as also from such direct declarations s "these, verily, are piled by mind," we understand that there is here an injunction of a sacrifice of knowledge. Just as the Dahara-Vidya and the like are regarded as sacrifices quite unconnected with any of the ritualistic ones, so, from the supplementary passages and from direct declarations such as those cited above, we understand that the sacrifice of knowledge is also unconnected with any of the ritualistic sacrifices. And there are instances where passages which merely assert are construed into injunctions, as for instance, "what one does with knowledge, that surely is more powerful." * [* Chha. 1-1-10.] This principle has been well explained in the Purva-Mimamsa III. V. 21. Wherefore it is but proper to maintain that these fires are only parts of a sacrifice of knowledge.

The Sutrakara now supposes an objection and answers it as follows:

(This view is in) no (way objectionable) because (the transfer of particulars from one to another) is seen even on account of some similarity, as in the case of death. No occasion indeed for the relation of space. (III. iii. 49)

"Each one of them is commensurate with the one mentioned above:" in these words the particulars connected with the fire built by bricks are transferred to the mental fires simply because of the similarity of results. The same fruit that accrues from the fire built of bricks through the sacrifice with which it is connected accrues also from these mental fires which form part of the sacrifice of knowledge. The Sruti does not certainly mean that these mental fires occupy the same amount of space as the fire built of bricks. We find particulars connected with one thing being extended to another on account of some point of resemblance, whatever that point of resemblance may be. The passage "He verily is death, He who is the person dwelling in this orb," identifies the person dwelling in the sun with Death simply because both are alike destroyers. Here, certainly, the person dwelling in the orb does not occupy the same space as Death. Thus, the identification being possible on account of any point of resemblance whatever, no objection can be taken to our view.

The Sutrakara states another reason as follows:

And from the sequel, such is the meaning of the passage; and they are appended because of the preponderance. (III. iii. 50)

From what follows in the Brahman, we understand that the passage speaking of mind built fire and so on means that these fires exist only in knowledge. The passage referred to runs thus: "that piled fire is this world, indeed," and so on. In this passage, the Sruti enjoins a Vidya (upasana) productive of a distinct fruit. The mind-built fire and the like are treated in a ritualistic section simply because of the details to be imagined in connection with these fires abound in that section. Therefore, these fires form part of the sacrifice of knowledge.

Adhikarana 30

Some (hold that it is not proper) because of the existence of the self (Atman) in the body. (III. iii. 51)

Now a doubt arises as to whether it is proper or not to contemplate in all meditations of the Supreme, the nature of Brahman as described above.

(*Purvapaksha*): Some hold as follows:

As the worshipper dwells in the body and manifests himself as the actor and the enjoyer, it is not proper to contemplate, in the meditations of the Supreme, the Paramesvara as the Self of such a one, - to contemplate as such Him who is Three-eyed and so on.

(*Siddhanta*): - As against the foregoing contention the Sutrakara says:

The opposite (should be contemplated because the self-realisation) depends thereon, as in the case of the realisation (of Brahman). No (incongruity) whatever. (III. iii. 52)

It is not that the Paramatman should be contemplated as the Self of the worshipper who manifests himself as the actor and the enjoyer. On the contrary, it is the opposite nature, as manifested in the one liberated from the mundane life, - *i.e.*, in the one by whom all sins have been shaken off, and so on – that should be contemplated, because the realisation of the true nature of the Self depends upon such contemplation. The realisation of the true nature of Brahman, for instance, depends on the contemplation of Brahman as He really is. The Sruti says:

> "According to what his will is in this world, so will he be when he has departed this life." * [* Chha. Up. 3-14-1.]

Accordingly, in as much as the worshipper should be contemplated as liberated from mundane life, as free from all sins, and so on, there is no incongruity whatever in contemplation the Paramesvara, - who has to be contemplated as the Self of the worshipper, - in His nature as the Three-eyed, and so on.

Adhikarana 31

What are connected with the subsidiary parts are not (confined to them alone). They are indeed common to all Vedas in all their recensions. (III. iii. 53)

A doubt arises as to whether those things which are enjoined in certain parts of the Vedas in connection with the subsidiary parts of the contemplation should be regarded or not as forming parts of all contemplations.

The Vedanta-Sutras with Srikantha Bhashya

(*Purvapaksha*): - Now a repetition of the Pranava in connection with the Dahara-Upasana is enjoined in the Kaivalya-Upanishad as follows:

"Having made the Atman the (lower) arani, and the Pranava the upper arani, by repeated churning the wise man burns up the bond." † [† Op. Cit. 11.]

In the Atharvasiras the smearing of the ashes is enjoined in connection with the Pasupata-Vidya (the contemplation of the Pasupati, the Lord of the souls), as follows:

"With the Mantra, 'Fire is the ashes' and so on, let him take up the ashes, rub on the limbs (with it) and touch them all. This is therefore the vow relating to the Pasupati, for the liberation of the soul from bondage."

Elsewhere the wearing of the ashes in three lines is enjoined in the words "Let him make three lines." * [* Kalagnirudra-Up.] As oneness with Siva is declared to be the fruit of this kind of worship, it must form a necessary part of the worship of the Supreme. Such things as are thus enjoined as parts of the worship of Brahman should (according to the Purvapakshin) be observed by the worshippers only in the case of those kinds of worship which are enjoined in the particular parts of the Veda referred to, because of their context; they cannot be common to all.

(*Siddhanta*): - As against the foregoing we hold as follows: There is no rule that the smearing of the ashes and the like which are enjoined in connection with the worship of Brahman should be confined to the students of those particular parts of the Veda in which they occur. On the contrary, they should be observed by all worshippers of Brahman, whatever Veda they study and whatever recension they follow. The sruti or direct declaration should prevail against what we may make out from mere proximity or context.

Or, no incongruity as in the case of the incantations, etc. (III. iii. 54)

Just as there is no incongruity whatever in using, in connection with a sacrificial rite common to all recensions, those incantations (Mantras) which occur only in certain recensions of the Veda in connection with that sacrificial rite, so too here.

Adhikarana 32

The whole is essential, as in the case of the sacrificial rite. So, indeed, the Sruti teaches. (III. iii. 55)

Now a doubt arises as to whether, in the case of the Vaisvanara-Vidya, the contemplation should be practised in separate parts or as a whole.

(*Purvapaksha*): - The sruti teaches that the heavenly region, the Sun, the Air (Vayu), the Ether (Akasa), Water, and Earth should be regarded respectively as the head, the eye, the vital air, the trunk, the urinary organs and the foot of the Vaisvanara, the Universal Man. A contemplation of each of these parts separately has also been enjoined in such words as the following, occurring in connection with the contemplation of the heavenly region, and so on.

"And whoever meditates on that Vaisvanara Self eats food, sees his desire, and has spiritual lustre in his house." † [† Chha. Up. 5-12-2.]

Accordingly, in as much as the word 'contemplate' and the declaration of the fruit mentioned in connection with each separately, it is but proper to practise the contemplation of each part separately.

(*Siddhanta*): - We say that the contemplation of the whole is essential. – To explain: After declaring that the heavenly region, etc., are the head, and so on, of the Vaisvanara who has to be contemplated as having the three regions for his body, the Sruti declares further that the realisation of Brahman is the result of the contemplation:

"But he who worships the Vaisvanara Self as a span long, and as identical with himself, he eats food in all worlds, in all beings, in all self's." * [* Chha-Up. 5-18-1.]

Now, the contemplation of the Vaisvanara as a whole is essential, as founded on proper authority when compared with the contemplation of Him only in part; for it is said that the former alone leads to the realisation of Brahman. The Sruti is not quite earnest when speaking of the contemplation of the Vaisvanara in part, or of its fruit. After enjoining, for instance, the sacrificial rite in the words "when a son is born one should offer an oblation of twelve dishes to Vaisvanara," the Sruti goes on: "What has been offered in eight dishes purifies him, as Gayatri, with spiritual lustre;" and so on. Just as the sruti is not quite earnest in speaking of the oblation of eight dishes or of its fruit, so too here (in the case of the Vaisvanara-Vidya). And the Sruti expressly declares that the contemplation of the whole is surely essential. In the section referred to, after the questions, "What Self, O son of Upamanyu, dost thou worship."..."What Self, O Prachinayogya, dost thou worship?", the answers are given in the words "I worship the Heaven, O Lord, O King." Having in these words taught the contemplation of the constituent parts, the sruti has declared here and there the fruits thereof in the words "He eats food, he sees desire," and so on. All this notwithstanding, the Sruti declares that evil would result from the contemplation of the separate parts, in the following words of the King:

"That, however, is but the head of the Self, and thus your head would have fallen (in a discussion), if you had not come to me." † [† Chha. 5-12-17.]

Wherefore, surely, the contemplation of the whole is essential.

Adhikarana 33

They are different, because of the difference in the designation, etc. (III. iii. 55)

Here a doubt arises as to whether in the contemplation of the Supreme we should combine together all the various descriptions of the Supreme, or contemplate each separately.

(*Purvapaksha*): - In the contemplation of the Supreme, we should combine all together, in as much as Brahman, the object of contemplation, is one and the same, though various contemplations are taught severally in the several recensions of the Veda.

(*Siddhanta*): - As against the foregoing, we hold as follows: Because of the impossibility of combining together the infinite number of contemplations taught in the Vedic texts which are infinite in number, the several contemplations are distinct from one another, since Brahman, though one in Himself, has distinct attributes. It has been shown that there may be such a distinction in the worship of one and the same Being, just as different cakes are offered to one and the same Indra when endued with different attributes, *i.e.*, according as He is addressed as the Kind and so on, or just as the sacrificial fire is worshipped differently according to the place occupied, as Garhapatya, and so on. Hence the conclusion that, because of the distinction in the designation and other such appendages, the contemplation of the Supreme taught in different recensions are different. This special section has been devoted to the same subject, only with a view to refute the theory that the Vedas do not enjoin contemplation or knowledge (jnana).

Adhikarana 34

They are so many alternatives, because their fruits are all alike. (III. iii. 57)

Thus, the contemplations of the Supreme in different forms have been treated of. A doubt arises as to whether, in the case of a devotee, they form so many alternative courses, or they should one and all be practised.

(*Purvapaksha*): - What is the prima facie view? It would seem proper that the Dahara-Vidya (the contemplation in the heart), the Sad-Vidya (the contemplation of the One Existence) and the like, should be practised in conjunction, because it is possible that more effort produces more fruit. There is nothing to show that they are so many alternatives.

(*Siddhanta*): - As against this view, we hold as follows: As regards one and the same individual, all the several contemplations of the Supreme form so many alternative modes of worship – Why? – because the realisation of the unsurpassed Bliss of Brahman, which is the fruit of the intuitive perception of Brahman, is the same in all cases. If the aim is attained by one upasana only, why should one resort to others which are of no use? Moreover, by one upasana, the immediate perception of the true nature of Brahman is attained in most intense meditation, because the devotee firmly regards himself as one with Brahman. By abandoning one and resorting to another, there will be only a wandering of the mind. Hence it is that they are all so many alternative courses.

Adhikarana 35

The interested ones, however, may be conjoined together at will, or not, because of the absence of the foregoing reason. (III. iii. 53)

Now, a doubt arising as to whether the principle laid down in the last preceding Adhikarana applies to the contemplation (Vidyas) which are intended to produce results distinct from the intuitive realisation of Brahman, we hold as follows: The principle established in the foregoing adhikarana does not apply to such contemplations; for, there is a distinction between the two kinds of contemplation. "Becoming a God, he goes to the Gods:" * [* Bri. Up. 6-1-2.] in these words the sruti gives us to understand that, in all contemplations of the Supreme in which the Supreme is contemplated as the Self of the devotee, the realisation of Divinity is attained while still alive, as a result of intense meditation. There is no evidence whatever to show that in the same way the interested (Kamya) contemplations, such as the contemplation of 'name' as Brahman, produce such intuitive realisation. As the interested contemplations are not calculated to produce the result spoken of, it would seem proper to practice as many of such contemplations as possible, with a view to produce a proportionately greater result. Hence the conclusion that one may resort to either one alone of such contemplations, or more.

Adhikarana 36

In the case of the members (of sacrificial rites), they follow (the rites) to which they relate. (III. iii. 59)

Now, again, a doubt arises as to whether the Upasanas connected with members of sacrificial rites, such as the Udgitha and the like, form part of the rites concerned, or they are independent.

(*Purvapaksha*): - Such a doubt having arisen, the argument on behalf of the prima facie view is stated by the Sutrakara as follows: The Upasanas relating to the Udgitha and such other members of sacrificial rites do, like those members themselves, form part of the sacrificial rites concerned, since, as in the case of the milk-pail and so on, no result is said to accrue from such Upasanas where the Sruti speaks of them.

And because of the commandment. (III. iii. 60)

Because there is an injunction implied in the words "let him contemplate the Udgitha," * [* Chha. 1-1-1.] and because no injunction is implied in the words "whatever he does with contemplation (Vidya)," † [† Chha. 1-1-10.] etc., we conclude that the Upasanas referred to, do form part of the sacrificial rites.

The Vedanta-Sutras with Srikantha Bhashya

Because of the rectification. (III. iii. 61)

"He who knows that the Udgitha is the Pranava, and the Pranava the Udgitha, rectifies, from the seat of the Hotri priest, any mistake committed by the Udgatri in performing the Udgitha;" ‡ [‡ Chha. 1-5-5.] in these words the Sruti impresses the necessity of conjoining the Upasana. For this reason, too, these Upasanas form parts of the sacrificial rites. The mistakes referred to consists in performing the Udgitha without knowledge or contemplation (Vedana). The Sruti, which speaks of rectification by other means in the absence of the knowledge, certainly points to the necessity of conjoining the knowledge or contemplation with the sacrificial rite. Because of this necessity, the Upasanas referred to, form parts of the sacrificial rites.

Because of the declaration that the attribute is common. (III. iii. 62)

"By that (syllable) does the threefold knowledge proceed. 'Om,' thus does the Adhvaryu priest give an order; 'Om'; thus does the Hotri recite; 'Om'; thus does the Udgatri sing." Thus the Pranava is associated everywhere; and since the Upasana is here spoken of as an attribute of the Pranava, it may be concluded that the Upasana is necessary part of the sacrificial rie. The word 'that', (occurring in the passage quoted above) referring to something that has just been spoken of, must here refer only to the Pranava combined with Upasana. Wherefore it cannot be made out that the Upasana connected with the Udgitha and the like do not form necessary parts of the sacrificial rites concerned.

(*Siddhanta*): - As against the foregoing the Sutrakara states the Siddhanta as follows:

Certainly no, because of the absence of the declaration that they go together. (III. iii. 63)

For the Upasanas to go together with the sacrificial rites is to form necessary parts of them. Because this is not declared in the sruti, the Upasanas do not form parts of the sacrificial rites. "What a man performs with knowledge that alone is more powerful;" * [* Chha. 1-1-10.] in these words we are told that such Upasanas are the means of producing distinct results of their own; they cannot therefore form parts of sacrificial rites. "Let him sing the Udgitha": here the sruti teaches merely that the Upasanas are related to the Udgitha; and therefore those Upasanas which are connected with the members of sacrificial rites are not necessary parts of those sacrificial rites.

And because of the revelation. (III. iii. 64)

"A Brahman priest who knows this saves the sacrifice, the sacrificer, and all the other priests:" † [† Chha. 4-17-10.] thus speaking of all being saved by the Brahman priest's knowledge, the sruti shows that the knowledge is quite necessary for the Udgatri and the other priests and that it does not therefore form a necessary part of the sacrificial rite. Wherefore it is but right to hold, as we have done above, that the Upasanas are not absolutely necessary for the sacrificial rites.

THIRD ADHYAYA – FOURTH PADA

Adhikarana 1

In the preceding section has been expounded the nature of the Paravidya, the supreme wisdom. And now, with a view to expound the nature of the *asrama dharmas*, - those duties which are enjoined on the several holy orders, - which are accessories to that wisdom, the Sutrakara declares that the end of man is attained through wisdom alone.

Thence is the end of man, because of the word. So says Badarayana. (III. iv. 1)

Thence, - that is from wisdom alone, - accrues the end of man, because of the following passages of the Sruti:

"The knower of Brahman reaches the Supreme." ‡ [‡ Tait. Up. 2-1.]

"Having known Siva, one finally attains peace." § [§ Sveta. Up. 4-14.]

So thinks the blessed Badarayana.

Now a doubt arises as to whether this is possible or not, because of the passages of the Sruti pointing both ways.

(*Purvapaksha*): - The prima facie view is stated as follows:

Being an appendage, it is mere arthavada concerning man, as in other cases. So thinks Jaimini. (III. iv. 2)

The end of man accrues not from knowledge. Why? For, it is the agent of actions that is declared to be one with Brahman in such passages as "Thou art That," where the words referring to the agent and Brahman are put in apposition to each other; and to view the agent as one with Brahman conduces to the elevation of the agent and thus forms an accessory of the ritual. As to the Sruti, however, speaking of the independent fruits of knowledge, we hold that it constitutes a mere Arthavada, on the principle enunciated in the Purvamimamsa (IV. III. 1). Accordingly, the end of man does not accrue from knowledge. So thinks the teacher, Jaimini.

Because it is seen to be the custom. (III. iv. 3)

Custom to the same effect is also seen. Asvapati Kekaya, who knew Brahman, says: "I am going to sacrifice, O Lords." * [* Chha. 6-11-10.] Thus we learn that ritual is essential even in the case of knowers of Brahman, such as Kekaya.

Because there is Sruti to the same effect. (III. iv. 4)

Knowledge is a mere appendage to ritual because, in the words "whatever one does with knowledge," † [† Ibid. 1-1-10.] knowledge is declared by the Sruti itself to form a part of ritual. The Sruti means that what one does is done with knowledge.

Because of the embrace. (III. iv. 5)

"Him do knowledge and work embrace:" ‡ [‡ Bri. Up. 6-4-2.] from these words we understand that knowledge and ritual are united in one and the same person; and therefore knowledge forms but an appendage of ritual.

Because of the injunction in the case of him who is possessed of it. (III. iv. 6)

Ritual is enjoined on one who has studied the Vedas till he has understood the meaning, as may be seen in the passages like the following:

"He who has learnt the Veda from a family of teachers, according to the sacred rule, in the leisure time left from the duties to be performed for the Guru, who, after receiving his discharge has settled in his own house, etc." § [§ Chha. 8-15-1.]

Wherefore, too, knowledge is an appendage of ritual.

Because of the rule. (III. iv. 7)

It has been definitely laid down as a rule that the knower of Atman should devote his life to ritual. "Only performing works here a man should wish to live a hundred years." * [* Isa. Up. 2] For this reason also, knowledge is an appendage of ritual. From that no good accrues to man.

(*Siddhanta*): - Now the Siddhanta is stated as follows:-

Because of the one above is taught, Badarayana's (is valid) because so it is revealed. (III. iv. 8)

Knowledge is not a mere appendage of ritual. On the contrary, Badarayana's view that by knowledge alone man attains his end holds good, because He alone who is a being other than the individual soul, other than the agent, is pointed out as the one to be known. So indeed the Sruti says.

"Let me be born manifold." † [† Chha. 6-2-3.]

"He is the Cause, the Lord of the lords of senses." ‡ [‡ Sveta. 6-9.]

"Superior to the universe is Rudra, the Great Sage." § [§ Mahana 10-19.]

In passages like these we find declared the superiority of Brahman who has to be known. Wherefore knowledge is not an appendage of ritual.

As to the contention that custom points otherwise, the Sutrakara says:

But equal is revelation. (III. iv. 9)

Custom is found pointing equally to the supremacy of knowledge, not alone of ritual exclusively. Revelation, indeed, points to the renunciation of ritual by knower of Brahman, as seen in the passages like the following: -

"This, indeed, said the Kavasheya sages who knew Him; 'for what purpose are we to study? For what purpose are we to sacrifice? What are we to do with offspring?'"

One should perform, as an accessory to knowledge, that work which is not accompanied with a longing for the result; whereas one should abandon that which is accompanied with a longing for the result. So, there being no incongruity whatever, it is ritual that forms as appendage to knowledge, while knowledge is of primary importance.

As to the argument based on the text "whatever one does with knowledge," the Sutrakara says:

Not universal. (III. iv. 10)

The passage "whatever one does with knowledge," does not speak of knowledge as common to call cases, in as much as it speaks of knowledge as if it has been already made familiar. And the knowledge which has just been familiarized is that concerning the Udgitha-Vidya. "Whatever one does with knowledge that alone becomes more virulent," in these words it is taught that the Udgitha-Vidya, the subject of the present section, is the means of making more powerful the ritual which is associated with it. Accordingly the Vidya does not form an appendage of ritual.

As to the contention based on the text, "Him do knowledge and work embrace," the Sutrakara answers as follows:

Division (is meant), as in the case of a hundred. (III. iv. 11)

"Him do knowledge and work embrace:" here, knowledge and work being productive of distinct results, knowledge accompanies (the soul) to yield its own fruit. Thus a division is meant here, when we say, for example, two hundred (rupees) has been realised by the sale of land and precious stones, we mean a division, namely, that land has been sold for a hundred (rupees) and that precious stones have been sold for a hundred.

For him who is possessed of the mere learning. (III. iv. 12)

Because the scriptural text "Having learned the Veda," etc., enjoins ritual only on him who possesses the mere learning, knowledge does not form an appendage of the ritual. The injunction concerning the learning of the Veda relates merely to the getting up of texts. Even supposing that it extends also to a knowledge of the meaning of the texts, the Vidya or knowledge spoken of (in the passage under consideration) is something different from that relating to the meaning of the texts. Vidya is that revolving in mind of a certain idea, which is enjoined in the words "let him contemplate (upasana)." Therefore (this knowledge which is under discussion) nowhere forms an adjunct.

Because there is no specification. (III. iv. 13)

In the passage "Only performing works here," etc., there is no specific reason found to show that the whole life of the enlightened sage should be devoted to ritual for ritual's sake. On the contrary we understand that this ritual is an appendage of Vidya, because it occurs in a section devoted to Vidya, beginning with the words "By Lord should be covered all this." Therefore Vidya does not form an appendage of ritual.

Or it is a permission, for the praise (of Vidya). (III. iv. 14)

The sequel says indeed that, though doing works always, one is not tainted by them, in virtue of Vidya. For the foregoing reason also, Vidya alone is of primary importance.

And some (read of the abandonment of ritual) on the impulse of desire. (III. iv. 15)

"What shall we do with offspring?:" in these words some speak of the enlightened sage's abandoning of house-holder's life on the impulse of desire. Therefore, too, Vidya appears to be of primary importance.

And (of) destruction. (III. iv. 16)

And some read of the destruction of all works brought about by Vidya. "His works, too, are destroyed, when, He, who is high and low, is seen." * [* Mund. Up. 2-2-0.] Therefore ritual is not of primary importance.

And (Vidya is found) among celibates; and indeed in the word (they are mentioned) (III. iv. 17)

Because we find Vidya among those holy orders whose ranks are composed of celibates, and because such cannot perform Agnihotra and other rites, Vidya cannot be an appendage of ritual. Indeed in the Vedic passage "Three are the branches of law," * [* Mund. Up. 2-2-9.] three orders of holy life are mentioned. Hence the conclusion that Vidya alone is of primary importance, conducing to the good of man, and that it should be combined with those of the prescribed works, as its appendage, which are not associated with a longing for the fruits spoken of primarily in connection with them.

Adhikarana 2

Jaimini (thinks there is) a backward reference, because of the absence of command. The Sruti indeed forbids. (III. iv. 18)

In the preceding section three orders of holy life alone are mentioned as the paths of religion, in the words "Three are the branches of law." Therefore there arises a doubt as to the existence of the fourth order of holy life.

(*Purvapaksha*): - Because of the absence of all injunction of the fourth order of holy life in the passage referred to, Jaimini thinks that the reference to the fourth order in the passage "wishing for that world (for Brahman) only, mendicants leave their homes." † [† Bri. Up. 6-4-22.] is intended as a praise of the upasana. Indeed, the Sruti forbids the fourth order in the words, "the killer of the son of the gods, indeed, is he who casts aside the sacrificial fire." ‡ [‡Tait-Sam. 1-5-2.] accordingly, there is a great evil in the abandonment of the sacrificial fire, and therefore no other order of life can be entered on by abandoning fire.

(*Siddhanta*): - Now, the conclusion is stated as follows:

It should be entered on, as Badarayana thinks, because of the Sruti pointing to its equality. (III. iv. 19)

Lord Badarayana regards that like the order of householders, etc., the other order also should be entered on. The evil connected with the abandoning of sacrificial fire must apply only to the order of householders, in as much as the Sruti speaks of all orders of holy life as of equal importance, as the following passages show:

"Three are the branches of law."

"Wishing for that world only mendicants leave their homes."

Hence the existence of the duties of the fourth order of holy life.

Or it is an injunction, as in the case of the carrying. (III. iv. 20)

"For, above he carries it for the Devas:" in this passage, (the carrying of the firewood above for the Devas) is enjoined, because it has not been enjoined anywhere else. So, too, in the present case, there is an injunction.

Or, there is even a direct injunction in the Jabala-Upanishad: "Having finished student's life, he should become a householder. Having become a householder or a forester, he should leave home." This passage cannot point to any restricted order; for, the Sruti says: "Having abandoned fire, or having lit no fire at all, on whatever day he is disgusted, that very day he should abandon home." For him whose mind (antha-karana or inner sense) has been purified on the ripening of the good acts of former births, it is possible to leave home while yet a student. But the prohibition contained in the passage,

"Having discharged the three debts, one should direct the mind to liberation. But he who resorts to it without having discharged the debts, goes downward." * [* Manu 6-35.]

refers to him who has not yet grown disgusted with the world.

Some hold that, because of the prohibition of the abandoning of sacrificial fire in the passage "the Killer of Devas' son is he who abandons the sacrificial fire," the leaving of home (*i.e.*, the fourth order) should be entered on only from the student's life, but not after entering on the life of a householder. If such were the case we can attach no meaning to the following injunction:

"Having become a forester, he should leave home ...Having abandoned fire, or having lit no fire at all, on whatever day he is disgusted, that very day he should leave home."

Wherefore there can be no restriction that one should leave home only from the student-life, or that one should leave home after having become a forester.

As to those who say that one should leave home only from the student-life, their meaning is as follows: There are only two orders of holy life, - one with fire, the other without fire. Of the two, the latter comprises the student and the mendicant, and the former comprises the householder and the forester. Of the two, the abandoning of home from the student-life is far preferable to the abandoning of home as resorted to by one who has first lit the sacrificial fire and then abandoned that fire. If the meaning were explained otherwise, then there would be a contradiction in the Sruti. Hence the necessity of the duties of all orders of life.

Adhikarana 3

If it be held that they are mere praises because of their referring (to parts of sacrifices), (we say) no, because they are new. (III. iv. 21)

"Let a man meditate on the syllable Om, called udgitha; ...That udgitha is the best of all essences, the highest, holding the highest place, the eighth." * [* Chha. 1-1.]

A doubt arises as to whether in the passages like the foregoing the contemplation of the udgitha, etc., as the best of all essences, etc., is enjoined or not.

(*Purvapaksha*): - What view suggests itself at first? It would appear that the contemplation of the udgitha, etc., as the best of all essences, etc., is not enjoined; but that, as in the passages "the (earth) is the ladle," "the heavenly world is the Ahavaniya," the predicating, - with reference to the udgitha, etc., which are parts of sacrificial rites – as the best of all essences, etc., are mere praises.

(*Siddhanta*): - No, because they are new. They are not mere praises, but the contemplation of the udgitha, etc., as the best of all essences, is surely enjoined, because they are new. And accordingly the argument relating to the ladle cannot apply here, because here there is no proximity to the injunction of the udgitha as there is in the case of the ladle. Wherefore, the contemplation of the udgitha, etc., as the best of all essences, etc., is certainly a subject of injunction.

And because of the word of injunction. (III. iv. 22)

"Let a man meditate on the udgitha."

Here a word of injunction occurs. For this reason too, there is an injunction as to the contemplating of the udgitha, etc., as the best of all essences, etc.,

Adhikarana 4

If it be held that they serve the purposes of pariplava, (we say) no, because such are specified. (III. iv. 23)

In the Vedantas, stories like the following are taught at the commencement of Vidyas:

"Pratardana, forsooth, the son of Divodasa, came by means of fighting and strength to the beloved abode of India." * [* Kaushi. 8-1.]

A doubt arises as to whether they are intended for pariplava or for the praise of the Vidyas.

(*Purvapaksha*): - What view suggests itself at first? That they are intended for pariplava. In the sacrifice of Asvamedha, the king shall be seated with his family and the Adhvaryu shall tell Vedic stories in their purpose. This is the act called pariplava, enjoined in the words "let him tell pariplava." † [†Asvalayana-Srauta-Sutra, 10-6-10.] Because of the injunction "they should relate all stories in pariplava," † [†Asvalayana-Srauta-Sutra, 10-6-10.] the stories occurring in the Upanishads are intended for pariplava.

(*Siddhanta*): - We answer as follows: They are not intended for pariplava, because such are specified. "On the first day should be related the story that Manu, the son of Vivasvat, is the king; ... and on the second the story that Yama, the son of Vivasvat is the king..."‡ [‡ Ibid. 10-7-1, 2.] In such words as these are specified the stories which are intended for pariplava.

As to the stories occurring in the Upanishads, the sutrakara says that, as forming one coherent whole with the proximate injunctions of Vidya, they are intended for the (praise of those) Vidyas:

And because in the same way they are connected as on. (III. iv. 24)

Just as the stories such as "He cried." * [* Tait. Sam. 1-5-1.] form one coherent whole with the injunctions of sacrificial rites, so also, these form coherent wholes with the injunctions of Vidyas, and, as such, they are certainly intended for praising the Vidyas.

The Vedanta-Sutras with Srikantha Bhashya

Adhikarana 5

And hence no necessity for lighting fire, etc. (III. iv. 25)

In a preceding adhikarana the existence of the final order of holy life was explained. A doubt arises as to whether there is a necessity or not for the lighting of the sacrificial fire, etc., as subserving Vidya.

(*Purvapaksha*): - What view suggests itself to us at first? Since ritual is enjoined as an appendage of Vidya, there is a necessity, even in the case of celibates who possess Vidya, for the lighting of sacrificial fire, etc., as subserving Vidya.

(*Siddhanta*): - As against the foregoing, we hold as follows: Their Vidya does not stand in need of the lighting of sacrificial fire etc. For we are given by the Sruti to understand that they have attained Vidya by renouncing ritual: "wishing for that world (for Brahman) only, mendicants leave their houses." † [† Bri. Up. 6-4-22.] But, their Vidya stands in need of the performance of those duties only which pertain to their own order, it being impossible for them to light the sacrificial fire, etc.

Adhikarana 6

And there is a necessity for all, because of the sruti enjoining sacrificial rites, etc., as in the case of a horse. (III. iv. 26)

In the preceding adhikarana it has been shown that the Vidya of those belonging to the fourth order does not stand in need of the lighting of fire, etc., since the latter is inconsistent with their order. Now, a doubt arises as to whether, in the case of the order of house holders, the Vidya stands in need of the rituals or not.

(*Purvapaksha*): - Now, we say that even in the case of the householders, Vidya does not stand in need of the ritual, such as the lighting of sacrificial fire; for, the ritual cannot form an appendage of Vidya, since it is not associated with it in the case of the celibates. As to the argument that Vidya (under discussion) stands in need of ritual, because the latter subserves Vidya as the prayajas, etc., subserve the Darsa and the Purnamasa, we ask, how does the adhana or the like ritual subserve Vidya? Does it subserve Vidya by way of contributing to the result, as the Prayaja subserves the Darsa? Or does it subserve Vidya by way of contributing to the very being of Vidya, as the husking of the paddy subserves the Darsa. It cannot be in the former way, since then, as a result of action, Mukti (liberation) would be non-eternal. If the latter were the case, then the analogy fails because such is not the relation between the Darsa and the Prayaja. Therefore ritual does not form an appendage of Vidya. Wherefore, even in the case of householders, Vidya does not stand in need of ritual.

(*Siddhanta*): - In the case of householders who have to perform the sacrificial rites, Vidya requires all rites such as Agnihotra, because the Sruti says, "Brahmanas seek to know Him by the study of the Veda, by sacrifice, by gifts, by penance, by fasting;" * [* Bri. Up. 6-4-22.] and the sacrificial rites, etc., are things commanded by the Paramesvara. Just as a horse, though a means of transit, stands in need of proper equipage for the purposes of transit, so also does Vidya stand in need of ritual. When freed from all longing for results, the Vedic ritual subserves Vidya by way of contributing to its very being, and liberation does not therefore constitute a result of the ritual. On the contrary, liberation (moksha) is the direct result of knowledge (jnana). Thus, in the case of householders, Vidya requires sacrificial rites, etc. In fact, in the case of all orders of holy life, Vidya should be necessarily associated with the duties of the respective orders; and it therefore stands to reason that Vidya should be associated with ritual.

Adhikarana 7

Still, he should be endued with calmness and subjugation, because of their being enjoined, and because, as the accessories thereof, they also should be necessarily observed. (III. iv. 27)

"Having becomes calm and subdued, quiet, patient and collected, he sees the Self in self." † [† Ibid. 6-4-23.]

"By faith, devotion, meditation, do thou know." ‡ [‡ Kaivalya-Up.]

In such passages as these it is declared that Vidya stands in need of calmness, subjugation of the senses, etc. A doubt arises as to whether, in the case of the order of householders, acquisition of these is possible.

(*Purvapaksha*): - As having to do with the sacrificial rites, they are concerned in many kinds of activity; and therefore, the acquisition of calmness and sense-subjugation, which consists in the cessation of such activity, is not possible in their case.

(*Siddhanta*): - As against the foregoing, we hold as follows: The householder, though engaged in the actions enjoined, should abstain from prohibited and interested actions, and thus cultivate calmness, etc., in as much as calmness, etc., faith, devotion and meditation are enjoined, and because, as the accessories of Vidya, they should be necessarily practised with a view to the acquisition of Vidya. *Calmness* (Sama) consists in the suppression of the subjective affections such as fondness and enmity. *Subjugation* (Dama) consists in withdrawing all senses from prohibited activities. *Quietude* (Uparati) is abstention from all prohibited and interested actions. *Patience* (Titiksha) is the endurance of pairs of opposites. *Collectedness* (Samadhana) of the mind consists in its being turned towards the Supreme Principle, it being at the time free from lassitude and other kinds of distraction. *Faith* (Sraddha) is that phase of pure mind (Sattva) in which it has conceived an aversion for all other sciences not conducing to the *summum bonum*, and in which it feels an intense longing for a familiar acquaintance with the Upanishad, the Supreme Wisdom, the science of the Paramatman. *Devotion* (Bhakti) is the Vedic ritual, constituting that service of the Supreme Being, Paramasiva, which is quite connected with the worship of any other God, which is effected by the threefold group of sense-organs, which forms that lofty eight-fold path of devotion. *Mumuksha* is an intense desire to obtain an intuitive vision of that mighty splendour of Liberation (Moksha Lakshmi) wherein the devotee is penetrated through and through by the Supreme Bliss; and this state of *Mumuksha* is attained through the attainment of calmness, etc., by him who is endued with *Vairagya*, - with indifference to all pleasures of this world and the next – and Viveka, the faculty of determining the real and the unreal. All these supreme virtues, from Viveka (discrimination) to Mumuksha (desire for liberation) – should be studiously practised by all orders of holy life seeking Vidya.

Adhikarana 8

And there is permission of all food when there is danger to life, because of revelation to that effect. (III. iv. 28)

In the Prana-Vidya (the contemplation of the Supreme as Life), the Sruti says:

"To him who knows this, there is nothing that is not (proper) food." * [* Chha. 5-2-1.]

This passage appears to teach that, in the case of him who is devoted to Prana-Vidya, all food is permitted. A doubt arises as to whether this is reasonable or not.

(*Purvapaksha*): - Since eating is a thing with which we are all familiar in other ways and is therefore not a thing fir to be taught by revelation, it is the permission of all food, which otherwise unknown to us, is the fit subject of injunction here.

(*Siddhanta*): - To this we reply as follows: Even in the case of him who is devoted to Prana-Vidya, the permission of all food does not extend to all time, but only when life is in danger. Indeed, even in the case Ushasti who is of great power and a knower of Brahman, we find the sruti teaching that resort may be had to the eating of leavings, only in case of extreme danger to life. The Sruti reads as follows:

"When the Kurus had been destroyed by hail-stones, Ushasti Chakrayana lived as a beggar with his virgin wife at Ibhyagrama. Seeing a chief eating beans, he begged of him. The chief said: 'I have no more, except those which are put away for me here.' Ushasti said: 'Give me to eat of them.' He gave him the beans and said: 'There is something to drink also.' Then said Ushasti: 'If I drank of it, I should have drunk what was left by another, and is therefore unclean.' The chief said: 'Were not those beans also left over and therefore unclean?' 'No,' he replied: 'for, I should not have lived, if I had not eaten them, but the drinking of water would be mere pleasure." * [* Ibid. 1-10.]

Wherefore, it is only when life is in extreme danger that permission to eat all kinds of food is given even to him who is devoted to the Supreme Vidya (Para-Vidya, the contemplation of the Supreme).

And because of the avoiding of contradiction (III. iv. 29)

Permission of all food is to be availed of only when life is in jeopardy, because of the necessity of observing purity in food as enjoined in the following passage:

"When aliment has been purified, the whole nature attains purity. When the whole nature has attained purity, memory is firm. When memory remains firm, then all the ties are loosened." † [† Chha. 7-26-2.]

And it is also said in the Smriti. (III. iv. 30)

That the permission of all food should be availed of only when life is in danger has been also taught in the Smriti:

"A man partaking of food from any source whatever, when life is at risk, he is not tainted with sin, any more than the lotus-leaf is tainted with water."

And hence the text about the rising above the impulse of desire. (III. iv. 31)

And accordingly, there is the scriptural injunction that one should rise above the impulse of desire:

"A Brahman should not drink liquor."

Thus, even in the case of the devotee of Vidya, permission of all food may be availed of only when life is at risk. Otherwise, as committing a prohibited act, he will prove an offender against the command of the Supreme Lord, Paramesvara.

Adhikarana 9

And even the duties of the order (should be observed) because they are enjoined. (III. iv. 32)

In the case of a house-holder (grihastha) who does not possess knowledge (Vidya) we understand that the duties of the order (asrama) such as sacrificial rites should be observed, because they are enjoined as such in the words "He should offer oblation into the fire throughout life," and that they should be observed also as the means of acquiring Vidya as declared in the words "the Brahmanas seek to know Him by sacrificial rites, gifts," * etc. [* Bri. Up. 4-4-22.]

And also as accessories. (III. iv. 33)

And we further understand that even in the case of one who possesses knowledge (Vidya), they should be observed, because they are enjoined as accessory to Vidya in the words "He who has known both Vidya and Avidya" * etc. [* Isa. Up. 11.]

Now, a doubt arises as to whether the sacrificial rites, etc., should be performed only once, or twice separately – as a means of Vidya when the man does not possess knowledge, and again as an accessory (anga) to Vidya when the same man has obtained knowledge in as much as they are enjoined both as a means and as an accessory to Vidya.

(*Purvapaksha*): - In virtue of the two injunctions, they should be observed twice.

(*Siddhanta*): - The Sutrakara says:

In any case, they are identical; because of the marks pointing both ways. (III. iv. 34)

Because of the two injunctions occurring in the two different contexts, the same sacrificial rites may be regarded as assuming two different forms; but they are nevertheless identical, in as much as their identity is recognised everywhere. Though, thus, the acts are identical in themselves, yet on the principle of *Samyoga Prithaktvas* * [* The same act enjoined in two different contexts may put on two distinct aspects.] there is no contradiction involved in viewing them in two distinct lights. Though performed only once, one and the same act may be regarded in two distinct lights in virtue of the double injunction. For instance, one and the same sacrificial post made of Khadira wood enters into an obligatory (Nitya and an optional Kamya, interested) rite in virtue of the following double injunction: "The sacrificial post can be made of Khadira wood"; and "in the case of one who desires manliness, they make the sacrificial post of Khadira wood." In the same way, the sacrificial rites, etc., are prescribed as a means of attaining Vidya in the case of one who does not possess it, and as an accessory of Vidya in the case of one who possesses it, and for these two purposes it will do to perform them only once.

And the Sruti declares that there is no overpowering. (III. iv. 35)

In the words "by Dharma he removes sin," † [† Mahana. 79.] the Sruti declares that, by way of removing the sin obstructing the rise of Vidya, the effect of the performance of the sacrificial rites is the removal of all the forces which may overpower Vidya. Hence no inconsistency such as the one urged above.

Adhikarana 10

(Vidya is possible even for those who stand) in the intermediate stages, because it is seen. (III. iv. 36)

It has been shown that Vidya is possible for those who belong to the recognized order of holy life (asramas). Now a doubt arises as to whether Vidya is possible or not for those who do not belong to any of the recognized orders.

(*Purvapaksha*): - The Snataka, - *i.e.*, one who has left the student-life but has not yet entered on the life of a householder, - and the widower are those who do not belong to any of the recognised orders of holy life. For them Brahmavidya is not attainable, because of the absence of the duties of a recognised order (asrama) which constitute the means of acquiring Vidya.

The Vedanta-Sutras with Srikantha Bhashya

(*Siddhanta*): - As against the foregoing we hold as follows: Vidya is quite possible even for those who do not belong to any of the recognised orders, in as much as we find it stated in the Sruti that Raikva and other such persons attained Vidya.

As to the contention that it is not possible because of the non-performance of the duties of any of the recognised orders, the Sutrakara says:

It is, moreover, declared in the Smriti. (III. iv. 37)

It is stated in the Smriti that even for those who do not belong to a recognised order Vidya is possible of attainment by means of prayers and the like:

"By prayer alone a Brahmana can attain perfection: as to this there is no doubt. Let him do anything else, or nor do it. A kind-hearted man is called a Brahmana." * [* Manu, 11.87]

Vidya is said to be possible of attainment by a special act. (III. iv. 38)

The Sruti states that it is possible to attain Vidya by means of special acts which are not confined to any of the recognised orders:

"By austerity, by celibacy, by faith, and by meditation, let him seek the self." † [† Prasna. Up. 1-2.]

Let the other be superior, because of the indicatory mark. (III. iv. 39)

It is better to belong to one of the recognised orders than not to belong to any, because the former enables one to accumulate more merit (Dharma). Moreover, the Smriti says "Let no twice born man remain for even a single day without belonging to one of the recognised orders." ‡ [‡ Daksha 1.] Thus, it is quite true that to belong to any of them. Still, in the extreme cases, the Vidya is possible of attainment even for those who are outside the pale of the recognised orders, by means of prayer and the like.

Adhikarana 11

For one who has become such, there can be no ceasing to be such, as Jaimini also thinks, because of the prohibition against ceasing to be such. (III. iv. 40)

Now, a doubt arises as to whether a descent to a former stage is allowed or not to those who have entered the order of celibates.

(*Purvapaksha*): - Even descent to a lower order is optional, like the ascent to a higher order which is taught in the following passage:

"Having completed student-life, let him become householder. He may even become a wanderer after retiring to the forest from home." § [§ Jabala Up. 4.]

The Vedanta-Sutras with Srikantha Bhashya

(*Siddhanta*): - As against the foregoing, we argue out our conclusion as follows: - For one who has ascended to the life of a perpetual student (Naishthika) it is not possible to come down again from it. For, there is a prohibition of the abandonment of that life. It is certainly prohibited by the Sruti in the words, "mortifying his body in the teacher's family till death." * [* Chha. Up. 2-23-2.] The following passages prohibit the descent:

"Let him go to the forest, and let him not come back."

"Having renounced fires, let him not return again."

And there exist no Scriptural passages permitting descent, as there exist those concerning ascent. Accordingly, since the Sruti expressly prohibit their descent, and since no passage in the Sruti is found permitting descent, those who descend down from a higher stage are not fit for Vidya. This is also Jaimini's view of the matter.

The Sutrakara proceeds to show that the man who has descended from a higher order cannot regain qualification for Vidya by means of expiatory rites:

Not even (the expiatory rite) conferring qualification (is possible), because, since the smriti speaks of them as fallen, it is impossible for them. (III. iv. 41)

In the case of a student who has broken the vow of chastity, the sacrifice of an ass is prescribed as the expiatory rite by which to regain his qualification for Vedic rites, as taught in the section of the Mimamsa treating of qualification for Vedic rites." † [† Purva Mimamsa 6-8-22.] Even this expiatory rite is not possible in the case of him who has descended down from a higher stage of life. The Smriti says:

"The man who, having once ascended to the life of a perpetual student, descends down from it, - for him I see no expiation, whereby that killer of the self may be purified."

The Smriti thus denying his qualification for the expiatory rite, he cannot regain qualification by that rite.

Some also (regard it as a) minor sin and (therefore claim the) existence (of expiation) as in the case of eating (forbidden food). This has been declared. (III. iv. 42)

Some hold that, as it is a minor sin, it admits of expiation, just as the eating of honey (on the part of a student) admits of an expiation. It has been said, "what is taught in the case of a student applies to the higher orders when there is no contradiction." That is to say, what has been taught in the case of an ordinary student (who in due course will enter on the life of a householder) applies to men of other orders, provided that it does not run counter to what has been expressly enjoined on those other orders.

But they should be kept outside (the pale), in either case, because of the smriti and custom. (III. iv. 43)

Whether it be a minor sin or a major sin, these transgressors are excluded from the path of the Vedic rites, etc. For, the Smriti says:

"I see no expiation whereby that killer of the self may be purified."

And they are excommunicated from the society of the orthodox. Wherefore, from all points of view, those who have fallen down from a higher stage, are not qualified for Vidya.

Adhikarana 12

Atreya thinks that it pertains to the sacrificer, because of the fruit (being assigned to him) by the sruti. (III. iv. 44)

The contemplation of the Udgitha, etc., has been taught. A doubt arises as to whether it has to be done by the sacrificer, or by his priests (Ritviks).

(*Purvapaksha*): - The contemplation of the Udgitha, etc., has to be done by the sacrificer himself, for it is he that is said to reap the fruit of the sacrifice acquiring more power, not the priests (Ritviks). So thinks Atreya.

Audulomi thinks that it is the duty of the priest. For that indeed is he paid. (III. iv. 45)

"Let the Udgatri priest who knows this shall say..." * [* Chha. 1-7-8] In these words occurring in the sequel it is expressly said that the Udgatri priest is the one who should contemplate. According to Audulomi, the act of contemplating is the duty of the priest.

(*Object*): - How can it be that the act is done by one person while the fruit goes to another?

(*Answer*): - For, the priests have been paid by the sacrificer for the performance of supplementary acts as well as of the main act. It is certainly for the performance of the sacrificial rites with all its supplementary acts that the priests are paid by the sacrificer. Therefore what is done by the priest forms the act of the sacrificer; and hence no incongruity in holding that the fruit of the act goes to the master of the sacrifice.

Adhikarana 13

The third is, like the sacrificial rites etc, enjoined in the case of the possessor of Vidya, because of the accepted sense (of the word). (III. iv. 46)

In the Kahola-Brahmana it is said:

"Therefore, let a Brahmana, after he has done with learning, seek to remain in childhood; then, after he has done with learning and childhood (let him be) a Muni." †
[† Bri. Up. 3-5-2.]

Having thoroughly acquired learning, i.e., having determined the main drift of the teaching of the many Upanishads, let a Brahmana seek to remain in childhood; that is to say, let him lead another mode of life, resembling childhood in so far as it is devoid of love and hatred, and the like. Having attained perfection in learning and the child-like state, then he is (to be) a Muni. Here a doubt arises as to whether the life of a Muni is the subject of an injunction or not.

(*Purvapaksha*): - As there are no such words as "He shall become a Muni," showing an injunction, it is not enjoined.

(*Siddhanta*): - As against the foregoing we hold as follows: - The third one, namely, the state of a sage (Muni) is enjoined, as another accessory, on the possessor of Vidya, in addition to learning and childhood, just as the sacrificial rites, etc., are enjoined. For, the word 'Muni' is familiar to all as denoting one who is given to profound meditation. This profound meditation which consists in constantly revolving the object of worship in thought is enjoined with a view to the perfecting of Vidya: the words "let him remain" being repeated in this connection. Therefore it is possible to make out an injunction of meditation.

Adhikarana 14

For the inclusion of all, verily does the Sruti conclude with the householder. (III. iv. 47)

A doubt arises as to whether Vidya is common to all Asramas, or confined to some only.

(*Purvapaksha*): - Since the student (Brahmacharin) is dependent on the teacher for the study of the Vedas, since the householder (Grihastha) is engrossed in the maintenance of the family, since the forest-dweller (Vanaprastha) is engaged in the hermit-life, knowledge and meditation are not possible for them. The Sruti connects Samnyasa with those who possess the knowledge of the Vedantic teaching in the following words:

"They who have determined the nature of things by their knowledge of the Vedantic teaching, those Yatis who, by Samnyasayoga, have purified their minds," * etc.
[* Mahana. 10-22.]

In connection with the practice of meditation (Dhyana), the Sruti declares that the devotee should be one "leading the life of the last asrama." † [† Kaivalya.Up.] Therefore, knowledge and meditation are meant for the last order of men, not for others.

(*Siddhanta*): - Vidya is quite possible for all orders of men. The possibility of Vidya for all orders of men is taught in the Chhandogya Upanishad in the following words:

The Vedanta-Sutras with Srikantha Bhashya

"He who...keeping up the memory of what he has learnt by repeating it regularly in some sacred spot,...he who behaves thus all his life reaches, the world of Brahman and does not return, yea, he does not return." * [* Chha. 8-15-1.]

Though the Sruti thus concludes with the householder, all orders are meant. So also, though the last order alone is mentioned in connection with meditation, other orders also must have been meant. Therefore, Vidya is quite possible for all orders of men. (In the Sruti quoted above in the Purvapaksha) 'Samnyasa' means renunciation of fruits, and "Yati" means one who has subdued the senses. All this is quite possible for all orders of men.

Adhikarana 15

Because, like the life of a muni, others, too, are prescribed. (III. iv. 48)

The Atharvasiras says:

"Having cut off desire, having thought over by reason the root of the aggregate of causes, having fixed the mind in Rudra, - in Rudra, they say, is unity, - in view of the eternal and ancient Rudra, who is food and strength, by austerity do ye restrain yourselves. This is the vow in honour of Pasupati."

This Pasupata-vrata, this sacred vow in honour of Pasupati, taught in the Atharvasiras is clearly taught in the Puranas. Now a doubt arises as to whether Vidya and Moksha are attained by those who devote themselves to this vow.

(*Purvapaksha*): - It would seem that they cannot attain Moksha, but that they attain only some minor results; for, this vow is not ranked among the religious orders; there is a limit to its duration; and it has been observed by Krishna and others with a view to obtain sons and the like fruits.

(*Siddhanta*): - As against the foregoing we hold as follows: Mukti itself accrues to those who observe this vow till death. The accomplishment of Vidya consists in deep meditation of Rudra, the Supreme Brahman. Like the life of a Muni, other duties belonging to the other orders, such as mendicant life, control of the body and the senses, are enjoined even in connection with the Pasupata-vrata. The meditation of Rudra, which is the severance of the bond (Pasa) and which produces Moksha, is enjoined on those who devote themselves to the observance of this vow. "They say unity is in Rudra. In view of the eternal and ancient Rudra, do ye restrain yourselves by austerity. With the Mantra 'Agni is the ashes,' etc., do ye take the ashes and touch the limbs smearing them all. Hence this is the vow sacred to the Pasupati, conducing to the release of the soul (Pasu) from the bond (Pasa)." † [† Atharvasiras.]

Therefore those who observe the Pasupata-vrata to the end of life attain to nothing short of Mukti (salvation) as the result of it.

As to the contention that it is not ranked among the recognised orders (asramas), the Sutrakara says:

Though not showing itself out (as an asrama, yet it is a means to salvation) as comprehending the essential features of an asrama. (III. iv. 49)

The Pasupatasrama, though not exhibiting itself as an independent asrama, is still an asrama by itself, known as Atyasrama or the transcendental order, and constitutes an independent means of reaching the Paramasiva, by virtue of celibacy and other attributes of an ascetic (which conduce to the attainment of Vidya) being comprehended in it. The Pasupata-vrata is of two kinds, life-long and temporary, as declared in the following passage:

"Either lasting till the death of the body, or lasting for a period of twelve years."

Of these two, that which lasts till the end of life and is called Atyasrama or transcendental order, leads to Moksha; whereas the other is a means of attaining some worldly enjoyment. Such is the distinction between the two. Thus the Sruti itself teaches that this vow (Vrata) has two aspects, - as a means to worldly enjoyment and as a means to Moksha – both securing Siva's grace. We should so interpret the texts as not to stultify the authority of this passage of the Sruti.

Adhikarana 16

The result is obtained in this birth in the absence of obstacles, as we see in the sruti. (III. iv. 50)

A doubt arises here as to whether the result of meditation accrues, to those who practise it as taught before, in this birth, or in a future birth.

(*Purvapaksha*): - Let us enquire. A man engages in the Upasana hoping that liberation may come to him in this very birth, but not in a future birth. Who does ever desire delay with regard to the result? Therefore the result in the form of liberation must accrue to him in this birth, if it should ever accrue to him at all. If not in this birth, it will never accrue at all.

(*Siddhanta*): - As against the foregoing, we hold as follows: In the absence of an obstacle in the shape of a strong karma of a different kind, the result of the upasana of the Supreme accrues in this birth. If there should be any obstacle, it will accrue in a future birth; just as the result in the shape of a worldly good does not necessarily accrue soon after the performance of the good karma which serves as a means to it; and will accrue in a future birth if there should be an obstacle present. And we are told in the sruti that Vamadeva and others reaped in a later birth the fruits of their investigation and study of Brahmavidya carried on in their past births. Hence no necessity, that the result of liberation should accrue in this very birth.

Adhikarana 17

Unlike (the sacrificial rites), there is no distinction in the result of liberation, because of the state of Him being determined (as the result). (III. iv. 51)

It has been established that, as in the case of the results accruing form mere works, the result in the shape of liberation accrues in the absence of an obstacle in the form of a strong karma of a different kind. A doubt now arises as to whether, on the same principle, there exists or not a difference in liberation accruing as the result of the different upasanas, as there is a difference in the case of the results of sacrificial rites.

(*Purvapaksha*): - It may appear that, like the results of mere sacrificial rites, liberation admits of distinctions. We are given to understand that different sacrificial rites produce different results: "Let him who desires Svarga perform the sacrifice of Jyotishtoma." "Let him who desires Svarajya or lordship in Svarga perform the sacrifice of Vajapeya." So too there must be a difference in the results of knowledge acquired through Upasana.

(*Siddhanta*): - As against the foregoing we hold as follows: Unlike the results of mere sacrificial rites, the result of Upasana-Jnana admits of no differences, in as much as it has been determined that the state of Brahman is the result of Upasana-Jnana. Since the state of Brahman which the possessors of Vidya attain is one and the same, there is no room for any kind of difference in the result here. It should not be urged that a difference in the digress of Upasana may give rise to a difference in the result; for, in the case of the acts of Upasana no results have been mentioned other than liberation. Brahman being one and the same, liberation which is the state of Brahman must also be one and the same. Hence no difference in the liberation accruing from different Upasanas.

FOURTH ADHYAYA – FIRST PADA.

Adhikarana 1

Frequent repetition (is meant) because of the instruction. (IV. i. 1)

In the third Adhyaya has been discussed in detail the nature of the worshipper (Upasaka), of the object of worship (Upasya), and of the several kinds of worship (Upasana), as also the duties of the various orders of holy life (Asramas). Here, again, in the fourth Adhyaya will be discussed the following topics: in the first pada, the mode of worship (Upasana); in the second pada, the departure, from earthly life, of Jiva, the worshipper (upasaka); in the third pada, the Path of Light (Archir), etc; and in the fourth pada, the state of the one who has attained to Brahman. Now the first Adhikarana (of the first pada) deals with the doubt as to whether one has to do once alone or to frequently repeat the act of knowing prescribed, as the means to Moksha, in the following passages:

"The Knower of Brahman reaches the Supreme." * [* Tai. Up. 2-1.]

"Knowing Siva, one attains infinite peace." † [† Sve. Up. 4-14.]

(*Purvapaksha*): - It should be done only once, because, on the principle that 'once done, the intention of the scripture is fulfilled," the act intended by the scripture in the words 'knowing (Jnana)' and 'realising (Vedana)' becomes accomplished when once done, as in the case of the Prayaja.

(*Siddhanta*): - As against the foregoing, we hold as follows. The act of knowing, prescribed as the means to Moksha in such passages as "the Knower of Brahman reaches the Supreme," should be frequently revolved; for, we understand that the act of knowing (Vedana) which is spoken of as the means to Moksha is of the form of meditation (Upasana), in as much as the two terms 'Know (vid)' and 'meditate (Upas)' are interchangeably used at the commencement (Upakarma) and the concluding portions (Upasamhara) of the following passages:

"Let a man meditate (upas) on mind as Brahman. ...He who knows (Veda) this shines and warms through his celebrity, fame and glory of countenance." ‡ [‡ Chha. Up. 3-18-1.]

"He who knows (Veda) what he knows, he is thus spoken of by me." § [§ Ibid. 4-14.]

"Teach me, O Lord, the Deity which you worship (upas)." * [* Ibid 2-3.]

And the word 'meditation (upasana)' denotes a continuous flow of thought. As to the Prayaja, etc., it is but proper to do them only once because their effects are invisible. In as much as the intuitive realisation (Sakshatkara), the result of knowledge (Vedana), is visible, this set should be repeated till its result is attained, as in the case of threshing the paddy.

And because of the indicatory marks. (IV. i. 2)

As pointing to this conclusion, the following passages (of the Smriti) may be cited:

"By *knowledge* of Isvara, the soul (Kshetrajnas) attains, it is deemed, the highest purity."

"Be he guilty of the major sins, or be he guilty of the minor sins, let a man practise *meditation* (dhyana) of Brahman, engaged therein for a quarter of the night."

"Let a man practise *Yoga* (*or Samadhi*) directed to the Atman."

"Let a man realise the Supreme Being (Purusha) who is of golden hue, who can be reached in the *dream-consciousness* (svapnadhi)."

And so on. Hence † [† Form the passages quoted above, it may be seen that the knowledge by which Brahman is reached is of the form of meditation (dhyana) and Yoga (Samadhi) consisting in the frequent repetition of one and the same thought.] the necessity of a frequent repetition of the knowledge of Brahman.

The Vedanta-Sutras with Srikantha Bhashya

Adhikarana 2

As the Self, verily, do they understand (Him) and teach also. (IV. i. 3)

In the preceding Adhikarana it has been made out that the meditation of Brahman should be repeated. Here follows the enquiry as to whether the Jiva or individual soul whose Atman is Brahman should regard himself as one with Isvara, or as distinct from Him.

(*Purvapaksha*): - It may at first sight appear that the proper course is for the Jiva to contemplate upon Brahman only as distinct from himself; for *firstly*, in the passage "superior to the universe is Rudra, the Great Sage," ‡ [‡ Mahana-Up. 10-19.] and in the Vedanta-Sutra I. i. 22, it is described that the Lord, the Para-Brahman, is an entity distinct from the Jiva, from the Pratyagatman, from the Pasu or individual soul, and secondly, the Siva can never become Brahman whose characteristic mark is Omniscience.

(*Siddhanta*): - No doubt, the Supreme Brahman called Siva is superior to the Jiva; still, the worshipper should meditate Him thus: "I am Brahman." For, even the worshippers of old, regarded Brahman as their own Self (Atman) thus: 'Thou, verily, I am, O Lord, O God; I, verily, Thou art" Though an entity quite distinct from the worshipper, the Supreme Brahman serves those worshippers all the same, by giving them His own being.* [* That is to say, by removing from them the state of bondage (pasutva).] And in the words "That Thou art," etc., they also give others, their pupils, to understand that Brahman is their own Self. Certainly, Mukti or liberation consists in attaining the state of Siva, that state which is full of unlimited supreme bliss and free from all taint. This attainment of the state of Siva is not possible except on the cessation of bondage (Pasutva) on the part of the Jiva, and the cessation of bondage cannot be brought about except by the meditation thereof (*i.e.*, of the state of Siva). Therefore, the worshipper, freed from servitude on the bondage being loosened by the continuous stream of the thought that "I am Siva," becomes Siva Himself. Indeed, the state of Siva consists in being the repository of that unsurpassed Bliss which is free from all traces of evil taint. And the Supreme Brahman is of quite the same nature. By constant meditation thereof the worshipper becomes of the same nature. Hence it is that all else is said to be unworthy of being meditated by the seeker of Moksha, in the passages like the following:

"The beneficent Siva alone should be meditated upon (by the worshipper) abandoning all else." † [† Atharvasikha.]

For, all scriptures teach that Mukti or liberation consists in the cessation of servitude (Pasubhava), of the identification with the body of a brahmana and the like, - and in the attainment of oneness with that Supreme Individuality (Paramambhava), with that Siva who is the immediate witness of His own inherent unsurpassed Bliss, and who is self-luminous, shining by his own light. Contemplation of oneness with Brahman lends the Upasaka to Mukti; otherwise there will be no cessation of *samsara*.

The Vedanta-Sutras with Srikantha Bhashya

Adhikarana 3

The Sutrakara makes a distinction:

(No meditation as Atman) in the symbol; not indeed is He (to be worshipped there.) (IV. i. 4)

In the passages like "let him meditate mind as Brahman," Chha. 3-18-1., we are taught to meditate Brahman in the mind and so on. Is Brahman to be meditated there as the Self (Atman) or as something different from the Self?

(*Purvapaksha*): - In such meditations of symbols as are enjoined in the passages "Let him meditate the mind as Brahman;" Let him meditate the Sun as Brahman," we are given to understand that, in meditating upon the mind, etc., we have to exalt them by regarding them as Brahman. Accordingly, in as much as the symbol has been regarded by the devotee as Brahman, what harm is there in regarding it as the Self (Atman)?

(*Siddhanta*): - As against the foregoing we hold as follows: The Self should not enter into the contemplation of symbols; for, in them it is not the Supreme Brahman that is meditated upon. On the other hand, it is the mind, etc., that are to be meditated upon as Brahman. Even supposing that in these cases the object of meditation is Brahman Himself conditioned by the mind, etc., it is not this conditioned Brahman that we should regard as the Self, in as much as the mind, etc., are not the essential attributes of Brahman and are therefore mere phenomena (Vikaras). It is the Brahman possessed of such attributes as unfailing will, etc., that we regard as the Self. Otherwise even the Self (Atman) would be subject to phenomenal charges. Therefore, the devotees should not meditate upon the symbol as the Self, seeing that there the Paramesvara is not the direct object of worship.

Adhikarana 4

Contemplation of Brahman (in the symbol is meant) because of His supremacy. (IV. i. 5)

In regard to the contemplation of symbols, a doubt arises as to whether the devotee should regard the symbols, -such as the mind, the sun etc., - as Brahman, or he should regard Brahman as the mind, etc.

(*Purvapaksha*): - We should regard Brahman as the mind, etc., and thus contemplate the Brahman, in as much as He alone is the dispenser of fruits.

(*Siddhanta*): - As against the foregoing we hold as follows: "Superior to the universe is Rudra; * [* Mahanar. 10-19.] in these words the sruti speaks of Brahman as the supreme; and therefore we should regard the mind and the like inferior objects as Brahman. In the ordinary world, indeed, one regards a man of inferior rank, such as a king's servant, as the king himself, and serves him as though he were the king himself. None, on the other hand, serves a king regarding him as a servant. Propriety indeed requires that all should bow down before that Being only who is Superior to all others. Accordingly, we understand that the Supreme Brahman is the Being before whom all should bow down, verily because; He is superior to all others. In the Mahanarayana-Up. 12, it is said that all worship should be directed to Him alone who informs all, to that Supreme Brahman whose attributes are mentioned in the Mantra, and to none else under any circumstances whatsoever.

Moreover, this Supreme Brahman (Parabrahman) has been defined to be the Being who is worshipped as the Supreme. To explain. The Taittiriya says:

"He, to whom all bow, is the..." Dharma is the forehead; Brahma is the upper jaw, sacrifice is the lower jaw, Vishnu is the heart; Samvatsara (Prajapati) is the organ of generation," * and so on. [* Tai. Aranyaka. 2-19.]

In this description of Simsumara, the Parabrahman or Siva is distinguished from Vishnu, the heart, and other members, simply because Siva is superior to all others, and He is designated as the head, the principal member, by an expression which embodies His essential character as the object of all worship. Even at the end of that section, the sruti speaks of Him alone as the Lord of all beings and as superior to all beings, and conclude by saying that He is the Being to whom all worship is ultimately due, because, He is superior to all: "My others, bow is to Thee, my bow is to Thee, all bow is to Thee." In the passages like "Bow to Thee, to Rudra, to Anger." * [* Tait. Sam. 4-5.] He is again and again referred to as the object of all worship, for the very reason that He is superior to all others. In the ordinary world, indeed, people worship him most who is great in power, and so on. Thus, the Supreme Brahman is the Being that is superior to all others, as the object of all worship, associated with Uma, possessed of diverse eyes, the One Being who can be designated by the term 'Isvara.' All symbols such as the mind become objects of worship because they are found pervaded by Him who is superior to all others, who is worthy of being worshipped by all. Hence the sruti speaking of such extremely low animals as dogs and kings of dogs, as the objects of worship, simply in view of their being pervaded by Brahman who is superior to all others.

Wherefore, in as much as lower beings are found to command our regard in virtue of their relation to the higher beings, we conclude that in contemplating the mind, etc., we should regard them as Brahman who transcends all.

Adhikarana 5

And the ideas of Aditya, etc., (should be contemplated) in the member, because it stands to reason. (IV. i. 6)

In the preceding Adhikarana it has been said that, because of Brahman's superiority, Aditya, and others should be regarded as Brahman, in our contemplation (upasana) of them. Now, a doubt arises as to whether, in such contemplations of members of sacrifices (Karmadigas) as are enjoined in the words 'He who burns here, upon Him let a man meditate as udgitha,' * we should contemplate Aditya, etc., as udgitha, or in the reverse order.

(*Purvapaksha*): - What would at first sight appear? It would appear that, in as much as udgitha, etc., and Aditya, etc., are both alike factors of sacrificial rites, and both alike manifested forms of Brahman, no fixed rule can be laid down as to the one way or the other.

(*Siddhanta*): - As against the foregoing, we hold as follows: Since Aditya and others are the objects of worship in sacrificial rites and are therefore superior, udgitha and the like which are mere members of sacrificial rites should be regarded as Aditya, etc., for, it is possible that the udgitha and other factors of sacrificial rites produce greater results, when improved by our contemplation of them as Aditya, etc. Indeed, the passage of the sruti – "Whatever one performs with knowledge becomes more powerful," * [* Ibid 1-1-10.] gives us to understand that the very thing which, when performed by itself, is possessed of power, is productive of greater results by way of becoming more powerful, when improved by knowledge. Thus, notwithstanding that both are alike essentially one with Brahman, and so on, still, because udgitha, etc., are enjoined as sacrificial acts, because udgitha, etc., are acts to be done and are, as such, means to ends, and because Aditya, etc., are things already existing and are, as such of a different nature from udgitha, etc., and do not constitute means to ends, we conclude that udgitha and the like factors of sacrificial rites should be contemplated as Aditya and so on.

Adhikarana 6

(One should be) seated, because of the possibility. (IV. i. 7)

It has been explained in what particular way one should practice contemplation. Now, ad doubt arises as to whether one should be necessarily seated during contemplation, or not.

(*Purvapaksha*): - Because the Sruti has nowhere laid down the rule that one should be seated during contemplation, and because contemplation, which is a mental process, is possible in all postures, there is no necessity for the upasaka to be seated.

(*Siddhanta*): - One should contemplate Brahman only when seated; for, to such a man alone one-pointedness of mind is possible. And the Sruti does enjoin that the upasaka should be seated:

> "At a retired spot, seated in an easy posture, pure, erect of neck, the head and the body;
>
> "Leading the highest order of life, restraining all the sense-organs, and having saluted his own Guru in devotion, regarding the heart-lotus unstained and quite pure, and in its centre contemplating Him who is free from all taint and grief;
>
> "The Unthinkable, the Unmanifest, whose forms are endless; Siva who is tranquil, immortal; who is the womb of Brahma, and who is devoid of a beginning, middle, or end; the one, who is Intelligence and Bliss; the Formless, the Wonderful;

"Him whose help-mate is Uma; who is the Supreme Lord, Mighty, Three-eyed, Dark-necked and Serene. Having meditated thus, the sage reaches Him who is the womb of all beings, the Witness of all, transcending darkness." ‡ [‡ Kaivalya-Up. 4, 5, 6 and 7.]

So says the Kaivalya-Upanishad. Wherefore, one should contemplate Brahman only while seated.

And because of meditation. (IV. i. 8)

And because by the following passages we are given to understand that Upasana, which brings about the break of the bond, is the same as Dhyana or Meditation:

"Having meditated thus, the sage reaches Him who is the womb of all beings." *[* Kaivalya-Up.]

"It is the Cause that should be meditated upon in the middle of ether (akasa). He who is endued with all powers, who is the Lord of all, the source of all God (Sambhu)." † [† Atharvasikha.]

"Only by the churning of meditation."

And the verb *Dhyai* is used in the case of persons whose bodily members are inactive, whose eye-sight is steadily fixed, whose mind is directed towards one object alone, as when we say "the crane meditates," over, one-pointedness of mind is quite necessary for Dhyana, which is an unbroken current of thought like the current of oil, interrupted by no alien thought of a different kind. Wherefore we should necessarily observe the rule concerning the sitting posture for success in Dhyana.

And (the word is used) with reference to the motionlessness. (IV. i. 9)

"The Earth meditates as it were; the mid-region meditates as it were." * [* Chha-Up. 7-6-1.] In such passages as these the word "meditate" is used because the earth, etc., are motionless; wherefore one should contemplate only when seated. Indeed, the current of meditation is possible only to him who is seated, as he is then motionless like the earth, etc.

And the Smriti says the same. (IV. i. 10)

"Having in a cleanly spot established a firm seat, neither too high nor too low, with cloth, skin, and *kusa* grass thereon;

"Making the mind one-pointed, with the actions of the mind and the senses controlled, let him, seated there on the seat, practice yoga for the purification of the self." † [† Bhagavad Gita. vi. 11, 12.]

In such passages as these, the Smriti enjoins that the upasakas should be seated; wherefore, one should contemplate Brahman only when seated.

Adhikarana 7

Where concentration (is possible), there (meditation may be carried on), owing to the absence of any difference. (IV. i. 11)

It has been said above that it is necessary that the Upasaka should be seated (during meditation). Now, a doubt arises as to whether as in the foregoing case, there is any rule, or none as to time and place.

(*Purvapaksha*): - It is but proper that there should be (a fixed rule). Just as a particular direction, a particular place, and a particular time are enjoined in the sruti with reference to sacrificial rites – "He who is going to engage in Brahma-Yajna shall do so in the eastern direction," ‡ [‡ Taitt. Ara. 2-11.] "Let him sacrifice by Vaisvadeva in a place sloping to the east;" "They sacrifice by Pinda-Pitriyajna in the afternoon;" – so also, it is but proper that, in this case also, there should be a rule as to the direction, etc.; for, the practice of Upasana is an act enjoined in the sruti.

(*Siddhanta*): - There is no fixed rule as to the direction, etc., in the case of Upasana. Concentration is indeed the primary requisite for meditation. Certainly this does not require a particular direction, time, or place. Where there does not exist any cause for attachment, hatred and other such evil passions, there indeed the mind attains concentration. So much alone is necessary, as taught in the sruti, "let him be seated at ease in a solitary place." ‡ [‡ Kaivalya-Up.] As to the statement "It attains infinite proportions when done in the presence of Siva," it refers to *Japa* or mere repetition of mantras. It does not refer to meditation, which, however, may be practised even there, provided that concentration, the primary requisite, is attainable. Wherefore, there is no rule as to time, place, or direction, in the case of Upasana, which is the same as meditation, and for which concentration alone is the necessary requisite.

Adhikarana 8

Till death (Upasana should be practised); for even then, it is seen. (IV. i. 12)

In the preceding Adhikarana it has been made out that the Upasana of Brahman requires no particular place, etc. But now we have to enquire whether it has an end or not.

(*Purvapaksha*): - Upasana may be practised as long as one may wish to do so. Otherwise, it may be stopped.

(*Siddhanta*): - Upasana should be practised day after day till death. It should never have an end, in as much as the sruti enjoins Upasana till death in such passages as the following:

"He who meditates thus day by day goes to Svarga." * [* Chha. 8-3-3.]

"He who behaves thus all his life reaches the world of Brahman." † [† Ibid. 8-15-1.]

The Vedanta-Sutras with Srikantha Bhashya

There should be no break, in the middle of the meditation of Brahman which leads to the state of Brahman. It is only when Brahman has been meditated upon by the Upasakas as their own Self without intermission that the state of Brahman manifests itself in those Upasakas. Hence it is necessary, for the manifestation of Brahman's nature, that the Upasakas should meditate, without intermission, upon the Supreme Brahman, who is omniscient, ever-satisfied, self-luminous, self-reliant, whose powers never fail, whose potencies are infinite. Accordingly the sruti says that Brahman's nature manifests itself in the Upasakas:

"In that most blessed form of Thine, O Rudra, which is gracious and attractive, which manifests dost pour Thy blessings from the mountain top, shine in Thy full splendour to us." * [* Tai. Sam. 4-5-1.]

To explain: *Rudra* is so called because, He expels (or causes to run away) from the Upasakas the intolerable misery of samsara which arises from various causes abiding in oneself as well as outside, and which has been running in a continuous stream of attachment for the body of Devas and the like, so that it has been firmly ingrained in one's nature by the beginningless sin (mala), karma and impressions (vasanas) of past experience. The supreme Brahman, Siva, the Supreme Lord (Paramesvara), is here addressed as Rudra. Rudra has a form which is gracious; *i.e.*, a form which is eternal, devoid of sin, and therefore supremely pure, most beneficent, the Highest Bliss itself. Because, it is gracious, it attracts the heart of all. It manifests itself in the sinless ones, *i.e.*, in those persons whose acts, both good and evil, have all been consumed in the fire of wisdom, - 'sin' standing for virtue as well. This form is also the most blessed one, because it is none other than the unsurpassed supreme Bliss spoken of in the sruti. "That is the unit of Brahman's Bliss." † [† Tai. Up. 2-8.] The Upasakas pray: "In that most blissful form, do Thou remove all good and evil acts of ours which have brought about our samsara, and manifest Thyself in Thy full splendour in our own essential nature."

Wherefore, in as much as Brahman's nature manifests itself in the nature of the worshippers (Upasakas), the meditation of Brahman which causes such manifestation, should be practised till death. There should be no break in it at any time whatever.

Adhikarana 9

From the attainment thereof (accrue) non-contact of the subsequent sins and destruction of the previous ones, because of the mention thereof. (IV. i. 13)

In the preceding section it has been explained with reasons how in the Upasakas, who are free from sins, the essential nature of Brahman clearly manifests itself. Now, a doubt arises as to whether, in the case of an Upasaka, a destruction of sins takes place or not.

(*Purvapaksha*): - It would appear at first sight that even in the case of Upasakas no destruction of sins can take place without the enjoyment of their fruits, since it is said that no action is exhausted even in hundreds of crores of ages (Kalpas), without its fruits being enjoyed. On the attainment of a body for the enjoyment of their fruits, further accumulation of Karma is inevitable; so that, there is no occasion for moksha.

(*Siddhanta*): - As against the foregoing we hold as follows: In the case of Upasakas, all sin is destroyed. – How? – As soon as the Upasana is commenced, destruction of previous sins and non-contact with the subsequent ones follow as a result of the Upasana itself. So indeed is it declared in the sruti:

> "As the soft fibres of the Ishika reed, when thrown into the fire, are burnt, thus all his sins are burnt." * [* Chha. 5-24-3.]

> "As water does not cling to a lotus leaf, so no evil deed clings to one who knows it." †
> [† Ibid. 4-14-3.]

Therefore, destruction of the previous sins and non-contact with the subsequent ones do accrue to the upasakas. As to the assertion that so sins can be exhausted without their fruits being enjoyed, it applies only to the unenlightened, and hence no contradiction.

Adhikarana 10

Of the other also (there is) in the same way non-contact, but on death. (IV. i. 14)

It has been proved that in the case of the enlightened sage there is no contact of sins. Now, a doubt arises as to whether there is a taint of good deeds (as opposed to sins or evil deeds) or not.

(*Purvapaksha*): - It is proper that there should be a destruction of sin, as it is opposed to Vidya or knowledge, but not of good deeds, since it would stand to reason that they should go along with Vidya as its necessary accompaniment.

(*Siddhanta*): - As against the foregoing we hold as follows: Even the good deeds of the sage do not touch him and are destroyed, in as much as their results are equally opposed to Moksha and therefore undesirable. The good deeds which are favourable to Vidya by way of securing good health and the like will be destroyed on the death of the body. But as to those acts which form a necessary accompaniment of Vidya, they do not taint the sage, as they are free from contact with objects of desire. Hence the conclusion that in the case of the sage there is no taint of good deeds either.

Adhikarana 11

But only those previous acts whose effects have not yet begun, because of its being marked as the limit. (IV. i. 15)

In the preceding adhikarana, it has been shown that in the case of the enlightened one there is a non-contact with the subsequent acts of merit and demerit and a destruction of the

The Vedanta-Sutras with Srikantha Bhashya

previous ones. Now a doubt arises as to the continuance or otherwise of those acts of merit and demerit which have already begun their effects.

(*Purvapaksha*): - In the words "all his sins are burnt" the sruti speaks of all sins without distinction. Therefore, as even the acts in question are among those done prior to entering on the path of Vidya, they, also must undergo destruction.

(*Siddhanta*): - As against the foregoing, we hold as follows: It is only such of the acts of merit and demerit done before entering on the path of Vidya as have not yet begun their effects, that undergo destruction; for, the sruti speaks of the death of the body as the limit:

> "For him, there is only delay so long as he is not delivered (from the body); then he will be perfect." * [* Ibid. 6-14-2.]

Hence no destruction of the Prarabdha-Karma, of the acts, which have already begun their effects.

Adhikarana 12

But the Agnihotra and others (contribute) only the effect thereof, as seen (in the scriptures) (IV. i. 15)

In the preceding Adhikarana it has been shown that good and evil deeds do not touch the enlightened one and are destroyed. It has been further shown that Upasana should be continued throughout life. But, now, a doubt arises as to whether even the performance of Agnihotra and other rites should continue till the death of the body or should cease in the middle.

(*Purvapaksha*): - It may appear that the Agnihotra and other rites need not be performed till death, in as much as it is supposed that, though performed, they undergo destruction. Who will have the mind to do a thing in the absence of utility?

(*Siddhanta*): - As against the foregoing we hold as follows: Agnihotra and the like should be performed till death as contributing to the very success of Vidya. Accordingly, indeed, the sruti says:

> "Brahmans seek to know him by the study of the Veda, by sacrifice, by gifts, by penance, by fasting." * [* Bri. Up. 4-4-22.]

The study of the Veda means the repeated japa or recitation of the Vedic mantras which treat of matters concerning Atman, which are calculated to produce the highest knowledge constituting the means of attaining the supreme Lord, Paramesvara. The Jabala-Upanishad says:

> "Then the students of Brahman thus addressed him: Tell us, O Lord, what mantra has to be recited whereby to attain immortality?" Yajnavalkya said: "It is by Satarudriya. These are indeed the names of the Immortal, and thereby one becomes immortal."

The Vedanta-Sutras with Srikantha Bhashya

In the Kaivalya-Upanishad it is said:

"That Brahmana who daily recites Satarudriya, he is purified by the sacred fires; he is purified by the air, he, is purified from liquor-drinking, he is purified from Brahamanicide. Taking his stand in the final order of holy life, let a man recite it always or, once; he attains the highest knowledge; the Ocean of Samsara undergoes extinction."

Here we are given to understand that by the recitation of the mantras called Satarudriya which treat of Brahman, that supreme knowledge which extinguishes Samsara is attained, and that the sins which are opposed to the knowledge undergo destruction. The recitation of Satarudriya is here said to bring about destruction of all sins, on the ground that it comprises the names of Siva who is immortal and free, through time without a beginning – as declared in the words "these indeed are the names of the immortal." From this it will be seen that even the recitation of the names of the Paramesvara – such as 'Siva,' – conduces to the destruction of all sins that may stand in the way of knowledge. The Sruti says:

"If even a chandala, if he should utter the word 'Siva', one may talk with him, dwell with him, eat with him."

Here indeed we are given to understand that the greatest sinner who is most impure attains highest purity by a mere utterance of the word 'Siva' denoting Brahman. Elsewhere also the sruti, after saying that in the case of the Brahmana who recites daily the Atharvasiras all sins are extinguished, declares also that he attains moksha, in the following words:

"Once reciting, he becomes clean, pure, and fit for sacrificial ritual. Reciting a second time, he attains the state of Ganapati; reciting it a third time he enters the Deva Himself."

And that the recitation of the Pranava causes the break of the bond (Pasa-vichchheda) is taught in passages like the following:

"Having made Atman the arani, and Pranava the upper arani, by practice of knowledge, by repeated churning, the wise man burns up the bond." * [* Kaivalya Up.]

So also elsewhere. Accordingly, since we are given to understand that the Vedic mantras treating of Paramesvara constitutes the means to Moksha by way of conducing to the knowledge of the Supreme, through destruction of all sins, the recitation of those mantras should be practised throughout life even by the enlightened sage. So also it is necessary to perform Agnihotra and such other sacrificial acts, dedicating their fruits to Paramesvara in as much as they are things commanded by him and constitute His worship. So, too, the observance of the injunction regarding gifts, etc., is necessary. Hence the conclusion that even for the enlightened sages it is necessary to perform Agnihotra and the like with a view to bring about the perfection of knowledge (Vidya). The worship of Lord (Isvara-upasana) takes the form of ritual (karma), austerity (tapas), recitation (japa), meditation (dhyana) and knowledge (jnana). *Ritual* (karma) comprises Agnihotra, etc; *austerity* (tapas) means *niyama* or self-imposed religious observance, or it may be Kaya-soshana, physical mortification;

recitation (japa) means repetition of Pranava and the like mentioned above. These form the means to moksha, by bringing about the extinction of sins. But knowledge and meditation are the direct means to moksha, as they cause the attainment of the condition of Brahman. Wherefore the observance of all these is necessary.

(*Objection*): - If the good deeds such as Agnihotra are intended for the development of knowledge, and if good deeds other than these, done in the past, have been destroyed on entering the path of Vidya, then what are those goods which, as said in the sruti, the friends of the sage inherit on his death?

(*Answer*): - The Sutrakara says:

(There are also deeds) other than these, - of which some speak of both kinds. (IV. i. 17)

Some, *i.e.*, the students of Satyayana recension of the Veda, read as follows:

"His sons inherit the property, his friends the good deeds, his foes the evil deeds."

The good deeds here spoken of are other than those – Agnihotra and the like – which are intended for the perfection of knowledge; they are the deeds whose fruition is obstructed by other and stronger deeds, and which, as capable of producing food, health, mental purity and the like which are consonant with knowledge, conduce to results favourable to knowledge and have not therefore been destroyed even by knowledge. These are the deeds spoken of – deeds of both kinds which precede and succeed knowledge.

It is indeed (said), "Whatever is done with knowledge," & c., (IV. i. 18)

"Whatever is done with knowledge, that alone becomes more powerful." * [* Chha 1-1-10] Here the sruti says that the purpose of the Udgitha-Vidya is the removal of obstruction in the path of the fruition of the act. Thereby the sruti implies the existence of obstruction, the fruition of some acts by other and stronger deeds. Hence the meaning of the sutra is that Agnihotra and the like should be performed with a view to the removal of the obstacles that obstruct the fruition of those acts which are favourable to knowledge.

Adhiakarana 13

After exhausting the others by enjoyment, he then becomes blest. (IV. i. 19)

Now we have to enquire whether those who, while possessing Vidya, hold certain responsible offices (in the administration of the universe), are entitled or not to Moksha, - as the result of their Vidya, - over and above the offices they hold.

(*Purvapaksha*): - If plurality of births be postulated for the enjoyment of the fruits of the prarabdha, - of the karma which has begun its effects, - then the knowledge attained in one birth disappears in the succeeding birth, so that whatever karma is done in the latter birth leads to enjoyment of fruits. Wherefore, owing to this possibility of a series of births, they (*i.e.*, the office-holders) do not attain liberation.

(*Siddhanta*): - As against the foregoing we argue as follows: The prarabdha-karma can but lead to enjoyment of Vidya acquired in the past, so that they (those office-holders) do attain liberation. They will not be subjected to an (endless) series of births; for, there is no cause. The interval of birth and death is like that of sleep; they do not bring about extinction of Vidya.

FOURTH ADHYAYA – SECOND PADA.

Adhikarana 1

Speech (is dissolved) in mind, because of our experience and the word. (IV. ii. 1).

And for this very reason all senses (follow) after (mind). (IV. ii. 2)

In the pada just closed, it was shown in what particular way, & c., the upasaka should practise upasana. This pada will treat of his departure from the body. The dissolution of speech and other sense organs in mind of the departing person is taught in the following passages: -

"Of this departing person, my dear, speech is dissolved in mind, mind in breath, breath in fire, fire in the Supreme Deity." * [* Chha. 6-9-6.]

A doubt arises as to whether this stands to reason or not.

Purvapaksha: - What is the *prima facie* view? Every effect, indeed, attains dissolution in its material cause (upadana), as we find that a pot is invariably resolved into clay, its material cause, and so on. The material cause of speech and other sense-organs is Brahman, not mind. Wherefore, it is proper that they should be dissolved only in Brahman.

Siddhanta: - As against the foregoing, we hold as follows: -

The Sruti says: -

"Of this departing person, my dear, speech is dissolved in mind" † [† Ibid.]

"The senses being dissolved in mind." * [* Prasna, 3-9.]

We actually see that at departure speech and other sense-organs cease to function even prior to mind. Therefore, speech first attains dissolution in mind; then all senses are dissolved in mind. As to the contention that an effect attains dissolutions only in its material cause, we say that it is not always the case. This law applies only to the dissolution of the thing itself. It is not meant here that speech and other senses are themselves dissolved in mind; only the cessation of their functions is meant here. Just as a burning piece of charcoal, when cast into a body of water, ceases to emit light, & c., so also it stands to reason that the functions of speech and other sense-organs are merged in mind, though mind is not their material cause. The dissolution of speech, & c., *i.e.*, of things which possess the functions, here stands for the dissolution of the functions, the functions and the things that possess those functions being here spoken of as identical by courtesy.

Adhikarana 2

This mind in breath, from the sequel. (IV. ii. 3).

The dissolution, in breath, of mind accompanied with speech and all other senses, is spoken of in the words, "Mind (is dissolved) in breath." † [† Chha. 6-8-6.] A doubt arises as to what kind of dissolution this is.

Purvapaksha: - Granted that it is the functions of speech and other senses that are merged in mind, seeing that mind is not their material cause (upadana). But as to mind itself, it is itself dissolved in breath (prana), in as much as breath is the material cause of mind. "Made up, indeed, of food, my dear, is mind, and made up of waters is breath; ‡ [‡ Chha. 6-5-4.] In these words, the Sruti teaches that, as made up of food, mind is made up of earth (prithivi) and that, therefore, as made up of waters, breath is the material cause (upadana) of mind; so that it is not contrary to reason to say that mind is substantially dissolved in breath.

Siddhanta: - As in the case of speech and other senses, so also in the case of mind, it is the functions of mind that are merged in breath, because of the sequel, "Mind (is dissolved) in breath" * [* Chha. 5-8-6.] Mind is not substantially dissolved in breath; for, breath cannot be the direct (upadana) or material cause of mind, since mind is not born from breath (prana). Wherefore, reason shows that it is only the functions of mind that are said to be merged in breath.

Adhikarana 3

It unites with the lord, because of the union therewith, etc., (being spoken of) (IV. ii. 4)

Erstwhile, the dissolution of the mind and all the senses in the breath was spoken of. Now a question arises as to where that breath attains dissolution.

Purvapaksha: - What, now suggests itself at first? From the words of the Sruti "the breath (is dissolved) in light" the breath attains dissolution in light.

Siddhanta: - As against the foregoing, we hold as follows: -

That breath then unites with the Jiva, the lord; it does not attain dissolution in light, because of the Sruti which speaks of its union with the Jiva in the passages like the following:

"Thus do all the senses gather round the
Self at the time of death." † [† Bri. 6-3-38.]

Now the Sutrakara proceeds to explain away the apparent contradiction of the passage "the breath (is dissolved) in light.

(It unites) with the elements of matter, because of the Sruti referring to them. (IV. ii. 5)

In the passages, "the breath (is dissolved) in light", ‡ [‡ Chha. 5-8-6.] the Sruti refers to 'light' as enjoined with the other elements of matter. Accordingly, there is no contradiction, since we are only taught here that the breath along with the Jiva unites with the elements of matter.

Not in the one alone; so indeed they teach. (IV. ii. 6)

Not in light alone does the breath attain its dissolution. For, the Sruti, which treats of the triplication, teaches its conjunction with the other elements of matter. Wherefore, since the breath along with the Jiva, unites with the elements of matter, there is no contradiction of the Sruti.

Adhikarana 4

And same up to the commencement of the passage. And immortality. (IV. ii. 7)

A question arises as to whether the departure that is here described is the same or different for the enlightened and the unenlightened, prior to the commencement of the passage starting with light.

Purvapaksha: - What suggests itself at first? In as much as mundane life and liberation are two quite different effects, the departure is different in the two cases of the wise and the ignorant.

Siddhanta: - As against the foregoing, we hold as follows: -

Prior to the commencement of the passage starting with the light, etc., the departure is quite the same for the wise and the ignorant. But the wise man effects the exit through the tubular passage (nadi) in the head and attains immortality, but not the others; here lies the difference. For, the Sruti says: -

"There are a hundred and one nadis of the heart; one of them enters the crown of the head. Moving upwards by it, a man reaches immortal; the other nadis serve for departing in different directions." * [* Katha. Up. 6-10.]

Prior to this, the departure is quite the same.

The Vedanta-Sutras with Srikantha Bhashya

Adhikarana 5

Because of the reference to embodied existence prior to union with Him. (IV. ii. 8)

It has been shown in the last section that the enlightened one makes his exit through the nadi in the head, and that then commences the journey on the Path of Light. Now there arises a question as to whether, in the case of the enlightened one who has departed from the body, a journey on the Path of Light is possible. The Sruti speaks of immortality being attained immediately after the death of the physical body: -

"When all desires which once entered his heart are undone, then does the mortal become immortal, then he attains Brahman here." * [* Bri. 6-4-7.]

And the Sruti speaks also of the journey on the Path of Light, in the words, "They go forth to light" † [† Chha. 6-10-1.]

Purvapaksha: - Now it would seem that journey on the Path of Light is impossible in the case of liberated souls, in as much as the liberated soul cannot start on the journey, owing to the impossibility of speech, etc., coming into life again after having been once absorbed in Brahman.

Siddhanta: - As against the foregoing, we argue as follows: - Embodied existence does not cease, because of the reference to a connection with the body, prior to the attainment of Brahman through the path of light. The Sruti merely says that the liberated one becomes immortal at once, because the actual attainment of immortality is to come off very soon. Wherefore in the case of the departing wise man, journey on the Path of Light is possible. Now as to the assertion that such a journey is impossible in his case, because of the absorption of speech, etc., the Sutrakara says as follows: -

And a (body) subtle in size (he has), because so we find. (IV. ii. 9)

Though he has departed from this body, the subtle body continues. Otherwise, owing to the impossibility of a journey, no conversation with the moon and the like would be possible. In the Sruti, indeed, in the Paryanka-Vidya, there is recorded a conversation taking place on the path of gods between the wise soul and the woman: -

"All who depart from this world (this body) go to the moon ... Verily, the moon is the door of the Svarga world. Now, if a man objects to the moon (if one is not satisfied with life there), the moon sets him free. But, if a man does not object, then the moon sends him down as rain upon this earth. And according to his deeds and according to his knowledge, he is born here again as a worm, or as an insect, or as a fish, or as a bird, or as a lion, or as a boar, or as a serpent, or as a tiger, or as a man, or as something else in different places. When he has thus returned to the earth, someone (a sage) asks, 'Who art thou?' And he should answer...." * [* Kaushitaki-Up. 1-2.]

So that, in the case of the wise man who has departed from the body, journey on the Path of Light is possible.

Hence not by destruction. (IV. ii. 10)

Hence, *i.e*, for the foregoing reasons, the Sruti, "Then does the mortal become immortal;" † [† Bri. Up. 6-4-7.] which speaks of the attainment of immortality, does not mean that immortality is immediately attained through a complete cessation of all connection with the body.

Because it is possible that such a subtle body exists somewhere without being altogether destroyed, warmth, which is the property of the subtle body is indeed felt somewhere, even when the wise soul departs from the body. Warmth is not the property of the gross physical body, as it is not felt in it after death. Hence also the possibility of the journey.

(If it be objected that this cannot be) because of the denial (we say that the senses depart) not from the embodied one. This indeed is clearly taught in the recension of some. (IV. ii. 12).

Objection: - The Brihadaranyaka teaches how the unenlightened soul departs from the body in the following words: -

"The point of his heart becomes lighted up, and by that light the Self departs, either through the eye, or through the skull, or through other places of the body. And when he thus departs, life departs after him, and when life thus departs, all the other vital elements depart after it." * And so on. [* Bri. Up. 6-4-2.]

Then, the Sruti, after concluding the subject so far as it concerns the unenlightened soul in the words, "So much for the man who desires", proceeds as follows: -

"But as to the man who does not desire, who, not desiring, free from desires, is satisfied in his desire, or desire the Self only, his vital elements do not depart elsewhere; being Brahman, he goes to Brahman." † [† Bri. Up. 6-4-6.]

As the Sruti here denies the departure of the wise soul, he directly attains Brahman here alone.

Answer: - No; for, in the words, "his vital elements depart not," ‡ [‡ Ibid.] the Sruti teaches that the vital elements of the departing soul who has started for a journey on the Path of Light are not detached from him. This idea is clearly conveyed by the words of the Upanishad in the recension of the Madhyandinas.

"As to the man who, not desiring, freed from desires, is satisfied in his desires, or desires the Self only, *from* him the vital elements do not depart."

And the Smriti also says. (IV. ii. 13).

The Smriti speaks of the wise one passing through the nadi in the head:

The Vedanta-Sutras with Srikantha Bhashya

"Among them, there is one going upward, making its way through the Solar region; thereby, he passes beyond the region of Brahman and attains the supreme goal."

Therefore, journey on the Path of Light is possible in the case of the departing soul of the wise man.

Some say that journey on the Path of Light is not invariable in all cases, in as much as in the case of those who are devoted to the Unconditioned the cessation of connection with the body here is itself their liberation.

Adhikarana 6

They (are dissolved) in the Supreme. So, indeed, the Sruti says. (IV. ii. 14).

In a former section, it was shown that Jiva conjoined with the senses becomes absorbed in the elements of matter including light (tejas). From the words "light (becomes dissolved) in the Supreme Deity," * [* Chha. 6-8-6.] we understand that light combined with other elements of matter and conjoined with Jiva attains dissolution in the Supreme Deity. Now, a doubt arises as to whether a dissolution of its very being in the Supreme Deity (Parabrahman) is here meant, or the mere undistinguishability of the two from one another.

Purvapaksha: -It would seem proper that the absorption of the very being of light is here meant. The Supreme Deity is, etymologically, none other than Mahadeva. It is Mahadeva who is spoken of in the Sruti as Parabrahman, the source of all beings, in the following and similar passages: -

"This Deity thought" † [† Chha. 6-3-2.]

"The one God (Deva) creating heaven and earth." ‡ [‡ Mahanarayana Up. 1-12.]

Therefore, it is but reasonable to suppose that in Him, the material (upadana) cause, all elements of matter, along with Jiva, attain dissolution in their very being.

Siddhanta: - The true theory, however, may be stated as follows: - Though Brahman is the material cause, the elements are not dissolved in Him by their very being. On the other hand, they only become undistinguishable from one another. There is no ground whatever why the mere union, once taught in the words, "speech becomes one with mind," I should be understood in quite a different sense here. Therefore, as in the case of the mind, etc., here too, the Sruti means only a cessation of function.

Non-separation (is meant) because of the text. (IV. ii. 15)

Because the text of the Upanishad speaks of union, it is quite reasonable to understand that mere non-separation of the elements of matter from Brahman is here meant.

Adhikarana 7

There is the blazing forth of the point of his seat; then within the gate illumined by it, in virtue of the knowledge and in virtue of the complementary contemplation of the path, (the wise one), helped by the Grace of the One in the heart, departs by the passage beyond the hundred. (IV. ii. 16)

In a former section, it was said that up to the starting point on the Path of Light, the process of departure is the same in the case of the enlightened and the unenlightened. Now we shall enquire whether there is any difference or no between the two at the time of their exit.

Purvapaksha: - In the words, "light is dissolved in the Supreme Deity", it is said that the wise as well as the ignorant is absorbed in the Supreme Cause, - the Highest God, the Supreme Brahman, the Supreme Light, - and remains there inseparable, for a time, resting himself. Therefore, their departure is quite the same, in as much as the Sruti speaks of the blazing up of the heart and so on in the case of both alike. The Sruti says:

"The point of his heart becomes lighted up, and by that light the self departs, either through the eye, or through the skull or through other places of the body." * [* Bri. Up. 6-4-2.]

Therefore, the departure being the same in both, there is no difference whatever between the two.

Siddhanta: - Such being the prima facie view, we say that our conclusion is that there is a difference between the two. To explain at length: - In virtue of the wisdom which takes the form of the worship of the Supreme Lord (Paramesvara) dwelling in the heart, and in virtue of the complementary contemplation of the Path of Light, the Lord, who is gracious to all, becomes propitiated; and when the enlightened devotee is glanced at by the gracious eye of the Lord which is capable of destroying all the sin that enshrouds His being and when the gate of his exit is illumined by His grace, he passes upwards by that nadi in the head which lies beyond the hundred ones. But not so the other; on the contrary, he passes out by the other nadis. So says the Sruti: -

"There are a hundred and one nadis of the heart, one of them enters the crown of the head. Moving upwards by it, a man reaches the immortal; the other nadis serve for departing in different directions." † [† Katha-Up. 6-16.]

Such is the peculiarity in the departure of the wise man.

All this amounts to this: - "Rudra abides in the heart of men." "The heart-lotus, which is free from dirt, perfectly pure;" ‡ [‡ Kaivalya-Up.] in such passages of the Sruti as the above as well as in the passages like "the Lord sits, O Arjuna, in the region of the heart in all beings," § [§ Gita. 18-51.] we are given to understand that the Supreme Lord (Paramesvara) dwells in the hearts of all men. He in whom Jiva with the functions of his senses becomes absorbed and is merged in sole communion; He whom – in the words, "Superior to the universe is Rudra, the Great Sage (Maharshi)," * [* Mahana. 10-19.] and "all verily is Rudra," † [† Ibid. 16.] – the Sruti declares to be above the universe as the efficient cause (Nimittakarana) thereof, and to be one with the universe as its material (upadana) cause; He whose supremacy as the Lord of the universe is taught in the words "One indeed is Rudra; they stand not for a second;" ‡ [‡ Sve. 3-2.] He then whom nothing else the seekers of liberation have to know, as taught in the words, "Siva alone is to be meditated upon"; § [§ Atharvasikha.] He of whom, - in the words, "Here indeed, when the life principles of a man depart from the body, Rudra imparts instruction to him about Brahman, the Saviour (the Taraka-Brahman), whereby he becomes immortal," ¶ [¶ Ramottaratapani.] – the Sruti says that He teaches to the enlightened devotees at death the Taraka-Brahman whereby they realise his true being; He who, as the object of all worship; is the Lord of all sacrifices; as the Sruti says, "Secure Rudra, the Lord of your sacrifice, for your protection;" € [€ Rig-Veda.4-3-1.] He who is the best doctor of the disease of Samsara, as addressed in the passage, "O Rudra, ... invigorate our sons by thy medicinal plants, for, I hear that Thou art the chief physician amongst physicians. £ [£ Ibid. 2-38-4.] He whose form and part Maya is said to be – in the words, "Maya, verily, be it known is the material cause, and Mahesvara is its possessor," ¥ [¥ Sve. Up. 4-10.] – that supreme energy (Paramasakti) called Maya which manifests itself in the variegated flower-show called the universe; - He, indeed, the Supreme Brahman dwelling in the heart – the Supreme Lord, whose form is supreme Bliss, who is the Consort of Uma, the Supreme Spirit (Paramatman), glances at the contemplating and devout aspirant – the devotee who has been constantly engaged in *Agnihotra* and other rituals enjoined as forms of Divine worship in the Sruti which constitutes the Divine command, who is completely free from the slightest mark of prohibited action, who has dedicated all fruits of his action to God, whose will has been completely surrendered to the Divine will, who has imbibed in full the immortal nectar of the knowledge of God, who has renounced all interested action as well as its fruit, who, having attained discrimination, etc., is solely engaged in devotion to God, seeking Divine Grace, - and, at the time of his leaving the body, the Lord, in all His Grace towards the devotee, directs towards him His gracious glance which wipes away all the stain of samsara. Then this devotee, with all the stain of samsara completely wiped away by the mighty Grace of God, and departing by the nadi of the head shone on by the resplendent Atman, reaches by the path of Light the supreme Divine abode which transcends all material universe, the unsurpassed bliss being its very nature; then attaining to a form like the Divine form itself, his nature partakes of the eternal unsurpassed bliss. Therefore, it is but proper to hold that there is a difference in the destinies of the enlightened and the unenlightened.

Adhikarana 8

Following the (sun's) rays. (IV. ii. 17)

In the preceding section, it has been shown that the devotee, who has obtained the grace of the Paramesvara abiding in the heart, departs by the nadi of the head. Now a question arises as to whether, in the case of the departing devotee, the upward journey is possible by night as well as by day.

Purvapaksha: - The view that first suggests itself is this: We are given to understand that the departing soul passes upward in contact with the sun's rays, as the Sruti says:

"When he departs from this body, then he departs upwards by those very rays." * [* Chha. 8-3-5.]

Certainly, contact with the sun's rays is possible only by day, but not by night.

Siddhanta: - As against the foregoing, we hold as follows: It is true that the departing soul of the enlightened devotee (Vidvan) passes upward only in contact with the sun's rays. But this contact is possible by night as well as by day; for, even at night, the sun's rays are present, as shown by the heat felt during summer nights. Hence the conclusion that, by night as well as by day, his soul passes upward in the wake of the sun's rays.

Now the Sutrakara refers to an objection and answers it.

If it be objected (that it) cannot (happen) at night, (we say) no, because the connection exists as long as the body exists; and so the Sruti says. (IV. ii. 18)

Objection: - It has been said that, even when one is dead at night, he attains Brahman, by passing in contact with the sun's rays. This is not possible; for death, by night is condemned in the following words:

"Day-time, bright fortnight, the period of the summer solstice, - these are good for the dying; but the opposite is condemned.

Answer: - No, because the bondage of samsara lasts only as long as the body lasts. For, the prarabdha karma, - *i.e.*, the sum total of the acts, which has brought about the present birth – continuing to operate even when those acts which will lead to bondage, but which have not yet begun to operate, have been destroyed by Vidya or knowledge, is operative only up to the close of the final bodily existence; and, therefore, when even the prarabdha ceases at the close of the last bodily existence, there remains no obstacle to the attainment of Brahman.

And the Sruti teaches accordingly: "For him there is only delay so long as he shall not be delivered from the body; then he shall be perfect." * [* Chha. 6-14-2.]

As to the condemnation of the night-time, it holds good only in the case of other persons. Wherefore, there is nothing unreasonable in the statement that, even when the enlightened devotee is dead at night, he can attain Brahman.

And hence even during the period of the winter solstice. (IV. ii. 19)

For the foregoing reason, i.e., only because there is no cause of bondage, the enlightened devotee (Vidvan) attains Brahman, even though he may die during the period of the winter solstice.

These two are taught in the Smriti with reference to the Yogins as things to be contemplated. (IV. ii. 20).

Objection: - It is with reference to the dying enlightened devotees that the Smriti speaks of certain periods of time as leading to a return of the souls and of certain other periods as causing no return:

"Now in what time departing, Yogins go to return not, as also to return, that time will tell thee, O chief of the Bharatas.

"Fire, light, day-time, the bright fortnight, the six months of the northern solstice, - then departing, men who know Brahman reach Brahman.

"Smoke, night-time, and the dark fortnight, the six months of the southern solstice, - attaining by these to the lunar light, the Yogin returns.

"These bright and dark paths of the world are verily deemed eternal; by the one, man goes to return not, by the other, he returns again." * [* Bhagavadgita. VIII.23-26.]

Therefore, it is unreasonable to maintain that the condemnation of the night-time and the period of the winter solstice refers to unenlightened persons.

(*Answer*): - This Sutra is meant as an answer to the foregoing objection. In the passages quoted above, the Sruti teaches that the two paths, called the path of the Pitris (Pitriyana) and the path of the gods (Deva-yana), are to be daily contemplated upon by those who are engaged in Yoga or contemplation as a necessary part of their Yoga, that they should contemplate daily that the enlightened souls pass by the Path of Light and that others pass by the opposite path. The Sruti does not, on the contrary, teach that any particular periods of time are suitable for the death of the enlightened devotees, for, the Smriti concludes in the following words: -

"Knowing these paths, O son of Pritha, no Yogin is deluded, wherefore at all times, be steadfast in Yoga, O Arjuna." * [* Ibid. viii.27]

And it is the Pitriyana and Devayana paths that are referred to in the second and the third of the verses quoted above. The word 'time' occurring in the first of the verses quoted above refers only to the whole host of the escorting gods (ativahika-gana), among whom the gods presiding over particular periods of time predominate. Wherefore, no objection whatever exists to the view that the enlightened devotees reach Brahman, even though they may die by night, or in the winter solstice, or in the dark fortnight. When the body dies, then Brahman is attained at once.

FOURTH ADHYAYA – THIRD PADA.

Adhikarana 1

By light, etc., as it is clearly taught. (IV. iii. 1.)

In the last pada it was taught that the contemplator departs from the body by the nadi of the head, the passage being lighted by the Grace of the Paramesvara dwelling in the heart.

The Vedanta-Sutras with Srikantha Bhashya

Now, we shall first enquire whether such a contemplator attains Brahman solely by the path of light, or it is possible for him to reach Brahman by some other way also.

Purvapaksha: - Indeed, in one place we are taught that it is also possible to reach Brahman without passing through the path of light. "Where the root of the hair divides, there he opens the two sides of the head, and saying Bhu, he enters Agni, saying Bhuvas, he enters Vayu, saying Suvas, he enters Aditya, saying Mahas he enters Brahman. He there obtains lordship." * [* Taitt. Up. 1-6.] Wherefore the path of light is not always necessary for reaching Brahman.

Siddhanta: - As against the foregoing view, we argue as follows. The enlightened devotee (Vidvan) reaches Brahman by the path of light solely; for in the Vidya of Five Fires (Panchagnividya) it is clearly taught that the path of light leads to Brahman, in the words "They go to light..."† [† Chha. 5-10-1.] In the passage of the Taittiriya-Upanishad quoted above it is not the path to Brahman that it taught; on the other hand, it is the attainment of the glory (vibhuti) of Brahman that is taught there. Wherefore the attainment of the Supreme is possible only through the path of light. According to some, there is no necessity for the path of light in the case of those who take to the contemplation of the unconditioned Brahman.

Adhikarana 2

(We should understand) 'Vayu' after 'year,' because of the generic and specific mention. (IV. iii. 2.)

A doubt arises as to whether in the order of the stages on the path of light as mentioned here (*i.e.*, in the Chhandogya-Upanishad) we should interpose the order mentioned elsewhere in the Sruti, or whether we should adhere only to the order found here. The Chhandogya teaches the order of the stages on the path of light as follows:

"They go to light (archis,) from light to day, from day to the light half of the moon, from the light half of the moon to the six months when the sun goes to the north, from the six months when the sun goes to the north to the year, from the year to the sun, from the sun to the moon, from the moon to the lightning. There is a person not human; he leads them to Brahman." § [§ Ibid. 5-10-1, 2.]

In the Brihadaranyaka, the wind (Vayu) is mentioned between the year and the sun:

"When the person goes away from this world, he comes to the wind. Then the wind makes room for him, like the hole of a carriage wheel, and through it he mounts higher. He comes to the sun." * [* Op. Cit. 7-10-1.]

The question is whether or not the wind should be interposed (between the year and the sun).

Purvapaksha: - Now it should not be interposed, because it does not occur in the Sruti between them.

The Vedanta-Sutras with Srikantha Bhashya

Siddhanta: - As against the foregoing we hold as follows: On the principle that we should gather together what is taught in different places on the same subject, the wind should be interposed after the year and before the sun. In the Brihadaranyaka itself, elsewhere, when speaking of the order of the stages on the path of light, the region of Gods, (Devaloka), is mentioned in the words "from the months to the region of the Gods, from the region of the Gods to the sun," and this Devaloka should come after the year, for, following the teaching of the Chhandogya we should interpose the year in this passage, and then the year will have to take its place after the months since it is a longer period than the months. The Devaloka is none other than the wind. The word 'Devaloka,' *literally* the region of Gods, denotes the wind as its generic appellation, whereas the word 'Vayu' denotes the wind itself specifically. Thus, as specific and generic appellations of the same thing, the words 'devaloka' and 'Vayu' refer to one and the same thing, namely, the wind. So before the sun we should interpose the wind. The Sruti says:

"The wind is the seat of the Gods."

"The wind that blows here, - this is the stronghold of the Gods."

Adhikarana 3

After lightning (comes) Varuna, because of (their) connection. (IV. iii. 3.)

The Kaushitaki-Upanishad reads as follows:

"Having reached the path of the gods, he comes to the world of Agni (fire), to the world of Vayu (air), to the world of Varuna, to the world of Indra, to the world of Prajapati, to the world of Brahman." * [* Op. Cit. 1-3.]

Here, the first place given to light, here designated as 'Agni,' is indisputable. As the relative positions of Vayu and the sun expressly assigned to them in the other Upanishads have a better claim to our acceptance than the one assigned here, they will have to be placed after the year in their due order. Varuna, too, and others being mentioned here, a doubt arises as to whether they can or cannot be placed in the path of light.

(*Purvapaksha*):- There being no rule by which to determine their position, they can find no place in the path of light.

(*Siddhanta*): - As against the foregoing we hold as follows: It is necessary to assign places to them in the path. It is but right to assign a place to the world of Varuna next after the world of lightning, because of their mutual relation. The mutual connection between lightning and Varuna is well known to all, in as much as Varuna is the lord of the water in the rain which is preceded by the lightning. After them should come the worlds of Indra and Prajapati, such being the only places that remains to be assigned to them. Thus there remains nothing inexplicable.

Adhikarana 4

They are guide, because of the mark (IV. iii. 4)

Now a doubt arises as to whether light, etc., are so many localities marking the stages on the path, or they are so many gods (Devatas) leading the wise devotees (to their destination).

(*Purvapaksha*): - It may at first appear that they are so many localities, since the path may have some marked stages. In common parlance people say, 'leaving the village, go the river, and then thou wilt reach the station of the herdsmen, so too, are light, etc.

(*Siddhanta*): - As against the foregoing we hold as follows. Light, etc., are certainly so many different gods identifying themselves with the path, and acting as leaders of the wise devotees. It is but right to conclude that light, etc., also are leaders, though not mentioned as such specifically as may be inferred from the fact that the person in the lightning is mentioned to be a leader: "There is a person not human, and he leads them to Brahman." * [* Chha. 5-10-2.]

Now it may be asked: Of what use are Varuna, &c., if the person in the lightning leads the souls to Brahman? The Sutrakara answers as follows:

Thence by the person in the lightning alone, as the Sruti says. (IV. iii. 5.)

After reaching the person in the lightning, that person alone leads them to Brahman, as the Sruti says: "There is a person not human; and he leads them to Brahman." Varuna and others are leaders in so far as they help the person in leading the soul. So, there is nothing inexplicable here.

Adhikarana 5

(He leads them to) the Created, says Badari, because of the possibility of passage to Him. (IV. iii. 6.)

A doubt arises as to whether the non-human person leads the devotees to the Brahman Himself or to someone else.

(*Purvapaksha*): - He leads them only to the Hiranyagarbha, the Created, for it is to Him, not to the supreme Brahman who is all-pervading that a passage is possible.

The Sutrakara gives another reason:

And because it is so specified (IV. iii. 7.)

Being specified in the words "I come to the hall of Prajapati, to the house," † [† Chha. 8-14-1.] it is to the abode of the Hiranyagarbha that the person leads the devotees.

But the mention of Him is due to proximity. (IV. iii. 8.)

The Vedanta-Sutras with Srikantha Bhashya

As to the mention of Brahman in the words "he leads them to Brahman," § [§ Ibid. 5-10-2.] it is due to the Hiranyagarbha's proximity to Brahman, and the Hiranyagarbha's proximity from his being spoken of as the first created being: "See ye the Hiranyagarbha who is the first-born." * [* Mahanarayana-Upanishad.]

As the dissolution of the creation, along with its lord he goes beyond it, as the Sruti says. (IV. iii. 9.)

Though the abode of the Hiranyagarbha is first reached, there is no contradiction of the Smriti which denies return to this world. For, at the dissolution of the world of the Hiranyagarbha, the souls of the enlightened pass on to the Highest goal which lies beyond the world of the created Brahman, along with the Hiranyagarbha the lord of the latter. Accordingly it is said in the Sruti: ...

"They in the Brahma-loka, at the end of the creation, are all released, on reaching the immortal one beyond."

Hence no inconsistency whatever.

And the Smriti also says. (IV. iii. 10.)

"At the time of dissolution, at the end of the great cycle, they all, along with Brahman, with regenerated souls, enter the Supreme Abode." From this passage of the Smriti too, we understand so. Thus we conclude that the host of the gods, from the god of light upward, leads the soul to the Hiranyagarbha first. Then, at dissolution, the supreme Brahman is reached by the soul along with the Hiranyagarbha. (Now follows another *purvapaksha*: -)

To the one beyond, says Jaimini, because He is primarily so. (IV. iii. 11.)

The gods on the path of light lead the soul to Narayana Himself, who is superior to the Hiranyagarbha; for Narayana can be called Brahman in the primary sense of the word, as He is the Parabrahman in His aspect as the upadana or material cause of the universe. So says Jaimini.

The Sutrakara gives a reason for the above:

Because we find it so stated. (IV. iii. 12.)

"He reaches the end of the path, that supreme abode of Vishnu." † [† Katha-Up. 3-9.] in these words we find it stated that the abode of Vishnu is the one reached by the soul.

For the following reason also, we hold that the soul is led to Vishnu.

And there is no reference to the Created. (IV. iii. 18.)

As to the passage "I come to the hall of Prajapati, to the house," * [* Chha. 8-14-1.] there is no reference to the created being, the Hiranyagarbha; for is possible that, as the protector of creatures, Narayana may be denoted by the word "Prajapati." And as to the passage, "They in the Brahma-loka, at the end of creation, are all released, on reaching that immortal one beyond," † [† Mahanarayana Up.] here, too, the word 'Brahman' refers to

The Vedanta-Sutras with Srikantha Bhashya

Narayana. Having dwelt in His abode, the Yogins, at the end of the great cycle, *i.e.*, on the last bodily existence coming to a close, they pass on to the Great Immortal Brahman who is above all, and become released. Hence no inconsistency. "These, indeed, are the designations of the Immortal," ‡ [‡ Jabala-Up.] in these words it is said that Siva, the Parabrahman, is the one who is called the Immortal, and the one who can be said to be ever free. Wherefore, on the death of the body brought into existence by the prarabdhakarma, the yogins dwell in the abode of Vishnu, till the completion of the fruit of the prarabdhakarma, and then, passing on to Brahman who is above all, they become free.

(*Siddhanta*):- Now the Sutrakara proceeds to state his own conclusion.

Badarayana maintains that (the person) leads (to Brahman) those who do not worship symbols; because there is a fault in both (the views given above). And he who is intent on Brahman (goes to Brahman Himself). (IV. iii. 14).

The worshippers of symbols are those who worship a sentient being or an insentient object merely regarding it as Brahman. But they who worship Brahman Himself who is above all are not said to be the worshippers of symbols. The worshippers of the Brahman Himself are led by the person to Brahman Himself and to none else, to that Brahman whom the Sruti describes as superior to all, as dark and yellow, as divers-eyed, - in as much as the Sruti teaches that the worshipper of Brahman Himself attains Brahman Himself: Having reached the highest light, he attains his true form." § [§ Chha. 8-3-4.]

"Him whose help-mate is Uma, who is the supreme Lord, Mighty, Three-eyed, Dark-necked, and serene: having meditated thus, the sage reaches Him who is the womb of all beings, the witness of all, transcending darkness." * [* Kaivalya-Up.]

In both the views given above there is a fault, in as much as they contradict the Sruti. He who is intent on Brahman, *i.e.*, the worshipper of Brahman Himself, goes to Brahman; he does not tarry on the way, because there is no use doing so. Being the Upadana or material cause of the Hiranyagarbha who represents the sum total of all creation, Narayana is superior to the Hiranyagarbha; superior even to Narayana is the supreme Brahman called Siva, the Nimitta or efficient cause, the Diverse-eyed, the Omniscient, the Omnipotent, the Ever-satisfied, the Self-reliant, the Self-luminous. So we read in the Sivasankalpa-Upanishad.

"Brahman is greater than the great; greater still than that great one is Hari; even greater than this one is Isa."

Elsewhere, too, we read "Brahman who is superior to Narayana." ‡ [‡ Mahanarayana-Up.] Having thus spoken of Brahman as superior to Narayana, the Sruti, in answer to the question – of what nature is Brahman? – proceeds to describe Brahman in the passage "The True, the Real," § [§ Ibid.] as one who, being the Omniscient, is never subject to error in thought or speech, as one who fills the whole universe with the rays of His Potency; as one associated with Uma, the Parasakti or Supreme Potency, who is inseparable from Himself, the great cause (paraprakriti) that supreme Light made up of highest bliss and pure intelligence, manifesting Herself in the form of the whole universe including the

Hiranyagarbha, which is evolved out of Narayana the highest sentient being, who in his turn is but one aspect of Her own being; as the Immutable, as the Three-eyed, as the supreme Brahman transcending all. In the words "superior to all is Rudra" || [|| Ibid.] He is said to be above the whole universe. Therefore it is quite unreasonable for the followers of the Vedas to imagine a higher being than this one.

<small>And the Sruti points out a distinction. (IV. iii. 15.)</small>

The Sruti itself distinguished the three – (1) Brahman who is above all (2) Vishnu who is an aspect of Brahman and who is the material cause (upadana) and (3) the Hiranyagarbha who is evolved from Vishnu – from one another as the passages like the following show:

"Brahma is greater than the great...even greater than this one is Isa."

"See ye the Hiranyagarbha the first born." * [* Katha-Up. 3-9.]

"Purusha verily, is Rudra." Wherefore the only reasonable conclusion is that the non-human person leads the soul to the abode of Siva, the supreme Brahman, that is beyond Brahma (the Hiranyagarbha) and Vishnu, - to that abode which is the supreme Light made up of supreme bliss.

As to the supposition (that the person leads the soul to Vishnu,) based on the passage "He reaches the end of the path, that supreme abode of Vishnu," we say that the word 'Vishnu' here denotes the Parabrahman. The end of the six-fold path, *i.e.*, that which lies beyond that path, can properly be no other than the abode of Siva, who is above all. Or to interpret it otherwise: the supreme abode or nature of Vishnu who manifests Himself as the universe is the supreme light, which is supreme bliss, itself; and this can be no other than the state of Siva, the Parabrahman, wherein dwelling Vishnu is not of the world though manifesting Himself as the universe. Hence no inconsistency whatever.

In reference to this subject some hold as follows: - As the Sruti says, "At the end of the great cycle, they are all released, on reaching the Immortal One beyond," † [† Mahanarayana-Up.] we should understand that those who worship Vishnu as the highest manifestation of Siva, the supreme Brahman, reach the world of Vishnu, - who is called Brahman (in the Sruti) because he is a manifestation of the supreme Brahman – and, with all the glory of Vishnu manifested is themselves, they, at the end of the cycle, when the last bodily existence comes to a close attain to Siva, the Supreme Immortal Being beyond, and then they are liberated. Thus the sruti teaches that those who worship Vishnu reach first the world of Vishnu and, then, after some interval, attain to the abode of Siva. Hence nothing inconsistent here.

FOURTH ADHYAYA – FOURTH PADA.

Adhikarana 1

On reaching (the Supreme Light), there is the manifestation in his true form, as the Sruti says. (IV. iv. 1.)

It has been shown in the last preceding section that those who have attained true wisdom, reach, by the path of light, the abode of Siva, the Parabrahman, - that abode which lies beyond the abodes of the Hiranyagarbha and Narayana, and which, being of the nature of the highest bliss, is known by the name of Svarga. In this pada, the Sutrakara proceeds to show how, in the case of those who have reached that abode, the manifestation of their true nature takes place. The Sruti teaches that he who has reached the Parabrahman, - the Great Luminary, the Supreme Light, - manifests himself in his true form: "Having risen from out of this earthly body, and having reached the highest light, (the serene being) appears in its own form." * [* Chha. 8-3-4.] Now a doubt arises as to whether this form which is attained by him comes into being at the time, or it has already existed.

(*Purvapaksha*): - It has not already existed in him. On the other hand, since the Sruti speaks of this form being attained, it must be something newly acquired, like Svarga.

(*Siddhanta*): - As against the foregoing we hold as follows: - When the Jiva reaches Brahman, his true form – similar in its nature to that of Brahman – which has already existed in him veiled by his sin, manifests itself on the removal of the sin. So we understand from the words "in its own form;" otherwise, the qualification "own form" will have no meaning, in as much as even the newly acquired form belongs alike to the Jiva. On the contrary, as we maintain, when the sin veiling the *true* nature of the Jiva has been removed by the Grace of Siva, the Parabrahman who is gracious to all, the *true* nature of the Atman, similar to the nature of Siva, comes into manifestation; it is not newly brought into existence, as the result of an act is. Since the Jiva's sin has existed from time without beginning, we can easily understand how he is subject to samsara or mundane life. Wherefore we conclude that when the Jiva is liberated, it is his true inherent nature, the pure consciousness and bliss endued with omniscience and other such attributes, - which bursts forth into manifestation.

(It is) the liberated one (that attains his true form), (as shown by) the original proposition. (IV. iv. 2.)

Though the Atman in himself has already existed, we maintain that, when the Jiva is freed from sin, the infinite bliss and the like manifest themselves in him; for, in the words "I shall explain him (the true self) further to you," the Sruti proposes to treat of him alone who is released from the waking and other states of consciousness brought about by sin.

Moreover,

The Atman (is meant here), as shown by the context. (IV. iv. 3.)

From the context we understand that the Sruti, in the words "I shall explain him further to you," proposes to treat of the Atman free from all sins, who forms the subject of the discourse; for, the Sruti starts with the words. "The Atman who is free from sin,...He it is that we must search out, He it is that we must try to understand," and says further on "I shall explain him to you further." Wherefore, we conclude that the liberated Atman, in whom the inherent attribute of sinlessness and the like have mentioned themselves, is of a nature and attributes similar to those of Brahman.

Adhikarana 2

Because (the liberated one) is found described without distinction. (IV. iv. 4.)

It has been said in the last adhikarana that the nature and attributes of the liberated one are similar to those of Brahman. Now, we have to enquire whether this similarity of the liberated (soul to Brahman) is consistent or not.

Purvapaksha: - Which of the two seems at first sight to be the case? It would seem that none of the souls, whether bound or liberated, can be similar to Brahman, in as much as the Sruti denies a second being similar to Brahman, in the passages like "Rudra is one and remains without a second."

Siddhanta: - As against the foregoing we state our conclusion as follows: - There does exist a similarity between Brahman and the liberated soul. – How? – For, in such passages as "The sinless one attains greatest similarity," and "the liberated one becomes equal to Siva," we find it taught that the liberated soul is similar to Brahman in nature and attributes; and it is this similarity that is taught by the Sruti in the words "He that knows Brahman becomes the very Brahman." The liberated Atman, in virtue of this similarity being attained, realises himself as in separate in nature from Brahman. As to the allegation that the Sruti denies similarity in the words "Rudra is one and remains without a second," it has reference to the fact that the Jiva has no concern with the operation connected with the universe. The Sutrakara, too, says in the sequel, "as may be inferred from the similarity in respect of mere enjoyment." Therefore the similarity meant here refers to the attainment of all objects of desire equally with Brahman. Accordingly the Sruti says: "He enjoys all blessings, at one with the omniscient Brahman." Hence we conclude that the liberated soul can be similar to Brahman.

The Vedanta-Sutras with Srikantha Bhashya

Adhikarana 3

It is in respect of Brahman's attributes, says Jaimini, as the Sruti's teaching, etc., shows (IV. iv. 5.)

It has been said above that, when the soul is liberated, his inherent nature, - similar to that of Brahman, self-luminous and endued with the attributes of sinlessness, etc. – manifests itself. A doubt arises as to whether similarity in both respects is possible or not possible.

(*Purvapaksha*): - The purvapaksha will now be stated by way of citing the views held by others. – Jaimini says that the manifestation of the true nature of the liberated soul, as declared in the words "he appears in his own form," refers to the attributes of Brahman, such as sinlessness, etc. It is these attributes of Brahman which are also inherent in the nature of the Pratyagatman or Jiva, as declared in the Sruti.

"The Atman who is free from sin... He it is whom we must try to search out, He it is whom we must try to understand,"

"He moves about there eating, playing, and rejoicing..."

Wherefore, according to Jaimini, the liberated one becomes equal to Brahman only in respect of the attributes above referred to.

In respect of consciousness alone, says Audulomi, because that is his nature. (IV. iv. 6.)

Audulomi holds that the liberated soul is equal to Brahman only in so far the inherent nature of both is consciousness (Vijnana) as the Sruti says:

"As a mass of salt has neither inside nor outside, but is altogether a mass of taste, thus indeed has this Atman neither inside nor outside, but is altogether a mass of consciousness." † [† Bri. Up. 6-5-13.]

"He is nothing but a mass of consciousness." ‡ [‡ Ibid. 4-4-12.]

Thus, as we find both the views upheld, we have to conclude that the liberated soul and Brahman are distinguishable as well as undistinguishable; but, as they cannot be both distinguishable and undistinguishable at the same moment, we have to conclude that they are distinguishable or undistinguishable under different conditions of time, & c.

(*Siddhanta*): - The Sutrakara proceeds to state his own conclusion: -

Though (the soul is) such, the attributes mentioned above do exist because of their mention, so that Badarayana finds no inconsistency. (IV. iv. 7.)

But Badarayana maintains that the liberated soul is, both by nature and attributes, equal to Brahman, because there is no inconsistency whatever involved in the view. Though in the words, "he is nothing but a mass of consciousness," it has been taught that the liberated soul is self-luminous, still the Sruti proceeds to teach. "The Atman who is free from sin...must be understood," thus showing that the attributes also mentioned above, such as sinlessness, pertain to the liberated soul. Wherefore, as the two aspects based on the teaching of the twofold authority are not inconsistent with each other, it is but proper to admit both. It is only in case of mutual opposition that an explanation should be sought for in the difference of the conditions of time, etc. Thus, we conclude that the liberated soul is like Brahman, self-luminous, as he is consciousness by his very nature, and that he is also endued with all excellent qualities, as it is declared that he is free from sin, and so on.

Adhikarana 4

By mere will (he secures all enjoyment) because so the Sruti teaches. (IV. iv. 8.)

It has been said above that the liberated soul, who is self-luminous, is of unfailing will, and so on. Now a doubt arises as to whether this is possible or not.

(*Purvapaksha*): - What is the view that first suggests itself? It would seem at first sight that, in the case of the liberated soul, his mere will, without the aid of external causes, cannot secure for him the objects of enjoyment, since that alone cannot produce the effect.

(*Siddhanta*): - As against the foregoing we hold as follows. By mere will, he can secure all objects of enjoyment, as the Sruti says:

"Thus when he desires the world of the Pitris, by his mere will the Pitris come to him." * [* Chha. 8-1-2.]

Wherefore, his mere will can secure for him all objects of enjoyment; there is no need for external causes.

And hence he has none else as his lord. (IV. iv. 9.)

For the very reason that he has attained to the nature of Brahman and is endued with sinlessness and other such attributes, he has none else for his lord; he is independent, never subject to Karma, since all karma has been destroyed. The Paramesvara does not control him, because he has gone beyond the sphere of the injunctions and the prohibitions which constitute His command and which have been in vogue in the long current of time. How so? – Because he has ceased to be a dependent being (*pasa*). And certainly, on the removal of sin, he has attained to the state of Siva Himself. His attainment of the state of Siva consists in his possessing all the unsurpassed blessed qualities free from the taint of all sin, - that is, - in being of the same nature as that of Siva. Now, the nature of Siva is made up of omniscience, etc. Therefore the liberated soul who is equal to Siva, has Siva's attributes such as omniscience, eternal knowledge, eternal happiness, perfect freedom, omnipotence, unfailing power, and endless resources. Samsara means the contraction of the self-knowledge (Atmajnana) so that, when the sin, the cause of contraction, is removed, the liberated soul attains omniscience. For the same reason, when ignorance, the source of samsara has been eradicated, the illusion also, by which the soul identifies himself with a large or a small body, ceases to exist. And because the liberated soul is devoid of decay, death, and grief, therefore, not being subject to karma, he is perfectly free. He is ever happy, because he rejoices in his own self, being solely immersed in the enjoyment of that unsurpassed bliss which constitutes his very nature; and he is therefore devoid of hunger, thirst, and so on. Because all his powers are ever unfailing, therefore his desires and his will are always realised. Hence it is that the liberated soul and the Paramesvara are spoken of in the Sruti as endued with the eight attributes, such as freedom from sin, etc. Wherefore it is but right to say that the liberated soul who is equal to Siva is perfectly independent.

Adhikarana 5

Badari maintains absence (of the body); for so says (the Sruti) (IV. iv. 10.)

It has been shown above that the liberated soul is self luminous, of unfailing will, and so on. Now comes the enquiry as to whether the liberated soul is embodied, or disembodied, or both.

Badari maintains that the liberated soul has no such organs as the body and the senses; for, the Sruti speaks of Brahman as disembodied, - the words "who is without parts, without actions," – and the liberated soul, who is of the same nature as Brahman, must also be disembodied.

Jaimini maintains existence (of the body), because of the alternatives spoken of in the Sruti. (IV. iv. 11.)

But Jaimini holds that the liberated soul has a body, because the Sruti speaks of him as putting on different phases of existence with bodies and the sense-organs.

"He becomes one, he becomes three, he becomes five." † [† Chha. 7-26-2.] and so on. Now the Sruti having spoken of the liberated soul as embodied and also as disembodied, a doubt arises at to what his true state is.

(*Purvapaksha*): - The truth is that the liberated soul is disembodied; for, the Sruti teaches that he has no external organs and the like in the following words:

"Seeing these pleasures by the mind, he rejoices." * [* Chha-Up. 8-12-5.]

And Brahman, too, is spoken of in the Sruti as devoid of external organs and the like, as one whose delight is in the Atman and prana alone, whose bliss lies in mind alone." * [* Tai. 1-6.] That is to say He takes delight in the Atman alone, not in any external object; He enjoys by the mind not by any external organ. Wherefore the liberated souls are ever in a disembodied state. As to the embodied state spoken of, it relates to the soul (in a state of bondage) whose conditions are different.

The Vedanta-Sutras with Srikantha Bhashya

(*Siddhanta*): - As against the foregoing view, the Sutrakara states his conclusion. (IV. iv. 12.)

Like the sacrifice lasting twelve days, both are possible, says Badarayana for the same reason. (IV. iv. 12.)

As the Sruti speaks of both embodied and disembodied states, the liberated soul exists in either way at will. So thinks the blessed Badarayana. Since the Sruti teaches both ways, the sacrifice lasting twelve days may be treated either as a *sattra*, or as a *ahina*, that is to say, either as a sacrifice in which a number of persons are engaged as primary sacrifices, or as a sacrifice in which only one person is engaged as a primary sacrificer. So, too, here. On the state of the soul who have risen to the height of Siva there is a pauranic text which reads as follows:

All-knowing, all-pervading, pure, all-full by nature, endued with strength equal to Siva's, gifted with supreme power, embodied as well as disembodied do they become at will." Wherefore the liberated souls may exist in either way.

The Sutrakara says that in the case of one and the same person the two states are possible at different times.

Because of the possibility (of enjoyment) in the absence of the body, as in a dream. (IV. iv. 13.)

The liberated one sometimes creates several bodies at will, and, entering into them, he wanders about. Sometimes, withdrawing the bodies, he remains. In the disembodied state, the liberated one enjoys the pleasure created by the Paramesvara, in the same way that in a dream a person in the state of bondage enjoys by the mind (manas) the pleasures etc., created by the Paramesvara. That is to say: - Just as in a dream a person enjoys with the mind alone, without the aid of the body and the sense-organs, the objects brought before his view by the Isvara, so also the liberated one enjoys the bliss which is the essential being of Brahman with the mind alone which forms part and parcel of his being.

When it exists, as in the waking state. (IV. iv. 14.)

During the existence of the body and other accessories created by his will, the liberated one enjoys all pleasures like a person in the waking state.

(*Objection*): - If it be possible for the liberated one to enjoy by way of perceiving material objects, then, as the liberated one will have to perceive also what is not desirable in the universe, he cannot be free from the contact of the miseries of samsara.

(*Answer*): - No; for, the liberated one never perceives the universe in an undesirable form. In point of fact, the whole of this universe appears to him as Brahman. So the Sruti says:

The Vedanta-Sutras with Srikantha Bhashya

"This then becomes Brahman, embodied in akasa, the True Being, the pleasure-ground of life, the bliss of the mind, full of peace, immortal." * [* Tait-Up. 1-6.]

In the passage preceding this one, - in the words, "He attains the heavenly kingdom, he attains the Lord of wisdom," – it has been said that the Yogin attains to the abode of Siva, the Parabrahman, the one essential bliss of the heavenly kingdom, that he attains to the Lord of wisdom, to that one who is the fountain source of all wisdom. Then, the question arising as to what the particular state of the liberated one may then be, the Sruti answers in the words "He is the lord of speech, the lord of the eye, the lord of the ear, the lord of knowledge." † [† Ibid.] he becomes the ruler of speech etc., in as much as they are all obedient to his own will. In the case of the liberated one who has attained to this state, - that is to say, who has risen to the state of Brahman embodied in akasa, and whose organs of speech, etc., are pure and obedient to his own will, -, then, i.e, on his attaining to that state, this whole universe becomes the Brahman Himself embodied in akasa, that is, Brahman clothed in the supreme splendour (akasa), *i.e.*, in His Supreme Bliss. That Supreme Power (Para-Sakti) which is the fountain-source of all being, the one homogeneous essence of ultimate being, light, and bliss, is what is called Paramakasa, the Supreme Splendour, forming the very being of Brahman, and which directly in the case of the Paramesvara and the liberated one, and ultimately in the case of others, is the means of realising their will and activity.

Accordingly the Sruti says:

"Who indeed could breathe, who could live, if this akasa, this bliss, did not exist? This one, indeed, makes one happy." * [* Tait. 2-7.]

"Bliss indeed is He; attaining that bliss, indeed, a person here becomes happy." † [† Ibid.]

In these words the Sruti teaches that the Parasakti is the object of universal experience. Accordingly the Sruti – beginning with the words "That is the unit (the highest) of human bliss," and ending with the words "That is the unit of Brahman's bliss," ‡ [‡ Ibid 2-8.] – teaches that the manifestation of bliss rises in an ever ascending scale up to Brahman according as the limiting conditions (upadhis) subside. As free from all limiting conditions, the bliss of Brahman and the liberated one is all full, as the Sruti says, "That is the unit of Brahman's bliss, and of the bliss of that man who is versed in the scriptural lore and unassailed by desire." § [§ Ibid.] The man here referred to is that person who has attained supreme knowledge and who performs the *agnihotra* and other sacrificial acts without longing for their fruits, while dedicating them all to Brahman. The bliss of such a man, who is liberated while still alive, and the bliss of Brahman are quite equal. No inconsistency is however involved in the Sruti teaching, at the same time, that such a man's bliss is equal to the bliss of lower stages, such as the human bliss; for, in the case of the Yogin who, by his superior Yoga has risen through the several stages, his yoga at the lower stages being yet imperfect his bliss manifested at those stages is spoken of as equal to the bliss of the beings who are on those levels. Hence it is that this one, this supreme Bliss, the final source of all, this supreme splendour, being in separate from the Supreme Being, is spoken of as Brahman, as the cause of the universe, in the words "He knew that Bliss was Brahman." * [* Ibid.3-6.] And the manifestation of this Bliss is referred to in the words "This was the wisdom attained by Bhrigu, founded in the Supreme Heaven." † [† Ibid.] Accordingly, in as much as the universe appears to the liberated ones as Brahman clad in His Supreme Splendour, they become immersed in the Supreme Bliss, and are, therefore, like Brahman, free from all contact of misery.

Adhikarana 6

Like a lamp he pervades, so indeed the Sruti teaches. (IV. iv. 15.)

It has been already indicated that the liberated soul becomes all-pervading in virtue of his power of assuming an infinite number of bodies at his own will.

(*Purvapaksha*): - Now one may suppose that the liberated soul cannot, properly speaking, be all-pervasive, because he is said to wander about like a limited being, in the following passages:

"In all worlds, he wanders about freely." ‡ [‡ Chha. 8-4-3.]

"These worlds he wanders through, eating the food he likes, putting on the form he likes." § [§ Tait. 3-10-5.]

Wherefore his assumption of several bodies can only be gradual, but not simultaneous.

(*Siddhanta*): - Just as a lamp enclosed within a jar pervades the whole room by its light on the removal of the limitation, so also does the liberated soul becomes all-pervasive by way of pervading the whole universe through his Sakti (Divine Power), on the removal of the sin which obscured his Sakti.

Accordingly the Sruti says:

"He is our kinsman and father. He is the dispenser. He knows all the heavenly abodes; in whom disporting, those who have attained immortality find their heavenly abodes in the third region." * [* Mahana. 1-15.]

"They at once spread over earth and sky, over all worlds, over all quarters, and over heaven; having snapped asunder the long thread of destiny, and seeing the One in all creatures, they become that One." † [† Ibid. 1-17.]

These verses occur in the section treating of Mahadeva, the Supreme God, the creator of the universe, and embodied in the whole universe. (The first verse quoted may be interpreted as follows: -) He, Mahadeva, our kinsman, our Father, the creator. He is the dispenser of all good. He knows all non-material heavenly regions. Now the sruti proceeds to say what purpose is served by His being our kinsman and knowing all regions. Those who have attained immortality and enjoy the bliss of freedom and always disport in Him, resort to the abodes they like, all full of spiritual splendour, and situated in that region of Mahadeva called heaven and which lies beyond Maya, forming the third region from here. That is to say: - The liberated ones, having attained immortality – with their bonds of confinement broken asunder when Mahadeva, the Parabrahman, the doer of all good like a kinsman and a father, has vouchsafed His grace, - dwell in the splendid abodes formed in their own region of Supreme Heaven, the third one from here.

Now in the next verse the Sruti teaches how they pervade the whole. – The liberated souls spread over the earth and sky with the rays of their own Divine power (Sakti); they spread over even the regions of the Hiranyagarbha and the like; they spread through the four quarters. Thus they dwell, pervading the whole universe. So that, omniscient as they are, they rend asunder the vast thread of destiny caused by Karma; and thus released from bonds of virtue and vice, they behold in all beings the one Being, Mahadeva, and become one with Him, one with all. Therefore, the liberated ones immersed in the one Being, Siva, do pervade the whole.

Thus, the liberated Jivas are of the same nature as Mahadeva and are spoken of as Devas, pervading the universe including heaven itself. It is they that are extolled in the Saman called Devavrata beginning with "Those Devas who abides in Heaven," etc. The Purana also says.

"They indeed are the very Devas who dwell in Heaven, the Devas who dwell in the Mid-air, (antariksha), the Devas who dwell on Earth; these Devas abide in their Divine vow."

Here the "Earth" means the Brahmanda; what is spoken of as "*Antariksha*" refers to the second region called Maya; what is here spoken of as "heaven" (Dyauh) refers to the third region, otherwise known as Paramakasa, the Supreme Light, the pure Divine Source, the abode of Siva. Hence the all-pervasiveness of the liberated ones.

Nescience refers to one of the two states of self-absorption and death; so indeed it is taught in the Sruti. (IV. iv. 16.)

(*Objection*): - The Sruti teaches the absence of the internal and external knowledge, in the case of him who has attained to Brahman: "Embraced by the all-knowing Atman, he knows nothing whatever, external or internal." * [* Bri. 6-3-21.] How then can the liberated soul pervade all by his divine power of knowledge."

(*Answer*): - This objection cannot be maintained. For, this want of knowledge on the part of jiva refers to either of the two states, namely, sleep or death. Regarding sleep the Sruti says:

He said: "Sir, in that way he does not know himself that he is it nor does he know anything that exists." *[* Chha. 8-11-1.]

And as to death it is taught as follows: "Having risen from out of these elements, he vanishes again in them. When he has departed, there is no more knowledge." † [† Bri. 6-5-13.]

Liberation being quite distinct from these two states, there can be no absence of knowledge. On the contrary, owing to the removal of the veil of sin (mala), the soul becomes all-knowing and all-powerful. So in liberation there can be no want of knowledge.

Adhikarana 7

Excepting activities connected with the universe, from the section and from want of proximity. (IV. iv. 17.)

It has been said that the liberated souls attain equality with Isvara in respect of the attributes of self-luminosity, pervasiveness, omniscience, etc. Accordingly equality even with respect to the creation of the universe is inevitable, because of the unqualified assertion, "He attains utmost equality." ‡ [‡ Mundaka 3-1-3.] When equality in respect of creation of the universe is once admitted, then as there would be many Isvara's, we would have to give up the theory that Isvara has no second. Therefore the question arises as to what sort of equality with Isvara is attained by the liberated souls: Does the equality comprehend the creation of the universe, etc., or does it not comprehend it?

(*Purvapaksha*): - What is the view that suggests itself? Because that Sruti – in the words "When he desires the region of the Pitris," etc., § [§ Chha. 8-2-1.] – teaches that, by mere will, he has the power to create the region of the Pitris, etc., because again the Sruti – in the words "through these region he wanders, eating the food he likes, putting on the form he likes, - * [* Tait. 3-10-3.] he is said to be active in all regions, as also because no limitations is made as regards the equality attained with Paramesvara, it may be concluded that the liberated souls are engaged also in the creation, etc., of the world.

Conclusion: - As against the foregoing view we maintain as follows: Though the liberated soul attains equality with the Paramesvara, his freedom as regards objects of enjoyment does not extend to the creation, etc., of the universe. Having regard to the section (in which the passages treating of the creation etc., of the universe occur), we conclude that such functions pertain to the Paramesvara. Take for instance.

"Whence, verily, these creatures are born." † [† Tait. 3-1.]

"Creating the heaven and the earth there is one Deva." ‡ [‡ Mahana. 1-12.]

In these sections treating of the creation of the universe, Jiva has no place at all. Therefore, the liberated soul has nothing to do with the creation, etc., of the universe.

If it be said that it is expressly taught, we say, no, for such teaching refers to what exists in the region of the hierarchy. (IV. iv. 18.)

If it be said that the liberated soul has to do with the activity connected with the universe, as expressly taught in the Sruti "through these worlds he wanders, eating the food he likes, putting on the form he likes," § [§ Tait. 3-10.] we answer: that it is not so taught. The passage teaches merely that he can command the enjoyments available in the regions of

Brahma and others of the hierarchy, because the passage refers to the enjoyment of the objects of desire. He has therefore nothing to do with activities connected with the creation of the universe.

Objection: - If so, then, as he is engrossed in the enjoyment, he is subject to change.

Answer: - The Sutrakara answers as follows:

And it is not subject to change, so, indeed, the Sruti describes its state. (IV. iv. 19.)

The bliss to be enjoyed by the liberated soul is not subject to change, is pure, is of the nature of all-full Brahman. So, indeed, does the Sruti describe its state.

"Bliss indeed is He: attaining that bliss, indeed, a person here becomes happy." * [* Tait. 2-7.]

And the nature of Brahman, indeed, is described as immutable in the following passages.

"Existence, knowledge, and infinite is Brahman." † [† Tait. 2-1.]

"Bliss is Brahman." ‡ [‡ Tait. 3-6.]

Hence the bliss of liberation is not subject to change, as the bliss of a bound soul (Pasu) is subject. That is to say: Wandering freely in the region of the hierarchical beings ranging from Sadasiva to Brahma, eating the food he likes, putting on the form he likes, putting on the form he likes, released from all sense of identification with the human and other bodies, with his three potentialities uncontracted, the liberated soul fully realises his all-pervading self, endued with the supreme Bliss and light, with Siva and Sakti held in homogeneous union in all their glories, immersed in the universe which has become of one homogeneous essence in perfect unison with Parabrahman. Accordingly, in the words "I am the food, I the food! I am the eater of food, I the eater of food, I the eater of food!" the Sruti teaches that the liberated soul regards his self as all-pervading, identifying himself with the whole universe including the experiencer and the objects of experience. The Self spoken of here is not the self of Samsara or mundane experience, in as much as it is all-full as embracing the whole universe. On the other hand this Self is quite free; it is quite distinct from the fictitious samsaric self which is limited as comprehending only the body of a Deva or some other being, thinking "I am a Deva," or "I am a man," and so on. Hence there is no connection whatever with the self of the world of matter or the self "*Aham*," refers to Siva and Sakti held in perfect unison. The thought of the liberated soul takes the form "The whole universe including food, etc., is nothing but that self." Hence the saying of the wise:

"The recognition of Siva and Sakti in perfect union, embracing the whole from '*a*' to '*ha*,' is spoken of as '*aham*,' since the infinite is void of attributes.

The Vedanta-Sutras with Srikantha Bhashya

"The syllable '*a*' is in the heart, and the syllable '*ha*' is in the twelve membered regions. Hence the sages look upon this (universe) as '*aham*,' the non-dual, resting in the shining Self."

Now, the song of the liberated soul who has entered the supreme abode of the unsurpassed Brahman, accompanying his meditation of the glorious word '*aham*' which denotes Siva who comprehends all universe, is not a thing which is enjoined here by the Sruti as incumbent on the liberated soul. On the contrary, the song referred to is intended to extol the state of the liberated soul with a view to indicate the highest flight of the enjoyment of Bliss. Wherefore, excepting the enjoying of Brahman's Bliss, the liberated souls cannot, of their own will, have anything to do with creation and other such activities.

So do the direct and the indirect (Revelations) reveal. (IV. iv. 20.)

The Sruti and the Smriti teach the same thing that has been taught above. The passages of the Sruti are such as the following:

"From the Atman sprang Akasa." * [* Tait. 2-1.]

The Smriti referred to includes the passages like the following:

"Waters alone did He create in the beginning." † [† Manu. 1-8.]

Therefore Brahman alone is the cause, etc., of the universe.

Now one may suppose: - Then, because perfect equality of the liberated soul with Brahman, *i.e.*, with Siva, is taught – in the passages like the following: -

"When the seer sees the brilliant maker and lord (of the world as the person who has source in Brahman, then he is wise, and staking off good and evil he reaches the highest oneness, free from passions;" * [* Mundaka. 3-1-3.]

"The liberated one can be equal to Brahman;" –

Therefore, whatever power Siva has, such as the power of creating the universe, all that power can accrue to the liberated one, without any limitation whatever. Otherwise perfect equality cannot hold good.

As against this supposition the Sutrakara says: -

And because of equality only as regards enjoyment. (IV. iv. 21.)

The equality of the liberated soul with Brahman refers merely to the enjoyment of all objects of pleasure. It does not refer to the creation of the universe and the like; for, then, there would be many Isvara's or Lords of the universe. The Sruti accordingly says:

"He attains all pleasures in unison with the omniscient Brahman." † [† Tait. 2-1.]

The Vedanta-Sutras with Srikantha Bhashya

Brahman is spoken of as omniscient because He is endued with that *chit* or consciousness which sees all things, which constitutes His very nature, His heart itself, manifested as the one supreme existence and light, and in virtue of which Brahman or Siva who is unconditional by time and space becomes omniscient, is the cause of all, abides in all things as their very self, is possessed of all powers, is of unfailing power, is independent of all, is ever satisfied, is of unsurpassed supremacy, is gracious to all, is the one bliss which all the liberated souls seek to attain. Only as endued with this power, even the Supreme Brahman is said to be omniscient.

Having attained perfect unison with Him, the liberated soul, too, with his inner sense, with his inherent thought or consciousness, attains all objects of desire; that is to say, he sees them all and rejoices. Accordingly the Sruti says.

"Seeing these pleasures with the mind, he rejoices." * [* Chha. 8-12-5.]

"The Mind is his divine eye." † [† Tait. 1-6.]

"Whose nature is true, rejoicing in the senses, delighted in the mind." ‡ [‡ Tait. 3-12-5.]

In these words it is said that even Brahman enjoys His bliss in the mind, not with the aid of the external organs. The wearing of the body and the senses by Brahman and the liberated soul is optional for them and subserves amusement; hence no room for any objection. Wherefore it stands to reason that the equality of the liberated soul with Brahman holds good only as far as enjoyment is concerned, in as much as we maintain that, as Brahman enjoys all objects of desire, so also does the liberated soul enjoy. Even in common parlance, as when we say "Devadatta is a lion" we speak of equality when we find agreement in respect of a few attributes; and therefore the assertion of equality (between the liberated soul and Brahman) is not open to objection.

No return, as so it is taught. No return, as so it is taught. (IV. iv. 22.)

It has been said that the liberated souls attain equality (sayujya) with Brahman, because of the similarity in respect of enjoyment, etc. Now a doubt arises as to whether even they do again return to Samsara at any time, or do not return. This doubt arises because we find that those who in virtue of a certain act of merit have attained to the position of Indra do return to Samsara.

(*Purvapaksha*): - What view may suggest itself to us here? In the words "having as much food as he likes and assuming as many forms as he likes, he enters (into these worlds)," we are given to understand that the liberated souls are associated with many bodies. When once they are associated with them, it is likely that they will again do good and evil deeds. When the great act of Divine worship which he had done before became exhausted through enjoyment in various ways, the liberated soul has to come back to the Samsara of mean pleasures under the force of the act or acts which ripen at the time. Accordingly, those who have risen to the height of Indra and the like return here on the exhaustion of their great meritorious act, and are born in the body of a Brahmana or the like. Wherefore those who have attained to the height of Brahman return to Samsara again, in as much as the enjoyment, which works by way of bringing together the objects of enjoyment and the enjoyer, only causes the exhaustion of the great meritorious act.

Siddhanta: - As against the foregoing we hold as follows. There is no return to Samsara for the liberated ones who have seen directly the Divine Light of Brahman and entered into His abode. Why? For, the Sruti teaches as follows:

"He who behaves thus all his life, reaches the world of Brahman and does not return, yea, he does not return." * [* Chha. 8-15.]

The Purana, too, after treating of the abodes of Brahma, Vishnu, and others, declares as distinct from them all the ancient abode of Siva, the Parabrahman, in the following words:

"The primeval abode of the Spouse of Uma is as resplendent as a crore of the suns; it is furnished with all objects of enjoyment, quite pure, eternal and imperishable."

"Having attained to that celestial abode the souls are freed from all troubles; they become omniscient, all-pervading, pure and all-full."

"They, according to their own will, become embodied or disembodied, with their body and the senses quite pure, with supreme powers endowed to them."

"In the case of those men who were devoted to Gnana and Yoga and have attained the supreme abode, there is no return again to the fierce region of Samsara."

We shall now explain the meaning of these passages: -

In the words "having reached the highest light it appears in its true form; that is the self;" * [* Chha. 8-3-4.] the Sruti, refers to the Supreme Light, attained by the liberated soul; the Supreme Brahman, associated with Uma; that Mighty Light whose splendour transcends the splendour of crores of the suns, and by whose light all this shines. So says the Sruti:

"The sun does not shine there, nor the moon and the stars, nor these lightning's, and much less the fire. When He shines, everything shines after Him; by His light all this is lighted." † [† Katha. 5-15.]

In the Atharvasiras also it has been described as follows:

"I am Paramesvara, the Supreme Lord; I am Akasa, the celestial Ether; I am the pure; I am the end and the middle; I am the Light in front and at the back; I am one and all; whoso knows Me and Me alone he knows all Devas."

The Smriti also says:

"Everyone should meditate on Siva, who has feet and hands everywhere; who has the head, the eye and the mouth everywhere; who is the mass of light that overspreads all."

The Vedanta-Sutras with Srikantha Bhashya

Beyond this is that Light, the Para-Brahman known as Siva, associated with Uma. The abode wherein He dwells, it needs no saying, is as resplendent as a crore of the suns put together. The same thing which in the form of consciousness is the unsurpassed light, is the seat of unsurpassed bliss and is therefore known as Svarga, as taught in the Sruti: "the region of Svarga enveloped in Light;" ‡ [‡ Tai. Ara. 1-27.] "Devas, verily, went to the region of Svarga, and these Devas asked Rudra," * [* Atharvasiras.] and so on; the abode here spoken of being the one beyond the fourth. So says the Uttara Gita: "the fourth and the one beyond the fourth is the abode of Siva devoid of evil."

The abode is primeval because it is beyond all lokas or regions, because it is the cause; below it and outside it are the seven envelopes of the Brahmanda as taught in the words "be it known that the envelopes of the Anda are outside the region of Siva." And it is primeval also because that is the abode of Brahman who transcends the whole universe including Brahman, because it has transcended all, as the Sruti says:

"Greater than the great is Brahma; beyond this great one again is Hari; and beyond Him even is Isa." † [Sivasankalpa-Up.]

It is the abode of Uma's Spouse, of Siva, the Parabrahman. In the words "Him whose help-mate is Uma, the Supreme Lord, the Ruler," ‡ [‡ Kaivalya-Up.] the Sruti teaches that Siva, the Lord of Uma, who is dark-necked and three-eyed, should be meditated upon and is the goal lying beyond the Prakriti of darkness. Moreover, having declared that Siva is the essential being of all, in the words "All verily is Rudra," § [§ Mahana. 16-18.] the Sruti concludes, "Homage to the golden-armed, to the Lord of Gold, to the Lord of the Mother, to the Lord of Uma." § [§ Mahana. 16-18.] By word the "Uma" which is synonymous with Pranava, the Supreme power of Parasakti, which is also the Supreme cause (Paraprakriti) is meant. In the words "Dark and Yellow is Brahman" the Sruti teaches that Brahman is harmoniously blended with her. Therefore the abode belongs to the Parabrahman, the Lord of Uma.

What else is it? It is furnished with all objects of enjoyment; it is always endowed with all objects of desire. Hence, verily, the Sruti, "He attains all objects of desire, with the omniscient Brahman," teaches that the liberated one attains all objects of desire in conjunction with Brahman.

Quite pure is the abode, because untouched by change, the Sruti giving us to understand that it is beyond all causes and effects, in the passages like the following:

"Him who is the witness of all, who is beyond darkness." * [* Kaivalya.]

"Who has colour like the sun, who is beyond darkness." † [† Sve. 3-8.]

Indeed, that abode wherein Siva abides is perfectly pure, because, unlike the products of matter (Prakriti), it does not give rise to attachment, hatred, greed and the like. That is to say, this abode is the Supreme reality, luminous, full of great bliss, the Supreme celestial Akasa, because the material products alone are said to be subject to creation and other processes, and because this abode is beyond those processes, it is eternal. It is the universe of the material Akasa that passes through the processes of creation, &c; it does not apply to this celestial abode which is composed of spiritual Akasa.

(*Objection*): - We are taught that everything except Siva is subject to dissolution, as the Sruti says:

"When what is beyond darkness is attained, then there is neither day nor night, neither being nor non-being, Siva alone there is." ‡ [‡ Svc. 4-18.]

How can this abode and the liberated ones be eternal?

(Answer): - No such objection can be raise here. For, the liberated souls and this abode are comprehended in the entity of Siva. These are equally blessed (Siva) as seats of perfect purity. Blessedness consists in being of a nature quite distinct from that of the bound soul (pasu) and his bondage (pasa) which comes within the sweep of the wheel of creation, etc. Thus, the abode of Siva which is distinct from the bound soul and his bondage, cannot be perishable.

This abode is imperishable, not subject to decay and growth, unlike Svarga etc., which are the results of acts admitting of increase and decay. Such it is declared to be in the Sruti, "He reaches the goal of the Path; that is the Supreme abode of Vishnu." * [* Katha 3-9.] The highest inherent nature of Vishnu is, indeed, the abode of Siva known as Paramakasa, the Spiritual ether, the goal of the six-fold Path, that which lies beyond the Path. It is the abode designated as Brahmaloka from which there is no return – which is spoken of in the following passage:

"He reaches the world of Brahman, and does not return, yea, he does not return." † [† Chha. 8-15-1.]

In the words "having attained to that celestial abode, the souls are freed from all troubles," and so on, the characteristic marks are given of those who have risen to that abode and who are equal to Brahman. Having attained the abode, that inherent divine nature of the great God which is beyond speech and thought, *i.e.*, having realised it by Gnana-yoga directed towards it, the souls become emancipated. They are completely freed from death and all sources of evil such as Avidya. That is to say, the liberated souls are free from all evil tendencies and qualities.

Next their blessed qualities are mentioned. They have attained the state of Siva, and are omniscient owing to the destruction of the taint of sin which has shrouded their knowledge; they become omniscient. As their power of knowledge extends to all regions, they become all pervading, as explained already in the Sutra IV. iv. 15. And being pure, with the state of Siva manifested on the removal of sin, they attain to a pure spiritual condition and become one mass, as it were, of consciousness. In the Sutra IV. iv. 7, it was shown that the soul becomes self-luminous, of unfailing will, and so on.

They become also all-full, they are ever satisfied, in as much as they are in their very nature the bliss unsurpassed and have attained all desires. It is their very nature to enjoy unchanging and unsurpassed bliss, as already explained in the Sutras IV. iv. 19.

Because they are thus all-full, their body and senses are perfectly pure; their body and the senses are no longer those which are subject to undesirable change. It is taught in the Sruti, - "He becomes one" * [* Chha. 7-26-2.] and so on, - that the liberated souls puts on several bodies at will. Therefore the body and the like which the liberated ones assume at will are all perfectly pure, because they are formed by Mahamaya. Their purity consists in not subjecting the soul to any undesirable change. In the words "The Lord by his Mayas is seen in different forms," † [† Bri. Up. 4-5-19.] the Sruti teaches that even Isvara assumes, by His powers of Mahamaya, many bodies, such as the one with dark neck. In the words "Ugra is of diverse forms with eternal bodies," † [† Bri. Up. 4-5-19.] the Sruti teaches that the bodies assumed by the Paramesvara, are not made of matter, are made of pure spirit (Vidya) and are eternal. Just as the Paramesvara assumes manifold pure bodies, so also the liberated souls.

They are endowed with Supreme powers, with the highest glories acting according to their own will, not having to demean themselves so as to do services to others. In the Sutra IV. iv. 9, it has been shown that the liberated soul is perfectly independent, not being swayed by Karma and the like. They, the liberated ones, are independent and are endowed with supreme powers.

They become embodied or disembodied of their own accord. They who have risen to the abode of Siva sometimes put on pure bodies and senses and enjoy pleasures therein, independently of the will of Isvara; sometimes, without the body and senses, and solely with their inherent mind, they enjoy all sorts of pleasure. This has been already shown in the Sutra IV. iv. 12, by way of explaining the meaning of some passages in the Sruti bearing on the subject. Accordingly the liberated one becomes embodied or disembodied at will. In the words "Homage to you all, to the disembodied and to the all bodied" * [* Rig. Sam. 2-13-9.] the Sruti teaches that those who have attained equality with Siva are without form and have manifold forms. When they become embodied, then whatever bodies – marked with dark neck and so on, - the Iswara assumes, all such bodies can be assumed by those who have attained equality with Him. In support of this some quote the Sruti. "Those who are dark necked, dark throated." † [† Tai. Sam. 4-5-4.]

Accordingly, those who are devoted to the knowledge conveyed by the Vedanta and to Yoga embracing all forms of self control and the like and directed towards the Paramesvara, ‡ [‡ Ibid. 4-5-11.] and who have thereby attained to that abode of Paramasiva which has been described above, - they who have become endowed with the attributes mentioned above and have become equal to Siva do not return again to the region of Samsara, which is one unsurpassed suffering and is therefore hard to endure; they will not again be subject to the life of Samsara.

Therefore, as taught in the words "he reaches the world of Brahman and does not return," those who have reached the eternal, imperishable world of infinite Bliss and Light belonging to the Lord of Uma, the Parabrahman, who is omniscient, omnipotent, possessing all glories, bestowing His grace on all, who is the object of all worship, who is devoid of all taint of evil who is the depository of all excellent and good qualities, who is possessed of diverse eyes, are endowed with omniscience and other virtues, and dwell there (in that world) without fear of return.

That is to say –

The liberated ones become blended with Brahman, with Siva who is one mass of unsurpassed bliss and light, and attain luminous bodies. They become omniscient, omnipresent, peaceful; they are the seat of the supreme eternal glories; from them all veils of sin have glided away; and they see Him everywhere; and He is their very being and self. As the sruti says "Where the gods having attained the immortal pass into abodes in the Third," * [* Mahana. 1-15.] they attain the abodes they like in His Supreme Spiritual world; and with all desire accomplished at their own will, they shine everywhere along with Him at all times. Thus the whole is quite consistent.

This commentary has been written by me, solely with the aid of Devotion, my way being illumined by service at the feet of Svetacharya.

(Finis.)

www.ingramcontent.com/pod-product-compliance
Lightning Source LLC
Chambersburg PA
CBHW030821230426
43667CB00008B/1311